MAXIMILIAN AND JUÁREZ

Jasper Ridley gave up his practice at the bar to become one of the leading historical biographers of England, winning the James Tait Black Memorial Prize for his biography of Lord Palmerston. He has twice stood for Parliament and is a Fellow of the Royal Society of Literature.

ALSO BY JASPER RIDLEY

Nicholas Ridley
Thomas Cranmer
John Knox
Lord Palmerston
Mary Tudor
Garibaldi (Phoenix Press)
The Roundheads
Napoleon III and Eugénie
The History of England
Statesman and Saint
Henry VIII
Elizabeth I
The Tudor Age
The Love Letters of Henry VIII (ed.)
Mussolini
Houses of Hanover and Saxe-Coburg-Gotha
(with John Clarke, edited by Antonia Fraser)

MAXIMILIAN AND JUÁREZ

Jasper Ridley

PHOENIX PRESS

5 UPPER SAINT MARTIN'S LANE
LONDON
WC2H 9EA

A PHOENIX PRESS PAPERBACK

First published in Great Britain
by Constable and Company Ltd in 1993
This paperback edition published in 2001
by Phoenix Press,
a division of The Orion Publishing Group Ltd,
Orion House, 5 Upper St Martin's Lane,
London WC2H 9EA

Copyright © 1992 by Jasper Ridley

All pictures courtesy of the Weidenfeld Archive

A CIP catalogue record for this book
is available from the British Library.

Printed and bound in Great Britain by
Clays Ltd, St Ives plc

ISBN 1 84212 150 2

To my daughter Barbara

✺ ACKNOWLEDGMENTS ✺

Her Majesty Queen Elizabeth II graciously permitted me to have access to documents in the Royal Archives and to publish the information which I obtained from them.

I wish to thank Susan Adrian and my daughter Barbara Ridley for driving me to nearly all the places in Mexico that are mentioned in the book and for their help with the illustrations; Senatore Arduino Agnelli for his kindness to me in Trieste; Jean Cadell for her advice on translations; Angus Cundey of Henry Poole and Company for information about Maximilian's measurements, which were in the records of his firm from 1861, when they made a suit for him during his visit to England; Dottoressa Rossella Fabiani for her information and assistance to me at Miramar; Catherine Johns for her help with the research; Señor Raoul Ortiz of the Mexican Embassy in London; Alice Rodman and Elissa Chandler for their hospitality in Baltimore while I was researching in Washington, D.C.; Dr. Michael Smith for information on medical matters; and Señor J. A. Velasco of Oaxaca for local information on Juárez's native village of Guelatao.

I also wish to thank the librarians and staff of the Bibliothèque Nationale in Paris; the British Library in London; the British Newspaper Library in Colindale; Canning House in London; the Library of Congress in Washington, D.C.; the London Library; the Museo Juárez in Mexico City; the National Archives in Washington, D.C., and the Military Reference Branch; the Public Record Office at Kew; the Royal Archives at Windsor Castle; and the Austrian Staatsarchiv in Vienna.

I thank my wife Vera for reading my typescript and for her most useful suggestions; Denis Jones for his help with photocopying; and my son John for reading the proofs.

� CONTENTS ✥

MAXIMILIAN
AND
JUÁREZ

❈ 1 ❈

DEPARTURE FROM MIRAMAR

SUNDAY, April 10, 1864, was a very warm day with a cloudless blue sky in the Austrian city of Trieste. By 10:30 A.M. hundreds of people were lining the road that led from the port along the shore of the Gulf of Venice to the palace of Miramar, four miles north of the town. Miramar was the residence of Archduke Ferdinand Maximilian, the brother of the emperor, Franz Joseph of Austria — Archduke Max, as the loyal people of Trieste affectionately called him.

They watched as four state carriages, preceded by mounted outriders, moved slowly along the road toward Miramar. The coat of arms on the carriage doors and the livery of the outriders were those of Archduke Max, but the black-coated gentlemen in the carriages were Mexicans, on a strange mission: they had come to proclaim an Austrian archduke as emperor of Mexico. Their leader, who had not set foot in Mexico for twenty-four years, was acting under the authority of an assembly of notables in Mexico City. The notables had been appointed by the commander-in-chief of the French army of occupation, which had reached the capital after fourteen months of hard fighting, but still controlled less than a third of Mexican territory.

A few minutes before eleven o'clock the Mexicans reached Maximilian's dream palace, which he had begun to build only a few years earlier. They saw a white edifice perched on a rock jutting out into the sea, a castle Norman in style but mid-nineteenth century in spirit, its square battlements adorned with an occasional baroque ornament, a product of post-Biedermeier romanticism. The leader of the Mexican delegation, Don José María Gutiérrez de Estrada, had been to Miramar several times before, but the Mexicans coming for the first time may have been surprised to see that the palace of the archduke, their future emperor, was a bungalow: only the ground floor had so far been completed. The grounds of the castle were swarming with people, for the gardens of Miramar were always open to the public on Sundays, though they had never been as crowded as they were today.

The Mexicans were greeted at the castle gate by Count Zichy-Metternich, the grand master of the household, who led them from the terrace into the hall, in the middle of which was a large billiard table. He took them through a number of small rooms, including Maximilian's bedroom, built to look like a cabin in a ship; none of the rooms was more than about ten feet high, but all were artistically decorated with elaborate paintings and hung with portraits of Maximilian, his ancestors, and other royal Habsburgs.

Count Zichy led them on until they reached the largest bedroom, the only room large enough to receive the Mexican deputation. The entrance hall was bigger, but the ceremony could not be held there because of the billiard table, too large to be stored anywhere else. A small table had been moved into the bedroom in place of its two beds; it was made of black and white marble, with curved legs of gilded wood, and the top was covered with little mezzotints of places in Rome. Maximilian wished to sign his acceptance of the throne of Mexico on this table, for it had been given to him by Pope Pius IX.

The Mexicans found the archduke and his Belgian wife, Archduchess Charlotte, surrounded by secretaries, officials, and Austrian and French diplomats. Maximilian wore the full-dress blue uniform of an admiral of the Austrian navy, with the Order of the Golden Fleece around his neck. He wore it well, for he was six feet two inches in height, well built and handsome, though a little fat for a man of thirty-one. His complexion was fair, and his hair and beard were golden, with the beard worn long and parted in the middle so that it ended in two points. His blue eyes were kind and dreamy, not like the eyes of a young man who had once confided in his diary the great satisfaction he experienced while watching the blood and agony of a bullfight.

Archduchess Charlotte, who wore a pink dress with the black sash of the Order of Malta on her breast and a diamond tiara on her dark brown hair, was impressive rather than beautiful. This determined young woman, who would soon be twenty-four, had a graceful figure and an imperious manner. Her face and mouth were strong and firm, but could soften into a charming and friendly smile. One glance at the faces of Maximilian and Charlotte revealed what all their friends knew: the archduchess was a much stronger character than her husband.

The Mexican delegates, in their black frock coats, stood together a few steps from the couple, and Gutiérrez de Estrada began his speech. He spoke in French, the language of international diplomacy, the second language of every European royal family, and the language of the soldiers of the foreign army of occupation that had invaded his homeland. He spoke only by implication about the civil war that had recently raged in Mexico, and made no reference to the liberal government of his enemy, Benito Juárez, who was still in control of part of the country. But he praised the emperor of the French, Napoleon III, and Maximilian and Charlotte, "a princess who is no less a queen by her graces than by her virtues and high intelligence." It was fitting that Maximilian, "a worthy scion of the Emperor Charles the Fifth and of the Empress Maria Theresa," should become the ruler of a people who had always adhered to Catholicism and the monarchy, those two great principles introduced to Mexico by "the noble and generous people," the Spaniards, who had "rooted out therefrom the errors and darkness of idolatry."

Maximilian replied in Spanish, the language of his new subjects. He and Charlotte had mastered Spanish well since they started to learn it two years before. He read from a script that had been prepared, discussed, corrected, and censored by his brother Franz Joseph and his ministers, and that he had finally accepted. He said that the documents they had presented convinced him that he had been chosen as emperor not only by the Assembly of Notables in Mexico City but by the overwhelming majority of the Mexican people. He promised that he would rule as a constitutional monarch and would grant Mexico a liberal constitution as soon as the present troubles were ended.

When he finished, the Mexicans applauded enthusiastically and cried out, "Long live the Emperor Maximilian of Mexico! Long live the Empress Charlotte of Mexico!" At the same moment, the imperial flag of Mexico, the red, white, and green tricolor, was unfurled above the palace of Miramar. Seeing the flag, the commander of the Austrian warships in the port of Trieste ordered the firing of a twenty-one-gun salute.

Monsignor Reditch, the almoner of Miramar, administered the oath to Maximilian, who swore to uphold the independence of Mexico and the inviolability of her territory, and to protect the welfare of the Mexican people. Then Maximilian and Charlotte, and the most important of the assembled dignitaries, crowded into the tiny chapel, which could hold barely a dozen people, for the service of thanksgiving, at which the *Te Deum* was devoutly sung by the chapel choir.

After lunch there was another ceremony at which the new emperor of Mexico signed a treaty with France. The Treaty of Miramar was being signed after nearly a year of haggling and bickering that had left

Maximilian with a feeling of resentment he would never be able to throw off completely. But on April 10 at Miramar there were only smiles and handshakes at the signing ceremony.

Maximilian spent nearly an hour signing other documents and appointing his ambassadors to the various European courts, and then retired to the library before the great banquet to be held in the evening. Alone at his large desk in the little room, his back to the window looking out at the sea, his face toward a portrait by Winterhalter of Charlotte as a child, he collapsed with exhaustion. When his servants came to help him change for dinner, they found him half unconscious, his arms stretched out on the desk and his head resting between his arms.

His physician, Dr. Jilek, was summoned. He was not surprised by what he found. He had been expecting a collapse of this kind for several weeks, as Maximilian's mood changed from elation to despair, from delight at becoming emperor of Mexico to grief at leaving his beloved Austria and forfeiting his right to the Austrian throne. Dr. Jilek's concern for Maximilian's health was one of the reasons he had opposed the Mexican venture. He was now rendering one of his last services to his patient, because he had said, very firmly, that he would not go with Maximilian to Mexico.

The doctor told the officials at Miramar that the archduke needed a complete rest and could not possibly attend the state banquet that evening. The archduchess — Dr. Jilek tried to remember to call them now the emperor and the empress — would have to preside in the emperor's place. Charlotte did this very well, apologizing for the emperor's absence and impressing everyone by her calm assurance and regal charm.

Maximilian and Charlotte were due to leave the next day for Mexico in the Austrian warship *Novara*, which Franz Joseph had placed at their disposal; they would call at Rome on the way to obtain the pope's blessing. But Dr. Jilek said that Maximilian was not fit to travel, and he was taken to a little cottage in the castle grounds where he could rest undisturbed. When the news spread in Trieste and the neighborhood that the departure was postponed, the local officials and leading citizens took the opportunity to pay one last visit to Archduke Max at Miramar. Maximilian was too ill to meet them, and Charlotte took his place. She also received the deputations from Venice and Fiume with unruffled poise.

By April 13 Maximilian had recovered, and it was decided that he could sail the next day. On the last evening there was not a cloud in the sky as Charlotte's lady-in-waiting, Countess Paula von Kollonitz, looked out the windows of Charlotte's apartments and for the last time saw the sun disappear into the sea to the west. The wind rose during the night, and by dawn the waves were breaking on the rocks beneath the palace, though it was another sunny day.

During the morning the leading citizens of Trieste came to Miramar to say goodbye to the archduke, who had been very popular with the townspeople during the years he lived at Miramar. Maximilian was well enough to receive them, but he nearly broke down when they handed him a farewell message signed by 12,000 local inhabitants.

At two in the afternoon of April 14, Maximilian and Charlotte and their escorts, watched by a large crowd that had assembled near the jetty, entered the launch that was to take them out to the *Novara*. A local band played the Mexican national anthem, but Charlotte turned to Countess Zichy-Metternich and whispered, "Look at poor Max. How he is weeping."

Miramar remained in sight for a long time as they sailed south along the Adriatic bound for the toe of Italy and Civita Vecchia, from where they would go to Rome. Great receptions and banquets were being prepared for them in Rome. But the people there were singing one of those ditties on current affairs that were so popular with the lower classes:

> *Massimiliano, non ti fidare!*
> *Torno al castello di Miramare!*

> Do not trust them, Maximilian!
> Turn back, go back to Miramar!

❋ 2 ❋

GUTIÉRREZ LOOKS FOR

AN EMPEROR

IF MAXIMILIAN could not make up his mind whether to be happy or unhappy at having been given the crown of Mexico, Gutiérrez de Estrada had no such ambivalence. His visit to Miramar on April 10 was the happiest day of his life. It was the end of a long quest. For twenty-two years he had traveled from his home in Rome to Paris, Vienna, and London to find an emperor for his beloved Mexico. At last he had found Maximilian. A week later he entertained Maximilian at a reception in his house in Rome. "All the most distinguished Roman aristocracy," wrote Paula von Kollonitz, "were gathered in the reception rooms of Señor Gutiérrez de Estrada: amongst them were many noble ladies, whose eyes sparkled as brightly as the diamonds on their necks and in their hair. . . . The old Gutiérrez wept for joy at the honor which fell to the lot of his family. He is an excellent, worthy man."

When Gutiérrez was born in Mexico in 1800, King Charles IV of Spain ruled over an empire on the American continent of more than five and a half million square miles. It included the whole of South America, except for the Portuguese colony of Brazil and the British, French, and Dutch territories in Guiana; all the mainland of Central America, except for British Honduras, as well as Cuba and other islands; and all of what is now the United States west of the Missis-sippi, as well as Florida. It stretched through 98 degrees of latitude, from Cape Horn in the south to the undetermined frontier — some three hundred miles north of San Francisco — with the largely unex-plored and sparsely inhabited territory called Oregon, after the great River Oregon, which was marked on all the maps but in fact did not exist. Oregon separated the Spanish Empire from the British colony of Canada and from Russian America, which was governed for the mad Czar Paul I by the Russian governor at New Archangel (Sitka). Spain,

Russia, Britain, and the United States all claimed sovereignty over Oregon, for Spanish, Russian, and British seamen had landed on the coast, and the American explorers Lewis and Clark had reached it overland from St. Louis.

In 1800 Spain ceded to France the territory known as Louisiana, between the Mississippi River and the Rocky Mountains. Three years later France sold it to the United States, and in 1819 Spain ceded Florida to the United States.

Of all the explorations and conquests by the Spaniards in the New World, Gutiérrez and his Mexican conservative friends were most proud of the conquest of Mexico by Hernán Cortés's small band of *conquistadores* in 1521. Cortés and his men had invaded Montezuma's Aztec Empire with two objects, to which they attached equal importance: to find gold and to win the heathen regions of America for Catholic Christianity. They found little gold, but located vast quantities of silver in the mines of San Luis Potosí, Guanajuato, and Zacatecas. By the nineteenth century these lodes were producing two thirds of the silver in America and had made Mexico the wealthiest of the four Spanish viceregalities governed for King Charles by his viceroys in Buenos Aires, Lima, Bogotá, and Mexico City. Mexico was "the jewel in the crown" of the king of Spain (as the British later called India). The *conquistadores* also enriched themselves by obtaining grants of large estates in Mexico, on which the native Indians were forced to work as serfs.

The Spaniards were equally successful in proselytizing. Almost as soon as they captured an Aztec town, they began to build a cathedral or church on the site of the temples where the Aztecs had performed their religious services and human sacrifices. The priests from Spain arrived immediately and set to work to convert the Indians to Christianity. They had great success, especially after an Indian peasant who had become a Christian had a vision of the Virgin Mary, only ten years after the conquest, in the village of Guadalupe on the eastern outskirts of Mexico City. The Church saw to it that Our Lady of Guadalupe became the patron saint of Mexico and placed great emphasis on her having appeared to an Indian; it showed how God could reward a member of the conquered race who accepted the true religion and was willing to obey and serve the Spanish masters whom God had placed above him.

The influence, power, and wealth of the Catholic Church in Mexico increased over the three centuries after the conquest. The pious kings of Spain gave the Inquisition, or Holy Office, in Mexico the same powers that it had in Spain to deal with those accused of heresy and vice; they had no right of appeal to any other court or even to the king himself. The bishops, who were usually sent out from Spain, became the most influential body in the viceregality. The Church acquired more and more land, and by the nineteenth century was said to own about half the land in Mexico.

Mexico was the most densely populated of the viceregalities; in 1800 it had some 6 million of the 17 million inhabitants of Spanish America. The capital, Mexico City, was the largest city in America, with a population of 169,000, larger than Rio de Janeiro with 135,000, or Lima with 87,000, or the rapidly growing city of New York with 60,000. Only one million of the inhabitants of Mexico were white. These were nearly all Creoles, that is, persons of Spanish origin who had been born in Mexico, though most of the more important positions in public life were held by *gachupines,* who had been born in Spain and sent out to the colony. About one million were *mestizos,* born of liaisons between the Spaniards and the Indians. There were 10,000 black slaves in the ports of Veracruz and Acapulco and along the Atlantic and Pacific seaboards, but no more had been imported from Africa because the Indian serfs could do all the necessary menial tasks.

The 4 million Indians in Mexico came from 182 different tribes speaking fifty-one different languages or dialects, most of which had no written alphabet. The natives were subjected to harsh economic and racial oppression. By the end of the eighteenth century, the king of Spain had officially abolished serfdom in Mexico, but the Indians were still forced, by discriminatory laws, police regulations, and economic forces, to work on the land owned by the Creoles. Although desperately poor, they were required to pay "tribute" and a variety of taxes and fees to the government and to the Church, and were kept in a position of inferiority by hunger and by social conventions.

In Mexico City on Sundays and holy days, the Creoles took their afternoon siesta, then emerged from their houses half an hour before sunset to stroll or drive down the Calle de Plateros and the Calle de San Francisco, through the Alameda, to meet their friends on the Paseo Nuevo. Meanwhile the Indians were working on the Paseo in the heat of the sun, climbing down into the ditch beside the causeway to scoop up water in buckets to throw on the road and clean it before the Creoles arrived in their carriages imported from Paris and Vienna, from New York and San Francisco.

In Mexico City and in many other parts of the country, during the rainy season from June to September, it rained heavily nearly every day between three and five o'clock in the afternoon, turning the gutters in the streets into fast-flowing streams; but there were always

Indians standing barefoot in the water, ready to carry Creoles across the street on their backs for a few cents.

During the religious festivities in Holy Week, an Indian could easily be found in every town to play the part of Judas, to be spat upon by the people who wished to show their hatred of Christ's betrayer. Dressed in his Judas costume, he would stand for hours in the corner of the *zócalo,* the great town square, his face drenched with the spittle of the faithful, to earn enough to get something to eat for himself and his family.

Not surprisingly, class hatred was very strong. In 1799 the bishop of Michoacán wrote that the Indians "are servants, menials, or laborers employed by the upper class. Consequently between them and the Spanish class there is the conflict of interests and the hostility which invariably prevails between those who have nothing and those who have everything, between vassals and lords." He thought that class hatred was stronger in America than elsewhere, for in America "there are no graduations between classes. . . . They are all either rich or poor, noble or vile." The Pomeranian nobleman Baron Alexander von Humboldt, who was very familiar with a society based on class distinction and inequality, was shocked when he went to Mexico in 1803 and saw the class oppression, the "monstrous inequality of rights and wealth" that existed there. Mexico, he wrote, was "the country of inequality."

Don José Gutiérrez de Estrada and his friends thought that this situation was right and proper. They believed that everything good in Mexico had been created by the Spaniards. They could not understand why, from time to time, some historian or archaeologist came from Europe to explore the ruins of ancient Indian temples or to search for records of a civilization that existed before Cortés came. Why should anyone be interested in pre-Spanish Mexico? It was a land not of civilization but of savages who indulged in human sacrifices to their pagan gods. The Mexican conservatives had far more sympathy with Archbishop Zumárraga, the first bishop of Mexico, who in the sixteenth century had destroyed twenty thousand statues of Indian gods and all except three of the thousands of manuscripts in which the Aztecs had recorded their history.

When the liberals pointed out that the human sacrifices of the Aztecs had been followed, within a few years, by the *autos-da-fé* in which Protestants and other heretics were burned alive by the Inquisition, the conservatives said that this was different. The Holy Office and the authorities in Mexico were defending Christianity from heresy. Their methods may have been a little harsh, but this was because of the cruelties of the age. The Inquisition in Mexico had not imposed a death sentence since 1715, though at the beginning of the nineteenth century it still fulfilled a useful task in protecting the flock from error.

The Mexican conservatives were equally hostile to the Anglo-Saxon influence, which was beginning to filter into Mexico from the United States. In fact, they believed that the trouble that had transformed America from a contented continent dominated by Spain into a turbulent area filled with radical revolutionaries, had originated in New England in 1775, when the British colonists had risen in rebellion against their king in Europe to uphold the right of colonials to control their political and economic destinies.

Then, the next year in Philadelphia, they had adopted Thomas Jefferson's Declaration of Independence, with its absurd and blasphemous statement that "all men are created equal." Was it not plain that God had created men unequal, some to be princes and some to be subjects, some to be lords and some to be serfs, some to be rich and some to be poor, some to be masters and some to be slaves? And the Americans themselves were hypocrites when they professed to believe that all men were equal, because they owned black slaves and had exterminated the Indians who inhabited the lands that were incorporated into the United States. Gutiérrez and his friends contrasted this typical example of Anglo-Saxon cruelty with the Christian actions of the chivalrous Spaniards, who had not exterminated the Indians in Mexico. They had compelled them to serve their Spanish masters, as God had intended, but had spared their lives and saved their immortal souls by converting them to Christianity.

What most distressed the conservatives about the American Revolution was the part that Spain, their beloved Spain, had played in bringing it about. When George Washington's army was starving at Valley Forge and the colonials faced defeat, France had entered the war against England, and Spain, France's ally, had joined in. The Spanish forces that invaded Florida, intercepted British ships at sea, and tried unsuccessfully to capture Gibraltar did not play an important part in winning the American War of Independence; but the Spanish pride of the Mexican conservatives led them to exaggerate the role of Spain, and their guilty consciences made them blame the folly of the well-intentioned but misguided King Charles III, who, in order to regain Florida from the British, had encouraged the idea of revolution throughout the whole American hemisphere.

The French Revolution had an even more serious effect on Mexico. The revolutionaries in Paris proclaimed the doctrine of liberty, equality, and fraternity, and the rights of man, which Pope Pius VI anathematized as evil and heretical, for man had no rights, only the duty to serve God in the station in society in which the Almighty had placed him by obeying his superiors, showing kindness to his inferiors, and believing and upholding the doctrines of the Catholic Church.

By 1794 seditious literature advocating the doctrines of the French Revolution was circulating surreptitiously in Mexico. The Inquisition immediately warned the viceroy and urged him to ban the publication of Thomas Paine's *The Rights of Man* and the reading in any college of any book about the French Revolution, "this deplorable event." The viceroy duly banned Paine's book; hearing that three hundred copies were being sent to Mexico from New Orleans, he ordered the customs officials to confiscate and destroy this "extremely abominable book," and assured the Inquisition that he would do all in his power to defend "the public tranquillity of these rich and precious dominions where flourish the most tender and true sentiments of religion, love, and loyalty to the King." The viceroy was most put out when he discovered that the chief agent of the revolution in Mexico was his French chef, of whom he was so proud. The chef, when not engaged in cooking his exquisite dishes for the viceroy's table, had been organizing the underground distribution of subversive books. The Inquisition found the chef guilty of propagating the "abominable doctrine of liberty and irreligion," and soon afterward he was deported, with all the other Frenchmen in Mexico.

After the French Revolution came Napoleon's invasion of Spain and the breakup of the Spanish Empire in America. In Buenos Aires, Lima, and Bogotá, the revolution was led by white liberals, who, after many years of fighting, achieved independence from Spain. In Mexico, the revolutionaries of 1810 were mostly Indians, though their leader was Father Manuel Hidalgo, a Creole priest, fifty-seven and already bald, who had spent his life ministering to the Indians on his father's estates and was shocked by their poverty and the injustices they suffered. Hidalgo was one of a long line of revolutionary priests, stretching back to Arnold of Brescia in twelfth-century Italy, who believed that Christ's religion should champion the poor instead of being a bulwark of the privileged ruling class. His followers marched under a banner that bore the picture of Our Lady of Guadalupe. Hidalgo not only demanded independence from Spain, but also denounced the rich, the nobles, and the officials as enemies of the people, and proposed that the goods of the rich be confiscated and divided between the poor and the state.

The viceroy sent the army under General Calleja to suppress the revolt, and the Creoles rallied behind him. The war was fought with great savagery on both sides. When Hidalgo's men captured the wealthy mining center of Guanajuato, they massacred the Creoles.

When Calleja recaptured the town, he ordered all the Indian inhabitants to assemble in the main square; then, not wishing to waste
powder and bullets on such riffraff, he told his men to cut the throats
of 14,000 of them.

After six months of fighting, the government forces defeated and
captured Hidalgo. He was condemned as a heretic by the Inquisition,
excommunicated, and degraded from the priesthood before being
taken to Chihuahua in the north for execution by a firing squad. After
he had been tied to a chair and blindfolded, the first volley shattered
his arm and his belly, but did not kill him. The second volley broke his
shoulder and ripped out his guts, but he survived. As the blindfold
slipped from his eyes, the soldiers saw the tears running down his
cheeks, which so upset them that their third volley also failed to kill
him. It was only after they had walked up to him and placed the
muzzles of their muskets on his heart that the fatal shot was fired.

The Inquisition ordered that the memory of so wicked a heretic
must be completely blotted out. Anyone who kept a copy of his
writings or his portrait was to be excommunicated, and this order was
so effectively enforced that no contemporary portrait of Hidalgo survives today.

The revolutionary struggle was carried on by another priest, a
mestizo named José Morelos. Unlike Hidalgo, he organized the rebels
into a disciplined force, forbade looting, and spared the lives of his
prisoners. This made no impression on General Calleja, who system-
atically executed every rebel he captured. It was only in the closing
months of the revolt, after all his protests to Calleja had failed, that
Morelos ordered reprisals, executing prisoners and burning the property of the government supporters. The rebellion was suppressed and
Morelos was shot in December 1815, after he had been degraded from
the priesthood and excommunicated as a heretic. One of the charges
brought against him by the Inquisition was that he had a portrait of
Hidalgo in his possession.

Most of the Spanish Empire had been lost, but Mexico, "the jewel
in the crown," was preserved for King Ferdinand VII when the allies
restored him to his Spanish throne after the defeat of Napoleon. He
did not have it long. In 1820 a revolution in Spain brought the liberals
to power in Madrid. They abolished the Inquisition and confiscated
the property of the Church, and they ordered the viceroy of Mexico to
do the same in the viceregality, to abolish slavery, racial discrimination, and trial by military courts, and to proclaim religious toleration.
When these instructions reached Mexico, the landlords, the Church,
and the army denounced them and proclaimed the country's indepen-

dence from Spain. They chose as their leader General Agustín de Iturbide, a Creole, a large landowner, and a devout Catholic, who had distinguished himself in suppressing the revolts of Hidalgo and Morelos. So national independence from Spain, which in the other viceregalities was won by liberal revolutionaries, was achieved in Mexico by conservative counterrevolutionaries.

As Ferdinand VII was virtually a prisoner of his liberal ministers in Madrid, the Mexican conservatives invited a Habsburg prince, Archduke Karl of Austria, to become their king. The deputation of leading conservatives who went to Vienna to offer the crown to the archduke took with them, as secretary to the delegation, the twenty-one-year-old Gutiérrez de Estrada. But the Austrian chancellor, Metternich, did not wish Austria to become involved in Mexico, and Archduke Karl refused the offer.

The conservatives then decided that Iturbide himself should become Emperor Agustín I of Mexico. The new emperor abolished the Inquisition and the discriminatory laws against Indians, but the Constitution prohibited religious toleration; only the Roman Catholic religion could be practiced. Army officers were required to take an oath to defend not only the nation and the state but also the Catholic Church.

In 1822 Metternich and Czar Alexander of Russia authorized King Louis XVIII of France to send an army into Spain to overthrow the liberal government and restore the absolute rule of Ferdinand VII. The liberals surrendered on a promise of an amnesty; Ferdinand promptly violated it and had the liberal leaders shot. The government in Spain was now as reactionary as the Mexican conservatives could wish, but they had grown used to independence, and successfully resisted the halfhearted attempts of Ferdinand VII to reconquer Mexico.

The liberals in Mexico did not like being ruled by Iturbide and persuaded one of his subordinate commanders, General Antonio López de Santa Anna, to overthrow the emperor. They were more generous to the defeated Iturbide than the conservatives usually were to their liberal enemies; he was allowed to leave Mexico. He went to England but returned to Mexico the next year and tried to make a revolution. When he was defeated and captured, the liberals did not give him a second chance. This time they had him shot.

It was not long before Santa Anna overthrew the liberal government and made himself dictator, and for the next forty years conservative and liberal governments succeeded each other repeatedly. Santa Anna was several times ousted by the liberals and then returned after another *coup d'état*. Gutiérrez and his friends claimed in 1861 that the struggles between the factions and the repeated military *pronuncia-*

mentos and revolutions had reduced Mexico to chaos and anarchy, and deplored the fact that there had been seventy-three presidents of the republic in forty years.

The Mexican liberals and their friends saw things differently. Eugène Lefèvre, a French radical who went to Mexico to help the liberal cause and became one of its leading propagandists, wrote in 1869, two years after the final triumph of the liberals:

> Every time that the Liberal Party, having had the good fortune to win an election, succeeded in forming a national government, by which I mean a government which did not agree to become the very humble servant of the priests, but which wished to make laws in favor of foreign immigration, of opening roads, of building railroads, of free public worship for all religions, of freedom of the press, of the reduction of tariffs, etc., etc. — the clergy organized a *pronunciamento* against the government and used their immense wealth to pay for it and their nefarious influence to ensure its success. . . . It was permanent civil war, always latent or patent civil war.

Gutiérrez, after returning from Vienna with the delegation that had failed to persuade Archduke Karl to accept the throne, had become a diplomat and a politician. After serving for a short time as foreign minister in Santa Anna's government, he resumed his diplomatic career and was sent to the embassy in Vienna, where he married the daughter of a French marquis. After the marquis's death, Gutiérrez's mother-in-law married an Austrian count, and became mistress of the household to Archduke Maximilian and Archduchess Charlotte. These ties increased Gutiérrez's respect for royalty and his growing discontent with republican regimes.

In 1840 Gutiérrez wrote a letter to President Anastasio Bustamante, who for a short time headed a liberal government in Mexico. It was a plea for monarchy — not the old absolute form but constitutional monarchy on the British and French model. After the English Revolution of 1688, the successful revolutionaries had not instituted a republic but had invited first William of Nassau and then George of Hanover to become their king. Even in France, the land of the revolutionary doctrines of 1789, the revolutionaries in 1830 had not tried a further experiment with a republic, but had chosen the constitutional monarchy of Louis Philippe. These constitutional monarchies had established freedom, law, and order, whereas republics had led to chaos and anarchy, to Robespierre, the Reign of Terror, and the guillotine.

Gutiérrez's letter to the president shocked the liberals. There was a great public outcry about it, and Gutiérrez was denounced as a traitor to the republic and banished from Mexico. He went to Europe and bought a house in Rome, from where he began his search for a European prince who would agree to become emperor of Mexico and for a European power that would send an army to force the Mexican people to accept him. It was suitable that this monarch be called an emperor rather than a king, because people spoke about the pre-Spanish empire of Montezuma; the first Christian ruler of Mexico, Charles V, had been an emperor; and Iturbide had called himself Emperor Agustín I.

In his letter to President Bustamante, Gutiérrez had referred to England, and to France after the revolution of 1830, as the great examples of successful constitutional monarchy; and he now turned to England and France. In 1842 he went to London to see the foreign secretary, Lord Aberdeen; but though Aberdeen agreed that constitutional monarchy was the best system of government and would be best for Mexico, he turned down Gutiérrez's suggestion that Queen Victoria's cousin, the duke of Cambridge, should become emperor of Mexico. The British government, he said, had no intention of sending an army to Mexico to impose this system on the Mexicans; that would not only be an unjustifiable interference in Mexican internal affairs, but would certainly involve Britain in trouble with the United States.

So Gutiérrez tried France, which only a few years before had gone to war with Mexico to obtain compensation for a French pastry cook who had suffered damage to his property during a riot in Mexico City; this was the "Pastry War" in which Santa Anna lost a leg and Mexico had to pay a war indemnity to France. But French honor having been satisfied and the pastry cook compensated, Louis Philippe's government had no wish to send another expedition to Mexico and would not allow Louis Philippe's son, the duke of Aumale, to accept the Mexican throne.

As the years went by, and Gutiérrez watched republican governments succeed one another in Mexico, he became more conservative. He no longer favored a constitutional monarchy on the English model, but preferred government by an autocratic conservative sovereign, like the monarchs of the Holy Alliance of Russia, Austria, and Prussia. In 1846 he went to Vienna and was received by Metternich, who was everywhere regarded as the leading champion of conservatism and the most hated enemy of the revolutionary republicans. Gutiérrez appealed to Metternich, as "the great protector of order and religion," to save Mexico from anarchy.

But Metternich was a realist in politics. He had long since realized that although he could suppress revolutions in Italy, Germany, and Poland, he could not prevent revolution farther afield; he had therefore reluctantly acquiesced in the revolutions in France and Belgium in 1830 and in the victory of the moderate liberals in Spain during the Spanish civil war of 1835–39. He knew that it was quite impractical to intervene in Mexico, especially as the United States would strongly resent it, and it would not be in Austria's interests to become involved in a conflict with the United States on the American continent. So Gutiérrez received much sympathy, but nothing more, from Metternich.

Gutiérrez went back to London to see the new British foreign secretary, Lord Palmerston. He knew that Palmerston was always willing to send the British navy to overawe foreign governments, as it had done in Naples, Greece, and China; Gutiérrez no doubt had visions of British gunboats off Veracruz frightening the Mexican liberals into surrender. But Palmerston was prepared to act only if British interests were involved or the safety or property of a British subject was threatened; and he, too, refused to intervene in Mexico.

Gutiérrez went to Madrid, hoping to persuade Queen Isabel to restore the Spanish Empire in Mexico by placing one of the Spanish princes on the throne. But the queen's ministers did not think that a Spanish expedition to Mexico would stand any chance of success, in view of the opposition of the United States.

Gutiérrez's hopes revived after Louis Napoleon Bonaparte's *coup d'état* of December 2, 1851, in Paris. Louis Napoleon, the nephew of the great Napoleon, had been banished from France at the age of seven, after the defeat at Waterloo. His mother was Hortense de Beauharnais, whose father, a leader of the French Revolution, had been guillotined by Robespierre when the revolutionaries fell out among themselves; she had married Napoleon's brother Louis, whom Napoleon had made king of Holland.

Hortense brought up her son to be in part a revolutionary and in part an enemy of the Revolution. She taught him that the only satisfactory compromise between the injustices and inequalities of the old regime and the horrors of the guillotine would be the rule of a member of the Bonaparte family, who would provide a government combining equality of opportunity with the preservation of law and order. This leader would win a popular mandate at a referendum before ruling as a dictator, would defend religion and the Catholic Church while granting religious toleration to other creeds, and would uphold the glory of France by pursuing a vigorous foreign policy and occasionally engaging in military interventions and successful wars.

Louis Napoleon lived for many years in exile in Switzerland and England and twice tried unsuccessfully to make a revolution in France. On the second occasion he was sentenced to life imprisonment, and was for six years a prisoner in the castle of Ham in northern France before he succeeded in escaping. During his exile and imprisonment he wrote several books in which he showed his interest in America and his anxiety about the growing power of the United States. One book, written at Ham in 1844, was about the prospect of building a canal across Nicaragua to link the Atlantic and the Pacific. The idea of a canal through the Nicaraguan lakes was attractive to many experts at the time, for it was not practicable to build a canal at Panama, where the continent was narrowest, because explosives powerful enough to blast through the rocky soil there had not yet been invented.

In some of his writings Louis Napoleon expressed socialist views, and he was sometimes accused of being a communist, but after the revolution of 1848 he was elected president of the French Republic with the support of the Conservative and Catholic parties. He sent an army to Rome and defeated Garibaldi's Red Shirts, overthrew Mazzini's Roman Republic, and restored the pope to power in the Papal States. In France he ruthlessly suppressed the "Reds" — a term that included those who called themselves Social Democrats, Communists, Jacobins, and Red Republicans. After his *coup d'état* of December 2, 1851, he arrested 30,000 of them and interned them in camps in Algeria and Cayenne.

Louis Napoleon was not the only European political commentator who was worried about the growing power of the United States. Others realized that the time might come when Europe, which for centuries had been the dominant continent, would be crushed between Russia and the United States, the two great powers to the east and the west. The population of the United States doubled every twenty-five years; 3 million in 1776, it had risen to 28 million by 1860. The prophets, assuming as usual that existing trends would continue, forecast that by 1963 the United States would have a population of 512 million.

There were also ideological reasons for mistrusting the United States, a republic that had repudiated monarchy. In Europe the words "republican" and "democrat" were terms of abuse in political controversy. Britain had her own reasons for disapproving of her disloyal former subjects in the United States. She had twice in the last seventy-five years been at war with them, and had several times been on the brink of a third war over some dispute on the United States–Canada border. In 1831, Palmerston had congratulated the British minister in Washington for his refusal to attend the celebrations on July 4 to mark the fifty-fifth anniversary of the Declaration of Independence.

The United States showed its contempt for the established conventions of the old monarchies. It refused to give its diplomatic representatives to the Great Powers of Europe the title of "ambassador" and insisted on calling them "ministers." It told them to refuse to wear the proper court dress when they were presented to the sovereigns to whom they were accredited and when they attended balls and receptions at court. American diplomats were often in contact with radical and even socialist revolutionaries, giving them moral encouragement when they made revolutions and United States passports to enable them to escape abroad when the revolutions failed.

When Tory landlords in England and Ireland had trouble with some agitator who was stirring up disaffection among their tenants, they would offer to pay his fare to the United States, where he could enjoy the doubtful blessings of living in a democratic country.

By this time the politicians and journalists in the United States were using a new phrase, Manifest Destiny. No one was quite sure who had first invented it, but everyone knew what it meant: it was the destiny of the United States to dominate the whole of the American continent. President James Monroe, in his message to Congress in 1823, had declared that the United States would not allow the European autocrats of the Holy Alliance to interfere in America. "The political system of the Allied Powers is essentially different from that of America. . . . We should consider any attempt on their part to extend their system to any portion of this hemisphere as dangerous to our peace and security. With any existing colonies or dependencies of any European power we have not interfered and shall not interfere." This reference to existing colonies did not satisfy the European powers, who firmly refused to accept the principles laid down by Monroe; and thirty years later, Manifest Destiny seemed to go far beyond the Monroe Doctrine.

By 1852 the *New York Herald* was calling for the extension of United States territory "from the Arctic Ocean to the isthmus of Darien" so that "every sea that laves the shores of North America will mirror the Stars and Stripes." The next year Senator Stephen Douglas of Illinois said that the destiny of the United States to expand could not be limited by international treaties. "You may make as many treaties as you please to fetter the limits of this giant republic, and she will burst them all from her, and her course will be onward to a limit which I will not venture to prescribe."

For many legislators from the southern states, the expansion of the United States meant the expansion of slavery. They had started with Texas. Within a few years of Mexico's achieving independence, United

States citizens from both free and slave states had migrated to Texas, and it was not long before they were demanding the independence of Texas from Mexico. The Mexican liberals supported them. In 1836, after capturing the Alamo and massacring the defenders, Santa Anna was defeated and taken prisoner by Sam Houston at the Battle of San Jacinto and forced to concede Texan independence. Almost immediately the supporters of slavery were demanding that Texas apply for admission to the United States, for while slavery had been abolished in Mexico, where there had never been more than a few thousand black slaves, it was flourishing in the southern United States, where the cotton gin had made it far more profitable than previously to have cotton picked in the fields by masses of slave laborers.

After nine years of independence, in 1845 Texas became the twenty-eighth state admitted to the Union. Within a few months President Polk used a frontier incident to declare war on Mexico and send two armies to win several glorious victories, to capture and occupy Mexico City, and to impose a peace treaty by which Mexico ceded California and the neighboring territories, amounting to two fifths of her soil, to the United States. Eager to preserve the reputation of being a non-imperialist power, the United States paid Mexico $15 million.

In 1853 Santa Anna, who had lost power in Mexico during the war but had regained it by another *coup d'état,* was in such financial difficulties that he agreed to sell yet another piece of territory to the United States. Mexico had now lost nearly half the land she had possessed when she had become independent from Spain thirty-two years earlier.

The Mexican War was popular in the United States, but an active minority opposed it. The Abolionists in New England and other opponents of slavery denounced the war as a conspiracy by the "slave power" in the South to acquire new slave states and thereby increase their influence in Congress. Some, including Congressman Abraham Lincoln of Illinois, who became very unpopular with his constituents, opposed the war as an unprovoked attack by the United States on a weaker neighbor.

Lieutenant Ulysses S. Grant, a recent graduate of the U.S. Military Academy, marched into Texas with his regiment. Forty years later, he wrote in his *Memoirs* that most of the army officers had no scruples about the annexation of Texas, "but not so all of them. For myself, I was bitterly opposed to the measure, and to this day regard the war which resulted as one of the most unjust ever waged by a stronger against a weaker nation. It was an instance of a republic following the bad example of European monarchies in not considering justice in their desire to acquire additional territory." But in spite of his feelings, Grant performed his duties as an officer under General Zachary Taylor and fought at Palo Alto, Resaca de la Palma, and Monterrey.

For several months, Grant served in the army of occupation at Tacubaya, a few miles east of Mexico City. Like other foreign visitors, he noticed that nearly all Mexicans were smoking cigarettes by the time they were ten. This seemed strange to Grant, for smoking had been strictly forbidden when he was a cadet at West Point, as it was among the officer corps in most armies of the world before 1850. He did not enjoy the bullfights that he watched in Mexico; the cruelty to the animals disgusted him as much as it fascinated Archduke Maximilian of Austria.

Gutiérrez de Estrada hated the United States. The war convinced him and his conservative friends that the Anglo-Saxons of the United States wished to conquer Mexico, and that the Mexican liberals, with their belief in republicanism, equality, and the rights of man, were agents of the United States working to weaken Mexico from within. Had not the liberal members of the town council at Desierto de Los Leones, near Mexico City, openly said in 1847 that they hoped the American soldiers would succeed in liberating the people of Mexico from the tyranny of Santa Anna? But most Mexican liberals took care not to say this publicly; on the contrary, when Santa Anna sold territory to the United States under the Gadsden Purchase of 1853, the liberals strongly denounced him for having betrayed his country to the foreigners.

Gutiérrez did not explain how the leaders of the American South, with their conservative sympathies, had caused the war with Mexico, while the liberal sympathizers and opponents of slavery in the United States had opposed it. He ignored such subtleties and became more obsessed every year with the threat of the two great evils, Mexican liberalism and United States expansionism.

But there was one ray of hope. The people of South and Central America, Latins by race and Catholic by religion, had closer emotional ties with Europe than with the Anglo-Saxon and Protestant United States. If some Latin and Catholic European power could establish a base of operations or a friendly regime somewhere in Latin America, it could check the expansion of the United States, maintain its share of trade with the Far East against competition from the United States, and prevent the United States from becoming sufficiently powerful to unite with Russia and dominate Europe. Gutiérrez hoped that Napoleon III, with his hatred of the "Reds," his support for the Catholic

Church, and his fear of the growing power of the United States, might be persuaded to erect this bulwark in Central America by sending troops to install a European prince as emperor of Mexico. But Napoleon III, like Aberdeen, Palmerston, Metternich, and the Spaniards, said that he sympathized but would do nothing. Gutiérrez was in despair; they were all afraid of the United States.

❊ 3 ❊

HIDALGO JOINS IN THE SEARCH

GUTIÉRREZ HATED the liberals more with every day that passed. They were not only traitors to their country and agents of the United States; they were Freemasons and traitors to God. Freemasonry, though it made fictitious claims to have existed in biblical times, had in fact begun in Scotland at the end of the sixteenth century, and became well established in England twenty-nine years after the Revolution of 1688. Its religion was the deism of the Age of Enlightenment; the Freemasons believed in a Great Architect of the Universe who could be the God of any denomination of Christians or the Jehovah of the Jews. Under the British constitutional monarchy and the rule of the Whig aristocracy, it became a respectable organization, with royal dukes as Grand Masters. But in the autocratic Catholic states of Europe, where Freemasons were regarded as heretics by the Church and subversive by the state because of their broadminded deism, their English origin, and the secrecy of their proceedings, they were suppressed and driven underground.

By the nineteenth century, the European organization of Freemasons, the Grand Orient, had taken a different path from the Freemasons in Britain. Not every Freemason was an active revolutionary, but most of them were sympathizers, and the Grand Orient lodges were a recruiting ground where the more dedicated members could be enlisted in the revolutionary groups of France, Italy, and Spain. The Grand Orient established lodges with the same revolutionary sympathies in Central and South America. Gutiérrez and his friends believed that the Freemasons and their secret society were responsible for the liberal revolutions in Mexico.

It was inevitable that liberals in Europe should come into conflict with the Catholic Church, which had been closely identified with the despotism of the absolute monarchy and was notorious for its persecution of dissenters. The last chance of avoiding the clash was lost when Pope Pius VI condemned the abolition of feudal privileges and the doctrines of the French Revolution in his encyclicals in 1791. Soon the revolutionaries in Paris were closing churches and suppressing Christian worship. The Catholic Church reacted by encouraging counterrevolutionary risings, in the Vendée and other provinces, that developed into a savage civil war.

In the nineteenth century the contest spread to Italy and Spain, where the Church opposed what it called "the Revolution"; when the ideas of the French Revolution reached Mexico, the war between the Church and the liberals developed there and was fought with the same cruelty as in Spain.

Of all the liberals, the one whom the Mexican conservatives hated most was Melchor Ocampo; they thought him a traitor to his class and to the memory of the benefactress who had found him as a small child playing in the gutter in Mexico City and had raised him to become one of the largest landowners in the state of Michoacán. No one knew who he was or how he had acquired the surname Ocampo, only that he had been adopted by Doña Francisca Xaviera Tapía, an unmarried lady of thirty-nine who lived with her younger brother at her *hacienda* near Maravatío in Michoacán. Not even the most malicious rumormonger dared to suggest that there was any improper explanation of her love for the little boy, because she was renowned for her virtue and piety. Unlike most wealthy women in her position, she never went to Mexico City for the social season, but traveled the eighty miles to the capital only once a year to take part in the religious ceremonies in Holy Week, and sometimes returned with another orphan to join the other children at Maravatío.

When she died, leaving no relatives — her brother had died earlier — she left all her property to Melchor Ocampo. He later studied law at Mexico City University, traveled in France and Italy, explored the sources of Mexican rivers, experimented with new farming methods on his lands near Maravatío, and read the 10,000 books in his library, which included the novels of Victor Hugo and the works of the French socialist writer Proudhon. He had four illegitimate daughters, whom he dearly loved and brought up on his *hacienda*; but despite his liberal doctrines about love and marriage, he went to great lengths to prevent them from discovering that their mother was also an orphan who had been adopted as a child by Doña Francisca and had joined the family at Maravatío.

The landowners of Michoacán were pleased when Ocampo entered politics, for it was the duty of a large landowner to play his part in the state and national governments. But they were disgusted when he became one of the most prominent leaders of the Liberal Party, serving as a deputy in the national legislature (the Congress), as minister of finance in a short-lived liberal administration, and as governor of Michoacán. They were particularly indignant when he became involved in a controversy in 1851 with the parish priest at Maravatío, Father Agustín Dueñas.

The liberals told a story about the origin of the controversy. A poor peasant of Maravatío who worked on Ocampo's lands lost a child, and asked Father Agustín to officiate at the little boy's funeral. When Father Agustín asked him to pay the usual fee, the peasant said that he could not afford to pay. Father Agustín refused to waive the fee. As the days passed, the peasant's neighbors became alarmed; they went to Father Agustín and told him that if the corpse was not buried soon, it would begin to stink. Father Agustín had a robust sense of humor; he was supposed to have said that the father had better salt the corpse and eat it before it went off completely. Ocampo stepped in. He paid Father Agustín's fee, and the priest officiated at the funeral. Ocampo then wrote a pamphlet attacking the privileges and greed of the clergy and denouncing them as cruel oppressors of the poor.

It is not a very likely story. Also, Ocampo made no reference to the incident in his polemic against Dueñas. It is reminiscent of the exaggerated stories told against the clergy that were featured in nineteenth-century liberal propaganda both in Europe and in Latin America — the kind of allegation that, at election time, is whispered on the doorstep, not published in the press. But it is quite likely that Dueñas did refuse to officiate unless he was paid his fee, however poor the bereaved parent or widow might be. He was a man of rigid principles who was determined to uphold, not his personal privileges but the rights and privileges of the Church, all the more zealously because he had once been a liberal. If these peasants were allowed, by a plea of poverty, to evade payment of the funeral fees, they would soon refuse to pay other ecclesiastical taxes; the poor should make sacrifices in order to perform their duty to the Church.

The conservatives were indignant with Ocampo. It was correct for him, a local landowner, to pay Father Agustín's fee as an act of charity to the poor peasant who worked on his land, but he had no business publishing pamphlets that attacked the privileges of the clergy. It was wrong of Ocampo to blame the Church for the misconduct of one priest. Had not Christ chosen Judas to be one of His Apostles in order to show that the most perfect body of men could contain one evil man among twelve and yet be a holy group?

Dueñas himself published a pamphlet replying to Ocampo's

charges, pointing out that, while the liberals always began by attacking the privileges of the clergy, their real aim was to destroy religion itself. "'Away with abuses!' they begin by saying, and then 'Away with the clergy!' and 'Away with the Church!'" Ocampo was unwittingly leading Michoacán "to freedom of faith and freedom of conscience, two aims that are as impious as they are fatal, and that in Europe serve as the banner of socialism." If God allowed these two principles to be established in Mexico, "it is certain that universal destruction would be our end."

Another hated liberal was the Indian Benito Juárez, who spoke only his tribal language, Zapotecan, until he was six or seven. He was born in a bamboo hut in the hamlet of San Pablo Guelatao, halfway up a mountain in the state of Oaxaca. Both his parents died before he was five, and he was brought up by his uncle, who taught him to speak Spanish and to read and write, for he thought the boy showed promise. The uncle threatened him with a severe beating if he was negligent in his studies, yet he intended that Benito should spend his life tending sheep on the hillside of Guelatao. So when Benito was twelve he decided to run away to his sister, who was a domestic servant in the city of Oaxaca.

On December 17, 1818, Juárez set out on foot over the mountains, determined to walk the forty miles to Oaxaca in one day, for it could be very cold at night, and the little mountain lions sometimes attacked children who slept on the hillside. At the top of the pass, he could look down on the valley of Oaxaca far below, and by nightfall he arrived at the house in the city where his sister worked. He was a very determined boy and would grow up to be a very determined man.

His sister was employed by a Creole merchant named Maza, who, impressed by Juárez's intelligence and character, arranged for him to stay with a Dominican monk in the city so that he could be educated for the Church. Juárez learned to speak Latin and French, but he was not attracted by the idea of becoming a priest, and his tutor, a broadminded monk, sadly agreed that it would be better if Juárez became a lawyer. Juárez soon built up a busy, though not very lucrative, practice, defending tenants before hostile judges in actions brought against them by landlords; but though he was a liberal in politics, he was not an extremist, and he was prepared to accept political and administrative office in Oaxaca under a governor who supported Santa Anna.

In 1847, at the end of the war against the United States, Juárez was elected governor of Oaxaca, and in the new situation created by Mexico's defeat, he openly came out against Santa Anna. While Santa Anna, hard-pressed by the liberal armies, was retreating toward the state of Oaxaca, Juárez called out the local militia and sent them to guard the border and repel any attempt by Santa Anna to enter Oaxaca.

Santa Anna, in later years, explained in his *Memoirs* why Juárez prevented him from entering the state.

> He could not forgive me for the fact that he had waited on me at table in Oaxaca in December 1828, in his bare feet and in a shirt and breeches of coarse cloth, in the house of Don Manuel Embides Asonbraba, for he is a native of such a low estate who has played a prominent part in Mexico, as everyone knows. A priest of the order of St. Dominic taught him to read and write and to wear shoes, and dressed him in jacket and pantaloons. I am not exaggerating, for General Don Manuel Escabar, who was present when Juárez was waiting at table, can confirm this.

By 1828 Juárez was twenty-two and had been wearing shoes, jacket, and pantaloons for a long time. He had just left his tutor to study law at Oaxaca University, but he may have put on Indian clothes and removed his shoes in order to earn some money by waiting at table, unless Santa Anna and Escabar were confusing him with someone else.

Santa Anna did not forgive Juárez for having kept him out of Oaxaca in 1847, and when he returned to power after yet another military *coup,* he had Juárez arrested and deported from Mexico. Juárez went to New Orleans to join the other liberal refugees, including Ocampo, and they established the Revolutionary Mexican Committee, with headquarters in the Cincinnati Hotel. Soon their funds ran out, and they had to leave the hotel and find the cheapest available lodgings on the top floor of a tenement building in the poorest district of the city. Juárez lived high up in a house in St. Peter Street in the intense summer heat during the cholera epidemic of 1854, earning a modest living by rolling cigarettes and selling them in the streets and wine bars. It was in New Orleans, under Ocampo's guidance, that Juárez became a convinced liberal *puro,* as opposed to the *moderatos.*

Juárez caught cholera. His friends, unable to send him to hospital, left him alone in his room to live or die. He lived; he was always a survivor.

The refugees kept in touch with events in Mexico and with the liberal General Alvarez, who was organizing a guerrilla resistance in the west against Santa Anna's government. Alvarez's supporters issued a manifesto at Ayutla calling for the overthrow of Santa Anna and the establishment of a liberal government. Juárez made his way to Acapulco on the Pacific coast and arrived at Alvarez's headquarters dressed in coarse Indian garments, perhaps in order to avoid detection on the journey. He offered to serve the revolutionaries in any capacity. Alvarez's son, not knowing Juárez's identity, asked whether he could read and write and then gave him a clerical job at Alvarez's headquarters. Alvarez and his son were embarrassed when they discovered that the little Indian, who they had thought might be illiterate, was the former governor of Oaxaca, and asked why he had not identified himself. "What does it matter?" replied Juárez.

He had arrived just in time to join the victorious liberal forces that entered Mexico City in August 1855 and forced Santa Anna to escape abroad. Ocampo, who had gone to Brownsville, Texas, when Juárez left New Orleans, intending to follow him, did not arrive until after the revolution had triumphed.

Alvarez soon handed over the leadership to another liberal general, Ignacio Comonfort, who became president of the republic. He appointed Juárez as minister of justice. Comonfort's government set out to limit the powers and privileges of the Church, but proceeded cautiously, conscious of the strong religious feelings of many Mexicans and of the influence of the Church over the people, not least over the Indians. Juárez introduced a bill which was passed by the Mexican Congress and became known as Juárez's Law (the Ley Juárez). It abolished many of the powers of the ecclesiastical courts and the legal privileges of the clergy, who became subject to the jurisdiction of the ordinary courts of law. The liberals also shocked the Church and the conservatives by introducing civil marriage, by allowing divorce for insanity and cruelty, and by ruling that no boy could marry until he was eighteen and no girl until she was fifteen, whereas by canon law the age limit had been fourteen for boys and twelve for girls. The conservatives also objected to the government's plan to provide state education for women.

Juárez's colleague, Minister of Finance Miguel Lerdo de Tejada, persuaded Congress to enact the even more controversial Ley Lerdo, which nationalized the property of the Church, closed most of the monasteries and nunneries, and stipulated that the clergy receive a fixed salary to be paid by the state. The government then sold the Church lands to private purchasers, thus giving them a financial stake in the reform.

The Comonfort government drafted a new constitution for Mexico. The president of the republic was to be elected for a term of four years, as was the chief justice of the Supreme Court. If for any reason the president was unable to act, the chief justice was to exercise his powers until a new president could be elected. Comonfort was elected president, and Juárez chief justice.

During the discussions on the new constitution, the liberals in Congress proposed the repeal of the provision in the constitution of 1824 establishing the Roman Catholic religion as the only religion lawfully practiced in Mexico. This was to be replaced by a clause proclaiming the principle of religious toleration. The Church rallied its forces to oppose the proposal, supplementing the arguments of its deputies on the floor of Congress with the noisy protests of its supporters in the public galleries. Some of the more moderate liberals also opposed the change on the grounds that it was premature. "If a majority of this assembly," said one of them, "declares for religious toleration, this will not become a law, much less a constitutional law. The country will repudiate it, and the law will remain a dead letter, as always happens with laws that run counter to the national will."

The liberal government did not dare to force the proposal through, and left it to a free vote of the deputies. After a heated debate the proposal for religious toleration lost by sixty-five votes to forty-four. The clerical supporters in the public galleries cheered and shouted "Long live religion! Death to the heretics!" "Jesus Christ never wished to kill," replied the liberal deputy Ignacio Ramirez, the only liberal leader who openly admitted that he was an atheist. He lost his seat at the next election, as did most of the other deputies who had spoken in favor of religious toleration.

The proposal for religious toleration having been lost, a compromise was adopted. The constitution of 1857 merely stated that the Catholic religion was the religion of Mexico, but omitted the provision that it was the only religion allowed by law. The Church denounced the new constitution. They did not fail to point out that Juárez and Lerdo, like George Washington in the United States and King Victor Emmanuel and Garibaldi in Italy, were Freemasons.

The archbishop of Mexico was an elderly and ineffectual man who was not suited to lead the Church's resistance to the liberals, but Monsignor Labastida, bishop of Puebla and Tlaxcala, had all the necessary leadership qualities and was eager for the fight. He was born into a poor Creole family, but had risen in the Church by his energy and ability. He had not developed any of the finesse of a diplomat or the polish of an aristocrat. The ladies who sat next to him at state banquets were disgusted by his table manners and by his habit of belching, but no one could accuse Labastida of a lack of antiliberal zeal.

In view of the Ley Juárez, the Ley Lerdo, and the constitution of 1857, Labastida and his colleagues decided that it was not enough to order the clergy to refuse absolution to anyone who swore allegiance to the new constitution; it was also necessary to overthrow the Comonfort government by a *coup d'état*. They sent a Jesuit priest, Father Miranda, to visit army barracks throughout the country to win the support of the commanders for their plan. Miranda persuaded several of the leading officers to meet secretly at Tacubaya, where they agreed to carry out the *coup*. He even succeeded in winning over Comonfort, who agreed to replace his liberal government by a junta of generals with himself at its head.

The *coup* was carried out on December 16, 1857. Comonfort persuaded most of his Cabinet ministers to support the *coup*; those who refused, like Juárez, were arrested. But in less than a month another of the army conspirators, General Félix Zuloaga, decided that he would be a better president than Comonfort, and Comonfort was forced to resign. His last act as president, before he left for New York, was to order the release of Juárez from prison.

Juárez decided that because Comonfort had resigned and Zuloaga had seized power illegally in Mexico City, under the provisions of the constitution the presidential powers had passed to him as chief justice. When he was released from prison he slipped out of Mexico City and set out on foot for the north. In Guanajuato, he found enough local support to enable him to proclaim himself the lawful president of Mexico in opposition to the junta that had seized power. His forces were defeated by Zuloaga's army, and though he shrugged off the setback by telling his ministers that "our cock has lost a feather," he was forced to retreat farther north. He reached Manzanillo on the Pacific coast, where he embarked on an American ship and traveled by way of Panama, Havana, and New Orleans to Veracruz, which had always been a liberal stronghold and was held by his supporters. He appointed Lerdo as his minister of finance and Ocampo as foreign minister. His government in Veracruz and Zuloaga's in Mexico City settled down to a three-year civil war, which became known as the War of the Reform.

Gutiérrez, in Rome, hearing the news from Mexico, was more convinced than ever that only a monarch imposed by European intervention could end the deplorable situation in his native country. He had the support of Santa Anna, who had given up hope that he would yet again be president of Mexico and was living in exile in the Caribbean island of St. Thomas. Gutiérrez found another useful ally — José Hidalgo, who had served for a time in the Mexican legations in London and Madrid but was now living in retirement in Paris. When he was stationed in Madrid, Hidalgo had often visited the house of the countess of Montijo, one of the leading society hostesses, whose daughter Eugénie had since married Napoleon III and was empress of the French.

Although Eugénie was soon to acquire the reputation among the liberals of being a ferocious partisan of the Catholic Church, she was not in fact an intolerant Ultramontane in politics, though she was a deeply religious woman. Her father, the count of Montijo, to whom she was very attached, had been a Spanish liberal; but after his death, her mother became friendly with the leaders of the Conservative Party in Spain, and Eugénie was brought up to be a pious Catholic in her home in Madrid and in the convent where she was educated in Paris.

Eugénie seems to have been very much affected by an incident that occurred in 1835 when she was nine, living with her parents in the Plazuela del Angel in Madrid during the civil war between the liberals and the Catholic armies of Don Carlos. As the Carlist forces advanced on Madrid, shooting all the liberals they captured, the rumor spread that the priests and monks were Carlist spies. One day Eugénie heard a great commotion in the square outside the house. The grown-ups told her not to look out of the window, but of course she did, and saw a liberal mob attacking the monastery on the other side of the square. They had got hold of an old monk and were repeatedly stabbing him with their knives, as the blood gushed forth. Eugénie was horrified, and never forgot what she had seen; for her, this would always be what "the Revolution" meant in practice.

When she was seventeen she tried to commit suicide after an unhappy love affair, by swallowing the heads of matches dissolved in milk; but she was given an emetic, and was saved. She bounced back, with the resilience she showed throughout her life, and became a heartless coquette, flirting indiscriminately with young noblemen and bullfighters, riding bareback through the streets of Madrid smoking a cigar, shocking her elders and fascinating the men. She sometimes crossed the French frontier to spend a holiday at the little fishing port of Biarritz, where she dared the fishermen to take her out in their boats when it was dangerous to go.

Her father had brought her up to admire Napoleon, and she was an ardent Bonapartist before she met his nephew. In November 1852 she was in Paris when Louis Napoleon was on the point of proclaiming himself Emperor Napoleon III. She was invited to go hunting with him in the forest of Fountainebleau, and as they rode ahead of all the others to arrive together at the kill, he fell in love with her. Two months later, to the surprise of all Europe, he married her. Her beauty, vivacity, and informality made her a popular figure in France and Europe; the men admired her charms, and the women followed her example in hairstyle and dress. She made Napoleon III's court the most brilliant in Europe, but her outspokenness sometimes embarrassed him. Not long after her marriage, when there was diplomatic tension between Spain and the United States over an incident in Cuba, she said in the presence of several foreign diplomats that it would one day be necessary for France to go to war with the United States. Her husband immediately told her not to talk nonsense.

She liked to spend a few weeks in September every year in her beloved Biarritz, and there Napoleon III built a house for her, the Villa Eugénie. As soon as it was known that the empress liked Biarritz, the aristocratic and wealthy families also went there, and the little fishing village that she had loved became a fashionable society resort.

In September 1857 Hidalgo went for a holiday to Bayonne, a few miles from Biarritz, and was walking in the street when Eugénie, on her way to a bullfight, drove past in her carriage. He took off his hat to salute her, and she recognized him, though she had not seen him since he had visited her mother's house in Madrid. She invited him into her carriage and told the coachman to drive to his destination. She said that she would like to meet him again and invited him to a barbecue that she was having in Biarritz a few days later. There Hidalgo told her about all the dreadful things that were happening in Mexico — how the liberals were attacking the Church and persecuting priests, monks, and nuns.

A few weeks later, after she had returned to Paris, Eugénie invited Hidalgo to the Tuileries Palace to meet Napoleon III. Hidalgo told the emperor what he had already told the empress, emphasizing that only the intervention of a strong European power could restore law and order and save religion in Mexico. Napoleon was sympathetic, but said that it would be impossible for him to intervene in Mexico, as it would involve France in difficulties with the United States. It was always the United States, the land of republicanism and democracy, that stood in the way of Gutiérrez's dream of an emperor for Mexico.

❄ 4 ❄

THE GENERAL AND THE INDIAN

THE MEXICAN CONSERVATIVES who had remained in Mexico were not as keen as the refugees in Europe or Santa Anna in St. Thomas on having a European prince imposed on them by an invading European army, for they hoped that they would be able to win their war against the liberals without foreign aid. As the War of the Reform entered its second year, in January 1859, they persuaded Zuloaga to resign, and chose as president of the republic his brilliant young second-in-command, General Miguel Miramón. He was descended from a family of French immigrants but had easily become assimilated with the Spanish Creoles. In 1846, at the age of seventeen he had enlisted in the army to fight the invaders from the United States and had shown great gallantry in several engagements. A landowner, a devout Catholic, handsome, brave, and a great success with the ladies, Miramón possessed a dashing temperament that made him ready not only to risk his life on the battlefield, but also to adopt a daring and aggressive policy in war and in politics. Once, when asked what connections and influence he had, he replied, "My sword is my influence."

He regarded liberals as the enemies of Mexico and of religion, and believed that it was his duty to God and his country to fight and destroy them without mercy. The conservatives could not have wished for a better leader in a civil war.

He was a very different figure from the rival president of the republic, Benito Juárez in Veracruz. Juárez, who was fifty-three in 1859, was just five feet tall, more dark-skinned than many Indians, and with a scar across his lips — perhaps the mark of a childhood beating from his stern uncle in Guelatao. He was abstemious in food and drink but very fond of cigars. He was said to have fathered a few bastards in his youth, but he was now a devoted husband to his spirited Creole wife,

Doña Margarita, the daughter of Maza, the merchant who had sheltered him when he first arrived in Oaxaca and who still employed
Juárez's sister as his domestic servant. Juárez had been living in Oaxaca for seven years when Margarita was born; they married in 1843,
when he was thirty-seven and she was seventeen. She bore him three
sons and nine daughters. Three of the daughters died in infancy, but
the other nine children survived, which was a much higher proportion
than was usual in nineteenth-century Mexico. Juárez was a devoted
father to all the children.

Doña Margarita was living in Oaxaca City with eight of the children, the eldest of whom was fourteen and the youngest a baby, when
Juárez left Mexico City and assumed the powers of president of the
republic. As soon as she heard that he had established his government
at Veracruz, she set off from Oaxaca with the children, to walk and
ride on mules across the mountains to Veracruz, 150 miles away,
facing not only the hardships of the journey but also the well-known
dangers of bandits and of any conservative forces they might encounter. They arrived safely a month later.

Juárez's manners were courteous and formal. He was soft-spoken
and hardly ever showed any emotion, but he was very determined,
and could be as hard as steel and ruthless. He was skillful in handling
his colleagues and in reconciling disagreements between them. He
adhered firmly to liberal principles and to the rule of law; but he
would break the law, and even the constitution, when he thought
there was no other way of saving his country and his cause. He was
accused by his enemies, and even by some of his supporters, of personal ambition; but insofar as it is possible to analyze a statesman's
motives, it is probably true to say that when he clung to power and
outplayed his rivals, he acted from a sincere belief that he was the only
man who could save Mexico. And he was probably right to think so.

Some conservatives despised him for being an Indian, but they
despised him even more for being a lawyer. The cynics said that
neither the conservatives nor the liberals had done much for the
Indians and that the forty years of struggle and civil wars was a fight
between the conservative landowners, priests, and army officers, on
the one hand, and the liberal lawyers and traders, on the other. The
conservatives also had among their leaders two Indians as full-
blooded as Juárez; but their Generals Tomás Mejía and Ramón Mendez were regular army officers. In Mejía's native mountains near
Querétaro the Indians were devoted to him and would follow wherever he led them; but many other Indians were liberal supporters.

A story was told about Juárez that the liberals were happy to repeat.
When he first arrived at Veracruz to head the government, he asked a

black woman who was a servant in his hotel to fetch him a glass of water. She rudely told him to fetch the water himself, which he did without protest or explanation. The next day, when the woman was serving the members of the government at a formal luncheon at the hotel, she was appalled to see the Indian presiding at the head of the table and being respectfully addressed as "Señor Presidente"; she fled from the room in panic.

But the conservatives more often told another story about Juárez. One day his officers went to tell him that the conservatives had attacked the town and that fighting was going on at the city gates. They urged him to mount his horse, put himself at the head of his troops, and lead them against the enemy. "I do not know how to ride a horse," replied Juárez as he lit another cigar and put his feet up on the sofa. It was only a story, but there is no doubt that Señor Licenciado Don Benito Juárez never made himself a general and never wore either the splendid military uniform of an army officer or the native dress of the Zapotec tribe, which his sister, the servant at Oaxaca, wore all her life. He wore the starched white shirt and the black stock, trousers, and frock coat, together with the top hat and cane, of a middle-class lawyer and professional man.

The liberals fought with fervor for their cause, countering the conservative slogan "Religion and Order" with "God and Liberty." But it was difficult for them to find generals to lead their armies against the professional officers commanding the conservative forces. Those army officers who joined the liberals often quarreled, accusing each other of disloyalty and of trying to become dictator; and they were reluctant to obey the orders of a government presided over by an Indian lawyer. But Juárez found General Santos Degollado, whom he appointed minister of war and commander-in-chief of the Federal Army. Degollado called on his soldiers to fight "for the sacred cause of democracy," denouncing the conservatives, "the hypocritical Pharisees who invoke the religion of Jesus Christ without believing in it or observing its maxims of fraternity and peace."

In October 1858 Degollado besieged Guanajuato, an important prize for the liberals. Its capture would impress the foreigners who had interests in its silver mines. The conservative General Blaucarte met Degollado in the house of the Prussian consul and agreed to surrender the city on condition that his life and those of his officers be spared and that they be allowed to go free. As soon as the surrender had taken place, the liberals entered Guanajuato and lynched several local conservatives, including an official who had executed a liberal mayor not long before. One of Degollado's officers shot Blaucarte dead, in full view of Degollado and his staff. Degollado demoted the officer to the ranks for this act of indiscipline but reinstated him a few months later, after he had distinguished himself in action.

The conservatives usually managed to be a little more ruthless than their opponents. In March 1859 Miramón, after recapturing Guanajuato and defeating the liberals in several battles, marched to Veracruz and besieged Juárez's capital; but yellow fever, the local scourge, forced him to lift the siege after a month, and he retired, discomfited, to Mexico City. Degollado had tried to seize the opportunity, while Miramón was at Veracruz, to make an attack on Mexico City, but Miramón's General Leonardo Márquez defeated Degollado at Tacubaya in a two-day battle on April 10 and 11.

Miramón arrived in Mexico City from Veracruz on the morning of April 11, and a few hours later received from Márquez a report on his victory and a list of the liberals who had been captured in the battle. Seventeen of the prisoners were officers. Degollado had escaped from the battlefield, leaving only his shirt, which was flown with the other trophies above Miramón's residence, the National Palace in Mexico City; but his second-in-command, old General Lazcano, was among the prisoners. Miramón immediately sent Márquez an order, which the liberals said was written on the notepaper of Miramón's mistress, Concha Lombardo, commanding him to shoot the seventeen officers. Miramón afterward justified this order on the grounds that these officers were deserters from his army who had gone over to the enemy, but he was acting on the assumption that any officer of the regular army who fought for the liberals against Miramón's government was a deserter and a traitor.

Tacubaya, which is today a suburb of Mexico City, was in 1859 a small country town where the wealthiest aristocrats, dignitaries, and businessmen had their country houses. Barron the banker, whose family had originally emigrated to Mexico from England and was one of the richest men in Mexico, had a mansion with a large garden at Tacubaya; the archbishop of Mexico's house and garden were almost as large.

During the battle, the liberals occupied the archbishop's house and set up a front-line hospital where their very inadequate medical services did what they could for their wounded soldiers. They were helped by Dr. Duval of Mexico City University, a British subject, who, with some of his colleagues, brought a team of medical students to Tacubaya to help care for the wounded on both sides. When Degollado retreated, the soldiers of the liberal army who were too seriously wounded to move were left behind in the archbishop's house. The head of the Medical Corps of Juárez's army, Dr. Sánchez, decided to stay behind with them and the military and civilian doctors who were caring for them.

Márquez received Miramón's order to shoot the seventeen officers at 5 P.M. on April 11. He immediately ordered his men to shoot all the other prisoners, as well. They began with General Lazcano. Some of Márquez's officers, who had formerly been Lazcano's subordinates, were in charge of the execution squad. They took the old man to the archbishop's garden, taunting and insulting him. He said to them, "It is cowardly and base to insult a dying man." They shot him in the back, the recognized military punishment for treason. Two captains and a lieutenant were shot, also in the back, a few minutes later.

Márquez's men then broke into the archbishop's house, where they found a scene that before their arrival was horrible enough — a scene often repeated in front-line hospitals in the mid-nineteenth century. Under the supervision of the surgeon, Dr. Sánchez, the doctors were ordering amputation of the arms and legs of all seriously wounded men. In the absence of anesthetics, the orderlies and students were giving the patients wine to make them drunk and holding them down on their beds by force while Dr. Sánchez performed the amputations.

Márquez's men arrived while the operations were being carried out. They ordered the doctors to stop operating and let the wounded soldiers bleed to death. Dr. Sánchez and all the doctors refused. Márquez's men then shot the wounded men. They also shot the doctors, orderlies, and students, who, they said, were giving aid and comfort to traitors and were therefore traitors themselves.

The liberal propagandists wrote many moving stories about the fifty-three martyrs who died in the Massacre of Tacubaya. Conscious of the deep religious feelings of the Mexican people, they were eager to convince them that the liberals were the true Christians and that the "reactionaries" who falsely claimed to be fighting for religion were really the successors of the Pharisees who persecuted Christ. Juan Covarrubias, a nineteen-year-old student of literature who had already written a number of unpublished short stories and poems before he enlisted in the liberal army, was told that he was to be shot. When he asked for a confessor, his captors said there was no time, so he distributed the money in his pockets among the soldiers of the execution squad and prepared for death. The officer gave the order to fire, but the soldiers did not shoot; when the order was repeated, only two of them fired. This did not help Covarrubias, for he was wounded by two bullets and was left to die. He was soon buried under a heap of other corpses, but was found, still alive, several hours later by other soldiers. They beat out his brains with their rifle butts.

Another young poet, Manuel Matías, aged twenty-four, had fought in the victorious liberal army at the Battle of Ocatlán, where he spared the life of a conservative officer who had been taken prisoner and was expecting to be shot. The young idealist gave him a horse and allowed him to escape. When Márquez's men told Matías he would be shot in the back as a traitor, he turned on them and said that he pardoned them, as they knew not what they did when they murdered those who were fighting for freedom. His words were interrupted by a hail of bullets, and he fell dead.

Agustín Jáureguy had not joined the liberal army and was living quietly at his house in Mexico City. But someone denounced him to the authorities there as a liberal, so on April 11 the soldiers took him to Tacubaya and shot him with the others.

The liberals wrote that Márquez should henceforth be called not "Leonardo" but "Leopardo" Márquez, and denounced him as "the Tiger of Tacubaya." Márquez was delighted, and announced that he would proudly assume the title. A few days after the killings, Márquez took part in the victory parade in Mexico City, wearing a sash he had been given by admiring conservative ladies. It bore the words "To Virtue and Valor. The gratitude of the daughters of Mexico."

❋ 5 ❋

THE GREAT POWERS
BECOME INVOLVED

THE BRITISH CONSERVATIVE foreign secretary, Lord Malmesbury, sat in the Foreign Office in Whitehall in London reading the dispatches from the British minister to Mexico, Mr. Otway, which had taken a month to reach him. He thought the Mexican civil war a nuisance, like all other civil wars in distant backward countries, for they interfered with the trading activities of British subjects and sometimes endangered their property and their lives. During civil wars the two rival governments were apt to impose emergency taxes on British subjects and to make them contribute to the "loans" that all the native inhabitants were forced, by threats and pressure, to pay, and that were supposed to be repaid but in practice never were. Often local military commanders in need of money to pay their troops adopted the simpler procedure of seizing the British subjects' property. Occasionally a British subject was killed in the crossfire between the combatants. A number of Englishmen and Scotsmen were living in Mexico. Some were connected with the silver mines of Guanajuato, Zacatecas, and San Luis Potosí. Others had purchased and developed agricultural land.

There were also British subjects in London who held Mexican government bonds for the repayment of money they had lent to Mexico in the early days of independence in 1824. The government showed no sign of repaying the capital protected by these bonds and sometimes defaulted on the interest due.

Mr. Otway, like the other foreign diplomatic representatives, had remained in Mexico City and recognized the conservative government at the start of the civil war. He thought that the best solution would be for Mexico to be annexed to the British Empire, and he wrote to Lord Malmesbury that he had met several wealthy and influential Mexicans who agreed with him. Malmesbury had no doubt that this would indeed be the best solution for Mexico, but he dismissed the idea and merely sent a British warship to cruise off Veracruz as an encouragement to Juárez's government to pay the interest due to the British holders of Mexican bonds. Any further intervention would lead to endless trouble, and perhaps to a war with the United States.

When Palmerston became prime minister again in June 1859, with Lord John Russell as his foreign secretary, the British government became a little more sympathetic to Juárez. They did not believe he was capable of governing Mexico and safeguarding the lives and property of British subjects; but Russell, with his strong Whig and anti-Catholic traditions, approved of the liberal measures against the Church, and was pleased when Juárez, in July 1859, issued a series of decrees that proclaimed religious toleration and completed the abolition of the privileges of the Church and the confiscation of its property. But an influential body of British Conservative opinion sympathized with the Mexican conservatives. Their journal, *The Saturday Review,* insisted that Miramón, with all his faults, was a Spanish gentleman, and preferable to Juárez, "a mere Indian" and "a sanguinary savage" who attacked the Church because he worshiped his tribal Indian gods.

Juárez took great care to protect the property of British residents. When General Degollado, fully conscious of the British reaction but desperate to obtain money to pay his troops, seized the silver (valued at $1.127 million) that British subjects in San Luis Potosí were sending to Veracruz for shipment to Europe, Juárez insisted on repaying the British owners, though it cost him the services of his best general, for Degollado resigned in disgust and withdrew into private life. Miramón was less accommodating and did not repay the $700,000 which British residents had deposited in the British legation in Mexico City and which Márquez forcibly removed from the legation.

The French government was more hostile than the British to the Mexican liberals. In the last months before the outbreak of the War of the Reform, the French minister in Mexico City, the count of Gabriac, had shown great hostility to the liberal government; and when Zuloaga and Miramón became president they received every encouragement from the French minister. The conservatives suffered from a disadvantage; because Juárez held the port of Veracruz, the liberals were in a much better position than they to trade with Europe and raise money to pay their troops from the customs duties in the port. By January 1859 Miramón was in considerable financial difficulties, even though the clergy had sold their plate and valuables and organized collections in the churches to raise money to help the government in its fight for God against the liberals and Freemasons.

Gabriac came to Miramón's help and put him in touch with a Swiss banker named Jecker, who offered to lend the Mexican government money on very advantageous terms for himself. Miramón agreed to issue to Jecker Mexican government bonds bearing 20 percent interest per annum. Jecker afterward stated that one of his partners in this transaction was the duke of Morny, Napoleon III's illegitimate brother and one of his most influential advisers; Morny was dead by the time Jecker disclosed this, and there is no corroboration of his statement, but it is very likely that Morny was connected with the Jecker bonds.

The Spanish government was even more hostile to Juárez, sending threatening and insulting notes to his government whenever a Spanish subject suffered some injury or slight at the hands of a local liberal commander.

The United States was the only foreign power that showed signs of supporting the liberals. There was strong sympathy for Juárez in the United States, especially among the Abolitionists, who identified the struggle of the oppressed Indians in Mexico with the campaign for the liberation of the black slaves. The *New-York Times* wrote that because Juárez was leading the fight for the freedom of an oppressed race that had for centuries writhed beneath the heel of the oppressor, he and the Mexican liberals were "abused and denounced from one end of Christendom to the other."

Other Americans supported Juárez for very different reasons. President James Buchanan, who viewed with alarm the drift in the United States toward secession and civil war on the slavery issue, devised a plan that, he hoped, would win public approval and result in advantage to the nation and glory for himself. Robert McLane of Maryland, Buchanan's emissary, presented to Foreign Minister Ocampo a proposal that the United States should recognize Juárez's government and send an expeditionary force to Mexico to help the liberals overthrow Miramón. In return, Juárez would cede Baja California to the United States and would uphold the rights of a railroad company based in New Orleans to build a railroad across the Isthmus of Tehuantepec, linking the Atlantic and the Pacific. Juárez would also grant the United States extraterritorial rights in perpetuity in the isthmus so that it could protect the rights of its citizens and the railroad company.

Ocampo did not like the proposal. The liberals had denounced Santa Anna for ceding territory to the United States under the Gadsden Purchase. If the liberals were now to cede Baja California, Miramón and the conservatives would make great political propaganda out of it, and the transaction might alienate many liberal supporters.

But Ocampo knew that they were not winning the War of the Reform, and with the constant threat of intervention from Spain, and perhaps from other European states, an alliance with the United States might be necessary. He eventually decided, very reluctantly, that he had no alternative but to accept the proposal. Juárez was more doubtful; he was prepared to agree to the railroad concession and the grant of extraterritorial rights in the isthmus, but not to the cession of Baja California or any Mexican territory.

On December 14, 1859, McLane and Ocampo signed the treaty, subject to ratification by their governments. Its terms had been published a few days before in the *New York Herald Tribune*; Miramón's newspapers in Mexico City also published them, and violently denounced Ocampo and the liberals as traitors to their country. Juárez withheld ratification until the treaty had been accepted by the United States Senate; but with the publication of the terms of the treaty by Miramón, most of the damage to the liberals had already been done.

Buchanan, in his message to Congress in December 1859, urged the Senate to ratify the treaty; but the congressmen were more concerned with what Buchanan called "the recent sad and bloody occurrences at Harpers Ferry," when John Brown and his band of eighteen white and black Abolitionists attacked the federal arsenal, hoping to provoke an uprising of the slaves and end slavery. The uproar following the raid and Brown's execution was one of the reasons the Senate rejected the McLane-Ocampo Treaty. In view of the talk of civil war in the United States, this was no time for the country to become involved in adventures in Mexico. The antislavery forces in the United States were suspicious of projects to acquire Mexican territory as a means to extend slavery, and the supporters of slavery were not eager to help Juárez and the Mexican liberals. The treaty was rejected by 27 votes to 18 in the Senate, and Juárez was relieved of the responsibility of having to decide whether to ratify it.

The Monroe Doctrine and the interests of the United States drove Buchanan's government to help the Mexican liberals even without the benefits promised by the treaty. In March 1860 Miramón again besieged Veracruz, shelling the town and killing thirty-eight women, children, and old men, while Juárez and his family withdrew to Fort San Juan de Ulúa across the harbor, for which action he was accused of cowardice by the conservatives. Miramón also tried to impose a naval blockade of Veracruz, though he had no navy capable of enforcing it. A Spanish warship, which had been cruising off Veracruz in the hope of frightening Juárez's government into paying compensation for losses to Spanish subjects, showed signs of joining in the blockade.

Two United States warships thereupon appeared and drove the Spanish ship away. The Spanish navy made no further attempt to intervene in Mexico.

When Degollado resigned, Juárez replaced him by a new commander-in-chief, General Ortega, who turned out to be the most successful general the liberals had found so far. He defeated Miramón in several engagements and closed in on Mexico City. Miramón made a last attempt to break through the encircling liberal armies, but on December 22, 1860, his forces were annihilated at Calpulalpam. Ortega entered Mexico City on Christmas Day and was received with great enthusiasm by the people. The foreign diplomats had been warned by Miramón that there would be looting and raping when the liberals arrived; but the troops behaved with perfect discipline, and no excesses were committed against Miramón's supporters.

The news of Ortega's victory at Calpulalpam reached Veracruz on the evening of December 23, when Juárez and his wife and the members of the government, in full evening dress, were attending a performance of Bellini's *I Puritani* at the opera house. The performance was interrupted while Juárez, rising in his box, read out the message from Ortega announcing the victory. The audience received the news with tumultuous cheering. The orchestra played the new Mexican national anthem, which had been composed to celebrate the constitution of 1857. Very few people in the audience knew the words, but they all knew and sang the "Marseillaise," for the French revolutionary song of 1792 had become the anthem of liberal revolutionaries in every country, though it was banned in the France of Napoleon III.

It seemed that at last it was the final victory of the liberal cause. But three days earlier, on December 20, South Carolina had seceded from the United States because Abraham Lincoln had been elected president. Ten other states were about to join South Carolina in the Confederate States of America. Everybody was talking of the forthcoming American Civil War.

No one was happier at the prospect than Palmerston. On January 1, 1861, he sent a letter with New Year's greetings to Queen Victoria, telling her that the last months of the old year had seen "the approaching and virtually accomplished dissolution in America of the great Northern Confederation." He had no doubt that the United States would cease to exist as a nation. This was good news for Palmerston, but a disaster for the liberals in Mexico.

❈ 6 ❈

THE ARCHDUKE MAXIMILIAN

IN JULY 1832, during the hottest summer in Vienna within living memory, two members of the imperial family were confined to their beds at Schönbrunn, the summer palace of Emperor Franz II on the outskirts of the city. The emperor's grandson, Napoleon Franz, was dying of consumption, and his daughter-in-law Archduchess Sophie was in labor.

Napoleon Franz, son of the great Napoleon by his second wife, Archduchess Marie-Louise of Austria, had been given the title king of Rome by his father the day he was born. Four years later, after the Battle of Waterloo, Napoleon abdicated in his favor and he was Emperor Napoleon II of the French for nine days, until the allied armies entered Paris and restored the Bourbon Louis XVIII. Napoleon Franz knew nothing about this at the time, for his mother had escaped with him to Vienna. He was brought up in Vienna while she lived with her lover in the Duchy of Parma, given to her by the victorious allies. Napoleon Franz was not allowed to keep any of his previous titles or to be called prince of Parma; but Emperor Franz's grandson had to be given a suitable rank, so he was created duke of Reichstadt, and when he grew up he was made a colonel in the Austrian army.

Napoleon Franz was treated with due respect at the court of his grandfather, who was very fond of him; but he was held as a virtual prisoner, because Metternich feared that the Bonapartists would restore him to the French throne. He wished to accomplish great things worthy of his father, and he resented that he was prevented from doing so by poor health and his position. The restrictions on his movements hampered the development of his sex life. When a pretty girl made eyes at him at the opera, Metternich became alarmed that she might be a Bonapartist agent sent to organize his escape. It was rumored that he was having an affair with the famous ballerina Fanny

Elssler, who took Vienna by storm in 1831; apparently the rumor started only because his servant sometimes took his letters to a friend and brother officer who happened to be living in the same hotel as Fanny Elssler. The duke of Reichstadt, a rather shy young man, showed no particular interest in Fanny or in any of the suitable young ladies he was allowed to meet.

Archduchess Sophie was the daughter of King Maximilian of Bavaria, who had allied himself with Napoleon and had sent Bavarian troops to fight for the French against the Austrians at Austerlitz and Wagram. When Napoleon started to lose, King Maximilian hurriedly changed sides and joined Austria and the allies, hoping that he had not left it until too late. He was much relieved when he escaped with no worse consequences than being obliged to surrender the Austrian territory that Napoleon had granted to him, and he was overjoyed when Metternich proposed a marriage between his daughter Sophie and Emperor Franz's second son, Archduke Franz Karl.

Sophie herself was much less happy when she was told that she was to marry the archduke. "Not *him!*" she cried, for Karl was dull, uncouth, and stupid. But she did her duty to father and country and married Karl in 1824. She was very unhappy at the Austrian court; she wrote to her parents that she hated Vienna and longed for her beloved Munich. Her only real friend at the Hofburg and Schönbrunn was the duke of Reichstadt, who was as lonely as she was. When she married the archduke, she was nineteen and Napoleon Franz was thirteen, and they soon established a relationship of devoted sister and younger brother. She called him "my old man" and "*mon petit choux.*"

Rumors about Sophie's relationship with her husband spread in the six years after her marriage because she did not produce a child. Then in 1830, when she was twenty-five, she gave birth to a son, who later became Emperor Franz Joseph. By then the duke of Reichstadt was nineteen, and it was whispered that he was Franz Joseph's father. Eighteen months later she was pregnant again with another son, who became Emperor Maximilian of Mexico. Again it was said that he was the son of Napoleon Franz.

These rumors, whispered at the time, were shouted from the rooftops a hundred years later by French journalists, novelists, and playwrights, and have been accepted by most of Emperor Maximilian's biographers. There is not a shred of evidence to support the rumors; of course, if there had been any evidence, it would probably have been destroyed by the parties or by the Austrian authorities. It was said that Sophie confessed, in a letter to her father confessor, that Maximilian was the son of Napoleon Franz and that the letter was found and destroyed in 1859, but there is no reason to believe this story. The only basis for it is a certain facial resemblance between Napoleon Franz and Franz Joseph and the fact that Sophie, childless after six years of marriage to the unattractive Franz Karl, produced a son when her close friend, the duke of Reichstadt, reached manhood. But even if Sophie had been prepared to be unfaithful to her husband, would she have had a sexual relationship with a boy whom she regarded as a child and a younger brother? Or, as she watched him grow up, did her affection for him extend to introducing him to the joys of sex, which he was too timid to engage in with other women?

The duke of Reichstadt's chronic chest complaint grew worse. On a very cold day in February 1832 he insisted, against his doctors' advice, on reviewing his regiment at a military parade in the park at Schönbrunn, and he became dangerously ill. In June the doctors told the emperor and his family that the duke's life was in great danger. The family thought it essential that he be given extreme unction, but they were afraid to suggest it to him. They took Sophie into their confidence, and she proposed to him that both he and she receive the sacrament, he because of his illness and she because of her pregnancy. This they did together in the chapel at Schönbrunn.

On July 6, as Sophie gave birth to Maximilian, Napoleon Franz was sinking fast. In 1832 women of quality were confined for a long time after their delivery, and Sophie had not yet risen from her bed when Napoleon Franz died on July 22. His mother, Marie-Louise, arrived from Parma in time to see him before he died, but Sophie was not present at the deathbed. When she was told of his death, she fainted, and the doctors feared that the news would retard her recovery and even endanger the health of her baby, but Maximilian thrived.

Again rumors were rife. If Maximilian was the duke of Reichstadt's son, then the death of the father when the son was a fortnight old made a sad and romantic story. Three years later Sophie gave birth to Archduke Karl Ludwig; her fourth son, Ludwig Viktor, was born in 1842. No one could suggest that Karl Ludwig or Ludwig Viktor was the son of Napoleon Franz.

The Austrian Empire was regarded by liberals everywhere as a bastion of absolutism. Though it was not quite as harsh a despotism as Russia, the dungeons in the Spielberg in Moravia were full of prominent liberal and nationalist leaders who were lucky if they emerged before they died there. Most of the empire was inhabited by subject peoples who considered themselves oppressed by the Austrians.

Emperor Franz died in 1835 and was succeeded by his eldest son, Emperor Ferdinand I. He suffered from epilepsy, and though he was well enough to marry a Piedmontese princess, they had no children. Metternich continued to rule the empire and to reject all proposals for reform. Meanwhile Sophie was bringing up her two elder sons, Franz Joseph and Ferdinand Maximilian; but people noticed that her personality seemed to have changed, that she had become colder and harder since the death of the duke of Reichstadt.

The two boys lived together in the Hofburg and at Schönbrunn, and in the summer went on holidays to Ischl, near Salzburg. They were different in character. Franz Joseph was tidy, systematic, and interested in military matters; Ferdinand Maximilian, usually called Ferdinand Max both by the family and by the people, was more dreamy and artistic, though he was a better horseman than Franz Joseph. The two boys were very close, and Ferdinand Max looked up to his more forceful elder brother with great admiration.

In 1848 revolutions broke out all over Europe. In March there were uprisings in Prague, Vienna, Milan, and Budapest. The emperor and the imperial family were at the mercy of the mob in Vienna. But the Austrian army in Lombardy and Venetia, under the command of the eighty-two-year-old Field Marshal Radetzky, won a number of victories over the Italian revolutionaries. Franz Joseph, who was eighteen, was serving in Radetzky's army. Maximilian, at sixteen considered too young to join his brother, was with the emperor, Sophie, and the rest of the family in the Hofburg.

In May a student demonstration in Vienna ended with the students forcing their way into the Hofburg and into the presence of the emperor. The imperial family fled to Innsbruck. A few weeks later, they thought it safe to return to Vienna, but soon there was another rising of the radical mob, in the course of which the minister of war was murdered. Again the imperial family escaped, and went to Olmütz in Moravia. Sophie, beside herself with indignation, wrote: "I could have borne the loss of one of my children more easily than I can the ignominy of submitting to a mass of students. In the future the shame of the past will seem simply incredible." It was fortunate for her that she could not foresee the future.

The empire was saved by Radetzky and Field Marshal Windischgrätz, and by the nationalist hatreds that divided the revolutionaries. Radetzky crushed the revolution in Italy, and Windischgrätz recaptured Prague and Vienna, though the intervention of a Russian army was needed to reconquer Hungary. Windischgrätz had twenty-three radical leaders shot in Vienna after trial by court-martial, and revolutionaries were executed and whipped in Lombardy and Hungary. Liberals throughout Europe were outraged by the executions and whippings, and public opinion in England was particularly incensed that women were whipped. But the Austrian imperial family, nobility, and middle class — and many of the people, particularly the peasants — regarded old "Father Radetzky" as a hero, and well worthy of the popular march that Johann Strauss the elder composed in his honor.

Archduchess Sophie was the most powerful personality in the imperial family. At the height of the revolution she summoned Windischgrätz and his brother-in-law, Prince Felix von Schwarzenberg, to Olmütz, where Schwarzenberg was appointed chancellor. Sophie, Windischgrätz, and Schwarzenberg thought that Emperor Ferdinand, whom his people regarded as an amiable idiot, was not a suitable head of state in this dangerous situation. The eighteen-year-old Franz Joseph, who had won his spurs in Radetzky's army and had the necessary youthful energy, aggression, and popular appeal, would be a much better leader of a counterrevolution.

Sophie persuaded Ferdinand to abdicate and her husband to relinquish his right to succeed to the throne. At a ceremony at Olmütz on December 2, 1848, Emperor Ferdinand abdicated, Franz Karl renounced his right of succession, and Franz Joseph began his reign, which was to continue until 1916. Maximilian was among the first to take the oath of allegiance to his brother, the new emperor. From then on, even when the two devoted brothers were alone together, he addressed Franz Joseph as "Your Majesty."

The young emperor wholly approved of the draconian policy of Radetzky, Windischgrätz, and Schwarzenberg, but the less military and more philosophical Maximilian was not happy about it. He noted in his diary that, although "we call our age the age of enlightenment. . . . In very many cities of Europe posterity will view with amazement and horror" the fact that military tribunals, without any process of law, "under the influence of hateful revenge, condemned people to death at a few hours' notice, perhaps because they wanted something different from what was desired by the power that stands above the law."

But only the most diehard supporter of Schwarzenberg and Radetzky could have feared that Maximilian was in any real sense a liberal. He was modern-minded in superficial ways. Like other members of the younger generation he smoked cigars and grew a beard, for beards were just coming into fashion, particularly among young radicals. He developed a great interest in botany, which was unusual in a member of a royal family. But his views on most matters were conventional and conservative.

He was a devout Catholic and went regularly to Mass and confession. He did his best to adhere to the rules of conduct his religion required of him. If he sometimes visited a prostitute, this was too common and venial a sin to be really reprehensible. He had a high sense of honor — the Habsburg code of honor, in which he had been brought up. He believed in absolute monarchy, though he did not exclude the possibility of establishing popular assemblies if this was the will of the monarch.

Maximilian was a man of strong principles. They were not the principles of the liberals, who believed in liberty, equality, and fraternity, in a constitution that granted to all men the rights of free speech, a free press, and freedom from arbitrary arrest, in parliamentary and legislative bodies elected by the people, either by universal or restricted suffrage. The supporters of absolute monarchy believed in obedience, in the duty of everyone, in whatever social class and position God had placed him, to obey his superiors and treat them with proper respect. He must give honest advice to his superiors but must always accept their decisions and carry out their orders. He must be kind and just to his inferiors, thank and reward them for loyal service, protect them in times of danger, and not abandon them if they were in trouble because they had performed their duty conscientiously. These were the principles that applied in the army and the Catholic Church, those two bastions of absolute monarchy, and they were the principles in which Archduke Ferdinand Max believed.

Once, when he was a young man, he wrote down twenty-seven rules of conduct he believed he should observe, and he always carried the paper on which they were written. "1. Let the mind rule the body and maintain it in moderation and morality. 2. Never a false word, not even out of necessity or vanity. 3. Be kindly to everybody. . . . 7. No abuse or obscenity. . . . 17. Never complain, for it is a sign of weakness." He admired the traditional English phlegm; rule 22, to "take it coolly," was written in English, though all the others were in German. But he would not have approved of the English gentleman's habit of sometimes eating with his tenants; his tenth rule was "Never joke with one's inferiors, never talk with servants." And of course there was rule 13: "Never mock at religion or authority."

Because Franz Joseph was so prominently identified with the army, it was thought proper that his brother should join the navy, and in 1850, when Maximilian was eighteen, he was given a command in the Adriatic fleet. The commander-in-chief, Admiral Dahlerup, thought Maximilian an able naval officer, and when Dahlerup resigned his command in 1854, his successor, Admiral Tegetthoff, was equally impressed by the archduke. During Maximilian's period with the fleet, the port of Trieste was enlarged, and he showed great interest in the work.

His mother encouraged his devotion to his duties as a naval officer, especially after she discovered that he was beginning a mild flirtation with Countess Paulien von Linden, the daughter of the king of Württemberg's minister in Vienna. He had danced with the countess at a carnival ball and afterward sent her flowers and a love poem. The following evening they both went to the opera, sitting with their parents in separate boxes. He smiled across at her, and she demurely raised the flowers he had sent and covered her face. He returned the next day to his ship in Venice, and soon afterward Paulien left Vienna, when her father was transferred to the Württemberg legation in Berlin.

A year later Maximilian accompanied Franz Joseph on a state visit to Berlin. Paulien von Linden and her parents were present at the great ball given in the emperor's honor. Franz Joseph paid particular attention to Paulien, but Maximilian did not speak to her. He looked at her sadly but gave no sign of recognition, and hurriedly went into another room. Paulien was sure that he was avoiding her because he had been told not to renew their relationship and that Franz Joseph paid her special attention to show everyone that she had done nothing wrong. She and Maximilian both realized that their difference in rank made any intimacy between them impossible; she was too low to be his wife and too high to be his whore.

In the summer of 1851 Maximilian went to the kingdom of Naples and stayed with his cousin, King Ferdinand, in his palace at Gaeta. Like many other nineteenth-century rulers, Ferdinand had started his reign intending to introduce liberal reforms but had turned into an extreme conservative when he saw that reforms only led to unrest and revolution. After his generals had suppressed the revolution in Sicily in 1848 by bombarding Palermo and other towns, Ferdinand was called "King Bomba" by the radicals; there were nearly forty thousand political prisoners in his dungeons.

While Maximilian was staying with King Bomba, he witnessed a disturbing incident. As he was driving with the king through the streets of Gaeta, a woman clasping a baby in her arms rushed toward the royal carriage; the wife of a political prisoner in the dungeons, she wished to ask Ferdinand to pardon her husband. The guards dragged her away, and as she resisted, the baby fell to the ground; the king's coachman drove on, leaving both the baby and the mother lying in the street. Maximilian was distressed by the incident, but the conclusions he drew were not hostile to the Neapolitan regime. He wrote in his diary: "The scene was a sad one, and illustrated the strong, perhaps exaggerated, feelings of the people of the south."

Despite all the protests of the liberals, the Austrian monarchy had not only survived and defeated the revolution but seemed stronger than ever, and there was a mood of optimism in the air. A great rebuilding program was carried out in Vienna, and wide new avenues with neoclassical buildings were constructed in the city center. Maximilian did not feel happy about the repressive measures in Italy and Hungary, but like all the Austrian establishment and most of the Austrian people, he believed that the empire was politically stable and militarily invincible, and that anyone, particularly any foreigner, who warned of the danger of refusing to make concessions was ignorant and impudent.

He was intensely patriotic and proud of everything Austrian. When he noted in his diary that English women were handsome, he hastened to add that when it came to waltzing, they were far inferior to Austrian girls. His only criticism of Austria was of the cold and wet climate of Ischl, which had only three or four really fine days in the year, though he had harsher things to say about the cold summers in Amsterdam and at Reichstadt in Bohemia.

Maximilian was sent with his ship on a tour of the Mediterranean ports, visiting Albania, Greece, and Smyrna. In Albania he met a sailor who had served as a pirate during the Greek War of Independence, and he listened with a mixture of disapproval and admiration as the old man told him how he had killed and tortured Turkish soldiers. He visited the local headman in an Albanian village and spoke with him in a friendly way, but he was annoyed when the headman, some years later, had the "impudence" to write to him at the Hofburg in Vienna.

He visited King Otto of Greece, who was his mother's cousin, for the Great Powers had decided that Greece should have a Bavarian prince as its sovereign. Maximilian noticed the corruption that prevailed everywhere in Otto's kingdom. In Smyrna he was embarrassed to see the naked slave girls in the market. "The sight of a naked woman frightens me," he wrote. "I am made to believe that sin is unbearably attractive."

At Gilbraltar he was entertained at dinner by the governor, Sir Robert Gardiner, a Tory general who had consistently refused asylum to radical refugees from Spain. Gardiner welcomed Archduke Ferdinand Max and proposed the health of the emperor of Austria in an appropriate speech that pleasantly surprised Maximilian, who had expected to hear the usual English criticism of Austrian oppression in Italy and Hungary. The archduke noted the quaint English custom by which the ladies retired toward the end of the dinner, leaving the gentlemen alone to drink their port, but unlike most visitors to England, he approved of this. "Many blame this habit as barbarous," he wrote. "I like it. The ladies ought to learn that they have to obey the men. The consequences of an exaggerated and senseless gallantry toward the ladies is shown to us by the immorality of France."

In Seville he was fascinated by the Spanish way of life, and proudly remembered that his Habsburg ancestor, Emperor Charles V, had ruled and lived in Spain. He loved the bullfights and the Spanish women, who did not faint at the sight of blood, like so many women in the decadent nineteenth century, but reveled in it, screaming with delight at the most horrible moments of the bullfight. He did not approve of the milder bullfights in Portugal, where the bull was teased and tormented but not killed.

For six years after Franz Joseph became emperor, Maximilian was the heir to the throne, but in 1854 Franz Joseph married Princess Elizabeth of Bavaria, with whom he had fallen in love, though Sophie had planned for him to marry Elizabeth's sister. The new empress was as determined a character as Sophie herself and more than held her own with her domineering mother-in-law. She soon gave Franz Joseph a son and heir. (Thirty-one years later this son, Rudolf, died in mysterious circumstances with his mistress, Marie Vetsera, at Mayerling.)

In 1856 Maximilian was sent on an official visit to the court of Napoleon III in Paris. Of course he behaved impeccably and made a favorable impression on Napoleon III and Eugénie; but in his private letters to Franz Joseph he expressed his low opinion of the unconventional upstart emperor and empress. He considered them *parvenus,* a word that often recurred in the letters, and he thought Napoleon III "utterly lacking in nobility." Napoleon reminded him "not so much of an emperor with a scepter as a circus master with a riding whip." He admitted that Eugénie was beautiful and "quite a thoroughbred, but essentially lacking in the august quality of an empress."

He was shocked at the way in which the emperor spoke openly about people and matters in the presence of his servants. "This seems to me typical of a *parvenu,* utterly lacking in that *esprit de corps* which makes one careful not to expose oneself before those in subordinate positions." He thought that the play acted before the court in the palace of St. Cloud was "very improper" and "ought not to have been acted before ladies," and that the emperor's obvious interest in all the pretty women "detracts greatly from his sovereign dignity."

At the state ball given in his honor, "the company was unbelievably mixed, and distinguished by their disgusting dress and tasteless behavior. Adventurers swarmed." He did not like the "*parvenu* etiquette" at the court of Napoleon III. "One can see, moreover, that his suite has formerly been that of a president of a republic; it is often hard for them to maintain themselves on a proper level. The behavior of the court ladies toward the empress, too, their shaking hands with her, their hearty friendliness, are a little shocking to our ideas of imperial etiquette."

He went on from Paris to the court of King Leopold of the Belgians at Laeken near Brussels, where he met Leopold's daughter, Princess Charlotte. They fell in love almost immediately and within a few months were officially engaged. King Leopold, who became Maximilian's father-in-law and exercised great influence over him, was called "the Nestor of Europe" by journalists because of the shrewd political advice he gave his relatives in the European royal families. He was a younger son of the duke of Coburg, the tiny German sovereign state that produced brides and bridegrooms for more powerful monarchs. His sister was Queen Victoria's mother and his brother was the father of Victoria's husband, Prince Albert. Leopold himself, when he was a young man, married Princess Charlotte Augusta, the granddaughter of George III of England, who was second in line of succession to the English throne; but eighteen months after the marriage she died in giving birth to a stillborn daughter.

When the sultan of Turkey's Greek subjects rose in revolt and won their independence, the Great Powers decided that Leopold would be the ideal sovereign of the new Greek state; but he refused the offer. He knew that if he accepted, he would be drawn into a conflict between Russia and Britain. Soon afterward he was offered another throne after a revolution broke out in Brussels in 1830 against the rule of the king of Holland, who had been given Belgium by the Allies in 1815. As the Great Powers would not accept such a radical idea as a republic, a king had to be found for the new state of Belgium. They agreed on Leopold, who accepted. Throughout eight years of war, blockade, and complicated international diplomacy before the independence and frontiers of Belgium were finally established, Leopold won the respect of all the Great Powers and of his Belgian subjects. Belgium became a model of a moderate constitutional country, with freedom of speech, a free press, and free elections; Leopold ruled as a constitutional king who followed the advice of his elected ministers.

This wise and upright sovereign had an emotional side to his nature that was more complex than his philosophical and political outlook. Toward the end of his life Leopold said that the only time he had been really happy was during the eighteen months he was married to Princess Charlotte Augusta. He was very much in love with her, and after her death never fell in love with another woman. Nine years after she died, when he was visiting Berlin, he went to the theater and saw an actress, Karoline Bauer, who bore such a striking resemblance to Charlotte Augusta that people who had met them both could hardly believe it. Leopold persuaded Karoline to leave the stage and set her up in a villa in Regent's Park in London and a cottage on the grounds of his house at Claremont, near Esher in Surrey, where he visited her nearly every day; but he wanted only to gaze at her and listen while she read aloud to him an uplifting story from a moral book. She grew tired of this platonic relationship and left him after a year.

When he became king of the Belgians, he thought it was his duty to marry again to provide a son and heir for his kingdom. To cement his alliance with France he married Princess Louise, the daughter of King Louis Philippe. She bore him three sons, but the first died in childhood, and the health of the other boys was not good, so Leopold thought he should make sure of the succession by having a fourth child. When he was fifty and his wife thirty-eight, this child was born, at Laeken on June 7, 1840. Leopold was disappointed that it was a girl, though Queen Louise was delighted and tried to win over her husband by suggesting that their daughter be named Charlotte. She was duly christened Charlotte Amélie, but for some years Leopold refused to show any interest in her. When the little girl was taken out of the royal nursery to attend her fourth birthday party, to which her father condescended to come, Louise wrote sadly to her mother, the queen of the French, "Poor child! She will probably never have such a happy birthday as this."

As Charlotte grew up, Leopold slowly thawed toward her. She was becoming a beautiful girl, with soft dark brown hair and deep brown eyes, and was also a very intelligent and serious child who impressed her tutors, her mother, and later her father, with her precocity. At thirteen she could speak perfect English and German as well as French, could recite correctly the dates of all the kings of England, and solve three fairly difficult arithmetic problems every day.

Like his nephew Prince Albert, the English prince consort, Leopold reacted strongly against the immorality of the society in which he had been brought up in the early years of the nineteenth century; and like Albert he preached morality to his children with the utmost seriousness and at great length. Princess Charlotte responded well to the continuous inculcation of moral values to which her father subjected her. She was a devout Catholic, for though Leopold was a Protestant he had agreed that she should be brought up in the faith of her mother and of the majority of his subjects. She went regularly to Mass and confession, and consulted her father confessor whenever any difficulty confronted her. She fully accepted the maxim that Leopold had impressed upon her: "Persons in high positions must particularly guard themselves against selfishness and vanity."

Leopold was sixty and Charlotte was ten when Queen Louise died, and as Charlotte grew into a beautiful young woman, her father became utterly devoted to her. His only fault was to be too protective; he prevented any man from approaching her, and he had a charming, but slightly ridiculous, habit of praising her beauty, intelligence, and moral qualities to all and sundry on every possible occasion.

As Charlotte loved dancing, and was a very elegant dancer, Leopold held many balls at Laeken. But Charlotte was not allowed to dance with any man who was not a member of a royal family, and not even royal princes or dukes were allowed to put an arm around her waist when they waltzed with her, for this was a privilege granted only to her brothers. When Leopold was young, the waltz was an immoral peasant dance which was danced in society only by those who recklessly disregarded all the proprieties; so it was rather advanced of Leopold to permit the waltz at all.

Charlotte was sixteen when Maximilian came to Brussels in the summer of 1856, immediately after leaving Paris. He much preferred the life at Laeken to the *parvenu* court of the Tuileries, and wrote to Franz Joseph, "By comparison with Paris, I was impressed here with a comfortable sensation of being once again among my own kind." He was delighted with Princess Charlotte, whose father, as usual, sang her praises without restraint. "I think she will be the most beautiful princess in Europe," said Leopold.

Leopold considered the possibility of a marriage between Charlotte and Maximilian, but Queen Victoria thought that Charlotte should marry Dom Pedro, son of the queen of Portugal. "I am sure that you would be more likely to secure Charlotte's happiness if you were to give her to Pedro than to one of those innumerable archdukes," she wrote to Leopold. But Charlotte had quite made up her mind to marry Maximilian. If that was what she wanted, Leopold was ready to let her have it. "My object is and was," he wrote to Victoria, "that Charlotte should decide as *she* likes, uninfluenced by what I might prefer." The engagement of Archduke Ferdinand Maximilian and Princess Charlotte Amélie was officially announced in November 1856.

There were difficulties about the dowry. Because Belgium was a constitutional state, this could not be settled merely by bargaining between the Austrian and Belgian Foreign Offices; the deputies in the Belgian Parliament had to be convinced that the dowry was not excessive. Maximilian now showed an aspect of his character that one would not have expected from his aloof, unworldly expression or from his twenty-seven rules of behavior. He loved money and was prepared to haggle in a most undignified way in order to get more of it. When he returned to Laeken at Christmas 1856 and Charlotte fell even more in love with him, he argued long and hard with Leopold to obtain a higher dowry than the Belgian Parliament was willing to give. Charlotte was determined. "The archduke is charming in every way," she wrote, and Maximilian got the dowry he wanted.

Maximilian was in Laeken during the silver jubilee celebrations to mark the twenty-fifth anniversary of Leopold's accession as king of the Belgians. He was present at the ceremony on New Year's Day 1857 when the parliamentary deputies came to Laeken and congratulated Leopold on the anniversary, and the leading deputies made speeches in praise of constitutional monarchy. Maximilian as usual behaved perfectly correctly, but he wrote to Franz Joseph, "For nearly five hours I had to swallow all the hackneyed phrases ground out to each other by the constitutional ruler and the various authorities and corporate bodies. . . . The whole affair was calculated to inspire the unprejudiced observer with a profound disgust for constitutional shams."

He was equally unimpressed by the ball in his honor that was held at Laeken a few days later, for it seemed as if anyone who wished to attend was allowed to do so. "The higher nobility of the land rubs shoulders with their own tailors and cobblers; all the English shopkeepers who have retired to Brussels for reasons of economy have access to the ball with their families." Still, it was better than the *parvenus* in Paris.

In the autumn of 1856 Franz Joseph decided that the time had come to relax the severity of the regime in his Italian provinces. If a more liberal policy was to be pursued in Lombardy, it would be advisable to replace Radetzky, who had been viceroy during the period of repression, with a less hated ruler. Radetzky, now aged ninety, could be retired on the ground of age, with due thanks for his services. Franz Joseph appointed Maximilian as Radetzky's successor. King Leopold strongly approved, and Maximilian and Charlotte, after their wedding in Brussels in the summer of 1857, went to Milan, where Maximilian took office as viceroy of Lombardy and Venetia.

The new viceroy was determined to do all he could to win the good will of the Italians. He and Charlotte learned to speak Italian; but it was not easy to make the people of Milan and Venice forget the harshness of Radetzky's rule, and only a few of the local aristocracy abandoned their policy of boycotting the official functions to which Maximilian invited them. On one occasion Charlotte was booed when she went to the theater in Venice. Maximilian was most upset and was convinced that it was all the fault of Napoleon III. "At Napoleon's prompting," he wrote to King Leopold, "our government in Italy has become the butt of journalists and revolutionary polemicists."

Maximilian's task was not made easier by Franz Joseph, who encouraged him to be liberal but reminded him that "severity must be exercised, yet with justice and without any trace of rancor." In a series of letters, he asked Maximilian how it was possible for the Italian tricolor flag to have been raised over the arsenal in Venice and why it had taken so long before the authorities hauled it down. And why was the demonstration of three hundred students in Padua against the regime allowed to take place? He advised Maximilian "to have recourse to severity in the event of even the smallest revolt." Franz Joseph also emphatically rejected Maximilian's advice that some measure of home rule be granted to Lombardy and Venetia, for this "would mean a weakening of the government's power of resistance against the Revolution and those who are in its favor."

In April 1859 Napoleon III and King Victor Emmanuel of Piedmont went to war against Austria, having made a secret agreement to liberate Lombardy and Venetia and annex them to Piedmont in return for the cession by Piedmont of Savoy and Nice to France. At the outbreak of the war Franz Joseph dismissed Maximilian as viceroy of Lombardy and Venetia so that the government of the provinces could be entrusted to the Austrian commander-in-chief in Italy, Field Marshal Franz Gyulai. Maximilian was sent to Venice to take command of the navy, but there were no naval operations during the war. After Gyulai was defeated by Napoleon III at Magenta, Franz Joseph dismissed him and took personal command of his army, but Franz Joseph too was defeated, at Solferino. Napoleon III was shocked by the high casualties at Solferino and alarmed at the Prussian troop concentration along the Rhine; he feared that if the war continued, it might develop into a revolutionary war that would give too much encouragement to the radicals. He therefore met Franz Joseph at Villafranca and agreed to peace terms by which Austria ceded Lombardy to Piedmont but retained Venetia.

By the end of the war Maximilian was completely disillusioned. He and Charlotte went to Madeira, where she stayed while he went on to Brazil, landing at Bahía and collecting the flora of the Amazonian forests, for he had always been interested in botany.

During his visit to Brazil he showed again his ambivalent attitude toward oppression and cruelty, his mixture of liberal and humanitarian sentiments, on the one hand, and his admiration for the energy, daring, and brutality of ruthless men of action, on the other. When he stayed on the estate of a Brazilian nobleman he was shocked to see the *chicote* and the *palmatória* with which slaves were flogged, and was particularly distressed at the cheerful way in which the master's children joked about flogging slaves. But at the same time he clearly admired a master who ruled despotically over hundreds of blacks whom he could quell and terrify with a single look and their fear of the *chicote*, and he had the greatest respect for a German immigrant who, after serving in the Prussian army, had gone to Brazil to make his fortune and had become the owner of a large estate and many slaves.

Maximilian wrote an account of his travels in Brazil and of his earlier travels in Albania and the Mediterranean (it was not intended for publication but was published soon after his death). His descriptions of the landscapes and his pen portraits of the people whom he encountered show his imagination, sensitivity, love of beauty, longing for new experiences, and gifts as a writer. He returned from South America enamored of the American continent and its warm climate, but disapproving of the system of slavery that existed in Brazil, for "the blacks are men and Christians, and by the law of God they are born free."

When he returned to Europe he spent much time supervising the building of the palace of Miramar near Trieste, where he and Charlotte lived when they were not in residence at Lacroma, the island off the coast of Dalmatia which Charlotte had bought for them. But the marriage was beginning to go wrong. He and she no longer slept in the same bedroom. Some people said that this was because he had caught syphilis from a prostitute in Brazil; but according to his valet, Grill, the estrangement began suddenly a little later, after Maximilian had returned to Miramar from a visit to Vienna. In Grill's version of the story, Maximilian caught syphilis from a prostitute in Vienna and infected Charlotte. Exactly the same tale was told about Franz Joseph and Empress Elizabeth after Elizabeth left Vienna and went off on her travels around Europe.

But Charlotte, passing the time in painting, swimming, and riding in the woods on her beloved island of Lacroma, showed no signs in public of being disillusioned with her husband. "I believe the day will come," she wrote to her old governess, "when the archduke will again occupy a prominent position. By this I mean a position where he will govern, for he was made for that and was blessed by Providence with everything necessary to make a people happy."

Then, in October 1861, the Austrian foreign minister, Count Rechberg, came to Miramar and asked Maximilian whether he would like to become emperor of Mexico.

⁜ 7 ⁜

NAPOLEON III

CHANGES HIS MIND

JUÁREZ, HAVING WON the War of the Reform, entered Mexico City on the morning of January 11, 1861, and was received with great enthusiasm by the inhabitants. Before leaving Veracruz, he had been urged by Robert McLane to show restraint in his victory and mercy to his defeated opponents, and the European diplomatic representatives in Mexico gave him the same advice as the United States minister. His supporters, remembering the Massacre of Tacubaya and other atrocities committed by the conservatives, did not feel so magnanimous; but the conservative sympathizers and foreign residents, who had been pleasantly surprised at the good behavior of the liberal troops after they captured Mexico City, were equally relieved to find that when Juárez's government took over, there were no massacres of conservative prisoners, no summary trials and executions, no guillotine, and no firing squads.

It was easier for Juárez to show restraint because most of the more hated conservative leaders had escaped. Miramón went into hiding and made his way secretly to Veracruz, where he embarked on a French warship, which then cruised off the Mexican coast with Miramón on board. The French captain refused to hand him over to the liberal authorities at Veracruz or to the British warships there, though the British government wished to question him about the theft of money from the British legation in Mexico City. The French warship took Miramón to Havana. Zuloaga and Márquez also escaped from Mexico City and went to Michoacán, where they organized armed bands and carried on guerrilla warfare in the mountains, less than a hundred miles from the capital.

Some of the conservative leaders went to Europe to join Gutiérrez de Estrada and Hidalgo. Miramón's minister in Paris, General Almonte, also joined the Mexican refugees when Miramón's government fell. Almonte was the illegitimate son of the priest Morelos, who had led the revolt of 1811. He began his political life as a liberal, but he later joined the army and supported Santa Anna, standing by his side to watch the slaughter of the defenders of the Alamo, and being taken prisoner with him at San Jacinto. He was minister of war in President Bustamante's government in 1840, when Gutiérrez published his letter to the president in favor of a constitutional monarchy in Mexico. At that time Almonte had issued an order to the army denouncing Gutiérrez as a traitor, but now the two men were allies in the fight against Juárez.

One prominent conservative leader did not escape. Miramón's brother-in-law, Isidoro Díaz, who had been a member of Miramón's government, was captured and sentenced by a military tribunal to be shot for treason. His wife and family pleaded with Juárez for his life. Juárez pardoned him and let it be known that he was considering granting an amnesty to Miramón's supporters. This aroused great indignation among the liberals, especially in the revolutionary clubs that modeled themselves on the Jacobin and Cordelier clubs of Paris in 1792. A meeting of the clubs at Mexico City University, attended by 5,000 members, sent a deputation to Juárez to protest the extent of the amnesty and the pardon for Díaz. Francisco Zarco, the brilliant editor of the liberal newspaper *El Siglo XIX* (The Nineteenth Century), wrote that if Díaz was pardoned and an amnesty granted to all the reactionaries, then "goodbye justice, goodbye liberty, goodbye public order."

In view of the protests, Juárez annulled Díaz's pardon and did not grant the amnesty. But Díaz was not executed, though he was kept in prison, and no steps were taken to arrest any of the other conservatives who were living peaceably in Mexico City and elsewhere in the territory controlled by the liberal government.

The liberals, like many revolutionaries and members of left-wing parties, were quarreling among themselves. Many of them criticized Juárez about the amnesty, and he and Ocampo were also criticized for having wished to cede Mexican territory to the United States under the McLane-Ocampo treaty. Degollado, who was himself under a cloud for having resigned from his post of commander-in-chief in the middle of the war, claimed that he had shown more courage than Juárez, for when Miramón's army bombarded Veracruz he, unlike Juárez, had not fled to the shelter of San Juan de Ulúa.

Ocampo thought that these quarrels were inevitable. "Unfortunately the Liberal Party is essentially anarchic," he wrote, "and will not cease to be so for many thousands of years. The criterion of our enemies is authority. . . . They obey blindly and uniformly, whereas when we are commanded, unless we are told how and why, we murmur and are remiss when we do not actually disobey and resist."

Throughout the civil war, Juárez had acted as president of the republic by virtue of his position as chief justice of the Supreme Court under the provisions of the constitution; now that it was possible to hold an election, he had to offer himself as a candidate for the presidency. Ortega, who had led the liberal armies to victory, resigned from Juárez's government and stood against him in the presidential election. Lerdo also stood as a candidate, but he died during the election campaign. Juárez was elected, obtaining 5,289 electoral votes against 1,989 for Lerdo and 1,846 for Ortega; but Congress confirmed Juárez's election by only 61 votes to 55. Ortega was elected chief justice of the Supreme Court and would therefore take over as president if Juárez were unable to act.

Ocampo, conscious of the unpopularity of his treaty with McLane, and wishing to spend more time on his model farm at Pateo near Maravatío, resigned as foreign minister. Juárez appointed Zarco to succeed him, and Ocampo went off to his farm, which he had not seen during all the years of civil war. Juárez urged him to return to Mexico City and play his part as a deputy in the debates in Congress. He warned Ocampo that he might be in danger from Márquez's guerrilla bands, which were active in the mountains of Michoacán, not far from Maravatío. But Ocampo remained with his daughters at Pateo.

On May 30, 1861, the daughters went to a party in Maravatío, leaving Ocampo alone in the house with a few servants. Late in the afternoon a small band of horsemen arrived at Pateo; they were led by Captain Cajiga, a Spaniard who had joined Márquez's band. Ocampo invited them to have a drink, but they refused and ordered Ocampo to mount a horse and come with them. As they rode through Maravatío, Ocampo asked to be allowed to visit his daughters at their party and say goodbye to them, but Cajiga refused. After two days' traveling they reached the village of Huapango, where Cajiga handed over Ocampo to Zuloaga and Márquez, who had temporarily established their headquarters there.

When the people of Maravatío saw Ocampo being taken through the town as a prisoner, they at once sent the news to Mexico City. *El Siglo XIX* voiced the indignation of the liberals, denouncing Márquez's "soldiers of religion" as worse than the savage tribes of Apaches and Comanches who kidnaped women and children. It demanded that a message be sent to Márquez informing him that unless Ocampo was released, the most prominent conservatives in Mexico City would be shot; if Márquez demanded a ransom for Ocampo, the ransom money should be collected from conservative supporters. The government gave orders to arrest Márquez's mother and Zuloaga's wife as hostages for Ocampo. Márquez's mother escaped, but Zuloaga's wife was seized. She was not harmed but was told to write a letter to Zuloaga asking him what ransom he required to free Ocampo.

Márquez and Zuloaga waited for twenty-four hours at Huapango, then, taking Ocampo with them, moved on to Tepeji del Río, which they reached on the morning of June 3. Here Ocampo was informed that he would be shot. His guards offered him a confessor, but Ocampo refused to confess; he told the priest that he did not need his intervention to make his peace with God. They gave Ocampo time to make his will, and then, at 2 P.M., a small detachment of troops rode out of Tepeji del Río with Ocampo toward the west. When they reached a clearing in the wood, the troop commander ordered Ocampo to dismount from his horse. As soon as he had done so, the soldiers shot him in the head and the heart, firing at such close range that Ocampo's face was blackened by gunpowder. They tied a rope under the dead man's armpits and hung the corpse on a tree, where it was found the next day by the messenger whom Juárez had sent with an offer to pay a ransom for Ocampo.

The body was taken to Mexico City and buried after the nonreligious funeral on which Ocampo had insisted, at which great crowds of liberals demanded vengeance on "the vile beast of Tacubaya, the execrable Leonardo Márquez" and on all the reactionaries. Márquez and Zuloaga issued a statement disclaiming any responsibility for Ocampo's death and asserting that Cajiga had kidnaped him without their authority; but no one believed them. *El Siglo XIX* condemned the attitude of the Church, which was always ready to denounce the liberal government if the civil authorities legitimated the bastard children of a priest, but had not uttered one word condemning the murder of Ocampo. There were rumors that the furious liberals would storm the prisons and lynch Isidoro Díaz and some other conservative prisoners; the European ministers in Mexico City urged Juárez to prevent such an atrocity. Juárez told them that he had already sent one of his youngest commanders, General Leandro Valle, to guard the prisons and protect the prisoners from the mob.

General Degollado, indignant at the murder of Ocampo and seeing an opportunity to redeem his reputation, went before Congress and asked permission to command an army that would crush Márquez and his guerrillas. The government and Congress granted his wish, and he set out for Michoacán with a small force composed largely of inexperienced recruits. As they advanced into the mountains they marched straight into an ambush prepared by Márquez. Most of Degollado's men fled, and Degollado himself was caught as he tried to escape, and was immediately shot.

When Degollado's horribly mutilated body was brought back to Mexico City, young General Valle volunteered to avenge Ocampo and Degollado. He led a force of eight hundred men into the mountains of Michoacán, but when he reached a point about a mile from where Degollado had been killed, he in his turn was ambushed. Many of his men were killed. He himself was captured and brought before Márquez, who told him that he would be allowed half an hour before he was shot. Valle replied that if he had captured Márquez, he would have allowed him three minutes.

At the place of execution, Valle was told that he would be shot in the back as a traitor. He asked to whom he had been a traitor; they told him he was a traitor to religion. After he had been riddled with seventeen bullets, his corpse was hung on a tree. Márquez released the other liberal prisoners whom he had captured and told them to return to Mexico City and warn the liberal leaders that he would treat them, and all purchasers of confiscated Church lands, as he had treated Valle. He would put less prominent liberals to forced labor, making them rebuild the monasteries and convents that the liberals had destroyed.

General Ortega took personal command of the new army that was sent against Márquez. His second-in-command was General Porfirio Díaz, who had distinguished himself in several battles in the War of the Reform. Ortega, more cautious than Degollado and Valle, avoided all ambushes set for him and forced Márquez's guerrillas to scatter and flee into remoter districts. Many of the guerrillas were captured, including Ocampo's abductor, Cajiga, and were immediately shot, but Márquez and Zuloaga escaped. From his headquarters in the mountains, Márquez was able to enter into correspondence with Father Miranda, and through him with Gutíerrez and his friends in Paris, who congratulated Márquez on his achievements.

The liberal government faced another problem: How were they to pay their foreign creditors and placate the foreign governments that demanded satisfaction for their subjects? Mexico was nearly bankrupt and could not pay. And now the foreign governments insisted that Juárez pay all the debts that Miramón had contracted during the civil war — compensation for the forced loans that Miramón had imposed, for the foreigners' property that had been seized, for the British subjects' money that Márquez had stolen from the British legation, and for the wholly unreasonable sums that Miramón had undertaken to pay to Jecker and the holders of the Jecker bonds.

It was a rule of international law, one that Palmerston and other European governments always insisted upon in dealing with backward nations, that the government of a country was responsible for the debts and acts of earlier governments and of those of its citizens who committed outrages against foreigners, even if these earlier governments and those citizens were its political opponents. But it was difficult to convince Mexican liberals, who had suffered so much at the hands of their conservative enemies, that they must now endure further hardships in order to compensate foreigners for the misdeeds of the conservatives, especially as the foreigners had suffered less from the conservatives than the liberals themselves had.

Juárez's government tried to negotiate a settlement of the debts with the British and French governments. They did not make any effort to reach an understanding with Spain, for the Spanish minister in Mexico City had openly sided with Miramón during the civil war. Juárez, accusing him of being in secret contact with the conservative guerrilla leaders, expelled him, together with the papal nuncio and the minister from Guatemala. But the British minister, Sir Charles Wyke, was not unreasonable. He was prepared to extend the time for repaying British creditors and to cancel part of the debts.

The French minister, Pierre Alphonse Dubois de Saligny, was more difficult. Apart from being the mouthpiece of a hostile government, he was an arrogant man who quarreled nearly as much with the other European diplomatic representatives in Mexico as he did with Juárez's ministers. Twenty years before, when he was the French minister in Texas during its short-lived independence, he had exaggerated an incident — his pigs were killed by his Texan neighbor in a dispute about the boundaries of their gardens — until it nearly led to a war between France and Texas. Strongly conservative in his sympathies, he took every opportunity to quarrel with the liberal government. In April 1861 he wrote to the French foreign minister that in view of "the state of anarchy, or rather of social dissolution, prevailing in this wretched country," a strong French naval force should be sent at once to the coast of Mexico "to provide protection for our interests."

But even Saligny seemed on the point of reaching an agreement about the French claims and the Jecker bonds with Manuel Zamacona, who in another government reshuffle had succeeded Zarco as foreign minister. Then on July 17 the Mexican Congress passed a resolution suspending payment of the interest due to all foreign creditors and bondholders. Zamacona, seeing the possible disastrous consequences of this provocation, urged Juárez to veto the resolution. Juárez refused; he was already sufficiently unpopular with the liberal extremists, and he dared not fly in the face of the passionate denunciations of the greedy foreign creditors by the liberal deputies in Congress and the writers in the liberal press.

As soon as Saligny heard of the resolution suspending payment of interest, he broke off his negotiations with Zamacona and prepared to leave Mexico. Zamacona asked him to wait for a few days in the hope that the decision of Congress would be reversed, but he refused. Sir Charles Wyke also protested the resolution and, though he stayed longer than Saligny, he too left Mexico City.

The European powers were encouraged to take a tough line with Juárez because of the news they had received from Washington. At 4:30 A.M. on April 12 the Confederate batteries in Charleston harbor had opened fire on the United States garrison at Fort Sumter, which surrendered after thirty-six hours' bombardment. The American Civil War had begun. Three months later, on July 21, a Union army of 18,000 men marched out of Washington, intending to capture the Confederate capital of Richmond, 115 miles to the south. They encountered the Confederate army at Bull Run, Virginia.

Many civilians drove out from Washington to see the first battle of the war. Some took picnic baskets with them, and several ladies called at army headquarters hoping to exchange a few words, during intervals in the fighting, with officers who had been their partners at regimental balls. The presence on the battlefield of onlookers with picnic baskets was a regular feature of warfare at the time; the picnickers had come out in the Crimea and in Italy to watch the battles of the Alma and Solferino. One of the civilians was a Mexican conservative, Rafael Rafael, who lived in New York. He had come to Washington to see the battle.

The Northern army encountered much fiercer resistance than it had expected, and retreated in disorder to Washington, with the civilian spectators retreating even faster than the soldiers. Rafael returned to New York and wrote to his friend General Almonte in Paris that he was convinced, after what he had seen at Bull Run, that the North was too incompetent, and the South too weak, to win the Civil War; if the Southern armies had had sufficient resources, they could have captured Washington after Bull Run. The war would therefore probably end in a stalemate and a compromise peace, but whatever the final result, it would last for years, not months. For the Mexican conservatives, this was the best possible scenario. Almonte hastened to tell the good news to his colleagues in Europe.

In September 1861 Hidalgo went to Biarritz, for he knew Napoleon III and Eugénie would be in residence there. Eugénie invited him to dinner at the Villa Eugénie. After dinner she went and sat at a little table with two of her ladies, and he joined her. Lowering his voice, he told her that he had just received a letter with confidential information that the British and Spanish governments were contemplating sending a naval force to Veracruz to seize control of the customs house and collect the customs duties until the British and Spanish creditors of the Mexican government had been paid. Eugénie rose and fetched Napoleon III, who came into the room reading a letter he had received from the king of Siam. She said to Hidalgo, "Tell the emperor what you have just told me."

Hidalgo told him, and as usual urged him to intervene to help the oppressed people of Mexico. Napoleon III said that the American Civil War had completely changed the situation. If Britain and Spain would support him, he would send an expeditionary force to Mexico; in the first place he would use only the navy, but if it appeared that the Mexican people wished it, he would help them to overthrow Juárez's government and install a European prince as emperor of Mexico. Yes, he was ready now to do what Gutíerrez and Hidalgo had been urging him to do for so many years.

But whom should they have as emperor of Mexico? It could not be a Spanish prince, for the Spaniards were hated in Mexico, and the Mexicans would fear that it was a step to make Mexico a Spanish colony once again. It could not be a member of the Bonaparte family, for the Great Powers, especially Britain, would not agree to see Mexico incorporated into the French Empire. The chosen candidate would have to be a Catholic. What about some of the lesser Habsburg princes and archdukes — the duke of Modena or archduke Rainier?

"Of course there is the archduke Maximilian," said Eugénie, "but he would not accept."

"No," said Hidalgo, "he would not accept."

Napoleon III agreed. "He would certainly not accept."

There was a short silence while Eugénie rose to her feet and stood there, gently tapping herself on the breast with her fan. Then she said, "Do you know? Something tells me that he *will* accept."

8

THE EXPEDITION TO VERACRUZ

NAPOLEON III HAD PLANNED IT carefully, in the way that he always planned — secretly, deviously, and taking no one into his confidence. As a young man he had been headstrong and had made himself a laughingstock by his rash and disastrous attempts at a military coup at Strasbourg and Boulogne; but in middle age he had become a skillful politician and diplomat. When Hidalgo revealed to him at Biarritz the secret information that Britain and Spain were about to send a naval force to Veracruz, Napoleon gave no indication that he knew all about it, that he had been discussing it for some weeks with the British and Spanish governments, and that it was he who had first suggested the idea.

More than forty years later, the French diplomat and historian Maurice Paléologue asked Eugénie when Napoleon III decided to intervene in Mexico, and "what gave him the final and decisive impetus." Eugénie replied, "It came in 1861 at Biarritz, from myself." She was referring to their conversation with Hidalgo in September. But two months earlier, in July, Napoleon had discussed plans to intervene in Mexico with the Spanish statesman General Prim, count of Reus, when he was on holiday at Vichy soon after the outbreak of the American Civil War. Napoleon had not then decided whom to choose as emperor of Mexico, but at Biarritz in September he and Eugénie and Hidalgo agreed to make the offer to Maximilian.

Napoleon's plan was that France, Spain, and Britain would send a joint force to Veracruz to seize the customs house and apply the duties to repay the French, British, and Spanish creditors. If he could persuade Britain and Spain to cooperate, it would remove any possibility of the United States interfering in support of Juárez; it would prevent the British government from condemning the French intervention; and it would stop Spain from acting alone and reconquering Mexico, which would defeat Napoleon's plans to bring Mexico under French influence. Once the three allies had seized Veracruz, their negotiations with Juárez about settling the foreign creditors' claims would almost certainly break down. Even if Juárez were to accept the exorbitant French claims for the holders of the Jecker bonds, Saligny could put forward new unacceptable demands and provoke a rupture. Then the French could persuade their British and Spanish allies to advance to Mexico City, overthrow Juárez, and install Maximilian as emperor. If Britain and Spain refused to agree, the French could do it alone and gain more influence in Mexico than if their allies had helped them. Maximilian, as emperor of Mexico, would be a barrier to United States expansion into Latin and South America, and in gratitude for French aid he would grant privileges to French capitalists in Mexico; perhaps he could even be persuaded to cede the state of Sonora, with its gold and silver mines, to France, though Napoleon would have to be careful about annexing Mexican territory.

Britain and Spain agreed to join in the expedition to Veracruz after they heard that the Mexican Congress had suspended interest payments on the foreign debts. Negotiations were taking place in London on the terms of the Three Power Convention under which they would act, but Napoleon had not yet told Britain and Spain about his plan to make Maximilian emperor. He had to choose just the right moment; if he told them too soon, Britain might withdraw from the proposed intervention, and Spain might decide to act alone and put a Spanish prince on the throne of Mexico. If he told them too late, they would accuse him of deception, of having lured them into the joint intervention by a trick. He would tell them when the negotiations for the Three Power Convention were almost, but not quite, complete, when it would be possible in theory, but very difficult in practice, for Britain and Spain to withdraw.

The more he thought about the plan, the more pleased he was with it. He thought it the best idea he had ever had; it was his *grande pensée*.

He had to approach Maximilian in the proper manner. One advantage in proposing Maximilian as emperor of Mexico was that it would please Franz Joseph and improve Napoleon's relations with Austria, with which he had been at war two years before. Under Habsburg family law, Franz Joseph, as head of the family, would have to give his consent before Maximilian could accept the throne of Mexico, so Franz Joseph would have to be approached first. But it should be an informal approach. Napoleon told Eugénie to ask the French foreign minister, Count Thouvenel, to mention the matter in a private letter to Prince Richard Metternich, the Austrian ambassador in Paris, who was on holiday on his estate in Bohemia.

The Mexican refugees could not wait. Hidalgo hurried back to Paris from Biarritz to tell Gutiérrez that Napoleon III had changed his mind and was now prepared to send forces to Mexico to install Maximilian as emperor; Gutiérrez went straight off to the Austrian embassy to tell the chargé d'affaires and to beg him to ask the Austrian foreign minister, Count Rechberg, to raise the matter with Franz Joseph.

During the next few years, Maximilian sometimes accused Franz Joseph of having first encouraged and then discouraged him from accepting the throne of Mexico; in fact, Franz Joseph, after his first discussion with Rechberg, adopted a position from which he never varied. He was very fond of his younger brother. Yes, Maxi had always been rather silly; as a child he had enjoyed embarrassing his elders by saying tactless things about eminent courtiers and foreign guests; and later, as a young man and governor of Lombardy and Venetia, his half-baked liberal ideas could have done quite a lot of damage if he had been allowed to carry them out. But Franz Joseph loved Maxi and would not stand in his way if he wished to become emperor of Mexico. He would not refuse his permission as head of the family, but Maxi must understand that he would be in this venture on his own, that Franz Joseph and the Austrian government would be in no way involved and would not give him any support. Franz Joseph also warned Maximilian that in his opinion it would be very unwise to accept the offer unless two conditions were fulfilled: first, that both Britain and France would support him in Mexico — and this meant not merely assurances of sympathy but definite treaty commitments to practical assistance; and second, that he would be accepted and welcomed as emperor by the majority of the Mexican people.

At the beginning of October 1861, Franz Joseph sent Rechberg to Miramar to explain this to Maximilian. Maximilian was not entirely surprised because for some years he had been receiving letters from Gutiérrez on the subject. Rechberg reported to Franz Joseph that Maximilian was eager to accept the throne of Mexico on the conditions Franz Joseph had laid down. Rechberg sent a reply to Gutiérrez which, though cautious, was by far the most encouraging that Gutiérrez had ever received from the Austrian government. Rechberg wrote to the Austrian chargé in Paris: "We therefore authorize you, Count, to inform Mr. Gutiérrez, in strict confidence, that the Emperor, our august Master, would not repulas a serious proposal made to him in this matter, and that His Imperial Highness the Archduke Ferdinand Maximilian would perhaps likewise not refuse to yield to the desire of the Mexican nation, should that nation call him to the throne." Rechberg added that it must be clearly understood that "to safeguard the dignity of His Imperial Highness the Archduke and of his august House," Maximilian's acceptance was conditional on his receiving the active support of Britain and France and on "a clearly expressed invitation to the Archduke from the people of Mexico themselves."

Napoleon III was very satisfied with the replies of Franz Joseph and Maximilian and was determined to ensure that the conditions on which they insisted were fulfilled. He would pledge French support and would try to obtain a similar pledge from Great Britain. As for the invitation from the Mexican people, he thought that this should not take the form of a plebiscite in Mexico, because, though he himself, in the Bonapartist tradition, had been elected emperor of the French in a national plebiscite, no Habsburg prince would wish to receive a throne by popular mandate. After the three allied powers had overthrown Juárez's government, they should convene a conference of Mexican notables, who would offer the throne to Maximilian. Napoleon had already told Thouvenel to suggest to the British foreign secretary, Lord Russell, that this Congress of Notables should choose a foreign prince to be their ruler. "Of course, the only legitimate pretext for an armed demonstration comes from our grievances, but I believe that it would be in the general interest to make of it the means whereby the Mexican nation itself could profit by the circumstances."

On October 9, Napoleon III himself wrote to his ambassador in London, the aged Count Flahaut, who fifty years before had been the lover of Napoleon's mother, Queen Hortense, and the father of her illegitimate son, the duke of Morny. In his letter Napoleon put forward Maximilian's name for consideration by the British government and asked Flahaut to show the letter to the British prime minister, Lord Palmerston.

> There is no need for me to enlarge on the common interest which we in Europe have in seeing Mexico pacified and endowed with a stable government. Not only has that country, which enjoys every natural advantage, attracted a great deal of our capital and many of our fellow countrymen, whose existence is continually threatened; but if it were regenerated it would form an impassable barrier to the encroachments of North America . . . and would provide an important opening for English, Spanish, and French trade.

The United States could not intervene because of the American Civil War, and "the outrages committed by the Mexican government have given England, Spain, and France a legitimate reason for interference in Mexico." He therefore suggested that Archduke Maximilian of Austria be made emperor of Mexico; it gave him particular pleasure to nominate a prince of a nation with which he had recently been at war.

Palmerston was unimpressed. He wrote to Russell that for fifteen years "people from Mexico" had been trying to persuade him to intervene in Mexico to place a European prince on the throne; but on looking into the matter it transpired that they wished to be provided with 20,000 European troops and "many millions sterling." No doubt it would benefit Mexico, and also the European powers, if the country were ruled by a European prince; but it would not be in Britain's interests to supply the necessary troops and money to achieve this. If Napoleon III chose to do so, Britain would wish him well but would not give any active support.

Russell was even more strongly opposed than Palmerston to Napoleon III's plan. He did not like the Mexican liberals' republican ideology and confiscatory measures, but he approved of their declaration of religious toleration and feared that the government of Maximilian and his conservative supporters might abolish it and persecute Protestants. He did not think that Napoleon's idea had much chance of success. "This project appears to have originated with the Mexican refugees at Paris," he wrote to Lord Bloomfield, the British ambassador in Vienna. "This class of people are notorious for unfounded calculation of the strength of their partisans in their native country and for the extravagance of their expectations of support."

Russell was also eager to avoid trouble with the United States, even when it was involved in a civil war. "Without at all yielding to the extravagant pretentions implied by what is called the Monroe Doctrine, it would be, as a matter of expediency, unwise to provoke the ill feelings of North America unless some paramount object were in prospect, and tolerably easy of attainment."

The Juárez government, faced with the threat of intervention by the three European powers, looked around for a powerful ally, and could find only one — the United States, which had taken nearly half of Mexico's territory in 1848 and was always eager to acquire more. After the indignation aroused in Mexico by the McLane-Ocampo treaty, Juárez was prepared to make an alliance with the United States only as a last resort; but he was now reduced to the last resort. His minister to the United States, Matías Romero, had no doubt which was the lesser evil for Mexico. "We find ourselves [facing] the hard alternatives of sacrificing our territory and our nationality at the hands of [the United States] or our liberty and our independence before the despotic thrones of Europe. The second danger is immediate and more imminent."

Juárez had sent Romero to the United States immediately after winning the War of the Reform against Miramón. Romero was a very able young lawyer from Juárez's home state of Oaxaca, who had worked in the government there when Juárez was governor. On his way to Washington, Romero went to Springfield, Illinois, to visit the new president-elect of the United States, Abraham Lincoln, and in February 1861 they had a long talk. Romero was both encouraged and discouraged by Lincoln's attitude. Lincoln said that he and many of his supporters had opposed the war against Mexico in 1846 and were determined to inaugurate a new policy of friendship toward the countries of Latin America. There would be no more imperialist aggression against Mexico. But he warned Romero that if, as seemed likely, war broke out in the United States between North and South, his government would not be able to protect Mexico against attacks from European powers, for the United States would do nothing to encourage the European powers to side with the Southern rebels.

Lincoln appointed as his secretary of state William H. Seward, a former governor of New York. Everyone had expected that Seward would be the Republican candidate in the presidential election, but after leading on the first ballot at the party convention, he had become deadlocked with his rival, Salmon P. Chase, thus allowing Lincoln to be chosen as the dark-horse candidate after the third ballot. When Seward heard that Spain, France, and Great Britain were planning to seize the customs revenues at Veracruz, he sent a protest and offered to pay all the debts Mexico owed their nationals if they refrained from mounting the expedition. He proposed that the United States take over the whole Mexican debt, paying the creditors 3 percent interest for five years, after which time the Mexican government would repay the United States at 6 percent, while Mexico would grant the United States a mortgage on the public lands and minerals in northern Mexico as security for the payment.

The Three Powers rejected the offer. Palmerston wrote mockingly to Russell that "the Washington government, inspired by a chivalrous sense of justice . . . proposes to pay the interest on the foreign debt of Mexico, I forget how long, taking a mortgage upon all the mineral wealth of Mexico." This scheme made no provision "for the punishment of the murderers of the subjects of the Three Powers, and . . . it lays the ground for foreclosure by this new creditor . . . and then further it tends to continue the present state of anarchy in Mexico."

Palmerston proposed instead, either to appease or to embarrass the United States, that the Three Powers invite the United States to join in the occupation of Veracruz. Romero begged Seward to accept this proposal so that the United States could exercise a restraining influence on the other three powers; but Seward did not wish to get involved. "It is very hard to have to declare war on a friend to contribute to saving him," he told Romero.

Señor Don Juan Antonio de la Fuente was a worried man. After the liberals had won the War of the Reform in Mexico, Juárez had dismissed Miramón's minister in Paris, General Almonte, and appointed la Fuente to succeed him. La Fuente's task was to prevent Napoleon III from invading Mexico. The Mexican liberals, after suffering for years, in prison or in exile, under the dictatorship of Santa Anna, had made a revolution, gained political power, and introduced their program of reform, only to be overthrown by another conservative *coup d'état* and involved in a particularly savage civil war. Now, having at last won this war, they were faced within a few months by the threat of attack by the most powerful army in the world, which was coming to support the defeated conservatives and to renew the reactionaries' attack on democracy.

La Fuente did not know how to stop the French plans. He was dealing with an enemy who was much stronger than the Mexican liberals and who was determined to force them into war, no matter what concessions they made or how much humiliation they were prepared to accept.

La Fuente waited anxiously in Paris. For four months the French government refused to accept him as the Mexican minister and continued to recognize Almonte. Then one day, to his delight and relief, he was invited to a diplomatic reception, but Thouvenel continued to refuse his requests for an interview. When at last he was summoned to the Foreign Office for talks, Thouvenel was cold and threatening; he told la Fuente that France would use "severe coercion" against Mexico if Juárez's government did not accede to all the French demands, including payment of the debt due on the Jecker bonds. La Fuente asked for an audience with Napoleon III but was repeatedly fobbed off with excuses until August 10, when he was granted an audience at Saint-Cloud. To la Fuente's surprise, Napoleon was charming and inquired about Juárez in a most friendly way, but he did not give la Fuente any reassurance about the threat to invade Mexico.

As usual, Napoleon III had handled the diplomatic negotiations very cleverly; he had succeeded in getting the reluctant British government to join in the intervention, thus providing a cloak for his real motives, and in preventing the Spanish government from acting alone. The Convention of London was finally signed on October 31, 1861. The Three Powers were to send their naval forces and 10,000 troops to occupy Veracruz. Spain would provide 7,000 soldiers under General Prim; France would send 2,500 under Vice Admiral Jurien de la Gravière; and Britain 700 Marines under Commodore Dunlop.

But Palmerston and Napoleon III had been warned by people who knew Mexico that Veracruz was one of the four most unhealthful ports on the Atlantic Ocean and that at this season of the year 20 percent of the Europeans who stayed in Veracruz died of *vómito,* the most dangerous form of yellow fever. It would be better if their troops advanced into the more healthful highlands in the interior. Napoleon realized that this could be made an excuse for going beyond Veracruz. He sent instructions to Admiral Jurien that climatic conditions, and the need to protect French subjects elsewhere in Mexico, might make it necessary to extend the area of his operations beyond Veracruz, and "that to strike at the Mexican government, or to render more effective the coercion exercised on it by the seizure of the ports, you may have to make a march into the interior of Mexico, even to Mexico City if necessary." But Russell instructed Sir Charles Wyke and Commodore Dunlop, in a dispatch that had been read and approved by both Palmerston and Queen Victoria, that the 700 British Marines could not suitably be employed inland, and "you will therefore under no circumstances allow the Marines to take part in operations against Mexico City."

As soon as the Convention of London was signed, preparations were made for the expedition to sail. On November 1 the British Lords of the Admiralty proposed that the three fleets should meet fifteen miles northwest of Cape San Antonio on the western tip of the Spanish colony of Cuba and sail together to Veracruz; within a week the first French ships had sailed from Toulon. But the captain general of Cuba was determined that the Spaniards should be in action first; the British and French ships were still in mid-Atlantic when the Spanish ships left Havana with 6,000 troops on board. They arrived at Veracruz on December 8. Their commander issued a proclamation stating that they had not come to interfere in the internal government of Mexico but only to compel Juárez's government to pay compensation to Spaniards who had suffered wrongs. They encountered no resistance, and by December 17 had landed and occupied the city and hoisted the Spanish flag over Fort San Juan Ulúa.

The French and British were not far behind. The fourteen French steamships carrying 2,500 men had reached Tenerife by November 24. "Sailors and soldiers!" said Admiral Jurien, "we are going to

Mexico." He reminded them of the words of Napoleon III: "Wherever the French flag flies, a just cause preceded it and a great people follows it." The French landed at Veracruz between January 6 and 8, 1862. The British Marines arrived at the same time, and General Prim arrived with another thousand men to take command of all the Spanish forces at Veracruz.

When the news reached Mexico City that the Spaniards were at Veracruz, President Juárez addressed the Mexican Congress. An English journalist, Charles Lempriere, was present; in view of all the talk in England about intervention in Mexico, he had decided to see for himself what was going on. He found the Congress very different from the House of Commons in London. The chamber was an immense semicircle, about two hundred feet in diameter, facing a raised dais under a canopy of red velvet, on which was the president's chair, also of red velvet. Above the chair hung the Mexican flag of green, red, and white. The session took place on December 15, a Sunday. Going there at 2 P.M., Lempriere found the public galleries "filled with all kinds of riffraff, both men and women, but there was no interruption or sound except from the members themselves, who made noise enough for all."

Juárez entered the chamber about 3 P.M. "amid an extraordinary din of cannons and trumpets." After bowing gracefully on all sides, he addressed the congressmen "in a clear and remarkably pleasant voice," telling them that the dreaded intervention from Europe had now taken place, and Spanish troops were in Veracruz. When he finished speaking, he was loudly cheered, and Congress voted him absolute powers to rule by decree during the emergency.

Three days later, Juárez issued his appeal to the people.

Mexicans! If they intend to humiliate Mexico, to dismember our territory, to intervene in our internal administration and politics, or even to extinguish our nationhood, I appeal to your patriotism to drive out those pestilent and hostile forces which have been the cause of our differences of opinion, to contribute your efforts and your blood, and to unite around the government in defense of the greatest and most sacred cause which exists among men and among peoples: the defense of our country. In defending ourselves in the war that has been forced upon us, we will strictly observe the laws and customs established for the benefit of humanity. Let the defenseless enemy nationals to whom we have given generous hospitality live in peace and security under the protection of our laws. Thus we will refute the lies of our enemies and show that we are worthy of the freedom and independence which we have inherited from our fathers.

Charles Lempriere, like most other foreign visitors, had a low opinion of Mexicans — lower even than of the natives he had seen on his travels in Bulgaria and Greece. He admitted that Mexican women were beautiful and "still retain the full power of the fan, the graceful arching of the neck and the far-darting glance which is the peculiarity of the Spanish race." But he thought that although all the men waltzed very well, "every man for years past, when he has secured office — no matter what, from the minister downward, with a few honourable exceptions — has thought of nothing but enriching himself at the public expense." He was surprised to see the great enthusiasm with which large crowds of old men, women, and children in Mexico City cheered the young conscripts, called up by Juárez's *leva*, who were leaving to join the army. The people escorted them to the Paseo, where mule-drawn coaches would take them to Veracruz, for the railroad had not yet been built any farther than Camerone, forty miles from Veracruz.

Archduke Ferdinand Max was very excited at the prospect of becoming emperor of Mexico. During the next thirty months he was to show extraordinary indecision about the Mexican adventure as he fluctuated between delight and despair, but his first reaction on October 4, 1861, was joy. He had been wondering what to do with his life ever since his dismissal from the post of viceroy of Lombardy and Venetia and his replacement as heir to the Austrian Empire by Empress Elizabeth's baby. Mexico, like Brazil, was in America, that unexplored and undeveloped continent of the future; many parts of Mexico had the warm climate that he loved; and what could be more fitting than that Mexico should be ruled by a well-meaning Habsburg prince, a descendant of the first Christian emperor of Mexico, Charles V?

His wife was even keener on the idea. Charlotte felt that Maximilian was wasting his talents at Miramar, and though she loved the house and her island of Lacroma, she would willingly sacrifice them and do her duty by accompanying her husband to Mexico and helping him as his empress. Four years later, when things were already becoming difficult in Mexico, she wrote from there to her old governess in Europe: "Put yourself in my place and ask whether life at Miramar was better than life in Mexico. No, a hundred times no! And I, for my part, prefer a position which offers me activity and duties, and even, if you like, difficulties, than to sit on a rock and look at the sea till I am seventy." At every stage Charlotte encouraged Maximilian to go to Mexico.

Franz Joseph and Count Rechberg were a little worried that the archduke was so eager. Franz Joseph was afraid that as usual Maxi would do something silly, that he would rush to accept before making sure that the conditions Franz Joseph thought essential had been fulfilled, and that he would tell Gutiérrez, who would leak the news to the international press. In this last respect his worst fears were realized, for on November 17 both the *Indépendance Belge* of Brussels and the *Kölnische Zeitung* of Cologne published a statement that the crown of Mexico had been offered to Archduke Ferdinand Maximilian.

Maximilian was annoyed that Franz Joseph and Rechberg thought he was rushing impetuously into the Mexican adventure. He told them he had decided to consult his father-in-law, King Leopold, before accepting and that it was Rechberg, not he, who had agreed to meet Gutiérrez. He himself had been holding Gutiérrez at bay while trying not to discourage a loyal supporter too much. He had refused Gutiérrez's suggestion of a visit to Miramar, for he thought it would attract too much attention, and had instead sent his secretary to meet Gutiérrez in Paris. And he was not the person responsible for the leak to the press.

Maximilian also consulted Pope Pius IX, who had once been a liberal but had been driven by his fear of revolution and mob violence into supporting conservative and absolutist regimes all over the world. Maximilian wrote to say he hoped that if he accepted the throne of Mexico, "I shall receive the sacred blessing which is so absolutely essential for me." Pius replied that the accounts he had received of the situation in Mexico "call forth our pity, and yours is a worthy task when you call upon religion and society to busy themselves with speedy remedies."

King Leopold did not disagree with the advice Franz Joseph had given Maximilian; he too believed that Maximilian should accept the throne of Mexico only if he received firm guarantees of support from both Britain and France and was invited to come by the Mexican people. But he was much more hopeful than Franz Joseph that these conditions would be fulfilled, and he immediately set about persuading his favorite niece, Queen Victoria, to support the scheme and to induce her government to guarantee the support that was essential for Maximilian.

On October 24, 1861, Leopold wrote to Victoria that he was pleased that "my neighbour" (Napoleon III) had turned his attention to Mexico. "It would be a great improvement to render gradually those ci devant Spanish colonies to civilisation and to render them useful to the rest of the world"; but as this could not be done "under existing circumstances of a revolution every fortnight," the French intervention was to be welcomed.

He received a discouraging answer from Queen Victoria's prince consort, his nephew Albert, who wrote to him on November 5, less than six weeks before Prince Albert died of typhoid fever at the age of forty-two. Albert wrote that Leopold could, if he wished, show his letter to Max and Charlotte, and warned them to be very careful before accepting the offer made to them by Napoleon III. "The Mexico plan is a dubious and dangerous one. As it comes from the Tuileries, one has to ask: what is its object? Can we believe that it is a lily-white scheme designed only to help Max and Charlotte?"

Prince Albert believed, on the contrary, that Napoleon's motive must be to restore the rule of the "priest party" and the Jesuits in Mexico and thereby win back the support of the Catholic Ultramontanes in France whom he had offended by his support for Italian unity in the war of 1859. As long as the United States would not tolerate a monarchy on its doorstep, any attempt to overthrow republicanism by force in America, instead of allowing it to destroy itself, could lead to a reaction against monarchy that would strengthen republicanism on both continents. "I very much hope that Max and Charlotte will not fall into a trap."

This letter did not convince King Leopold and had still less effect on the king's son, Prince Leopold, duke of Brabant (afterward King Leopold II of the Belgians, notorious for his many whores and for introducing slave labor into the Congo). Prince Leopold was enthusiastic about the offer to his brother-in-law and was sure that Maximilian would soon be emperor not only of Mexico but of a larger empire. "Once you are firmly established in Mexico," he wrote to Maximilian, "it is probable that a great part of America will place itself under your rule."

After keeping Gutiérrez waiting for nearly three months, Maximilian at last agreed to have him come to Miramar. He arrived on Christmas Eve and stayed five days. On the evening of Christmas Day Maximilian told him that if the Mexican people invited him to be their emperor, he would accept.

Gutiérrez urged Maximilian to get in touch with Santa Anna, who was living in exile on St. Thomas, for he knew that Santa Anna would support the plan to make Maximilian emperor. Gutiérrez also suggested that Monsignor Labastida, the bishop of Puebla, who was living in Rome, be sent to Mexico to work for Maximilian as soon as the French established a foothold there. Labastida had already told the Austrian minister in Rome of his support for Maximilian and had convinced him that the best elements in Mexico had always preserved an "essentially antidemocratic character," and that only the "friends of order" — the conservatives, the Church, and the majority of the landowning class — could be relied upon "to put an end to anarchy" in Mexico.

As soon as Gutiérrez left Miramar, Maximilian went to see Franz Joseph, who was visiting his one remaining Italian province, Venetia. The two brothers met in Venice on New Year's Eve and had a long talk about Mexico. Maximilian was so certain that he would go to Mexico that he discussed in detail the problems that would arise when he left Miramar. Unless Maximilian, in his enthusiasm, misunderstood what his brother said and misrepresented his view in the memorandum on their talk that he wrote that evening, Franz Joseph was very helpful. He agreed to provide an Austrian warship to take Maximilian to Mexico and "guns, bridging equipment, and artillery officers" for a force of Austrian and Belgian volunteers that would enroll for service in Mexico; all of them should be Catholics.

They discussed the question that always interested Maximilian so much — money. Maximilian would continue to receive his annual grant of 100,000 florins, and Franz Joseph would advance him another 200,000 florins ($100,000) for his immediate expenses. Maximilian would make Santa Anna duke of Veracruz or of Tampico, whichever title he preferred, and he would receive the same salary, 36,000 scudis, he had received as president of Mexico. Either Maximilian's brother Archduke Karl or Franz Joseph himself would buy Miramar from Maximilian, and alternative employment would be found for the servants who would not be going with him to Mexico.

Napoleon III agreed that Santa Anna should be contacted, but he and Eugénie had formed an adverse opinion of Gutiérrez when Hidalgo introduced him to them in January 1862. Gutiérrez's opinions about religion struck them as too intolerant. Napoleon prided himself on being the defender of the Catholic Church against the Reds and the godless radicals, but he believed in toleration for other religions and certainly did not wish to displease his English allies by conniving at any persecution of Protestants in Mexico. Eugénie, though she was often accused of being an intolerant Spanish Ultramontane, completely agreed with Napoleon about this. After their meeting with Gutiérrez, she complained that it had been like talking to Philip II of Spain, that great persecutor of heretics. Napoleon had a much higher opinion of General Almonte, who was a strong supporter of the conservatives but expressed himself a little more tactfully than Gutiérrez. Napoleon advised Maximilian to use Almonte's services in Mexico.

In January 1862 Almonte and Labastida went to Miramar and spent several days with Maximilian. They assured him of their support, and he was eager to accept their help. During their stay, Maximilian signed an agreement with Almonte on what should be done in Mexico. They agreed that until Maximilian's arrival, the country should be governed by a council of regency consisting of Almonte, Santa Anna, and Labastida; they also agreed on the number of marquises, counts, and barons whom Maximilian would create. He was to recognize all the existing titles of nobility of the Mexican aristocracy.

But Almonte was the cause of Maximilian's first doubts about Mexico. Napoleon III proposed that Maximilian pay $200,000 to cover part of the cost of Almonte's visit to Mexico. Maximilian approved of Almonte's going to Veracruz, but he refused to pay. Richard Metternich in Paris thought that Maximilian had gone so far in encouraging Napoleon III that it would be difficult for him to refuse to contribute the $200,000, but Maximilian would not pay anything at all. This demand for money removed for the first time some of Maximilian's euphoria about Mexico.

His doubts grew when he heard of the firm refusal of the British government to give him any active help. British support had been one of the conditions on which both Franz Joseph and King Leopold had insisted, and Maximilian had relied on Leopold's close friendship with Queen Victoria to win over the British government. But Palmerston and Russell remained as determined as ever not to become involved.

Maximilian was beginning to doubt. Should he abandon the Mexican adventure? Had it not always been a condition of his acceptance that Britain as well as France should pledge her active support? He remembered all his former hostility to Napoleon III, whom he had condemned as a *parvenu* and as the man responsible for all the unrest in Italy. He wrote to Rechberg that he would not accept the throne of Mexico unless he was supported by Britain against future threats from the United States, adding, "From the very beginning of our negotiations the thought has continually recurred to me that there was a danger of an unlimited extension of French power . . . In my opinion, the Emperor Napoleon wishes to dominate Mexico without appearing to do so in the eyes of Europe." All Napoleon's actions in the Mexican negotiations had convinced him "of the evident desire of the Emperor of the French so to manage the affair that the future sovereign of Mexico will be quite unable to free himself from his tutelage."

By April 1862 Maximilian had almost decided not to go to Mexico.

9

Saligny Wants War

All the allied forces had landed at Veracruz by January 8, 1862, and immediately encountered difficulties. Juárez had ordered the Mexican people not to collaborate with the invaders. Many of the inhabitants of Veracruz had left town, and the peasants and traders in the surrounding country were not sending supplies. The allies found the filth and the yellow fever which they had been warned to expect. The requisitioning officers, wandering through the town to locate suitable accommodation for the soldiers, found an open sewer in nearly every street. They requisitioned a disused hospital for some of the British soldiers, placing the others, together with some of the French and Spanish troops, in Fort San Juan de Ulúa. On the first night, seventeen of the British soldiers in the old hospital fell seriously ill, and soon the number rose to seventy-seven. More than 10 percent of the British force were out of action.

The allied high commissioners held their first meeting in Veracruz on January 9. Both France and Britain were represented by their ambassadors to Mexico, Saligny and Sir Charles Wyke, and by the commanders-in-chief of their expeditionary forces, Admiral Jurien de la Gravière and Commodore Dunlop. General Prim, count of Reus, was the only Spanish representative on the commission; but as he was a senator in Madrid and had formerly been employed on several diplomatic missions, he was well able to deal with the political and diplomatic problems as well as with those which confronted him as commander-in-chief of the Spanish forces in Veracruz. He acted as chairman at the meetings of the high commissioners.

When Prim was a young man he had been a liberal, and under the rule of the conservative dictator General Narváez, he had taken refuge in England and France to escape a sentence of six years' imprisonment in the Philippines; but a more moderate conservative government had granted him amnesty, allowed him to return to Spain, and employed him on military and diplomatic duties. At the age of forty-seven he still retained some liberal sympathies, but he kept his political views to himself. He had married a Mexican woman, whose uncle, Gonzales Echeverría, was minister of finance in Juárez's government. It was not long before the Mexican conservatives, and Saligny, Napoleon III, and Eugénie, had convinced themselves that Prim was a secret agent of Juárez and was working to sabotage the aims of the Three Powers.

At their first meeting, Admiral Jurien proposed that in view of the shortage of supplies, the allies should send forces to Tejería and Medellín, some twenty miles from Veracruz, to obtain food, for he believed that the Mexican peasants would be very willing to sell them to the allies if they were no longer prevented from doing so by Juárez's soldiers. Prim agreed to Jurien's proposal, and so, reluctantly, did Wyke and Dunlop, although their instructions from the British government were to advance no further than Veracruz. The allied troops obtained the supplies they wanted in Tejería and Medellin; the Mexican forces retreated as the allies advanced and did not attempt to stop them.

On January 13, the allied high commissioners discussed how they would set about obtaining satisfaction of their claims against the Mexican government. Mexico owed more money to the British than to all their other creditors combined. The British claims against Mexico amounted to 69 million Mexican piastres, or silver dollars.* The Mexican government admitted that they owed about $9 million to their Spanish creditors and $2,860,000 to the French. But the British government realized that Mexico could not afford to pay its debts in full. The allies could seize the customs house in Veracruz, which was Mexico's chief source of revenue, but their claims would absorb 79 percent of the customs dues, and the Mexican government could not operate if its income was reduced by that amount. Wyke therefore proposed that the allies open negotiations with Juárez, presenting him with a detailed list of their subjects' claims and discussing how much the Mexican government was prepared to pay.

Prim agreed, but Saligny presented the draft of an ultimatum that he proposed be sent to Juárez. Without giving any particulars of the debts due to the French creditors, he demanded that the Mexican government agree to pay $12 million to cover all debts due to French

---

*About £14 million or 346 million French francs. The Mexican piastre was almost equal in value to the U.S. dollar; there were five French francs to the dollar, and about five dollars to the pound sterling.

subjects up to July 31, 1861, with France reserving the right to claim a further sum as compensation for injuries suffered since then. Juárez's government was also to recognize its liability to satisfy in full the claims of the holders of the Jecker bonds for an additional $15 million.

Wyke and Prim thought Saligny's ultimatum very unreasonable; Mexico could not be expected to pay $12 million to its creditors without any details being given as to how this figure had been arrived at. They thought the amount excessive; it would take up another 15 percent of the customs revenues of Veracruz, leaving only 6 percent for the Mexican government; and they objected to the claims of the holders of the Jecker bonds. While recognizing in principle that the government of a country must be held responsible for the debts incurred by previous governments, they thought it unfair to require Juárez to pay interest at 30 percent per annum to Jecker and his associates on money that Jecker had lent to Miramón to enable him to wage war against Juárez, who at the time of the contract had publicly announced that he would not recognize or repay any loans made to Miramón. The French were demanding that Mexico pay, over the years, $15 million in return for the $750,000 paid by Jecker to Miramón.

And why was the French government making such demands on behalf of a Swiss banker? The French explanation was that, as Switzerland had no diplomatic representative in Mexico, France was acting on behalf of Swiss citizens there. But the Swiss government had asked the United States, not France, to represent its interests in Mexico. In 1862 no one except Jecker and his closest intimates knew that Napoleon III's illegitimate half-brother and influential minister, the duke of Morny, held 30 percent of the Jecker bonds.

Even the French Foreign Office was surprised that Saligny was demanding $12 million; they thought that $10 million was nearer the correct figure. But Saligny privately told Prim that although he thought $10 million was the right amount, he had been ordered to ask for $12 million, and had to follow his instructions. He left Prim with the impression that the figure of $12 million had been arbitrarily fixed by Napoleon III himself.

Prim afterward stated that when Jurien, at the meeting of the allied high commissioners, read out that part of Saligny's ultimatum referring to the Jecker bonds, Wyke and Dunlop protested and said "with one voice 'That claim is inadmissible, the Mexican government will never accept it; before tolerating it, they will go to war, and the arms of England will never support such injustice.'" But Saligny would not reduce his demands. It was only after Dunlop said it would be unfortunate if the ultimatum destroyed the cooperation between the allies which had been created with such long and laborious negotiations that Saligny agreed to the British and Spanish request to postpone sending his ultimatum until after the allies had sent envoys to Mexico City to negotiate with the government.

Saligny hated Juárez and his party. He wrote to Montluc, Juárez's consul general in France, who was a personal acquaintance of his, and explained that when he first came to Mexico

> I welcomed the triumph of the Liberal Party as the beginning of an era of peace and prosperity for this unhappy republic, but . . . this so-called Liberal Party lost no time in suppressing all liberty and substituting for the brutal and stupid despotism of Miramón the dictatorship of Mr. Juárez, who is both an idiot and a rogue. This so-called Liberal Party is nothing but a collection of people with no respect for law or religion, with no intelligence, no honor, no patriotism, who have never had any political opinions except robbery.

Saligny put the matter more frankly to the paymaster general of the French forces in Veracruz: "My only merit lies in having guessed that the Emperor intended to intervene in Mexico and in having made this intervention necessary."

Wyke, writing to Russell about the meetings of the high commissioners, told him that Saligny's ultimatum was "perfectly outrageous" and "so insulting" that it would be impossible for the Mexican government to accept it. Russell agreed; he thought that the French demands "could only be put forward in the hope that the Mexican government would not fail to reject them and would afford thereby a *casus belli* for the allies." He instructed Lord Cowley, the British ambassador in Paris, to urge Thouvenel to modify the demand for $12 million. Thouvenel agreed to have the figure reexamined by a committee consisting of the secretary of the French legation in Mexico, the French vice consul at Veracruz, and a French businessman in Mexico, but he refused to have a representative of the Mexican government on the committee. Cowley told Thouvenel that he thought Saligny's ultimatum was just an excuse for the French to remain in Mexico. Thouvenel did not deny it. "No doubt such was the emperor's wish," he replied.

Napoleon III had meanwhile decided to send another 4,000 troops to Veracruz. The British government did not like it, but Napoleon explained that for the honor of France there had to be as many French as Spanish troops in Veracruz.

Juárez received the allied envoys with courtesy in Mexico City, but he made it clear that he would defend the independence of Mexico from foreign intervention. According to Wyke, he indulged in "an immense amount of verbiage to the effect that Mexico is a great nation." He sent his foreign minister, General Doblado, to meet Prim on February 19 at La Soledad, twenty-five miles from Veracruz. Doblado was very conciliatory. He suggested that as the allied troops in Veracruz were suffering from the heat and the diseases of the "hot lands," they should advance into the highlands near Orizaba, some sixty miles inland from Veracruz, where the climate was more healthful for Europeans. He said that the Mexican government would allow the troops to go there if the high commissioners recognized Juárez's government and entered into negotiations about the debts, and on condition that if the negotiations broke down and the allies declared war, they would withdraw to their previous positions in Veracruz. This proposal served a double purpose for the Mexicans: it was a friendly gesture to appease the allies, and it deprived the French of the argument that it was necessary to advance to Mexico City to escape danger to the soldiers' health.

When Prim returned to Veracruz with Doblado's proposal, Saligny objected to entering into any agreement with Juárez's government, but he was overruled by Admiral Jurien, and the high commissioners endorsed the Convention of La Soledad. Saligny agreed under protest and wrote to Paris complaining of the conduct of Jurien and the British and Spanish commissioners.

Juárez, though conciliatory to the allies, was harsh toward Mexicans who collaborated with them. On January 25 he issued a decree under the emergency powers that had been granted to him by the Mexican Congress. He decreed that any foreigner who made an armed invasion of Mexico without a declaration of war, any Mexican who voluntarily served in the forces of such an invader, and any Mexican or foreigner living in Mexico who invited foreigners to invade or to alter the form of government of the republic, or who voted or administered laws in territory occupied by the invading force, would be guilty of a crime against the independence and security of Mexico, and on conviction by court-martial would suffer the death penalty. Saligny denounced the decree and said that it showed the barbarous nature of Juárez's regime.

Although Saligny objected to the Convention of La Soledad, the French troops were happy to take advantage of the provisions, which allowed them to leave Veracruz for the Orizaba district. During their seven weeks in Veracruz 29 French soldiers had died of diseases, and 159 were in hospital. They set out on the exhausting journey at 6 A.M. on February 26, marching as the French army always marched, not together in step, but with each man walking at his own pace. By midday many of the soldiers, weakened by the unhealthful conditions in Veracruz, had fallen far behind their sturdier comrades; the officers of the leading column lost sight of two thirds of their men. Admiral Jurien, riding back along the line of march, was shocked to see the state of his troops and was glad that they were in no danger of being attacked by the Mexicans. All the men had arrived at the first day's camp by nightfall, but by the time the army reached La Soledad, having climbed the pass that separates the hot lands of the coastal plain from the highland plateau, they had traveled only twenty-four miles in four days.

They halted for two days at La Soledad and when they went on toward Orizaba they left behind 80 men who were classified as sick and 200 who were unfit to march. They reached Orizaba on the ninth day after leaving Veracruz. Here they rested again before going on to their final destination at Tehuacán, where they were to stay. When they marched into Tehuacán five days later, they were in much better shape, though 122 men arrived in ambulances.

On March 6, while the troops were on the march, General Count Charles Ferdinand de Lorencez arrived at Veracruz thirty-seven days after leaving Cherbourg, with 4,474 men and 616 much-needed horses. They soon moved on to Tehuacán, where they joined Jurien's troops.

The Spanish troops went to Córdoba in the same area. The original plan was for the British to stay in Orizaba; but the British government had ordered them not to go beyond Veracruz, and Wyke and Dunlop told Prim they were worried about the arrival of the French reinforcements under Lorencez and were therefore particularly eager not to get involved in any French ventures deeper into Mexico. They decided not to avail themselves of the Mexican offer to go to Orizaba, but to reembark on their ships just outside the port at Veracruz.

Meanwhile the Mexicans were assembling their forces, as the people answered Juárez's call to join the Eastern Army and defend their country from the foreign invader. The enthusiasm of the volunteers in Mexico City, which had impressed the English journalist Charles Lempriere, was not found everywhere; there were still many sympathizers with the Conservative Party, and even some of the liberal supporters were slow to volunteer for the Eastern Army. Like some of the revolutionaries in the countries of Europe, they were more eager to fight their conservative neighbors than conservatives in the ranks of a foreign invading army a thousand miles from their homes.

There was a good response to the call in Oaxaca, Juárez's home state, and also the home state of the rising liberal leader Porfirio Díaz. At the age of thirty-two Díaz was a veteran of the war against the

United States, the rebellion of 1852, and the War of the Reform, and had recently been elected to Congress and promoted to the rank of general. He had served in the campaign against Márquez's guerrillas in Michoacán. The people of Oaxaca were divided politically, as were the people in most of the Mexican states. Many admired Juárez and his achievements as governor of Oaxaca, his program of building roads, of providing universal education, and prohibiting child marriages; but others deplored the liberal government's suppression of the monasteries. The city of Oaxaca was captured by Miramón's forces during the War of the Reform, but in the last months of the war, Díaz drove them out and regained Oaxaca for the liberals.

The people of Oaxaca suffered more from natural disasters than from civil wars. A few hundred people had been killed in the sieges and street fighting between Díaz and the conservatives, but thousands had died of smallpox in 1851 and 1852, and of cholera and in an earthquake in 1854.

In February 1862 more than a thousand men from Oaxaca marched northeastward to join the Mexican Eastern Army. As usual in Mexico, the soldiers were accompanied by their wives and women, who cooked and cleaned for their men in the army. The First Oaxacan Brigade marched to the village of San Andrés Chalchicomula, about forty miles northwest of Córdoba, which was the headquarters of the Eastern Army, and camped around a large barn in which the Eastern Army had stored 46,000 pounds of gunpowder. On the afternoon of March 6 the women lighted fires in front of the barn and began, as usual, to cook food for the soldiers. Many local tradesmen, knowing that the women would be preparing the food, came around to sell tortillas and beans.

It was a windy day, and the wind blew a spark into the barn, where it ignited the gunpowder and caused a tremendous explosion. In a moment the ground was covered with corpses, with severed arms, legs, and heads, and pools of blood. When it was possible, some days later, to count the victims, it was found that more than 1,500 people had been killed — 1,042 soldiers, 475 women, and some 30 of the local traders. Two hundred more had been wounded, many of them losing a limb or their eyesight. Some of the wounded were carried to the neighboring houses and cared for after a fashion, but the medical services of the Eastern Army were quite unable to cope with a disaster on this scale.

Admiral Jurien heard the news just as his troops were arriving at Tehuacán, some forty miles from San Andrés. He thought that he ought to alleviate the suffering; and it was a good opportunity to show that the French, as they claimed, had come to Mexico to rescue, not to oppress, the Mexican people. He sent some French army doctors to aid the wounded at San Andrés. Their skill was invaluable, and they saved many lives that would otherwise have been lost.

The Mexican conservatives, as usual, were less generous than the French toward their enemies. When Father Ignacio Merlin, one of the canons of the cathedral in Oaxaca, was invited to serve on the committee set up to organize relief for the victims of the explosion, he refused; he would do nothing to help godless liberals. "Señor Merlin, a faithful representative of his class," wrote the liberal Oaxacan newspaper *La Victoria*, "refuses to belong to a humanitarian organization, not because he is too busy, but to show the world that it is not to the clergy to whom one should run when it is a matter of rescuing the unfortunate." Four weeks later the liberals in Oaxaca suppressed the convent of St. Catherine of Siena, which had been erected in 1576, driving out the nuns and converting the building into government offices. (Today it is the Hotel Presidente.)

The explosion at San Andrés was a disaster for the liberals. There were only a handful of survivors from the First Oaxacan Brigade. Nearly 10 percent of the whole Mexican Eastern Army had been killed by the negligence of one of their own men and by a stroke of misfortune.

Napoleon III sent General Almonte from Paris to Veracruz; as Maximilian refused to pay his travel expenses, Napoleon paid them himself. Miramón also arrived at Veracruz. The British government had not forgiven Miramón for seizing the money in the British legation in Mexico City in 1860, and to Saligny's annoyance Dunlop announced that if Miramón landed at Veracruz he would be arrested and tried on a charge of theft. Prim agreed to let him go to Havana.

Wyke and Prim were also worried about Almonte, for they thought that Juárez would interpret his arrival as an attempt by the allies to interfere in the internal politics of Mexico. Doblado protested against Almonte's presence in the territory occupied by the allied troops; but Saligny rejected Doblado's demand that Almonte be expelled from Mexico. He worked closely with Almonte, and together they got in touch with some of Juárez's generals, hoping to persuade them to desert and join the allies.

Almonte contacted General Uraga, the commander-in-chief of the Mexican Eastern Army. He assured Uraga that the French had come not to conquer Mexico but to free the Mexicans from the tyranny of Juárez. Uraga was noncommittal, but he did not reject Almonte's advances out of hand. Juárez became suspicious of Uraga and dismissed him from his position as commander-in-chief. In his place he appointed General Ignacio Zaragoza, a young man who wore spectacles and looked more like a graduate student than a Mexican military leader.

Almonte also entered into communication with General Robles Pezuela, who had fought for Miramón in the War of the Reform but had been pardoned by Juárez and allowed to live quietly in Mexico City. Juárez's agents found out that Robles had been writing to Almonte. Robles was not arrested but was ordered to live in the town of Sombrerete in the state of Zacatecas, nearly 400 miles from the district where the allied troops were stationed, and to give his word of honor not to leave the town.

Almonte invited Robles to meet him at Córdoba, and Robles set off on the journey with a friend who was in touch with French officers. They had nearly reached Córdoba when they were stopped by Mexican army sentries at a roadblock. Asked where they were going, the two men spurred their horses and galloped off. One of the sentries, like many Mexicans, was an expert with the lasso; he lassoed Robles as he rode away and pulled him off his horse, though the other man escaped and reached the French camp.

Robles, who had broken his arm when he was pulled from the horse, was taken to Zaragoza's headquarters at San Andrés, where he was tried by court-martial under the decree of January 25 on a charge of attempting to collaborate with the invaders. He was found guilty and sentenced to death.

Juárez's minister of finance, Gonzales Echeverría, and the minister of justice, Jesús Teran, were negotiating with Wyke and Prim at Orizaba when the news arrived that Robles had been sentenced to death. Wyke and Prim told Echeverría and Teran that it would make a favorable impression on the allied high commissioners and facilitate the negotiations about the debts if the death sentence on Robles was not carried out. Echeverría and Teran sent a letter by messenger to Zaragoza's headquarters, urging Zaragoza to postpone the execution until an appeal for a pardon could be sent to Juárez in Mexico City. The messenger left Orizaba at 7 P.M. but lost his way as he rode through the dark night in stormy weather, and when he arrived at San Andrés at 11 A.M. the next day, he was told that Robles had been executed by a firing squad five hours earlier.

Saligny declared that the barbaric Juárez government had committed a hostile act against France by executing a gallant officer who had wished to enter into relations with the French. Wyke regretted the execution; although he censured Robles for rebelling against his government and for breaking his parole, he thought him a kindly man who, during the War of the Reform, had never committed atrocities, as Márquez and other generals of his party had done. Russell believed that the French were to blame for Robles's death, as it was the inevitable reaction of the Mexican liberals to the news "of the Representatives of a defeated Party, landing under the protection of 7000 men who had invaded their Soil."

Everyone in the French camp at Tehuacán was expecting orders from Paris to begin the war against Juárez. Saligny assured Jurien that the majority of the Mexican people hated Juárez's tyranny and that the French would be welcomed as liberators. Jurien doubted this. "They hate us here," he wrote to Thouvenel; "the foreigner in arms is always odious." Saligny pointed out that Jurien must not judge Mexico by Veracruz, which had always been a liberal city. When the French reached Puebla, on the road to Mexico City, they would be warmly welcomed, for Puebla was as Catholic and conservative as Veracruz was liberal.

The Jesuit Father Miranda, who had played such an important part in organizing the conservative *coup d'état* that overthrew Comonfort's government in 1857, had arrived with the other Mexican refugees from Europe at Veracruz. He showed Saligny a letter, from a friend in Mexico City, that complained bitterly about Juárez's January 25 decree against traitors. The decree "leaves us no choice but to take up arms. . . . After the decree of the 25th, what can be expected of such people? How many victims will there be before those gentlemen [the French soldiers] arrive? For the love of God, urge them to move and to come straight to this city, or we are lost."

Jurien was not convinced, but he had no doubt that the French could get to Mexico City without difficulty as soon as they received orders from the emperor. On March 24 he wrote to Lorencez that they would be in Mexico City within a month.

Prim tried to warn Napoleon III that he was making a big mistake in overthrowing Juárez's government and installing Maximilian. He wrote to him from Orizaba on March 17 and pointed out that in Mexico, unlike the countries of Europe, there was no deep-rooted aristocracy that could be relied upon to support the monarchy, and that Mexico had as its neighbor the United States, where the people had a strong attachment to republican doctrines and fiercely opposed the idea of monarchy:

Far be it from me, Sire, even to imagine that Your Imperial Majesty's power is insufficient to erect in Mexico a throne for the House of Austria. . . . It will be easy for Your Majesty to lead Prince Maximilian to the capital and to crown him King; but this King will find no support in the country, except from the Conservative leaders, who did not think of establishing the monarchy when they were in power and only think of it now that they are dispersed, defeated, and in exile. Some rich men too will accept a foreign monarch who will arrive supported by Your Majesty's soldiers, but this monarch will have nothing to sustain him on the day that this support is withdrawn, and he will fall from the throne erected by Your Majesty as other earthly powers will fall on the day when Your Majesty's imperial cloak will cease to cover and defend them.

This reference to "other earthly powers" was to the pope, whose temporal power in Rome was protected by Napoleon III's troops. Prim's forecast was as accurate about Rome as it was about Mexico.

Napoleon III was very angry when he received Prim's letter, and Eugénie was even more angry. Prim had been the first person to whom Napoleon, at Vichy in July 1861, had confided his plan to intervene in Mexico and place a European prince on the throne; the Spaniards had been the first to demand satisfaction from Juárez's government and to send troops, under Prim's command, to Veracruz. Now Prim was lecturing him and telling him to abandon the whole venture. He attributed this to Spanish resentment at his having chosen an Austrian rather than a Spanish prince to reign in Mexico, or to Prim's having been seduced into supporting the Mexican liberals by his Mexican wife and her uncle in Juárez's government. He sent an official note to the Spanish government, which was published in the French government newspaper *Le Moniteur* on April 2, asking them to recall Prim from Mexico and replace him with another commander.

Napoleon had already committed himself before he received Prim's letter. On March 20 Thouvenel sent instructions to Saligny and Jurien, informing them that the French government had repudiated the Convention of La Soledad. He mildly censured Jurien for having approved it; he recalled Jurien to Paris and appointed Lorencez as commander-in-chief in his place; he endorsed everything that Saligny had said and done; he told them to adhere, without any amendments, to Saligny's ultimatum of January 12, and to present it immediately to Juárez's government, whatever the reaction of the British and Spanish high commissioners. If Juárez did not accept the ultimatum, they were to start military operations at once and advance to Mexico City. They were barely to allow Juárez the opportunity of complying with their demands. "His Majesty hopes," wrote Thouvenel, "that you will not allow yourselves to be stopped by any evasive and fallacious reply from Juárez's government, and that you will march on the capital with as much promptitude as the means at your disposal permits." French honor required them to adhere to the terms of the Convention of La Soledad and withdraw from their positions in the highlands to Vera-cruz, and they were to begin the retreat and begin military operations as soon as the Spanish troops had withdrawn from their positions and were out of the battle zone.

To remove an anomaly, on March 26 the Swiss citizen J. B. Jecker became a naturalized Frenchman and a subject of Emperor Napoleon III, who six days earlier had decided to go to war to enforce Jecker's claims against Mexico.

When Thouvenel showed la Fuente a copy of the instructions he had sent to Saligny and Jurien, la Fuente realized that this was war, and that he could do no more good in France. He asked for his passport and broke off diplomatic relations between France and Mexico. He sent a last note of protest to Thouvenel. "Mexico is not as weak as Spain was under Napoleon I. Mexico may be conquered, but will never submit, and will not be conquered without having given proof of the courage and virtues which are not credited to her." Napoleon's "enterprise, ruinous and terrible for us, will be the same for its instigators."

On April 9 the allied high commissioners held their last meeting at Orizaba. Wyke and Prim protested the French decision to allow Almonte and Miranda to go to Córdoba. "Nobody entertains more respect for General Almonte personally than I do," wrote Wyke to Jurien, "but your Excellency must surely be aware that he is the recognized head of that party led by the infamous Marquéz, Cabos, and others now in arms and at open warfare with the established Government of Mexico. . . . Your other protégé, Padre Miranda, is a man whose very name recalls some of the worst scenes of a civil war which has proved a disgrace to the civilization of the present century." Prim and Wyke announced that as France was obviously interfering in Mexico's internal affairs, Spain and Britain would withdraw from the joint intervention.

The high commissioners were able to agree on their last note to Doblado, informing him that, owing to their disagreements, they would act independently of each other. The French troops would withdraw to their former positions in the hot lands, and as soon as the Spanish forces, which would be leaving Mexico, had passed this point, probably about April 20, the French army would start its operations.

Doblado, in reply, expressed Mexico's appreciation of "the noble, loyal, and considerate conduct of the English and Spanish commissioners," and informed Saligny and Jurien that though Mexico would never be the aggressor, she would defend her independence and meet force with force.

When Russell sent Wyke a copy of a report from Cowley in Paris about the French negotiations with Maximilian, Wyke understood what Saligny had been up to. "The French Agents," he wrote to Russell, "were from the first determined to upset this Govt. in favour of the re-actionary Party, thro' whose means they expect to get the ArchD. elected K. of Mexico."

Wyke and Dunlop met Doblado at Puebla, the nearest place where they could be sure of not encountering the advancing French army. Prim would have gone with them if he had not felt obliged to supervise the embarkation of the Spanish troops at Veracruz. On April 30 Wyke and Dunlop signed a treaty with Doblado settling the British creditors' claims by a compromise: Mexico would pay the British creditors $13 million. The first installment of $2 million would be paid at once; the balance of $11 million would be paid as soon as Mexico had obtained a loan from the United States to cover the amount, and in any case within sixteen months. Each quarter, as they received the money from the United States, they would pay it over to the British government. It was almost identical to the agreement that had been reached between Zamacona and Wyke in Mexico City in July 1861 but had then been rejected by the Mexican Congress. Now Juárez, under the emergency powers he had been granted, had authority to confirm the treaty without referring it to Congress, and he did so without delay.

The British and Spanish governments confirmed their high commissioners' termination of the joint intervention; but the British government repudiated the Convention of Puebla. They did not object to the financial settlement, but they would not agree to the involvement of the United States. "H. M. Govt. think that the Manner in which a Treaty between Mexico & the U.S. is recognised, is objectionable as, were the Treaty brought into operation, it might possibly affect the Independence of Mexico. . . . H. M. Govt. therefore decline to ratify these Conventions."

Both Britain and Spain recalled their forces from Veracruz without having signed any agreement with Juárez's government, leaving the field clear for the French to act alone in Mexico.

In Britain, public opinion was divided. King Leopold of the Belgians came to London in February 1862, hoping to persuade the government, the press, and Queen Victoria to support French intervention and the plan to place Maximilian on the Mexican throne. He may have had some success with the press, for both *The Times* of London and the *Morning Post* published editorials sympathetic to Maximilian's candidature. *The Times* strongly approved of the plan to overthrow republican democracy in Mexico and asked whether "those demoralized and bloodthirsty half-castes, uniting the vices of the white man with the savageness of the Indian," were "the people who were to teach not only effete Spain but even France and England the lesson of self-government."

But this did not change the policy of the British government. If the French succeeded in making Maximilian emperor of Mexico and imposing law and order there under a constitutional sovereign, Britain would view the change with varying degrees of approval — more from Palmerston, less from Russell. But the British government would not abandon its policy of strict neutrality and nonintervention in the war between Napoleon III and Juárez.

King Leopold was least successful with Queen Victoria. When she heard about the end of the Convention of London and the collaboration between the Three Powers in Mexico, she wrote to Russell, "The conduct of the French is everywhere disgraceful. Let us only have *nothing* to do with them in future in any proceedings in other countries."

Public opinion in France meant more to Napoleon III than public opinion in England. Until 1860 his regime had been a dictatorship in which the press could not criticize the government without fear of suppression, and socialists and radicals ran the risk of being arrested and imprisoned in internment camps in Algeria or Cayenne. But in November 1860 Napoleon had relaxed the dictatorship and allowed free political discussion, though the government retained and occasionally used its powers to censor and prosecute its critics. Five members of the liberal opposition — Jules Favre, Ernest Picard, Émile Ollivier, Louis Darimon, and Jacques Louis Hénon — had succeeded in getting elected to the legislative body, the Corps Législatif, at the general election of 1857 and at subsequent by-elections, despite all the pressure and discrimination applied by government officials in favor of progovernment candidates. The band of five was free to criticize all aspects of government policy, including its Mexican policy, in the chamber, but it was hopelessly outvoted in the division that followed the debates.

Favre and his colleagues did not oppose Napoleon's policy of seeking redress from Juárez for the wrongs suffered by French creditors, but they asked that Napoleon open negotiations with Juárez instead of trying to overthrow his government by force. "Governments are no more entitled than private individuals to kill their debtors in order to make them pay up," said Favre. The prime minister, Auguste Billault, whose chief duty was to defend the emperor's policy in the Corps

Législatif, rejected this demand. Addressing the opposition deputies with all the courtesy that parliamentary procedure required, he regretted that "the Honorable Monsieur Favre" and his colleagues should throw doubt on the justice of France's cause at a time when French soldiers were shedding their blood for this cause in Mexico. When Billault spoke in the debate on March 13, 1862, the news had not yet reached Paris that Admiral Jurien had agreed to the Convention of La Soledad. "Our troops are going to Mexico City," said Billault. "Having set out on February 20, they must be there already."

Napoleon III always wished to know how the public reacted to his policies. He ordered the *procureurs généraux* (district attorneys) in every department of France to report regularly to the minister of the interior on what the public was thinking in their districts. The *procureurs généraux* were ordered to be strictly truthful in these very confidential documents; and though they sometimes inserted a sycophantic phrase, they seem on the whole to have reported frankly and truthfully.

In the autumn of 1861 and the following winter, the reports from all over France told the same story: a lack of interest in Mexico, a complete failure to appreciate the emperor's farsighted projects in Central America and the advantages it would bring, politically and economically, to France. This feeling seemed to be increasing in the spring of 1862. The *procureur général* of Nancy reported on April 5 that there was little interest in colonial expeditions in Mexico, despite the advantages France had derived from her expeditions to China and Cochin China. The *procureur général* of Lot-et-Garonne wrote more strongly from Agen on April 6: "The Mexican expedition is having a rather disagreeable effect on opinion; people readily admit that it was necessary after the injuries and robberies to which our nationals were subjected, but these injuries and robberies are not well known."

In intellectual circles in Paris there was harsher criticism in private from opponents of the government. In March 1862 the writer Marco de Saint-Hilaire said to the English economist Nassau Senior that Napoleon III had made many mistakes but that "the worst of them probably is the Mexican expedition. It will complete the ruin of our finances and as I said before that ruin will ruin the dynasty."

But Napoleon III did not think that the support of public opinion was necessary in so easy a campaign as the one that was about to start in Mexico. General Lorencez had 7,300 soldiers under his command; deducting the sick and those who had to be left in the rear to guard vital installations in Veracruz and elsewhere, he had 6,000 men whom he could lead to Mexico City. Lorencez thought that this would be an easy task. On April 25 he wrote to Marshal Randon, the minister of war, in Paris: "We are so superior to the Mexicans in race, in organization, in discipline, in morality, and in elevation of feeling, that I beg Your Excellency to be so good as to inform the emperor that, at the head of 6,000 soldiers, I am already master of Mexico."

❧ 10 ❧

THE FIFTH OF MAY

AT ORIZABA, Saligny and Jurien issued a proclamation to the Mexican people: "Mexicans! We have not come here to take part in your disputes; we have come to put an end to them. . . . The French flag has been planted on Mexican soil; this flag will not retreat. Let wise men greet it as a friendly flag. Let madmen fight against it if they dare!"

General Almonte also issued a proclamation, in which he proclaimed himself president of the Republic of Mexico. Zuloaga, who since Miramón's departure had claimed to be the rightful president and the leader of the Conservative Party, now resigned the office in favor of Almonte and withdrew from active politics. Márquez, the Tiger of Tacubaya, the murderer of Ocampo, responded to the French appeal. After being defeated in Michoacán he had remained at large in the mountains to the north of Mexico City at the head of a guerrilla band of 2,500 men. He set off across country with his followers, hoping to link up with the French army.

Lorencez was ready to begin his march to Mexico City. If his army had been in Veracruz, the men would have had to climb the mountain range to reach the plateau of the temperate lands, and then ascend the steeper mountain range that separates the temperate lands from the high plateau of the cold lands, where Puebla and Mexico City are situated. Thanks to the Convention of La Soledad, the bulk of Lorencez's men were already at Tehuacán and Orizaba in the temperate lands. But it had been a term of the agreement at La Soledad that if the allies repudiated the convention and went to war with Mexico, they would withdraw to their former positions in the coastal plain. Lorencez announced that the honorable traditions of the French army required him to observe the convention; the French troops duly set out from Tehuacán, marching east and intending to descend the pass to the coastal plain.

There were 340 French soldiers in the hospital at Orizaba, and Lorencez asked Zaragoza if they could stay there. Zaragoza agreed, on condition that no fit French soldiers remain in Orizaba. He promised that the soldiers in the hospital would be safe and well cared for under the protection of the Mexican army, and assured Lorencez that he had not forgotten how the French doctors had cared for his wounded men after the explosion at San Andrés. On April 18 the French officers decided to move the sick men to another hospital in Orizaba. Most of them were taken in ambulances, but a few, who were well enough to walk, went on foot through the town, carrying their small arms with them. When this was reported to Zaragoza, he protested to Lorencez that the French were violating their agreement by keeping some fit soldiers in Orizaba.

The French had by now reached Córdoba in their march back to the hot lands, but were still on the plateau. From there Lorencez wrote to Zaragoza, explaining that the soldiers who had walked through the streets in Orizaba were some of the 340 wounded men who Zaragoza had agreed could remain there. Zaragoza accepted the explanation, and wrote to Lorencez, apologizing for having misunderstood the position.

But Lorencez did not wait for a reply. He decided that Zaragoza's original protest showed that the liberals were about to murder the French soldiers in the hospital at Orizaba. This made it impossible for him to continue his withdrawal to the coastal plain; he could not abandon his sick soldiers to the mercy of the Juárist barbarians. Prim, who was passing through Córdoba on his way to Veracruz, told Lorencez that his sick soldiers were as safe in the hospital at Orizaba as they would be in Paris. But Lorencez ordered his troops to turn about and march to Orizaba. Once again, as at Rome in their operations against the Roman Republic and Garibaldi in 1849, the French army under Napoleon III had gained an important military advantage by violating the terms of an armistice, and had found a plausible excuse for doing so.

Because the French had broken the Convention of La Soledad, Zaragoza could not defend the passes below Orizaba, and he withdrew to his second line of defense, the steeper pass of Aculzingo, rising from Orizaba to the high plateau through the thick forests that covered the higher parts of the pass. He stationed 4,000 men with eight cannons at Las Cumbras, near the top of the pass. On April 28 Lorencez sent his men up the pass in the face of Mexican fire. After a sharp fight, which lasted from 1:30 to 5 P.M., the French drove back the Mexicans and reached the summit, with only two men killed and thirty-six wounded. It was the relatively easy victory they had expected.

Once on the high plateau, they advanced rapidly toward Puebla as Zaragoza retreated. He had ordered his men to scatter propaganda leaflets in French on the ground across which the French would advance. Lorencez sent an advance party on ahead to collect and burn the leaflets before the rest of his men arrived; but many of the soldiers saw them and wrote about them in their letters to their families in France.

By May 4 the French had reached the village of Amozoc, a few miles north of Puebla, and Lorencez decided to attack the city at once. Saligny, relying on the information he had received from Mexican conservatives, had told him that the French would be welcomed as liberators and greeted with flowers by the people of Puebla.

Puebla, with 80,000 inhabitants and over 150 churches, was surrounded by a chain of forts. On the north side were Forts Loreto and Guadalupe; on the south, Fort del Carmen; on the west, Forts San Xavier and Santa Anita. Zaragoza placed some of his 6,000 men in the forts, and held others in reserve in the city, where he had erected barricades in most of the streets as a last line of defense. His chief anxiety was the reaction of the people, for Puebla had always been a conservative stronghold. Like Saligny, he expected them to welcome the French.

A few days earlier, Saligny had heard from Márquez, who was not far away and was hastening to join the French with his 2,500 guerrillas. Márquez sent an Indian scout through Zaragoza's lines with a message for Saligny; it was written on a piece of paper hidden in one of the handrolled cigarettes the scout carried on him. The scout reached the French headquarters and gave the letter to Saligny, who became more confident than ever that the French would be welcomed at Puebla. But in case there was more resistance than he expected, he passed on to Lorencez the advice he had received from Mexican conservatives who knew Puebla: Lorencez should not attempt to enter the city from the north side, the direction of Amozoc, but from the east.

Almonte had accompanied the French army to Amozoc. He knew Puebla well, for he had both captured and defended it during the civil wars. He advised Lorencez to march around the city and attack it from the west, and he said that Puebla had never been taken from the north. But Lorencez decided to march straight from Amozoc toward Puebla and to bombard and capture the northern forts.

On the morning of May 5, the French advanced to within 2,000 yards of Fort Guadalupe, the first of the forts in their path on the ridge north of Puebla, about half a mile from the larger Fort Loreto beyond it. At 11 A.M. their artillery began to shell Fort Guadalupe. Several of the shells fell within the fort, killing some of the defenders and causing damage to the walls. After a while Lorencez ordered the artillery to advance and to resume the bombardment from closer range; but from their new position the angle of vision and of fire was less satisfactory, and during the second bombardment no shell hit the fort or did any damage to the Mexicans.

After an hour and a half the French had spent nearly half their ammunition, and Lorencez sent in his infantry to capture Fort Guadalupe. They came under strong musket fire from the Mexicans in the fort, and from others sheltered by rising ground halfway between the two forts. The Mexican artillery in Fort Loreto was also turned on the French infantry. Two French colonels were killed as they led their regiments to the attack, and soon the corpses of the French were piling up in front of the walls of Fort Guadalupe. Once a French soldier succeeded in climbing the walls and hoisting the French flag over the fort, but he was killed a moment later and the flag thrown down. Zaragoza ordered his cavalry to attack the French infantry in front of the fort, and Porfirio Díaz led the charge.

Zaragoza was waiting for the rain, for during the previous week there had been a heavy downpour every day in the afternoon. It came at three o'clock, with a thunderstorm that drenched the combatants, obscured visibility, and made the ground in front of the fort slippery. At 4 P.M. Lorencez ordered the retreat. The French marched down from Fort Guadalupe to a position at the foot of the hill and waited for the Mexican counterattack. It did not come, and the French erected their tents and spent the night listening to the Mexicans cheering and celebrating their victory by singing Mexican songs and the "Marseillaise," which to the French was "*our* 'Marseillaise,'" although Napoleon III had banned it in France and it was the anthem of liberal revolutionaries everywhere, including Mexico.

The French had lost 462 men killed and wounded in the day's fighting; 8 had been taken prisoner.

Despite this setback, the French waited confidently for the Mexican attack the next day; but Zaragoza had a healthy respect for the French army, which since its victories in the Crimea and in Italy had won an international reputation as the best army in the world. He was probably as surprised as the French that his men had defeated them, and he would not press his luck too far. In a period of history when modern weapons had given the defensive a big advantage over the offensive, it was one thing to repulse a French attack on a fort and another to attack and defeat them in the open field. The important thing was the effect on the morale of his men and on Mexico's international prestige of having defeated the French on May 5; this would be lost if the victory were immediately followed by a defeat.

Lorencez waited two days for Zaragoza's attack, and then on May 8 began his retreat to Orizaba, for he could not renew his advance with his depleted force, and there was no place nearer than Orizaba where he could establish a base. With the French in full retreat, Zaragoza could claim a great victory. In his dispatch to the minister of war on May 9, he wrote that the French army had fought bravely but that Lorencez had shown his incapacity in the attack. "The national arms, Citizen Minister, covered themselves with glory, and through you I congratulate the first magistrate of the Republic. I can affirm with pride that the Mexican army did not once turn its back on the enemy during the long struggle that it had to sustain." He stated that he had 3,602 men engaged in the battle, and that the French had lost 1,000 men killed and wounded and between 8 and 12 prisoners.

The French disputed his figures. They said that he had understated his own strength and exaggerated the French losses, and that the Mexicans had had 12,000 men engaged, outnumbering the French by two to one. But though Zaragoza had overestimated the French losses and understated the numbers of his men, it seems that both armies were about equal in strength, with 6,000 engaged on each side.

Juárez made the most of the victory. He decreed that the Fifth of May should rank as a national holiday with the Sixteenth of September, the day on which Hidalgo began the revolution of 1810, and that the city of Puebla should henceforth be called the city of Zaragoza. The people continued to call it Puebla; it was called Zaragoza only in official government documents and in articles in the patriotic press. It was not long before even the officials and journalists began to call the city Puebla-Zaragoza so that people should know what place they were talking about.

In Puebla itself, few celebrated the victory of the Fifth of May, for Saligny was right in believing that most of the inhabitants had been preparing to welcome the French. Zaragoza was disgusted, and on the same day that he issued his triumphant order of the day he wrote in a private letter to the government that he would like to burn Puebla because the inhabitants were bad, lazy, and selfish and were lamenting the victory of the Fifth of May.

Lorencez assured his troops that they had nothing to be ashamed of and, without actually naming him, threw the blame on Saligny. "We had been told a hundred times that the town of Puebla called for you with all their hearts, and that the inhabitants would rush to follow you as you marched and to cover you with flowers. It was with the confidence derived from these false statements that we appeared before Puebla." It was not a very convincing excuse; a general should be prepared for the enemy to receive his men with gunfire, not flowers.

On the last stage of Lorencez's retreat to Orizaba, during his descent from the Cumbres de Aculzingo, he met Márquez and his 2,500 horsemen. The troops reached Orizaba on May 18. Zaragoza followed with 14,000 men, including 6,000 under General Ortega, who had arrived from the north too late to take part in the battle of the Fifth of May. Zaragoza took up his position on the slopes of the Cumbres de Aculzingo and bombarded Orizaba without doing much harm to the French.

That night at nine, the young French Captain Détrie led his unit of seventy-five men on a reconnaissance toward the Mexican lines. Encountering some enemy soldiers, he attacked them, having no idea in the dark that he was engaging the advance guard of the Mexican army. The Mexicans, not expecting the attack and confused in the darkness, panicked and fled up the mountainside, causing more confusion and panic among their comrades, who suddenly found themselves in the midst of a battle. Détrie and his men continued their attack all through the night, and at 3 A.M. they were joined by another seventy-five men, who had come to reinforce them. By morning the Mexicans had fled, leaving Détrie in possession of the pass of Cerro Borrego. The French had lost two men killed and twenty-eight wounded, including Détrie himself, who had suffered a severe wound; but they had killed or wounded two hundred Mexicans and captured two hundred prisoners, one regimental flag, and three pieces of artillery.

No one has ever satisfactorily explained why the Mexican soldiers, who had fought so well at Fort Guadalupe on May 5, performed so badly at Cerro Borrego thirteen days later. One of the French officers who took part in the action attributed the victory to a general misunderstanding. He thought that if he and his companions had known the strength of the forces that occupied the pass, they would never have attempted to dislodge them with seventy-five men, and that the victory, due to the exceptional vigor of Captain Détrie, had been possible only because the darkness of the night prevented the enemy from seeing how few troops the French had and the French from realizing the difficulties and dangers of their undertaking.

The Mexicans naturally did not publicize their defeat or allow it to cast a shadow over the public celebrations of the victory of the Fifth of May; but the debacle of Cerro Borrego had far-reaching results. It revived all the sense of inferiority, the reluctance to face the great French army, which had obsessed the Mexican commanders before May 5. They launched no further large-scale attacks on the French position at Orizaba, and allowed them to stay there until they could obtain reinforcements from France.

The news of the Fifth of May took more than a month to reach Europe, and until it arrived there Napoleon III and his supporters lived in happy ignorance, convinced that Lorencez was on his way to Mexico City. *Le Temps* wrote on May 23 that Admiral Jurien de la Gravière was advancing on Mexico City with such speed that even when taking into account the difference between the French and the Mexicans — "the French people placed very high and the Mexican people very low" — it was nevertheless a great achievement. On May 31 *La Patrie* reported that French troops entered Puebla on May 2 and were cheered by the population, who had illuminated the city in their honor.

Napoleon and Eugénie had still not heard about the setback when Eugénie wrote on June 7 to Archduchess Charlotte, who had opened a correspondence with her, and to whom she hoped she would soon be writing as one empress to another. After denouncing Wyke and Prim for accepting the Convention of La Soledad, Eugénie wrote, "Here we are, thanks to God, without allies." Since France had acted alone, freed from English and Spanish restraint, all the men in Mexico were "grouping themselves around Almonte, who, only yesterday an outlaw, is today dictator of all the provinces which we have recently overrun. The next mail will probably bring us news of our arrival in Mexico City."

On the same day Napoleon wrote to Maximilian that the news from Mexico was very good, now that they had at last abandoned Prim's "groping and ridiculous advances" to Juárez's government. "I am most anxious to know what has been going on for the last month. General Lorencez wrote to me that he reckoned on being in Mexico City by May 25 at the latest."

The news about the Fifth of May first reached Europe through the Prussian minister in Mexico, Baron Wagner, who wrote to his government about the events. The Prussian foreign minister sent a copy of Wagner's dispatch to Bismarck, who was Prussian ambassador in Paris (his last diplomatic post before unexpectedly being invited to become prime minister of Prussia the following September). Knowing how eager Napoleon III was to receive news from Mexico, Bismarck showed him Wagner's dispatch, though he wrote to Berlin that he was sure that Napoleon would not be grateful for the information.

The first reaction of Napoleon III's journalists to the news from Puebla was to lie. On June 13 *La Patrie* wrote that news had come from Veracruz on May 15 that the French army had won "a very glorious battle" before Puebla "in which the Mexican troops, much superior in numbers, were completely defeated"; that the French would enter Puebla the next day; and that "the alarming rumors that the English newspapers continue to spread" were untrue. *Le Constitutionnel* also denied the reports of a French defeat. But the truth could not be suppressed for long, and Napoleon decided to use it for his own advantage. He now had another reason for intervening in Mexico — to avenge the defeat of May 5, to restore French prestige, to vindicate the national honor. He decided to send 20,000 troops to Mexico. On June 18 *La Patrie* was still putting on a brave face; although admitting that there had been a slight check in Mexico, they wrote that reinforcements were being sent "not to relieve our army at Puebla, but to reinforce the results our brave soldiers have certainly obtained on the road to Mexico City."

Napoleon appointed General Élie Frédéric Forey to replace Lorencez as commander-in-chief, for though he sent a reassuring message to Lorencez, he told him that he had mismanaged the attack on Puebla and should not have issued his order of the day blaming Saligny. Forey, a tall, red-faced man in his late fifties with a splendid white mustache, had played an important part in winning army support for Napoleon's *coup d'état* of December 2, 1851, and had distinguished himself in the Crimea and in Italy.

On July 3 Napoleon wrote a letter to Forey, which was published, with some omissions, in *Le Moniteur*. After praising Saligny — "I do not doubt that if his advice had been followed, our flag would now be flying over Mexico City" — he laid down the objectives of French policy in Mexico. Forey must protect, and accept the help of, Almonte and all Mexicans who supported the French intervention; he must protect religion, but must not invalidate the sale of Church lands by the liberal government; and all his political decisions were to be only temporary, until the Mexicans could decide their destiny for themselves after the French had entered Mexico City. He must not force any form of government on Mexico, but if the Mexicans wished to have a monarchy, France would support this, and Forey should suggest that they choose Archduke Maximilian as their sovereign. "The Prince who may mount the Mexican throne," wrote Napoleon in a passage that was omitted from the published version, "will always be forced to act in the interests of France, not only from gratitude but even more because his country's interests will be in accordance with ours, and he will not be able to maintain himself without our influence."

Why was France sacrificing the lives of her soldiers and her money to find a throne for an Austrian prince? Because "the prosperity of America is of concern to Europe, for it feeds our industry and gives life to our commerce." It was in France's interest for the United States to be powerful and prosperous, but not for it to acquire control of the whole of the Gulf of Mexico and to dominate all Central and South America, including the Isthmus of Panama, because in that case "there would henceforth be no other power in America than the United States." But if, thanks to the French army, a stable government could be established in Mexico, "we shall have erected an insuperable barrier against the encroachments of the United States." This last passage was deleted from the published version and replaced by a sentence not included in the original letter: "We shall have restored to the Latin race on the other side of the ocean its force and its prestige."

While all the Mexican conservatives, from Almonte to Márquez, joined the French and fought in what Lorencez and Forey officially called "the Franco-Mexican army," the French liberals living in Mexico enthusiastically supported Juárez, and organized propaganda appeals to their fellow countrymen not to allow Saligny and Almonte to mislead Napoleon III into sending them to destroy the freedom of Mexico. The French newspaper in Mexico City, Le Trait-d'Union, wrote that "it would be too preposterous if the France of '89, the France of Solferino, should become in Mexico the advocate and the soldier of retrograde ideas and of shameful clerical reaction."

Once again, as with the explosion at San Andrés, it was chance, not the French, that struck the heaviest blow at the Mexican liberals. In September 1862 Zaragoza died of typhus. General Ortega succeeded him as commander-in-chief.

Zaragoza had wished to launch an attack to wipe out the French at Orizaba and Veracruz before the reinforcements from France arrived, and Ortega was also considering this idea. Juárez vetoed it. He was convinced that the Mexicans could defeat the French only by guerrilla warfare. He continued to make friendly gestures to the French, returning the wounded soldiers who had been captured on May 5 and their medals, which had been found on the battlefield, and agreeing to exchanges of other prisoners. But he had no illusions that Napoleon III would leave him and his people in peace. When Montluc wrote to him from France about the opposition in liberal circles there to the Mexican expedition, and the efforts he was still making to persuade Napoleon to abandon his intervention, Juárez replied to Montluc on August 28, 1862: "There is no point in having illusions, dear sir; the imperial government has taken the decision to humiliate Mexico and to impose its will upon her. This truth has been confirmed by the facts; there is no other help for it than to defend ourselves."

The Mexicans were waging guerrilla war against the French in the areas around Veracruz and Orizaba. Small units of French soldiers who ventured into the villages were attacked, straggling French soldiers were murdered, and Mexicans who collaborated with the French were killed. In Tampico, which the French had recently occupied, several of their soldiers were knifed in the street.

In France, Napoleon III was not going to rush things. There must be no repetition of the premature advance on Puebla and the defeat of May 5. This time the ground would be patiently and methodically prepared, with a slow buildup of massive superior military strength. In September Forey sailed for Mexico and took over command from Lorencez, and troops continued to arrive in Veracruz. The need to avenge the defeat, to show the Mexicans and the world that France was the greatest military power on earth, who could conquer a backward nation if she really put her mind to it, had swung over French public opinion and ended the apathy and opposition in France to the Mexican expedition. The author Prosper Mérimée, who had known Eugénie when she was a child in Spain and was in high favor at the Tuileries, wrote in his diary: "The Mexicans have been stupid enough not to let themselves be beaten by a handful of Frenchmen, and now there is not a man in France who dares to say that it would be better to negotiate with Juárez than to pelt him with cannon balls, which are very expensive."

In the Corps Législatif, Prime Minister Billault explained that French honor must be avenged, and the deputies enthusiastically voted the funds he demanded for the new expedition to Mexico, with only the opposition liberal deputies opposing the government's Mexican policy. The great majority of the French public took the same view. In July 1862 the reports of the *procureurs* from all over France told the same story. At Agen, at Amiens, at Bordeaux, at Colmar, at Metz, at Nancy, and at Orléans, the prople had hitherto not appreciated the importance of the Mexican expedition and had not supported it; but now, "despite all the able and perfidious words of Monsieur Jules Favre," their attitude had changed. After the failure of the forces at Puebla, the whole population realized that "the honor of the French flag was involved," and demanded "that our arms receive an overwhelming satisfaction."

Franz Joseph was as skeptical as ever about the plan to make Maximilian emperor of Mexico. The attitude of the British government continued to be ambiguous: if Napoleon III could succeed in establishing a monarchy in Mexico and impose law and order there, this would be a very good thing; but they were doubtful how far he could succeed. In October 1862 Russell, who was more skeptical than Palmerston, again warned Napoleon III not to get involved in Mexico. In a dispatch to Lord Cowley, which he authorized him to show to Thouvenel, Russell reminded him of what had happened fifty years before when Napoleon I had tried to conquer Spain against the will of the Spanish people. The end of the story "is well known, and might serve as a warning, if experience was not always bought and never borrowed."

Maximilian was still uncertain about what to do. In May 1862 he told Rechberg that although he had at first been attracted by the idea of becoming emperor of Mexico, if the throne were offered to him now he would refuse it. But he continued to toy with the idea of accepting. From time to time the possibility arose that he might go somewhere else. In February 1863 a revolution broke out in Poland against the Russian government, and the czar had to send an army to suppress it. A movement arose among the Polish revolutionaries in favor of inviting Maximilian to become king of Poland; but Franz Joseph would never have agreed to this, and within a few months the Russians had crushed the revolution.

A more practical possibility was Greece. When Maximilian's cousin Otto of Bavaria, who had been chosen king of the Greeks in 1832, was deposed after a revolution in Athens, the Great Powers looked for a new king. The British government thought Maximilian might be a suitable choice. On February 19, 1863, Russell wrote to King Leopold suggesting that Maximilian become king of Greece, and he took the opportunity to warn Leopold and Maximilian again of the dangers that would face Maximilian in Mexico: "The Government here can think of no one more worthy to occupy a difficult but honourable post than Your Majesty's son in law the Archduke Ferdinand Maximilian. . . . But I am told that the Archduke has his aspiration turned towards Mexico rather than Europe. Let him depend upon it, that no Prince introduced by a French Army can take root in the affections of the Mexican People." Russell was sure that Napoleon III's support for the reactionary party in Mexico, the Mexican suspicion of foreigners, and the republican feeling of the United States "will cause the failure of any European candidate for the throne of Mexico."

But Maximilian would not consider the throne of Greece and was annoyed that he had been offered it, for he thought that it was a trick to deprive him of Mexico. "They will not leave me in peace for a moment," he wrote. "They wish to make me absolutely ridiculous,

Figaro here, Figaro there, every day a new crown, including the crown of Poland."

Every year in January Napoleon III addressed the Corps Législatif when he opened the new parliamentary session. In his speech in January 1863 his reference to Mexico was brief and majestic. "Expeditions to China, to Cochin China, and to Mexico have proved that there is no country, however distant, where an affront to the honor of France remains unpunished." The chamber passed a vote of confidence in the government's Mexican policy by 245 votes to 5. Billault said that the whole of France had arisen against these five isolated voices.

The French refugees in England could attack Napoleon's Mexican schemes more strongly than the deputies in Paris. Edgar Quinet published his *L'Expédition du Mexique* in London in 1862 to protest French policy in Mexico, even if his voice could not be heard in France. In 1781, he wrote, Frenchmen had gone to America to bring freedom to her people; in 1862 they were going there to suppress freedom. Napoleon III wished to conquer Mexico in order to lay a mine under the United States, which was regarded all over the world as a fortress of republican freedom and democracy. Quinet was not impressed by calls to defend the honor of the flag. He thought that whenever an absolutist ruler wished to have his subjects blindly scurrying about to fulfill his orders, he spoke about "the honor of the flag."

Karl Marx took the same view. He strongly supported the liberal struggle in Mexico, with all the more zest because he believed that his two bugbears, Palmerston and Napoleon III, were behind the French intervention. On November 20, 1862, he wrote to Friedrich Engels, complaining that in Paris "even the so-called radical bourgeois are speaking about 'the honor of the flag.'"

Miss Sara Yorke was a very self-reliant and rather precocious young lady from a Louisiana family who lived in Mexico City. Her brother, an engineer, was helping to build the railway that one day would run from Veracruz to Mexico City, though so far only forty miles of the track had been built between Veracruz and Camerone. Sara was being educated in Paris, where she stayed in the house of Monsieur Achille Jubinal, an eminent antiquarian who was a member of the Corps Législatif. Jubinal disapproved of Napoleon III, and in the privacy of his house strongly criticized the government's policy in Mexico; but he did not join the five opposition deputies in the Corps Législatif and was careful what he said in public, remaining on friendly terms with prominent supporters of Napoleon who often bought his antiques.

Sara had just celebrated her fifteenth birthday in March 1862 when she heard that one of her brothers in Mexico had been murdered by bandits and that she would have to return to Mexico City to help look after her family there. A few days before she left Paris, Jubinal took her to a sale of his tapestries in the Rue Drouot, where they met the duke of Morny and his Russian wife, the former Princess Sophie Trubetskoi, a tall, cold beauty with a splendid mane of golden hair. Jubinal told Morny that Sara was going to Mexico and that he was worried for her safety. "Oh," said Morny, "by the time she arrives there, we will have changed all that. Lorencez is there now; our army will then be in Mexico City; the roads will be quite safe. Have no fear." The duchess of Morny was charming to Sara, who many years later, when as Sara Yorke Stevenson she had become a distinguished archaeologist and a pioneer of women's education, still remembered how kind and encouraging the duchess had been.

Sara reached Veracruz after an uneventful sea voyage and set off on the more dangerous journey by coach to Mexico City. She could not take the direct road by Orizaba and Puebla without passing through the front line between the French and Mexican armies; but the coach company paid the local guerrilla leaders to allow the coach to travel unmolested by a different route. The journey from Veracruz to Mexico City took nine days. They stayed each night at primitive but friendly inns, whose staffs kept a supply of blankets in the hall ready to wrap around the travelers as they walked to the hotel, in case the coach had been held up by bandits who had robbed them of all their clothes.

Sara arrived safely in Mexico City and settled down to life in the capital during the summer and winter of 1862–63 in a smart apartment. She soon became involved in social life. Society continued to attend balls, bullfights, and the theater as usual, undisturbed by the knowledge that the French army was at Orizaba; for everyone seemed to think that the victory of May 5 had won the war. There was a good deal of crime in the city, with robberies and occasional kidnappings; men who ventured out after 8 P.M. took care to carry revolvers or knuckledusters as a protection against attack, and to walk in the middle of the street, avoiding the dark alleys and doorways.

The foreign residents in Mexico City were a little anxious that they might be attacked by the people, especially after the Prussian minister, Baron Wagner, was assaulted and seriously wounded in the street; but the rumors that there would be a massacre of foreigners on September 16, the Mexican National Day, was entirely unfounded, and with a few exceptions the people obeyed Juárez's appeal to avoid all demonstrations against foreigners who lived peaceably in Mexico.

The government intensified its repressive measures against the Church, which had openly sided with the French. Only in Guadalajara did the Church hierarchy respond to the government's call to rally against the foreign invader; and Labastida, the bishop of Puebla, ordered the clergy to refuse all spiritual solace to soldiers in the liberal army, even when they were wounded. Juárez hit back with the decree of August 30, 1862, which dissolved Church organizations everywhere except in Guadalajara and made any priest who advocated disobedience to the law liable to three years' imprisonment. He also banned religious processions in the streets and prohibited the clergy from wearing their ecclesiastical vestments outside their churches.

The French army spent the summer of 1862 and the following autumn and winter on the alert, but largely inactive, at Orizaba and Veracruz, except for occasional expeditions into the countryside to pursue and destroy the guerrilla bands who attacked their transport and sometimes raided their outposts. The soldiers began to complain that their high command was doing nothing except distributing leaflets to them containing the text of Billault's speeches in the Corps Législatif in reply to Favre's speeches, which the Mexican liberals were handing out to them. Boredom was one of the troops' main problems. The army organized theatricals to pass the time and discovered some unexpected talent among the soldiers, some of whom risked the mockery of their comrades by acting women's parts.

On the evening of August 10, 1862, a dress rehearsal took place in the garrison theater at Orizaba of one of the latest Parisian successes, *Michel et Christine*. Halfway through the rehearsal the alarm sounded; some guerrillas had launched an attack on the town. The actors quickly changed out of their men's and women's costumes and into their army uniforms, and seized their weapons to fight the enemy, whom they repulsed after a three-hour battle. The next evening the performance of *Michel et Christine* passed off without interruption.

Soldiers acting the part of women provided an entertaining diversion, but the troops wanted real women. They found three young and beautiful women at Manuel Gonzalez's wine bar in Veracruz, where, along with Manuel's wine and the antics of an organ-grinder who made monkeys dance to his music, there were the three dancing girls, all under twenty, all skillful performers of the provocative local dance that combined the *cachoza* and the *bolero,* and all with the Christian name Dolores. The French soldiers frequented Gonzalez's wine bar, admiring the three Doloreses while their genial host filled and refilled their glasses.

One evening three French artillerymen spent some happy hours at Gonzalez's wine bar, but on their way back to their barracks they felt the first pains, and staggered into the cavalry barracks in agony. They were rushed to the military hospital, where the doctors diagnosed that they had been poisoned, and saved their lives by giving them an emetic just in time.

Before the night was out the French military police had called at the wine bar. But Gonzalez had gone. Having performed his mission in Veracruz, he had hastily left to join the guerrillas in the countryside. The three Doloreses were still there; they were arrested and tried with five other defendants by a French court-martial on a charge of being accessories to attempted murder. Two men were sentenced to death, and a woman who had supplied the poison received a sentence of life imprisonment. Dolores Barajos was sentenced to imprisonment with hard labor for ten years, but Dolores Arellano and Dolores Carrajal were acquitted. The three Doloreses had their brief moment of international fame, being prominently featured in the Paris press before they disappeared from the public gaze, one of them to endure, day after day, the harsh monotony of prison life in Fort San Juan de Ulúa, and the other two to continue living and dancing for as long as their looks lasted and they avoided yellow fever and *vómito* and other dangers of life in Veracruz.

❀ 11 ❀

SEWARD APPEASES NAPOLEON III

THE PORT OF MATAMOROS, at the northeastern corner of Mexico, was thriving. Fifty yards away, across "the turbid yellow waters of the Rio Grande" (as an Austrian officer called them), was Texas, which during the last twenty-five years had been a province of Mexico, an independent republic, and the twenty-eighth state of the United States, but was now one of the eleven states of the Confederacy. Texas, by joining the Confederate States of America, had provided a long land frontier with Mexico, which greatly helped the Southern cause.

Early in the Civil War the North gained naval ascendancy and was able to cause great damage to the South by blockading its Atlantic ports and stopping the export of cotton to Europe and the import of war matériel and other supplies. But exports and imports could leave and arrive through Matamoros. Wagon after wagon, loaded with cotton, traveled slowly from Missouri, Arkansas, and Louisiana across the plains of Texas to Brownsville, then in barges across the Rio Grande to Matamoros, through the customs control there, downstream for twenty miles to the little port of Bagdad on the Gulf of Mexico, and in oceangoing ships to Havana in Spanish Cuba and Belize in British Honduras, and on to Liverpool, Le Havre, and other ports in Western Europe. The ships, barges, and wagons made the same journey in reverse, carrying shoes, blankets, cloth, powder, lead, saltpeter, and sulphur, and even the latest Paris fashions for the Southern belles in Atlanta, Charleston, and Richmond. Three hundred ships a year arrived from Europe. The bulk of the trade was carried in English, Spanish, German, Danish, and Russian ships.

This busy and lucrative trade attracted thousands of people to Matamoros. In two years its population increased sevenfold, from 7,000 to 50,000. There were sailors in port, agents of the foreign shipping companies stationed there, tradesmen who opened shops to supply them, whores and brothelkeepers, United States federal agents spying and reporting to Washington, Confederate agents counterspying and reporting to Richmond, pro-Union refugees from Texas, deserters from the Confederate army, and Mexicans who came to take jobs in the customs service, where they could make a fortune on bribes to issue licenses allowing goods coming from and going into Texas to pass through customs.

The government in Washington received their agents' reports from Matamoros on the extent of the trade, but they could do nothing to block this hole in their blockade of the South. In March 1863, when eighty-two ships from Europe arrived at Bagdad, Captain Bailey, commander-in-chief of the Union fleet enforcing the blockade, reported that unless the trade through Matamoros could be restricted, the object of the blockade would be largely frustrated. But this could be done only if the United States were prepared to violate Mexican sovereignty or international law by capturing or blockading Matamoros, which would have been a grave political blunder. It would be likely to bring the United States into conflict with Britain and France, for a British and a French warship, the *Phaeton* and *Le Bertolet*, were usually cruising in the Gulf off Matamoros, ready to intervene to protect the merchant ships; Palmerston and Napoleon III might have seized on an incident there as an excuse for war with the United States.

At the outbreak of the Civil War, Confederate President Jefferson Davis immediately realized the importance of friendly relations with Mexico. He sent a government official, John T. Pickett, to Mexico to offer friendship to Juárez, hoping to enter into diplomatic relations with his government. Pickett hinted that the Confederate government might return to Mexico some of the territory that the United States had annexed in 1848, but Juárez refused to have anything to do with him. Not only his liberal sympathies but also political realism made him realize that the Mexican liberals must ally themselves with Abraham Lincoln and the North, not Jefferson Davis and the South. Juárez continued to be on excellent terms with the United States minister in Mexico City, Thomas Corwin, who was very popular in Mexico because he had opposed the Mexican war in 1846. Juárez granted Corwin's request to allow a force of Union troops from California to land at the Pacific port of Guaymas and march through Mexican territory to protect Arizona from a Confederate attack. As for Pickett, he got drunk in a bar in Mexico City and was arrested for disorderly conduct and expelled from the country.

But Matías Romero had a difficult task at the Mexican legation in Washington. William H. Seward, the secretary of state in Lincoln's administration, was a charming man and an able politician, but he tended to swing from one extreme to another. During his thirty years in politics, he had sometimes delighted the Abolitionists by declaring that to abolish slavery was a higher duty than to obey the Constitution, but then had tried to win the Republican nomination for the presidency by opposing the Abolitionist program of his rival, Salmon P. Chase. As governor of New York he had nearly precipitated a war with England by prosecuting for murder a Canadian soldier who had killed a United States citizen on the American side of the frontier while helping to suppress a rebellion in Canada; and he had pandered to popular chauvinism by his inflammatory calls for expansion of American territory. But whatever other causes he had sometimes supported, he had never been a friend of Mexico.

At the outbreak of the war against Mexico in 1846, Seward had expressed his delight that the United States had reached a new stage in its development, the stage of "territorial aggrandizement," for "our population is destined to roll its resistless waves to the icy barriers of the North and to encounter Oriental civilization on the shores of the Pacific." In 1860 he called for the annexation of New Brunswick and Nova Scotia, "what remains of Mexico," all the West Indies and Central America, and Russian America (Alaska). He told his son that he aimed to extend the United States "up to the pole and down to the tropics."

When, to his great annoyance, Lincoln beat him for the Republican nomination, Seward was convinced that, being Lincoln's intellectual superior in every way, he could treat the president as a pawn and conduct foreign policy on his own. On the eve of the outbreak of the Civil War, without consulting Lincoln, he drew up a plan by which North and South would compose their differences and unite to launch a "war of conquest" that would change a "threatened dismemberment of the Union into the triumphant annexation of Canada, Mexico, and the West Indies." If Spain and France objected, he would declare war on both of them. But after Lincoln discovered and ridiculed his plan, and the Civil War began, Seward efficiently carried out Lincoln's policy of avoiding difficulties with the European powers until the war was over.

When Romero visited Lincoln at Springfield, Lincoln warned him that if civil war broke out in the United States, his government would not be able to help Mexico against a European aggressor. When the war began, and Southern resistance proved much more formidable than had been expected, there was a very real danger that Britain and France would recognize the Confederacy and even intervene on their side. Lincoln became more than ever determined not to antagonize France by helping Juárez.

About the American Civil War, public opinion in Europe was divided, with a few exceptions, along clear political lines. German revolutionaries, French socialists and radicals, and English liberals and Abolitionists, from John Bright and Victor Hugo to Garibaldi and Marx, supported the North in the war against slavery and for republican democracy. Napoleon III and Eugénie, Pope Pius IX, Spanish Catholic reactionaries, and English Tories supported the South and were delighted to see the United States falling apart. The Spanish conservative newspaper *El Pensamiento Español* wrote that "the model republic of what *were* the United States" showed that a society cannot survive if its object is the welfare of man and not service to God. The United States, which had come into being by rebellion, was now "fighting like a cannibal and it will die in a flood of blood and mire. Such is the real history of the one and only state in the world which has succeeded in constituting itself according to the flaming theories of democracy."

Palmerston was equally pleased to see the disintegration of "the *Dis*united States," though, as the head of a liberal government, with many members of his Cabinet supporting the North, he could not do as much for the South as he would have liked. But he seized his opportunity when a United States warship stopped a British ship, the *Trent*, in mid-Atlantic and removed James Murray Mason and John Slidell, two well-known Southern politicians who were traveling to Europe as the Confederate government's unofficial diplomatic representatives in London and Paris. The British government, with the eager support of Napoleon III, protested the seizure and sent troops to Canada; Lincoln and Seward gave way and freed Mason and Slidell. The threat of British intervention on the side of the South continued, for the Union blockade of the Confederate ports was causing an acute shortage of cotton and severe economic distress in Lancashire and France.

Mason in London and Slidell in Paris set to work to persuade Palmerston and Napoleon III to recognize the Confederacy as a lawful government, as a preliminary to entering the war on the side of the South. Every time the South won a victory, the possibility of recognition by Britain and France increased; every time the North defeated the South, the possibility receded. On two occasions Napoleon III proposed that Britain and France recognize the Confederacy; but each time the pressure of the liberal members of Palmerston's Cabinet, and of public opinion in Britain, persuaded Palmerston to refuse. Napoleon decided to postpone recognition by France until Britain agreed to do the same.

Lincoln and Seward were determined to avoid at all costs provoking Napoleon III. They hoped to reach an informal understanding with him that if France did not recognize Jefferson Davis's government, the United States would do nothing to help Juárez.

On February 14, 1862, Romero told Seward of the danger of an imminent French attack on Mexico. Seward's reply was most discouraging. He said that all parties to the disputes between Mexico and the allied powers must show a sincere desire to negotiate a peaceful solution of their differences. This statement was as futile as it was self-evident and meant that the United States would do nothing to stop the French from conquering Mexico.

The French intervention in Mexico aroused strong feelings in South America, where opinion was divided, as in Europe, on party and ideological lines. The emperor of Brazil and the right-wing military dictator of Guatemala welcomed the French intervention, which would save Mexico and religion from liberal tyranny; the liberal governments of Ecuador, Peru, Chile, and Argentina supported Juárez and wished to do what they could to help him. In January 1862 Manuel Corpancho, who had just been appointed Peruvian minister to Juárez's government, went to Washington to suggest to Seward that a pan-American congress of all the states of the continent should be summoned to discuss taking action to defend the Mexican republic. Seward refused to meet Corpancho on the specious grounds that it would be improper for the United States secretary of state to discuss the situation with a Peruvian minister who was accredited to Mexico and not to the United States.

Two months later the Chilean minister in Washington, Federico Astaburuaga, who was perfectly properly accredited to the United States, also raised the matter with Seward, suggesting that the United States should call a pan-American congress and make at least a public moral gesture against French intervention in Mexico. Seward told Astaburuaga that the United States would not accept a monarchy in Mexico, but he refused to call a pan-American congress or to make any public declaration on the subject. Instead he sent a circular to all United States diplomatic representatives abroad, in which he stated that Britain, France, and Spain had informed the United States that their only aim in Mexico was to redress their grievances and that the president of the United States entertained no doubt as to their sincerity and fully accepted their declaration that they did not intend to change the form of government in Mexico.

By April 1862 a duly accredited Peruvian minister had arrived in Washington; he proposed to Seward that the United States and all the states of Central and South America issue a declaration that they would never recognize the Southern Confederacy or tolerate the establishment of a foreign potentate on the American continent. Seward refused to agree and said that such a declaration might endanger the relations of the United States with the European powers. The South American states considered convening a pan-American congress themselves. Seward told them that if they did, the United States would refuse to send a delegation and would publicize its refusal.

American diplomats abroad found it hard to carry out Seward's instructions and restrain their indignation about Mexico, especially after the publication of Napoleon III's letter to Forey of July 3, 1862, even with the important omissions. The United States minister in Madrid, Gustave Koerner, spoke to the Spanish foreign minister in January 1863 and told him unofficially that the United States would take some suitable action to prevent a monarchy being permanently imposed on the people of Mexico. When Seward heard about this, he rebuked Koerner, telling him that the United States completely accepted the French assurances about their intentions in Mexico and would remain strictly neutral in the war between Mexico and France. He sent Dayton in Paris a copy of his dispatch to Koerner, and told Dayton to read it to Thouvenel.

The French troops in Veracruz and the hot lands were suffering from yellow fever. Forey wondered whether it would be possible to recruit some black troops from Africa who would be more acclimatized to the heat and more resistant to tropical diseases. He had already replaced French troops with the Foreign Legion in the most unhealthful areas, and he wrote unashamedly to Marshal Randon, the minister of war in Paris: "I left the foreigners, rather than Frenchmen, in a position where there was more disease than opportunities for glory."

The French government thought it might look to Egypt for black soldiers, for the Egyptian authorities regularly kidnapped blacks in the Sudan and used them for forced labor in Cairo and Alexandria. Egypt was in theory a province of the Turkish Empire, but the office of khedive, the sultan's viceroy, had become hereditary in Mehemet Ali's family, thanks largely to the support France had given Mehemet Ali in the 1830s. Napoleon III now asked the khedive to show his gratitude for French support by selling him 1,500 kidnapped black conscripts for service in Mexico.

Because Egypt was not an independent state, foreign policy was in the hands of the Turkish government. Foreign powers were represented only by consuls in Alexandria; their legations and ministers were in Constantinople. The illegal agreement between France and the khedive was kept secret in the hope that the blacks would be on board a French warship bound for Mexico before the sultan heard about it, and before Palmerston, who was suspicious of the links between France and Egypt, could stop the plan.

The French frigate *La Seine,* sailing from Toulon and carrying French troops to Cochin China, docked at Alexandria on January 1, 1863. The troops were taken by the usual route across the Isthmus of Suez (the French were still building the canal) to embark on another ship at Suez to take them on to Saigon. *La Seine* remained in the port of Alexandria. On January 7, 50 young black men were press-ganged in the street and dragged onto the ship, where they were joined by 450 black soldiers who were already serving in the khedive's army. Egyptian soldiers and police sealed off the area and prevented the blacks' protesting wives and families from approaching the ship, which sailed early the next morning for Veracruz.

The United States consul general in Alexandria, William S. Thayer, made a strong protest to the khedive's government, against both the brutal manner of enlistment and the act of hostility to a friendly neighbor of the United States, the Republic of Mexico. Thayer asked whether the troops had been sent on the sultan's orders, which meant that Turkey was at war with Mexico, or without his knowledge, in which case Egypt had revolted against the sultan. The khedive's minister, after first avoiding Thayer and then lying to him, finally admitted that the blacks had gone to Mexico, but said that the sultan knew nothing about it and the khedive had sent only 500 men, even though the French had asked for 1,500. Thayer wished to take the matter further and to demand that the khedive bring the men back, but when he reported to Washington, Seward told him to take no further action, as it was no concern of the United States if the khedive sent troops to Mexico.

The 500 blacks arrived at Veracruz and were enrolled in the French army. They won high praise from Forey, from their commanding officers, and from their French comrades for their courage in the face of the enemy; and, as Napoleon III had expected, they proved much more able than the French soldiers to resist disease and carry out their duties in the hot lands.

Juárez's greatest need was to obtain arms from the United States; but the United States Neutrality Acts prohibited the export of arms to belligerent countries or the enlistment of volunteers to fight for them in wars in which the United States was neutral. When the French minister in Washington asked Seward whether the United States intended to enforce the Neutrality Acts against liberals in the United States who wished to send arms and volunteers to Juárez, Seward assured him that the laws would be enforced. Apart from the question of relations with France, the United States government was suspicious about any contract for the export of arms, because there had been cases in which Confederate agents had arranged for arms to be exported from the United States to Canada, and had then sent the arms surreptitiously through the Union blockade to the Confederate states.

In the summer of 1862 Romero asked Seward if the United States would grant Juárez a loan of $30,000, or preferably $40,000, to enable him to buy arms in the United States and also a license to export them to Mexico, as there were no armament factories in Mexico capable of producing the arms needed to fight the French. Seward said that the government could not make a loan from the Treasury to Mexico, as this would annoy Napoleon III, but that Romero could try to raise the money from private investors. Romero succeeded in raising enough money to buy 36,000 muskets, 4,000 sabers, 1,000 pistols, and ammunition from an arms dealer in New York, and asked the United States Treasury for an export license for the arms. After a delay, the license was refused. Seward told Romero that this was not because of any pressure from him, but because Edwin Stanton, the secretary of war, had said that the arms were needed for the United States Army.

As reinforcements for the French army continued to arrive at Veracruz, the supply department ran into a difficulty: a shortage of horses for the cavalry and of mules for transport. To save space on the transport ships, the French War Office had decided to send only a few horses from France, expecting to obtain in Mexico the other horses and mules they needed. But there was a shortage of the right kind of horses in Mexico, and most of the inhabitants, either from patriotic motives or from fear of Juárez's decree of January 25, refused to sell horses and mules to the French. The French minister in Washington therefore asked Seward to allow the French army to buy horses, mules, and wagons in the United States and export them to Veracruz; Seward agreed.

For Romero, this was the last straw. The United States, the only friend and protector of Mexico, was not only refusing to allow arms to be sent to Juárez, but was sending horses, mules, and transport wagons for the forthcoming French offensive. Were not these as much weapons of war, he indignantly asked Seward, as the arms he had not been able to send to Juárez? Seward replied that the United States Army needed the arms, but not the horses, mules, and wagons. Romero thought that was just an excuse.

A fortnight later, on November 21, 1862, Lincoln signed a proclamation prohibiting all exports of arms from the United States for the duration of the Civil War. After this, Juárez had to rely on illegal gun running from New York to Matamoros and from San Francisco to Mexico's Pacific ports.

The United States minister in London, Charles Francis Adams, acted on his own initiative to help Juárez. He asked the British government for a license for the English firm of Howell and Ziman to send a consignment of goods on a chartered ship to Matamoros, and stated that the goods were sent for "creditable purposes." He did not reveal that they carried arms purchased for Juárez by his supporters in Britain. When the truth came out, Seward apologized to the British government and censured Adams, though he did not recall him to Washington.

While Lincoln and Seward, despite their sympathy for Juárez, hampered his struggle against the French in order to placate Napoleon III, Juárez, for all his admiration for Lincoln and the Northern cause, was unable to prevent trade with the Confederacy from continuing at Matamoros. He issued a decree banning it, but he could not enforce the decree. General Santiago Vidaurri, governor of the states of Tamaulipas and Nuevo León, was in control at Matamoros, and although in theory he acknowledged the authority of Juárez's government, in practice he did what he liked in his territory. He was not prepared to forgo the customs revenues and the bribes paid to him and his officials by the Confederates for allowing cotton to come out and munitions to go in through Matamoros.

In March 1863 Jefferson Davis sent an agent to Orizaba to suggest to Forey and Saligny that the French send a squadron to occupy Matamoros, thus striking a double blow at Juárez and at the United States. It would close Juárez's last outlet to the Gulf of Mexico and the Atlantic, and if the French held the port, the United States Navy would not attempt to capture or blockade Matamoros. Saligny thought this was a very good idea and hoped that it would be followed by an alliance between France and the Confederacy; but the French were unable to sail to Matamoros because two thirds of the crews had yellow fever.

So the Confederate government turned to Vidaurri, and by increasing the bribes persuaded him to ignore Juárez's orders and to encourage the trade at Matamoros. Without consulting or even informing Juárez, Vidaurri signed a treaty with the Confederacy by which he agreed to extradite all deserters from their army who fled to Matamoros; to allow Confederate troops to pursue deserters, or any other enemies, across the border into Mexico; and to expel from Matamoros all United States agents and spies. Juárez could do nothing to stop Vidaurri from carrying out the treaty. He could not coerce the governor of Tamaulipas when the United States had not allowed him to buy even enough arms to fight the French.

Romero thought there was nothing more he could usefully do in Washington. On January 19, 1863, he wrote in disgust to Juárez and suggested that his government break off diplomatic relations with the United States, or at least recall him to Mexico so that he could join the army. Juárez was too wise to follow Romero's advice, and though he reluctantly recalled him, he soon persuaded him to return to Washington, where he remained for thirty years.

Romero never again gave foolish advice to his government, and he soon understood that he could do more good in Washington than in the army in Mexico. But he realized that he would have to adopt new methods. It was no use trying to persuade Seward, or even Lincoln, not to appease Napoleon III. He must organize support for Mexico in the United States by propaganda through the Mexican clubs and refugee organizations, through the radical political groups, through influential members of Lincoln's Republican Party, through public rallies and speeches at well-publicized banquets, through the press, and above all in Congress. He must create a climate of opinion in the United States that no president or secretary of state could resist. It would take a long time, but it was the only way.

✖ 12 ✖

"PUEBLA IS IN OUR HANDS"

IN FEBRUARY 1863 General Forey was ready to begin his campaign. He had under his command 18,000 infantrymen, 1,400 cavalry, 2,150 gunners, 450 engineers, an administration corps of 2,300, and Márquez's 2,000 Mexican soldiers. He had fifty-six cannons and 2.4 million rounds of ammunition. His subordinate commanders were General Félix Douay and the fifty-two-year-old General Achille Bazaine, who had risen through the ranks and been promoted to the rank of general during the siege of Sebastopol.

Before leaving Orizaba, Forey called on his troops to "march to the victory which God will give you" for the cause of "order and liberty." They must be merciful after victory but terrible in battle, and "soon you will plant the noble standard of France on the walls of Mexico City amid the cry of 'Long live the Emperor!'"

But Forey was worried about what the guerrillas would do when he began his offensive against Puebla. Could they seriously interfere with his supply lines? The full-time guerrillas were helped by part-time fighters. Mexican liberals of all classes, including some upper-class gentlemen, would sometimes take part in a night's operation with the guerrillas. The village shopkeepers, whose social position was higher in Mexico than in Europe, were usually sympathetic to the guerrillas, giving them supplies and entertaining them in their houses. Most of the inhabitants of Veracruz were on their side, including the foreign merchants there, especially French traders who had settled in Veracruz. Many of these Frenchmen were liberals and republicans; others wished to remain on friendly terms with their Mexican customers, who would still be there when the army of occupation had left; still others were afraid of what would happen to them if they helped the French invaders in defiance of Juárez's January 25 decree.

The guerrillas were very active near the little town of Medellín, only eight miles from Veracruz, and around Alvarado and Tlacotalpán, forty miles south of Veracruz on the coast. The many streams and little rivers that intersected the countryside impeded the French operations, for the guerrillas had broken down the bridges and removed the boats and barges. Small groups of guerrillas often came into Veracruz to make contact with their supporters there and supply them with leaflets to distribute surreptitiously to French soldiers.

When the allied forces first occupied Veracruz, the guerrillas prevented any supplies from entering the town. But this policy proved to be counterproductive. The allies sent troops into the villages to seize the food, and the Mexican peasants resented losing money by being unable to trade with the city. The guerrillas then changed their tactics and granted permits to the villagers to trade with Veracruz, provided that they paid a tax to the guerrillas on the supplies sent there. The villagers paid, either willingly, as a contribution to the patriotic cause, or resentfully, as extortion money to bandits.

The French formed a special unit to fight the guerrillas, the *contre-guérilla*. It was composed not of ordinary soldiers but of special recruits, men who were tough, fearless, and merciless. Some of them were Mexicans, but others came from France, England, Spain, Greece, Italy, Holland, Switzerland, the United States, and South America. Most had come to Mexico hoping to make their fortunes and had failed, but there were also seamen who had jumped ship; a slave trader from Havana who had been ruined when the blacks in his ship died of typhus; American citizens who had taken part in raids on Guatemala; unsuccessful hunters of bison around the Great Lakes; and planters from Louisiana who had been ruined by the Civil War. One came from a completely different background: Count Émile de Kératry had resigned his post as an attaché at the French embassy in Naples in order to serve with the army in Algeria. He was afterward sent to Mexico, where he persuaded the authorities to transfer him to the *contre-guérilla*.

The *contre-guérilla* was placed under the command of Colonel de Steklin, a Swiss officer who was serving as a mercenary in the French army. He was helped by two gunboats that cruised off the coast to the north and south of Veracruz and opened fire on any band of guerrillas they spotted. Naval Captain Rivière, who served on one of the gunboats, believed that "morality can only be inculcated into perverted people by terror, not by persuasion." The *contre-guérilla* acted on this principle. Kératry wrote that he and his comrades spilled and lost much blood.

Forey was not satisfied with Steklin's conduct of counterguerrilla operations. He thought that Colonel Du Pin, an elderly man who had won many military decorations in past campaigns, would do better. Du Pin had served in China and had taken part in the sack of the emperor of China's summer palace in Peking, when the palace was burned, the gardens dug up, and the priceless antiques in the palace destroyed by the French and British to punish the emperor for the tortures that had been inflicted on French and British subjects imprisoned in the palace. Du Pin, instead of throwing the antiques into the flames, had taken them back to Paris and sold them for a great deal of money. This was a violation of military discipline, and he had been cashiered; but Napoleon III had personally intervened in his favor, and he was taken back into the army and sent to Mexico.

On February 14, 1863, three days before Forey began his advance on Puebla, Saligny gave a ball for French officers and the local Mexican aristocracy at the house he had rented in Orizaba. During the ball, Forey took Du Pin aside and offered him the command of the *contre-guérilla*. Du Pin accepted and asked Forey to improve morale and discipline in the *contre-guérilla* by providing the men with a special uniform and by giving them higher pay than the French soldiers in other regiments. Forey was not happy about the high rates of pay, which he thought would arouse resentment in the army, but he agreed, as it was necessary to provide good incentives for enlistment in the *contre-guérilla*.

Kératry, too, was at Saligny's ball. Looking around at the Mexican gentlemen dancing the waltz and the *habañera,* he wondered how many of them would go home after the ball to change out of their evening dress before joining the guerrillas in some action that night. He thought that perhaps the next time he saw them they would be dangling at the end of a rope, hanged at Du Pin's order.

Du Pin, wearing a colonel's red and black pelisse, with yellow boots and Mexican spurs, an enormous sombrero on his head, eight or nine decorations on his chest, a revolver on his thigh, and a saber hanging at his horse's saddle, won the respect and affection of his men and terrified the enemy. Captain Rivière wrote delightedly that the Mexicans in the hot lands were so frightened of Du Pin that they would not come within fifty leagues of him.

Eleven days after Du Pin took command of the *contre-guérilla,* a Spaniard named Perez Lorenzo came to his headquarters at Medellín. He told Du Pin that he was a trader in fruit and lived on a nearby ranch. The day before, some guerrillas had come to his ranch and tied him to a post while they raped and killed his pregnant wife before cutting open her body and throwing her unborn child in Lorenzo's face. Lorenzo told Du Pin that he knew where the murderers had gone and offered to show the *contre-guérilla* the way to their camp. Du Pin was suspicious that it might be a trap to lure his men into an ambush, but after tying Lorenzo's arms behind his back, the *contre-guérilla* allowed him to lead them to the guerrillas' camp. The guerrillas were taken completely by surprise, and before they could resist, the *contre-guérilla* killed or captured many of them. They hanged all the prisoners from the branches of trees. "It was the first visiting card left by the French *contre-guérilla* on the bandits of the hot lands," wrote Kératry.

Lorenzo, who was now trusted by the *contre-guérilla,* offered to show them the way to other guerrilla hideouts. One evening, as they marched into a village, Lorenzo pointed out one of the villagers as a sergeant in the group of guerrillas who had killed his wife. The *contre-guérilla* seized the man and hanged him on a tree in the moonlight. The next day Lorenzo disappeared, and the *contre-guérilla* never saw him again. Had he invented the whole story in order to use the French army to get rid of his enemies? Was he a conservative who wished to see the French exterminate a group of liberal guerrillas and had lied about the rape and murder of his wife? Or had he spoken the truth, and been captured and killed by the guerrillas? The *contre-guérilla* did not care; they had killed and hanged some men who were either guerrillas or bandits, which was good enough for them.

When Du Pin came to a village, he went to the largest house, assuming that it was the home of a leading local citizen, and demanded food for his men. He seized a number of villagers at random as hostages and announced that if the food were not produced promptly, he would shoot the hostages. This always had the effect of sending the inhabitants scurrying around to find food and drink and all the supplies Du Pin required. Du Pin sometimes ordered more food than he needed to make the villagers believe that his numbers were larger than they were. After his men had eaten what they wanted, he destroyed any remaining food.

Du Pin knew that the little town of Tlaliscoya, between Tlacotalpan and Alvarado, was a center for guerrillas. As the *contre-guérilla* entered the town one evening, all the lights in the houses were extinguished. Du Pin told the inhabitants that he needed boats to operate on the little river. They told him there were no boats in the town. Du Pin established his headquarters in a large house on the river belonging to a leading citizen, Señor Billegras, and arrested six of the leading town notables. He set two of them free and told them to bring at least two boats to the house by five o'clock the next morning. If the boats did not arrive, he would burn the houses of the two notables; and every half hour after 5 A.M. he would shoot one of the four other notables and impose a fine of $1,000 on the inhabitants of Tlaliscoya. The boats were at Billegras's house by 5 A.M.

The *contre-guérilla* found a musket in Billegras's house and ordered the other notables to impose a suitable punishment on Billegras. They fined him $500, which he immediately produced; the money was shared among the members of the *contre-guérilla* before they left Tlaliscoya.

The inhabitants of Tlaliscoya were now well and truly frightened of the *contre-guérilla*. The next time Du Pin and his men arrived, they illuminated the town with lamps in every window and in the town square to celebrate the arrival of the *contre-guérilla* and in honor of the French intervention in Mexico. Du Pin said that he would give them even better illumination, and ordered his men to set fire to the huts on the outskirts of the town, which he thought had been used as shelter by the guerrillas.

The *contre-guérilla* made a night raid on a ranch two miles from Medellín and found in a banana grove a number of muskets and a carbine they could identify as having been stolen from French army stores. The grove belonged to an old man named Munos and his son. Du Pin brought the father and son back to Medellín, and after summoning the inhabitants to the town square by a roll of drums, announced that Munos and his son would be hanged the next day on the great tree in the square. A deputation of notables in Medellín came to Du Pin to ask him to pardon the two men, but he refused. In the evening the women came to beg for mercy, many of them, according to Kératry, wearing elegant *mantillas* over their pretty shoulders. Du Pin refused to receive them. Kératry wrote that they left, sadly disillusioned about the famous gallantry of French officers.

Next morning new ropes were fixed to the tree in the square in preparation for the execution, but Du Pin had let it be known that there was a way in which he might be induced to spare the lives of Munos and his son. More than four hundred of the inhabitants came to Du Pin's tent, shouting again and again: "Long live the intervention! Long live the emperor of the French! Long live the French!" Du Pin then agreed to pardon and free the two men, because the whole population "had shown so clearly their support for the new order of things."

Du Pin was sure that the whole area really supported the guerrillas and would shelter them as soon as he and his men had left. It was vitally important to prevent the guerrillas from attacking the railway line to Camerone and the road to Orizaba and Puebla, so he burned every ranch in the area.

Juárez had concentrated his forces at Puebla and was ready to fight the decisive battle of the campaign in defense of the city. He had 22,000 men under the command of General Ortega. They included not only Mexicans but also some Spanish deserters from Prim's army, a few English adventurers, some volunteers from the United States, and a larger number of European liberal revolutionaries, refugees from the absolutist governments that had regained power in Europe after the defeat of the revolutions of 1848. They were eager to fight for freedom against Napoleon III. Apart from the women who always accompanied the Mexican army, there was one woman, aged twenty-three, who had been allowed to join the army and fight after her husband had been killed. She had fought so well on the Fifth of May that she was promoted to the rank of lieutenant colonel.

Juárez visited his men at Puebla and called on them to resist the invader.

> The Emperor Napoleon III persists in inflicting the horrors of war upon a people who have always generously bestowed their favors and sympathies upon Frenchmen. . . . His aim is to humiliate us, and to destroy a free and popular republic in which the privileged classes have been completely removed. . . . Mexico, the American continent, and free men of every nation pin their hopes on you, because you will be defending their cause, the cause of liberty, humanity and civilization.

The fortifications of Puebla had been strengthened since the previous May. All the forts around the city were well defended, and barricades had been erected in the streets, ready for street battles and house-to-house defense.

When the French again reached Amozoc and advanced toward Forts Guadalupe and Loreto, they adopted very different tactics from those of May 5, 1862. Forey invested the city and placed his troops in positions where they could attack the forts on every side. He completed this operation by March 16, which, as he and his men proudly remembered, was the birthday of Napoleon III's little son, the prince imperial.

He decided to launch the first attacks against Fort San Xavier, to the west of Puebla, and his artillery began bombarding the fort on March 23. After four days' bombardment, Bazaine, who was in command of the operations against the fort, sent in the infantry. They were driven back and were repulsed again in another attack the next day; but in the third assault, on March 29, they succeeded in capturing the fort after fierce fighting. Bazaine's second-in-command was killed in the last, successful attack. Twenty-six other officers and men were killed and 189 wounded. General Douay's chief of staff was seriously wounded and died of his wounds a fortnight later. The Mexican losses were heavier: 600 men were killed and wounded; 200 were taken prisoner.

Forey had hoped that the capture of Fort San Xavier would lead to a rapid collapse of the defense, but the Mexicans withdrew to houses only fifty yards from the fort and continued their resistance from there. The French soon realized that they would have to fight for every house in the street. They eventually succeeded in capturing several of the houses, but they could not take either the barracks at Number 26 or the house at Number 34. Officers leading the attacks were shot down as they entered the houses, and units that succeeded in capturing a house were counterattacked by the Mexicans and taken prisoner. After a week's house-to-house fighting, Forey, worried about his losses, called off the infantry attacks and ordered mining operations to begin. But the sappers encountered hard rock, which they could not pierce, and were unable to mine the houses.

By April 11, 7 French officers and 56 soldiers had been killed, and 39 officers and 443 soldiers had been wounded. Forey called a council of war. Some of his officers advised him to abandon the siege and march on toward Mexico City; but Forey thought that it was essential for French prestige and morale to capture Puebla, and he ordered the siege to continue.

The propaganda war went on. During pauses in the fighting, the liberal army threw leaflets in French into the French positions with quotations from Victor Hugo's *Napoléon le Petit* and appeals to the soldiers drafted by French liberals in Mexico City. "You are soldiers of a tyrant; the best of France is on our side. You have Napoleon; we have Victor Hugo." When Hugo heard about this statement, he sent a message to the defenders of Puebla. "It is not France that makes war on you, it is the empire. . . . Valiant men of Mexico, resist. . . . The empire, I hope, will fail in its infamous attempt, and you will conquer."

As the street fighting went on day after day, the Mexicans used the churches and monasteries as strong points in the defense. The French found the convent of Santa Ines particularly hard to capture. On April 25 they launched an attack on the convent in which nine of the ten officers taking part were killed. Altogether the French lost 27 killed, 127 wounded, and 137 taken prisoner.

One of the more daring of Bazaine's officers was Marquis Gaston de Galliffet, captain of the tenth regiment of the Chasseurs d'Afrique, who later achieved international fame and opprobrium for his part in suppressing the Paris Commune of 1871. As a young subaltern he had won a bet of five hundred cigars by leaping into the Seine on his horse, Laura, wearing his shako and saber, from a high rock overlooking the river at Melun. Now, at thirty-two, he was already a veteran of the Crimean War, in which he had been wounded and had won the Legion of Honor.

He led his company in the attack on Fort San Xavier on March 29 and emerged unscathed, but three weeks later, during another attack at Puebla, he received a serious stomach wound. When his lieutenant came to help him, Galliffet ordered him to continue the attack; then, holding his entrails in place with his hands, he staggered to the medical post, and his life was saved.

In Paris, Napoleon III was impatiently awaiting news of the capture of Puebla; the public was surprised as the weeks passed without an announcement that the city had fallen. The general election for the new Corps Législatif was to be held on May 31, and Napoleon relied on good news from Puebla arriving in time to influence the election result. Even after the setback of May 5, 1862, no one in France or Europe had expected the Mexican resistance in Puebla to be so prolonged.

Napoleon's exasperated ministers blamed their two bugbears, Wyke and Prim, for the delay. If the allies had advanced on Mexico City when they first landed at Veracruz in January 1862, they could easily have reached and captured it; but the opportunity had been lost by the folly of Prim and Wyke in agreeing to the Convention of La Soledad.

Juárez called on his old party leader, General Comonfort, to emerge from retirement and lead an army of 7,000 men to relieve Puebla. Comonfort responded to the call and advanced to within a few miles of the city; but instead of attacking the French, he contented himself with destroying the crops in the surrounding villages to prevent the French from acquiring food. The Mexican guerrillas were intercepting the French supply wagons traveling from Veracruz to Puebla. This made it necessary for Forey to detach troops from the operations at Puebla to guard the supply lines to Veracruz, for the contre-guérilla alone could not cope with this problem.

Forey had among his troops the men of the French Foreign Legion. The Legion had been formed in 1831 for service during the conquest of Algeria, and after having been sent to take part in the Spanish civil war in 1835, had been permanently stationed in North Africa. It was now serving in Mexico.

Forey sent the third company of the Foreign Legion to escort a supply convoy from Veracruz to Puebla. It was commanded by Captain Danjou, who had lost his left hand a few years before and wore an artificial hand. He had sixty-four men under him, most of them Poles, Italians, Germans, and Spaniards. On April 30 the Legionnaires were marching through the village of Camerone when they were attacked by several hundred Mexican guerrillas. The Legionnaires retreated to a barn in a farmyard, which they used as a defense post to fire on the guerrillas; but the guerrillas entered the nearby farmhouse, and fired on the Legionnaires from its windows.

By 9 A.M. the weather had become very warm, and the Legionnaires suffered from thirst; they had only the wine in their knapsacks to drink. As the fighting continued, more guerrillas arrived, until there were 1,200 men against the 64 Legionnaires. The Mexican leader called on Captain Danjou to surrender, but he refused.

At 11 A.M. Danjou was killed by enemy fire, and his second-in-command, Lieutenant Villain, took charge until he was killed three hours later, after which Second Lieutenant Mautet took command. The guerrillas set fire to some straw to burn the barn and force the Legionnaires out; but the Legionnaires managed to extinguish the flames and continued to resist amid the smoke. By 6 P.M. only Moutet and four other Legionnaires were still alive, and Moutet led them out of the barn in a last suicidal bayonet charge. They were crushed by the guerrillas, but the guerrilla leader stopped his men from killing these last five men, and took them prisoner. Two of them, including Moutet, died soon afterward of their wounds, leaving three survivors in the Mexicans' hands. A fourth Legionnaire, suffering from eight wounds but still alive, was later found buried under a pile of corpses after the guerrillas had left with their three prisoners.

The French afterward erected a monument on the battlefield in honor of the heroes of Camerone, whose courage is still commemorated by the Foreign Legion on April 30 every year.

Forey sent Bazaine to lead a surprise attack on Comonfort's relieving army. Leaving Puebla at 1 A.M. on the night of May 7–8 with a force that included Márquez's troops, Bazaine marched west along the road toward Mexico City and then cut across country toward Comonfort's position on the hill of San Lorenzo. At one point they were challenged by Comonfort's sentries, but Bazaine ordered one of Márquez's men to reply in Spanish and fooled the sentries into thinking that they were a force of Juárez's soldiers. They climbed the hill and reached Comonfort's camp, and at five A.M. launched an unexpected attack. Comonfort's men were routed, and though some of them fought bravely, they eventually fled in all directions.

The news of Comonfort's defeat had a depressing effect on the defenders of Puebla. On May 12 the French captured a fort on the south side of the city and broke through the defenses at that point. Ortega was running short of food. On May 16 he approached Forey and asked for an armistice. When it was refused, he told his men that though they had fought heroically he was now forced to surrender because of lack of food and ammunition. He had in fact a considerable amount of ammunition left but was very short of food. He ordered the soldiers to destroy their cannons and their remaining stocks of ammunition to make them useless to the enemy; but they did not do this very effectively, and left undamaged for the French 117 cannons fit for use and 17,000 rounds of ammunition.

Ortega surrendered Puebla to the French at 4 A.M. on May 17, after a siege of sixty-two days. Although he and his chief officers surrendered, he emphasized that he was not surrendering on behalf of his men, and he told his soldiers to try to escape through the enemy lines to continue the fight another day. Many of them succeeded in escaping, but most were taken prisoner by the French.

The French had to decide what to do with their more than 12,000 prisoners. Their Mexican allies had a simple solution: they suggested to Forey that all the captured officers be shot. Forey indignantly rejected this proposal. He respected Ortega and his men for the gallantry with which they had defended Puebla and for the humane way in which they had treated the French prisoners they had captured during the street fighting. Forey offered to release the officers if they would give their word of honor not to serve against the French. As they all refused, he decided to send them as prisoners to France. The rank and file were given the opportunity of volunteering to serve in Márquez's army, and 5,000 of them agreed to do so. Some 2,000 others were set to work removing the barricades and clearing up the damage in Puebla. The remaining 4,000 were sent to work on the railway, which was being slowly extended from Veracruz toward Mexico City.

On May 19 Forey entered Puebla in triumph and was welcomed by the clergy at the cathedral as the deliverer who had saved them from the godless liberals. A *Te Deum* was held, and the religious celebrations in the city continued for two days. Both French and Mexican flags were hoisted over Puebla to commemorate the victory of "the Franco-Mexican army" of Forey and Márquez.

The 1,508 officers who had been taken prisoner were to be sent to Veracruz and put on a ship for France. They were asked to give their parole not to escape, but they refused. The French propagandists afterward accused them of having given their parole and broken it; but the French historians most sympathetic to the intervention in Mexico who wrote a little later admitted that the officer prisoners had refused to promise that they would not escape. It was not easy for the French to spare the men to guard them properly. When the time arrived for them to leave Puebla, only 950 of the officers could be found; the others, including four generals, had escaped. Another 400 escaped on the journey to Veracruz, including Ortega himself, who escaped at Orizaba, and Mariano Escobedo and Porfirio Díaz, who got away somewhere on the road. A total of 530 officers, including 13 generals, arrived in France.

Napoleon III was awaiting with increasing anxiety for the news from Puebla. To his great disappointment, it did not come by election day, May 31, and, despite all the manipulation of the voting and the pressure applied by government officials in favor of the government candidates, the liberals increased their numbers in the Corps Législatif from 5 to 25. They did especially well in Paris. Napoleon later told Austrian Ambassador Richard von Metternich that he had been half-dead with anxiety for a fortnight before the news finally arrived from New York on June 10, to be followed by Forey's official dispatch to Marshal Randon, the minister of war: "Marshal, Puebla is in our hands." Considering the length and severity of the fighting, the French losses in the whole campaign had not been heavy — 185 killed and 1,039 wounded.

Napoleon wrote to Forey that the news had "filled us with joy. . . . While I bitterly deplore the probable loss of so many brave men, I have the consolation of knowing that their death was not in vain, either for the interests or the honor of France, or for civilization."

❈ 13 ❈

In Mexico City

ON THE NIGHT of May 30, 1863, Sara Yorke was getting ready to go to bed when she heard the sound of marching feet in the street outside her house in Mexico City. She looked out the window and saw by the moonlight hundreds of soldiers tramping along the Calle de San Francisco. Most of them were not wearing uniforms, but only white shirts and loose baggy trousers, and they carried no equipment except muskets and boxes of cartridges slung over their shoulders. As usual with the Mexican army, they were accompanied by their women. They were the remnants of the defeated army of Puebla passing through the city without stopping and going toward the north. They marched in complete silence, neither singing nor speaking to each other. Sara thought that they looked utterly dejected.

Next morning there was great activity in the street. Horsemen kept galloping past Sara's window, and many wagons were being loaded. From time to time someone she knew drove past and waved goodbye. She did not realize what was happening until an attaché from the United States legation called and told her that the government and the civil servants were leaving the city, with the army and all the police force.

When Juárez heard of the fall of Puebla, his first reaction had been to try somehow to raise another army and make a desperate defense of Mexico City. But his generals told him that he had only 6,000 men available to resist Forey's 25,000 victorious troops. Their opinion was confirmed by Porfirio Díaz, who made his way to Mexico City after escaping from the French. He told Juárez that it would be impossible to defend the capital.

On the morning of May 31, Juárez addressed a hastily convened session of Congress. He announced that it would be necessary for the government to leave Mexico City and temporarily establish the capital of the republic in the city of San Luis Potosí, some two hundred miles to the north. He promised Congress that he would continue the struggle and would never surrender to the invader, because "adversity, Citizen Deputies, discourages only contemptible peoples." Congress passed a vote of confidence in the president.

Juárez waited till nightfall, then lowered the national flag that flew over the presidential palace, kissed it, and cried, "Long live Mexico!" He entered his carriage and drove north through the night.

As soon as he had left, the citizens of Mexico became alarmed. What would happen to the city without a government, an army, or a police force? Would there be rioting and looting? They were even more anxious when they remembered that Márquez and his soldiers were serving with the French army. If Márquez's men entered the city ahead of their French allies, they might massacre every inhabitant they suspected of being sympathetic to the liberals.

The foreign consuls organized a vigilante squad of 700 of their male nationals to keep order in the city; then they set off for Puebla to tell Forey that Juárez and the liberal army had abandoned the capital and to ask him to send his army there as soon as possible to maintain law and order. On the way they met Bazaine and the French advance guard, but he sent them on to Forey. When the people of Puebla heard why the consuls had come, they ran out into the streets cheering and shouting, "Long live France! Death to Juárez!"

The consuls also suggested to Forey that it would be better if Márquez's men were not the first to enter Mexico City. Forey was a little stiff, and explained that he could not alter his plan of campaign to suit the convenience of the inhabitants of Mexico City and the foreigners there; but he held back Márquez until Bazaine and the advance guard had entered. On the evening of June 7, after an anxious week, Sara Yorke heard the music of a Wagner march and went to bed happy, knowing that the French had come and that she and her family were safe.

Next morning Bazaine and his staff arrived with the rest of the advance guard, and Sara went out on her balcony to watch them. Two French officers looked up and ogled her. She was not surprised, for although she had only recently celebrated her sixteenth birthday, she had been brought up in Parisian high society. She reflected that it was probably the first time for many months that the officers had seen a young white woman, though in fact they must have met quite a few among the conservatives who had welcomed them so enthusiastically at Puebla.

Forey himself made his ceremonial entry two days later, riding at the head of the army with Almonte on his right and Saligny on his left.

It was a glorious, sunny day, and thousands of people turned out to watch. It seemed to Sara Yorke that everyone was cheering the French, but young José Luis Blasio, who eighteen months later became Maximilian's secretary, thought that while the aristocracy and middle classes were enthusiastic, the lower classes were silent.

Bazaine had appointed General Mariano Salas, a seventy-two-year-old conservative who had never played a prominent part in political or military life, as head of a provisional administration. Salas met Forey as he entered and handed him the keys of the city — a historical and symbolic gesture, for Mexico City no longer had any gates or walls. Then Forey and his officers attended a *Te Deum* at the cathedral. Forey had given express orders to Bazaine that Márquez and his men should ride in triumph through the city, and they were received by the conservatives in the crowds with even greater enthusiasm than the French.

At the start of the campaign, Forey had received precise instructions from Napoleon III about his relationship with the Mexican conservative leaders. He was to accept aid from all Mexicans who offered to help him and to tell them that they must decide for themselves the kind of government they were to have; but Forey himself was to exercise the real power. "Wherever our flag waves you must be absolute master," Napoleon had written to him on August 3, 1862; six months later the emperor put it a little differently: "You must be master in Mexico City without appearing to be."

Forey was to appoint a provisional government of Mexican conservatives and make them obey his orders. He was to suppress the liberal *puro* extremists and Juárez's supporters and force everyone to accept "the intervention," but he was to try to win over the moderate liberals. He was to protect religion from the excesses of the Juárists and to recognize the Roman Catholic Church as the only official religion, but he was to compel the conservatives and the Church to accept religious toleration and to recognize the titles of those who had purchased Church lands. He was to allow freedom of the press, subject to the system of warnings that existed in France, allowing the government to suppress, after three warnings, any newspaper that criticized its policies too freely. Every evening the editor was to send the proofs of the next day's newspaper to the censor's office.

After Juárez left Mexico City, the conservative newspaper *El Cronista de México* which Juárez had recently suppressed, reappeared on June 3, acclaiming the victory of the Franco-Mexican army and the end of "the liberal tyranny," which was "the most barbaric tyranny possible." A new conservative journal, *La Sociedad,* appeared on June 10, the day of Forey's entry into the city. It declared that the people had tears of gratitude in their eyes as they gave thanks for deliverance from the Red flag and from the government that had seized the property of the Church. But the delight of the conservatives in the upper and middle classes was a little diminished when they found that as owners of the larger houses in the city, they had French officers and soldiers billeted in their homes.

Sara Yorke was required to accept two naval officers. She did not want to have strangers living in the house and made this very clear to the two officers when they arrived; but "they turned out to be perfect gentlemen, and completely won us over by their unvarying good breeding under shabby treatment. Before long we were, and remained, the best of friends." While the officers were being charming to Sara and her sister, their orderlies were making love to Sara's Indian servants.

Forey had ordered all his officers and men to be on their best behavior, and it did not take them long to become friendly with the women. French officers escorted young women of good family to the theater, attended balls and parties at their houses, and readily accepted the role of the *novio*, or suitor, who in the traditional Mexican way wooed his lady in a most stylized and decorous fashion. The officers introduced a new word, *noviotage,* into the French language. There were quite a number of marriages of Mexican women to French servicemen, both among the higher and the lower classes.

Forey did all he could to encourage these friendships. Three weeks after the French entered the city, a great ball for French officers and the upper and middle classes was held at the Teatro Nacional. Several prominent citizens refused to attend, but 3,000 people came. *La Sociedad* called it "an eloquent protest against the past."

Señor Don Eustacio Barron, the banker, was always to the fore. His grandfather had come to Mexico as a poor immigrant from England, but Don Eustacio had become one of the richest, as well as one of the tallest and broadest, men in the country, and was said to be worth $30 million. He was the chairman of the bank Forbes and Company, which had branches in several provincial towns as well as in Mexico City, and was a major shareholder in the English Mining Company of Pachuca and in gold-mining companies in California, with commercial interests in San Francisco and in steamships on the River Amur at Vladivostok. He gave balls and parties for the French officers at his house in the Calle de San Francisco and at his splendid country villa at Tacubaya.

When they first arrived, the Chasseurs d'Afrique established their cavalry barracks on the Alameda, where the aristocracy and middle classes assembled every day for their morning promenades. The

French closed the Alameda to all civilians. This caused great annoy-ance, but a few days later the cavalry moved off and the Alameda was again open to the public. Forey ordered a military band to play there every day from 10 A.M. to 1 P.M. He himself often went there while the band was playing and talked to the people, especially to the children, who became fond of the tall old gentleman with the heavy white mustache, in his full-dress uniform of blue trousers and jacket, huge leather boots, and gold-laced hat. When he arrived in the Ala-meda the children ran up to him, shouting, "Here comes Don Forey, our friend!" He bought them toys and sweets and allowed them to sit on his knee and play with his medals and his sword.

Although the children liked Forey, the liberals did not, not even the moderate liberals, whose support Napoleon III hoped to win, for in political matters Forey followed the advice of Saligny and Almonte. He restored the old Spanish titles of the nobility, which had been abolished by the republic after Mexico became independent. He al-lowed the traditional religious procession through the streets on Cor-pus Christi Day to take place three weeks late, for on Corpus Christi Day Juárez was still in Mexico City, and he had banned all religious processions in the streets. The moderate liberals might not have ob-jected to the procession, but they were incensed at the decree that compelled all the people in the streets to raise their hats or curtsy when the procession with the Host passed by. The moderates also objected to the decree that confiscated the property of a number of prominent liberals unless they declared their support for the interven-tion and the new government in Mexico City.

Forey lost no time in setting up the provisional government. He nominated thirty-five prominent Mexicans to become members of a junta that would establish the future government of the country. Nearly all the members of the junta were conservatives, and ten of them had held office in Miramón's government. The junta nominated three regents to rule the country for the time being: Almonte, General Salas, and Bishop Labastida. Bishop Ormeachea of Tulanciago was appointed as a deputy on the Regency Council till Labastida, who by this time had been appointed archbishop of Mexico by the pope, returned to Mexico City. Almonte was chosen to be president of the council.

Napoleon III was happy. He could now bask in the glory of the capture of Puebla and Mexico City. It had taken a long time; there had been surprising setbacks; and it was a pity that the news of Puebla had not arrived before election day in France. But he still had a comfortable majority in the Corps Législatif, and the French people were less worried about Mexico. The reports from the *procureurs* on public reaction were not entirely satisfactory. The news had been received with enthusiasm in Besançon, Bordeaux, Colmar, Douai, Metz, Rennes, and Agen; but there had been a disappointing lack of interest and satisfaction in Aix and Amiens, and the inhabitants of Poitiers and Riom had welcomed the French victory only because they thought that it meant the end of the Mexican expedition and that the troops would soon be coming home.

The government propagandists really let themselves go. One of them revealed that Napoleon III had said the Mexican expedition would be "the most beautiful page of my reign," and this had now been shown to be true. The author of *The Capture of Puebla* hailed "this new victory of the invincible army, which is the proper name for the French army," under the leadership of "Napoleon III, this great man before whom even his enemies prostrate themselves." When Spain and England, thinking only of their own interests, withdrew from the joint intervention, it had been necessary to show the world "that France, guided by the greatest man in history, will refuse to retreat before any danger in order to safeguard her honor and to protect suffering humanity." Prince Henry de Valori wrote that the capture of Puebla and Mexico City had added to the heroic list of occasions when God had acted through Frenchmen.

The victory in Mexico unleashed a spate of anti-American propaganda in France. One writer believed that the United States and its ally Juárez were aiming at world domination. Victory in the Civil War and in Mexico, and the Monroe Doctrine, was only the first stage of their plan. "To cross the Atlantic and to carry American domination into Europe was the second." Another author claimed that the people of the United States had always hated the French, and revealed that a few years earlier the producer at the French theater in San Francisco had been shot dead in the foyer by a well-known bandit. The bandit had then ridden through the streets of San Francisco on horseback day after day for a month, without the authorities making any attempt to arrest him. Napoleon's propagandists did not fail to point out that though France was rich enough to be able to pay for glory, she should reward herself for her efforts by annexing the Mexican provinces of Sonora and Chihuahua, with their deposits of copper, mercury, and silver; if France did not take them, they would in due course be seized by the United States.

The celebrations of the victory in Mexico continued in France throughout the summer. On July 20, while Napoleon was on holiday at Vichy, the enemy flags captured at Puebla were brought to him by Marquis Galliffet, who had not yet fully recovered from his wound and was walking with the help of crutches. Napoleon walked through the park with Galliffet on their way to Mass, and the trophies were carried in triumph through the town. The capture of Puebla and Mexico City was the central theme in the festivities on August 15, the birthday of Napoleon I, which under the Second Empire had replaced February 24 (the day on which the Revolution of 1848 had broken out) as France's National Day. In Paris, which had its hottest day for ninety-eight years, the Champs de Mars was illuminated and decorated with a giant letter N and references to Puebla and Mexico City; and by government decree similar celebrations took place in 33,000 communes throughout France.

Napoleon III was reasonably pleased with foreign reactions to his successes in Mexico. On Bismarck's advice, the king of Prussia sent Napoleon a message of congratulation on the capture of Puebla. The British government, though cautious about welcoming the events in Mexico, seemed a little less skeptical about Napoleon's plans than they had been a year before, and influential British journals applauded his success. "Napoleon the Third is a monarch of rare genius," wrote *Blackwood's Magazine*. "Of all the projects of Napoleon III, this is the one which is most to be applauded for the good which it will accomplish for the world at large." However much Britain might view with suspicion his designs in Europe, he was to be congratulated on having refused to endure the insolence of "a full-blood Indian like Juárez." *The Times* was pleased that the French had finally triumphed over "one of the most degenerate and despised races of either hemisphere."

Napoleon was less happy about the course of events in the United States. A month after the French entered Mexico City, the North won the Battle of Gettysburg and captured Vicksburg, which ended any chance that Napoleon III might persuade the British government to join with him in recognizing the Confederacy; and though the Southern sympathizers, including the London *Morning Post,* continued to believe in a Confederate victory, most observers now thought that the North would eventually win. But there was still much fighting to be done, and Lincoln and Seward were still determined not to antagonize France.

❊ 14 ❊

BAZAINE AGAINST THE CHURCH

AND THE GUERRILLAS

FOR JUÁREZ in San Luis Potosí, the prospects were bleak. He had not been able to persuade any of the ministers of the four legations that still remained in Mexico — the United States, Ecuador, Peru, and Venezuela — to go with him to the north. All of them, even his friends Corwin of the United States and Corpancho of Peru, had insisted on remaining in Mexico City, because it would be easier to communicate with their governments and protect the interests of their nationals from there. In Corpancho's case it was also true that he could do more to help Juárez in Mexico City. Several liberals who were wanted by the French and by the Mexican conservatives were hidden in the Peruvian legation, and Corpancho was able to send useful information to Juárez in the diplomatic bag. When Bazaine and Almonte discovered what he was doing they expelled him from Mexico. Corwin could do nothing like this for Juárez, in view of Seward's policy of strict neutrality.

The liberal journalists had gone to San Luis Potosí, where Zarco launched a new journal, *La Independencia Mexicana,* to succeed *El Siglo XIX.* In the first issue on June 15, 1863, he declared that the lawful republican government of Mexico would continue the struggle until the end and would eventually shatter the hopes and illusions of Napoleon III. In the meantime Napoleon was flying high, and Juárez seemed to be sinking. Favre and Thiers in the Corps Législatif in Paris urged the government to open negotiations with Juárez, now that the defeat of May 5 had been avenged and French honor vindicated by the capture of Puebla and Mexico City; but Eugène Rouher, who since Billault's death had been the emperor's spokesman in the chamber, ridiculed the idea. "Negotiate with Juárez?" he asked contemptuously. "After we have defeated him at Puebla? After our army has triumphantly entered Mexico City? When we are pursuing his fleeing hordes to Querétaro, Guanajuato, and San Luis Potosí?"

In this grave hour, the liberal politicians in San Luis Potosí were playing their favorite game of quarreling among themselves. Juárez wished to form a new government that would include all the most important liberal leaders, with Doblado as well as Zamacona and Zarco. Doblado agreed to join the government, but only if Zamacona and Zarco were excluded and left San Luis Potosí. Juárez tried to reconcile them. As army commander in the district, Doblado signed an order expelling Zamacona and Zarco from the city. The two men appealed to Juárez, who revoked the order and thought he had persuaded Doblado to accept his decision. But two days later Zarco wrote to Juárez that Doblado had told him that although he had revoked the expulsion order to please Juárez, he would nevertheless send soldiers to remove Zarco by force unless he left San Luis Potosí within a week. Juárez again talked Doblado out of it, but Doblado refused to join the new government that was formed on September 8.

The one glimmer of hope came from the United States, where Romero's propaganda campaign seemed to be having some effect. It was helped by the Union victories in the Civil War in the summer of 1863, by the shock felt in the United States when the news arrived that the French had entered Mexico City, and by the publication in Paris of a brochure, *France, Mexico, and the Confederate States,* which was known to have been written by Michel Chevalier, the former Saint-Simonian socialist who had become an ardent supporter of Napoleon III and was regarded as his unofficial spokesman. In this pamphlet he argued that though France went to war for glory and civilization, the Mexican expedition would bring her great commercial advantages; but he believed that if it was to succeed, it must be accompanied by French intervention in the American Civil War on the side of the Confederacy.

An English translation of *France, Mexico, and the Confederate States* was published in New York as the work of Chevalier. It caused anger and alarm, for the *New-York Times* declared that it was undoubtedly inspired by Napoleon III himself. The journalist Vine Wright Kingsley wrote a review of the pamphlet, in which he criticized by implication Seward's appeasement policy toward France and stated that if Napoleon III persisted in his conquest of Mexico and recognized the Confederacy, the United States must be prepared to go to war with France, "let the foreign secretary pipe what strains he may."

The regents in Mexico City soon set about complying with Napoleon III's wishes by asking Maximilian to be their emperor. They chose 231 eminent persons, nearly all of them conservative supporters, to form the Assembly of Notables, which met in the National Palace in the city on July 10, 1863, and passed four resolutions. The first, that "the nation adopts as its form of government a limited hereditary monarchy under a Catholic prince," was carried by 229 votes to 2. The second resolution, that the monarch should bear the title of emperor of Mexico, and the third, offering the crown to Archduke Ferdinand Maximilian of Austria, were carried unanimously. The fourth declared that if Archduke Maximilian refused to accept the crown, it should be offered to any other Catholic prince selected by His Majesty Emperor Napoleon III. This was carried by 222 votes to 9.

The people of Mexico City, whatever they believed about monarchy or republicanism, were convinced that the whole thing had been stage-managed by the French. They said that the French had paid for the smart uniforms and frock coats in which the notables had appeared at the meeting of the Assembly.

Maximilian had been one of the first to congratulate Napoleon III on the capture of Puebla and Mexico City. He wrote to Napoleon that "with the assistance of Your Majesty's mighty hand" the people of Mexico would be freed from anarchy and that England would soon abandon her reluctance to support "Your Majesty's noble efforts." The news from Mexico had produced another change in Maximilian's attitude: all the doubts about going there that he had felt in May 1862 now disappeared, and his original enthusiasm revived.

On August 8 Maximilian received a telegram from Napoleon telling him that the Assembly of Notables in Mexico City had offered him the throne. He was delighted and wrote to Napoleon assuring him of his eagerness "to lend a hand in the work of regenerating Mexico." But he thought that as a Northern victory in the American Civil War now seemed likely, he would require, as emperor of Mexico, a treaty of alliance with France and Britain by which they would guarantee to defend Mexico against attack for a period of fifteen or twenty years. He hoped that King Leopold would be able to persuade Queen Victoria to make her government give this guarantee. But Russell adamantly refused to do so.

Napoleon confidently assured Maximilian that all opposition in Mexico to the French intervention would soon be ended and that "the summer will not go by before Mexico is pacified and transformed." Maximilian agreed with this optimistic forecast. On September 12 he wrote to Napoleon that all the news from Mexico confirmed "that wherever the expeditionary forces appear, they are received as liberators" and that the whole country would be pacified "in a few months." But in the autumn of 1863 the French controlled only the country between Veracruz and Mexico City, and even in parts of this area the guerrillas were active.

In a village near Cotastla, between Veracruz and Orizaba, the wealthiest local tradesman, Señor Molina, was a supporter of the guerrillas. He was entertaining them at his house when Du Pin and the *contre-guérilla* made a sudden raid on the village. The guerrillas got away just in time. They had tethered their horses to the fence in front of Molina's house. As they struggled to untie the ropes, Molina seized a machete and cut through the ropes, and the guerrillas rode away as the French came down the village street.

The French seized Molina and one of his cousins who was staying with him. When they searched the house, they found letters from the guerrilla leaders to Molina. Du Pin ordered that Molina and his cousin be executed immediately. Molina's wife asked Du Pin to spare their lives, but he refused, and the two men were shot before her eyes. She stood calm and motionless while the execution was taking place, but as Du Pin mounted his horse, she said to him, "Colonel, you will die within a week." He did not reply, and as he rode away she burst into tears.

On September 29 Du Pin went to Veracruz to make arrangements to pay his men's wages; he let it be known that he would be leaving Veracruz on October 1 on the 2 P.M. train to La Soledad. But he secretly left the city early in the morning. The 2 P.M. train, which was guarded by a small detachment of French troops, including some of the black soldiers who had come from Egypt, was derailed as it passed through the wood of La Pulga in a cut between two high banks. The soldiers and other passengers who managed to climb out of the toppled coaches were fired on by guerrillas from the top of the banks on both sides. The French and Egyptians fired back, but many of them were killed when cavalry reinforcements arrived for the guerrillas. Some of the wounded survivors afterward reported that at the height of the attack a woman appeared and asked whether Du Pin was among the dead. They believed that it was Señora Molina, who had paid the guerrillas a large sum of money to attack the train. But guerrillas did not need to be paid to derail a French troop train, which they succeeded in doing on several occasions on the short stretch of railway line between Veracruz and Camerone.

The French shot and hanged guerrillas and imposed collective fines on towns and villages in areas where the guerrillas were active; but Napoleon III wrote to Forey that he had heard that Mexicans feared the bastinado and exile more than death, and urged him to use flogging as a punishment. Forey and his officers carried out Napoleon's instructions, and Mexicans who resisted the French were whipped.

Captain Henri Loizillon, who had served with distinction in the Crimea, was a loyal army officer but had mildly liberal views. He arrived in Mexico in October 1862 and fought at Puebla. He wrote regularly to his parents in Paris during the two-month siege, telling them that Puebla would be captured within a week and that they would be in Mexico City soon afterward. After he arrived in the capital he met Mexican liberals who objected to the conservative policy Saligny was advising Forey to carry out, to the decrees forcing people to raise their hat when the religious processions passed by, and to the threat to confiscate the property of Juárez's supporters. He felt uncomfortable that the French army was enforcing such policies in Mexico, and he wrote about his feelings to his parents and to one of their friends in Paris, Madame Hortense Cornu.

Forty years earlier, Hortense Cornu's mother, Madame Lacroix, had been a domestic servant in the household of Napoleon III's mother, Queen Hortense, in Switzerland; as a little girl Hortense Lacroix had spent many hours playing in the garden with Queen Hortense's little son, Prince Louis Napoleon. They became close friends, and their friendship continued when they grew up and she married. Napoleon once wrote to her that their friendship could have been so deep and lasting only because there had never been anything sexual in it.

Hortense Cornu became a socialist and was pleased when Louis Napoleon wrote books in favor of socialism during his exile in London and in prison at Ham, where she regularly visited him. But she was outraged when he carried out his *coup d'état* of December 2, 1851, and imprisoned 10,000 socialists and radicals in internment camps in Algeria and Cayenne. She wrote to him that she was breaking off relations with him and would never speak to him again. He was sad and told her that she had misjudged him. Some years later, he wrote to tell her how deeply he regretted that their friendship had ended, and invited her to visit him at the Tuileries. She refused to come, but in March 1863 he tried again, and this time she relented. After this she often visited him at the Tuileries. He consulted her about his personal problems with Eugénie and his mistresses and about his political difficulties, and she helped him with the research for his biography of Julius Caesar.

When Hortense Cornu received Captain Loizillon's letter from Mexico, she went straight to the Tuileries and showed it to Napoleon. He told her that he did not wish his army in Mexico to be the tool of clerical reaction. A few weeks later he appointed Forey a marshal of France and recalled him to Paris, explaining that Mexico was too limited a theater of war for a marshal of France to operate in. In July

1863 he appointed Bazaine to succeed Forey as commander-in-chief in Mexico. The army was pleased at Bazaine's appointment, for they believed it was his victory over Comonfort that had won them Puebla. He also had the advantage of being able to speak Spanish; he had learned the language and had acquired a young Spanish wife when he served with the French troops in Spain on the liberal side during the Carlist War.

Napoleon also recalled Saligny, whom he had backed through thick and thin against Wyke, Prim, Jurien, and Lorencez. Saligny was furious. Neither Forey nor Saligny would leave Mexico. Forey gave as his reason that he did not wish to travel through the hot lands in the summer. The French soldiers made up a song, "Will They, Won't They, Go?" Bazaine wrote to both Marshal Randon and Napoleon III, pointing out that it was usual in the French army for the emperor's orders to be promptly obeyed. Eventually Forey and Saligny left. The Mexican conservatives were distressed to see Saligny go; they raised $100,000 by public subscription as a parting gift to him.

Bazaine had great ability, vigor, and determination but very little tact. Eugénie believed that French policy in Mexico should be an iron fist concealed in a velvet glove, but Bazaine did not trouble to conceal the iron fist. He knew what Napoleon wanted him to do and saw no reason to conceal his intentions of carrying out his emperor's wishes, however much the people in Mexico resented it. His job was to maintain the authority of the French army in Mexico, to force the people to obey it, to crush the resistance of Juárez's supporters, and to stop the Church and the Mexican conservatives from pursuing a policy of religious intolerance and reaction. When he took over from Forey, Napoleon wrote to him, "Prevent the reaction in Mexico by making them feel that it is always the sword of France which is in command." Bazaine made the regents repeal the decrees to which the moderate liberals had objected.

Bazaine was fully complying with the recognized laws of war in distinguishing between the regular Mexican liberal army, against whom the French had fought at Puebla, and the guerrillas, who operated as irregulars behind the French lines. Any act of hostility against the French army was to be tried by a court-martial consisting of three officers, one of whom must hold the rank of colonel or above. Wherever possible, one of the three officers was to be a Mexican serving under the French. The accused was to be allowed the services of an interpreter, and, if he wished, of an officer who was a lawyer assigned to him by the court. There was to be no appeal from the decision of the court, which would be by majority verdict, and all sentences, including that of death, were to be carried out within twenty-four hours. But Bazaine did not object if his officers, in cases of emergency, executed guerrillas without the formality of a court-martial.

The guerrillas, too, sometimes shot their prisoners. When they captured government officials who had collaborated with the French or accepted some office in the administration of the regents, they sentenced them to death and executed them under the provisions of Juárez's decree of January 25. In January 1864 the liberal guerrilla leader Colonel Garma raided the town of Irapuato near Guanajuato and captured the political prefect there who had been appointed by the regency. Bazaine sent a communication to Garma, telling him that if the prefect was harmed, he would shoot a number of prisoners in his hands, including the nephew of the Juárist General Barragan, who would be the first to be shot. In this case the prisoners were exchanged.

When there was an attack on his soldiers or on the railway line near Veracruz, or any other guerrilla activity, Bazaine imposed a collective fine on the inhabitants of the nearest town or village. In the worst cases he ordered the town or village to be burned. In March 1864, after a guerrilla incident near the village of Tlacolulan, in the Jalapa district, Bazaine ordered his Mexican subordinate, General Liceaga, to burn the village. Liceaga had scruples about doing this, and asked Bazaine to spare Tlacolulan. Bazaine wrote to Liceaga that he realized he had acted with the best intentions, but "you have perhaps rather forgotten that there is in Mexico City a commander-in-chief of the Franco-Mexican army. . . . I repeat that Tlacolulan must be destroyed. . . . A severe example is necessary in this country. If you will not do it, despite my orders, I can have it done by a handful of soldiers whom I will send to that area."

Bazaine interfered in every detail of the administration. The political prefect in Mexico City, who was in charge of the police there, received more of his directives than anyone else. The prefect was ordered to stop money from being smuggled out of the city to the guerrillas in the surrounding countryside under Nicolás Romero; to prevent the Mexican police from arresting drunken French soldiers, who were always to be reported to, and arrested by, the French military police; and to suppress gambling at monte and other games of chance, on which Mexicans wasted so much time instead of getting on with their work. Bazaine even issued orders to the police about traffic regulations in Mexico City: they were to prevent coachmen from driving their carriages three abreast and racing against each other through the streets.

Bazaine sometimes intervened to protect the victims of the government's repression. When he heard that political suspects were being detained for long periods without trial in the same prisons with convicted prisoners, he ordered the authorities to separate them and to expedite the inquiries into the suspects' cases. He ordered the release of an old man who had been arrested because he had refused to sign a declaration supporting the intervention, and of a number of men who had been imprisoned because of mistaken identity. And he ordered that Doblado's wife should merely be kept under observation, and arrested only if she tried to communicate with her husband in Juárez's territory.

He was quite prepared to take on the Mexican clergy. Many priests, in accordance with the directives the bishops had issued in 1857, refused to administer last rites to purchasers of the confiscated property of the Church unless they agreed to return the property. When Bazaine heard of such cases, he ordered the local bishop to compel the priests in his diocese to administer last rites. If the bishop told Bazaine that it was none of his business, Bazaine asked the regents and Archbishop Labastida to discipline the bishop.

There was trouble, too, when the wife of a French officer on Bazaine's staff went to Mass wearing the latest Paris fashions. The officiating priest was shocked, for Mexican women went to church dressed in black and heavily veiled and usually sat on the floor in the church. When the priest made a rude gesture in the direction of the officer's wife, her husband complained to the vicar of San José, the priest's superior. The vicar disapproved of the priest's conduct but said that the costume worn by European women was unsuitable for attending church in Mexico and that the Mexican clergy were entitled to refuse them admission to their churches if they were improperly dressed. Bazaine was furious. He wrote to Labastida that in view of the fact that the French were as good Catholics as the Mexicans, French women were justified in going to church in European dress, and he told Labastida to order his clergy to admit them.

One day in October 1863 Bazaine, escorted by his Zouave guards, marched in, uninvited, to a meeting of the three regents in Mexico City and ordered them to issue a decree recognizing Juárez's nationalization of Church lands and the titles of the purchasers of the lands. Almonte signed, and old Salas, as always, followed Almonte. Labastida refused, and Bazaine dismissed him from the regency. The Supreme Court, which since the establishment of the regency had been composed of conservative judges, ruled that Bazaine's action and the decrees Almonte and Salas had issued in Labastida's absence were unconstitutional. Bazaine thereupon ordered Almonte and Salas to dismiss the judges of the Supreme Court.

Labastida replied by excommunicating all those who took office under the regency, by organizing a petition signed by government officials protesting Almonte and Salas's action, and by ordering the doors of the cathedral to be closed on the following Sunday when the French soldiers normally attended Mass. Labastida expected to be arrested; he left his archiepiscopal palace and slept in a different house every night. Bazaine decided not to make a martyr of him by arresting him; but he banned the publication of the sentence of excommunication, dismissed from government service all the officials who had signed Labastida's petition, and said that he would open fire with cannons at the cathedral doors if they were not opened to admit the French soldiers to Mass. The doors were duly opened and the French admitted, and Labastida's resistance collapsed.

Soon the conservative clergy were saying that Bazaine was worse than Juárez, and that he was, like Juárez, a Freemason. Labastida wrote that the Church had never been so fiercely persecuted, not even by Juárez, as it was by Bazaine and Almonte. Gutiérrez agreed. "If they must introduce the principles of the routed and fugitive Juárez," he wrote, "why did we and our protectors and allies make so many sacrifices?"

Juárez and his supporters, still suffering from their own divisions, could for once sit back and rejoice at the split in their enemies' ranks. They announced that they would continue to oppose both the Mexican reactionaries and the foreign invaders.

The conservatives were basing their hopes on Maximilian. It was Maximilian who, at Gutiérrez's suggestion, had asked the pope to make Labastida archbishop of Mexico; surely Maximilian, as emperor, would support the archbishop and the rights of the Church and would overrule Bazaine in a way that Almonte and Salas as regents could not.

The Assembly of Notables in Mexico City sent a deputation to inform Maximilian that the people of Mexico invited him to be their emperor. The delegates went first to Paris, where they were joined by Gutiérrez and Hidalgo, who accompanied them to Miramar. They were received by Maximilian on October 3, 1863. Gutiérrez, as spokesman for the delegation, offered Maximilian the crown, saying that "as soon as the Mexican nation had been given back its freedom by the powerful hand of a magnanimous monarch" it had looked to Maximilian as a Catholic prince who could "restore the splendid heritage which we were unable to preserve under a democratic republic."

Maximilian had spent some time drafting his reply. He had submitted the text to Franz Joseph, who made Maximilian delete his opening sentence: "The Emperor, as the august head of our House, and I are deeply moved" by the Mexican invitation. Franz Joseph told Maximilian that he was not in the least moved by the Mexican offer. He insisted that all references to himself be removed from the speech and that no Austrian official be present when the delegation was received at Miramar. The whole Mexican project was Maximilian's personal affair, in which neither the Austrian emperor nor the government was in any way involved.

Maximilian said in his speech that he was willing to accept the throne of Mexico; that guarantees would be necessary; that he must be sure the offer was supported by the majority of the Mexican people; and that he intended to reign as a constitutional sovereign. After the ceremony he told Gutiérrez privately that he was a little worried as to whether the Council of Regency and the Notables in Mexico City represented the Mexican people. He pointed out that although he had been shown resolutions of support for the invitation passed by the population of sixty-six localities, these were all small villages in the vicinity of Mexico City and Veracruz. Gutiérrez assured him that the great majority of the Mexican people were eagerly awaiting him. He told Maximilian that his portrait had been displayed in a number of places in the country, and that wherever it was shown, the people removed their hats as they approached it. Gutiérrez did not find it difficult to convince Maximilian of the truth of this statement, because Maximilian wanted so much to believe it.

Franz Joseph was not pleased when he read the report of the speech, for Maximilian's reference to guarantees was unspecific, and he did not clearly state the condition on which Franz Joseph had told him to insist: the guarantee of support from both France and Britain. Napoleon III approved of most of the speech, but warned Maximilian that "it is not by *parliamentary* liberty that a country in the grip of anarchy can be regenerated. What is needed in Mexico is a *liberal* dictatorship, that is to say, a strong power which shall proclaim the great principles of modern civilization, such as equality before the law, civil and religious liberty, an upright administration, an equitable judicial procedure." A constitution should not be granted until several years after the country had been pacified. Maximilian explained to Napoleon that he had mentioned his intention of ruling as a constitutional sovereign chiefly to satisfy public opinion in England and even in Austria.

Maximilian was now determined to go to Mexico and would not listen to any contrary advice. In July 1863 Richard Holdreth, the United States consul in Trieste, ventured to write a letter to his imperial neighbor at Miramar assuring him that he was concerned only with "your honor, and that of the illustrious family to which you belong." He warned Maximilian very bluntly of the dangers he would encounter if he accepted the offer that had been made to him ostensibly by the Mexican people but really by the French army of occupation. "I have to observe in the first place that the Mexican people are born democratic, having a desperate and native antipathy to kings and to aristocrats. I have to add further that in this respect the Mexicans are certain of a very warm sympathy on the part of the government and people of the United States. The United States will never tolerate for a day a monarchical government, or any government supported by any European power in Mexico."

He also warned Maximilian that Napoleon III, who was opposed by Victor Hugo and by so many Frenchmen, would not reign forever in France. "The Bonapartes will be expelled, and in spite of the current idea of the superior tact and prudence of Napoleon III, the nephew will follow the fate of the uncle." But Holdreth overstated his case when he wrote that if Napoleon III did not immediately withdraw his troops from Mexico, the United States would send an army of veterans to drive him out and would blockade the Gulf of Mexico. Maximilian knew very well that while the American Civil War continued, Lincoln and Seward would do nothing of the kind, and that Holdreth must be writing without their authority.

The only person whose warning might have had any effect on Maximilian was his father-in-law, King Leopold, but on the question of Mexico the Nestor of Europe was not as wise as usual. He not only did not discourage Maximilian from going to Mexico, he encouraged him to hope that he could persuade Queen Victoria to reverse the policy of the British government and give Maximilian the guarantee he wanted. In September 1863 Charlotte went to Brussels to see her father, and wrote a full account of her talks with "dear Papa." He told her that it was essential for Maximilian to have the French guarantee and that although England would not give a guarantee because she was afraid of the United States, she would eventually be forced to go to war with the United States. Leopold said that in Mexico Maximilian would have to establish a press that was free but subject to repressive laws. "There is no contradiction here, because we recognize only the liberty to do good, not to do harm."

Franz Joseph was much more doubtful than Leopold about Maximilian's prospects. In August his foreign minister, Count Rechberg, raised the matter again with the British ambassador in Vienna, Lord Bloomfield, asking him to confirm the impression he had formed that the British government would not give a guarantee to Maximilian in Mexico. Russell's reply to Bloomfield could not have been clearer: "I have to state to Your Excellency that Count Rechberg is right in supposing that Great Britain would not guarantee the Throne of Mexico to the Arch-Duke."

It seemed clear to Franz Joseph and Rechberg that Maximilian was rushing into the Mexican adventure without insisting on the original conditions. On December 7 Rechberg wrote to Maximilian, urging him to think again, because it was still not too late to withdraw; if he did withdraw, Napoleon III would no doubt be put out, but Napoleon could do nothing about it and would get over it. Rechberg wrote that it was quite certain that Britain would never give the guarantee; could Maximilian be sure that Napoleon III would really keep his army in Mexico to protect him for as long as necessary and that he would not come to some agreement with the United States at Maximilian's expense?

But Maximilian preferred the letters he received from Gutiérrez, saying that all Mexicans "without exception" were praying to God "that the sovereign which He has given them" would soon come. Maximilian had quite decided to go to Mexico as soon as possible.

Rechberg's anxieties were well founded, for he had heard from Wyke that Napoleon had already begun to have doubts about his Mexican policy. Wyke, who had returned from Mexico to London, visited Paris in November 1863 and had a long talk with Napoleon. It was a purely private visit, but the British Foreign Office knew all about it. Wyke gave Napoleon the same warning that he had given Saligny at Orizaba and that Russell had so often repeated to Thouvenel: it would, in the long run, be impossible for France to maintain Maximilian on the throne of Mexico. Napoleon did not disagree. "I have got into a bed of nails, I realize that, but the affair must be settled." He wished it were possible to be an ally of the new Mexican Empire without standing bail for it. He was worried that when his troops reached the Rio Grande they might become involved in clashes with the Americans, and he wished above all to avoid war with the United States. But he did not want to admit that he had made a mistake, for that would be fatal to his prestige in France.

Wyke duly reported the conversation to Russell and to Maximilian's advisers. He may not have realized that when Napoleon discussed politics in a private conversation he usually gave the impression that he agreed with the other person. His statement to Wyke closely resembled what he had said to a friend in 1849 when he sent troops to crush Mazzini's Roman Republic and restore the pope: "We had to finish this wretched Roman affair by cannon shot. I deplore it, but what can I do?" However reluctantly, Napoleon was again ordering his troops, this time in Mexico, to kill republicans and Reds with their cannon shot.

The risk that French troops might one day be withdrawn from Mexico could to some extent be offset by the recruitment of volunteers from other nations to enlist in Maximilian's new Mexican army. Maximilian thought that both his native country and Charlotte's would be willing to provide volunteers. Already in the autumn of 1861 Franz Joseph had promised that he would allow the recruitment of volunteers in Austria.

Rumors about these Austrian volunteers reached the United States minister in Vienna. He was John Lothrop Motley, a native of Boston, a lawyer, diplomat, novelist, historian, and political pamphleteer. Having resigned from the diplomatic service to write *The Rise of the Dutch Republic,* which won him international renown, Motley had been recalled to diplomatic duties by Lincoln at the outbreak of the Civil War. All his background and instincts as a New England Protestant and liberal, with his hatred of Spanish Catholic absolutism and aggressive religious warfare, so vividly expressed in his books about the sixteenth century, made him deeply involved in the current events in Mexico. He expressed his feelings in letters to his old college friend at Göttingen University, Otto von Bismarck, to whom he still wrote with surprising frankness, seeing that he was now United States minister to Austria and Bismarck was prime minister of Prussia.

But with his broad humanity and his novelist's sensitivity, Motley could nevertheless sympathize with the predicament of Archduke Maximilian, whom he considered "a somewhat restless and ambitious youth" with "literary pretensions," as shown in the accounts of his travels. In September 1863 Motley wrote to his friend Dr. Oliver Wendell Holmes in Boston that the hot summer in Austria had parched all the earth, leaving "nothing green here but the Archduke Maximilian, who firmly believes that he is going forth to Mexico to establish an American empire, and that it is his divine mission to destroy the dragon of democracy and re-establish the true Church, the Right Divine, and all sorts of games. Poor young man."

Motley reported to Seward about the plan to raise volunteers in Austria to fight in Mexico, and he wished to raise the matter with Rechberg. Seward forbade this. He wrote to Motley that France had invaded Mexico and the two nations were at war, but the United States was strictly neutral and had neither the right nor the wish to intervene in Mexico to overthrow or to defend a republican or a monarchical form of government. Motley had to console himself with the thought that Austria, like the United States, would remain neutral with regard to Mexico, and that Franz Joseph had behaved very well in the whole business and had done his best to discourage Maximilian.

It was Maximilian's misfortune that when he acted from the highest motives, the result was usually harmful. His scruples about accepting the throne of Mexico only if he had popular support led to more fighting and killing. While he was expressing doubts as to whether the invitations he had received from the Assembly of Notables in Mexico City and the villages around Veracruz were a sufficient indication of the wishes of the Mexican people, Napoleon III thought it would be desirable to conquer more of the country and induce more towns to invite Maximilian. In November 1863 Bazaine launched an offensive against Juárez's troops in the north. He divided his forces, sending one army under Márquez to invade Michoacán, and the other under Mejía to march on San Luis Potosí. Both Márquez and Mejía advanced rapidly, and the liberal resistance seemed to crumble before them.

Thus Márquez returned at the head of a Franco-Mexican army to the state where he had murdered Ocampo and Valle and from which he had been driven by Ortega two years before. Lieutenant Laurent, who was sent to Márquez with a message from French headquarters, was fascinated to see the man about whom he had heard so much. Márquez was very small, with feet the size of a child's, and a big, bushy black beard. He spoke in a quiet voice, but when Laurent looked into his steely eyes he could well believe all the stories that had been told about his cruelty; no one had ever questioned his honesty and devotion to duty. Laurent described him as "gloomy, stern, fanatical."

General Tomás Mejía, aged fifty-five, was more than ten years older than Márquez. Mejía was a small, full-blooded Indian with a slim waist, broad shoulders, and an enormous head with piercing black eyes. He gave the impression of being lethargic, even lazy, but he was an indefatigable chaser of women and recklessly brave in battle. He was worshiped by his men and by all the Indians of his tribe in the mountains near Querétaro. Less than three weeks after the start of the campaign he had captured San Luis Potosí, defeating 4,000 liberal troops and capturing eight cannons. Juárez and his government left the city hastily, on their way to Saltillo.

Ten days later Mejía entered Guanajuato. Bazaine, who had come from Mexico City to join the army, wrote on December 12 to Napoleon III: "Sire, Your Majesty's soldiers have been masters of Guanajuato since the 9th. They entered it without firing a single shot, amid the acclamation of the population, particularly the Indian people."

On January 5, Bazaine captured Guadalajara, and the liberal commander, General José Maria Arteaga, retreated toward Colima. The

French soldiers boasted that they were conquering Mexico with their legs, not their bayonets.

In Paris, Madame Bazaine was having an affair with an actor, who had left his previous mistress for the general's Spanish wife. The discarded mistress was very jealous; she wrote to Bazaine about his wife's affair, then gleefully informed the actor that she had denounced him. He told Madame Bazaine, who went straight off to the Tuileries, confessed everything to the emperor, and begged him to prevent the discarded mistress's letter from reaching Bazaine. Napoleon feared that if Bazaine learned of his wife's infidelity, he would be distracted from his military duties, so he ordered the post office to intercept and detain the letter. It was too late; the letter was already on a ship bound for Veracruz, and there was no way that an order to intercept it could reach Mexico City in time.

Bazaine was campaigning near San Luis Potosí when the letter reached army headquarters in Mexico City. In his absence, his aide-de-camp opened the letter and read it. He decided, on his own initiative, to burn it and not tell Bazaine about it. A few weeks later Madame Bazaine died. The news was officially communicated by the War Office to Bazaine, who mourned the death of his faithful wife.

Bazaine announced that any liberal officer or soldier who surrendered and signed a declaration accepting the intervention would be welcomed and invited to take part in the reconstruction of the country under the regency and the future empire. Many liberals took the opportunity and surrendered, and it became the practice for them to be taken into the Franco-Mexican army with the same rank that they had held under Juárez, though Bazaine, who mistrusted their loyalty, was not happy about this policy.

After Bazaine's victory at Guadalajara, three liberal generals surrendered, including Uraga, whom Juárez had suspected in the first days of the intervention, but had been forced to employ because of a shortage of other generals. Even Doblado and Sebastián Lerdo de Tejada (the brother of Miguel Lerdo de Tejada), who was foreign minister in Juárez's government, got in touch with Bazaine through intermediaries, and they too might have submitted if Bazaine had been more flexible. But when they wrote about an armistice or negotiations or guarantees, he would have none of it. There was not to be another Convention of La Soledad. They must submit unconditionally to the intervention and the regency, and there was no need for guarantees, because they could read the proclamations that Forey, Bazaine, and Almonte had issued, offering them the opportunity of helping to build the new Mexico. They could see that these promises had been fulfilled in the case of their colleagues who had already surrendered.

Doblado and Lerdo decided to continue the struggle; but Doblado hoped it would be possible, despite Bazaine's initial response, to negotiate some compromise peace with the regents. General Ortega, who had defended Puebla so valiantly, agreed with him. They met with José Maria Chávez, an old man of seventy who had formerly been governor of Aguascalientes, and the three agreed that it would be best if Juárez resigned as president of the republic, because it was politically impossible for the French to negotiate with him. They persuaded five other liberal officers and politicians to join them and, using these five as stalking horses, asked Juárez to resign.

Juárez had hardly arrived in Saltillo after his journey of more than two hundred miles across the uninhabited scrubland from San Luis Potosí, when the five called on him. They said tactfully that they understood from Ortega, Doblado, and Chávez that he found the burdens of his office tiring and would like to resign. He told them firmly that he did not feel in the least tired and had no intention of resigning. This ended the attempt to get rid of him.

But Juárez encountered fresh difficulties and sorrows, both political and personal. His illegitimate son Tereso, born as a result of a love affair he had had before his marriage, was serving in the liberal army and had been taken prisoner by Mejía's men in the battle for San Luis Potosí. Juárez was as devoted to Tereso as to his twelve legitimate children. It may have been some consolation to him that Bazaine was still insisting that his commanders treat the captured soldiers of Juárez's regular forces as prisoners of war. Juárez's former leader, Comonfort, who had once betrayed the liberal cause but had recently returned and had served loyally at Puebla, was killed in a skirmish with a band of Mexican conservatives in the French service. There was a shortage of money and of arms after the loss of the weapons at San Luis Potosí. Juárez wrote to Matías Romero in Washington and urged him to secure as large a consignment of arms as possible in Philadelphia and smuggle them to him in contravention of the United States laws.

In March 1864 the Italian General Ghilardi, leading a guerrilla band near Zacatecas, was captured by General L'Hériller's men. Ghilardi was particularly hated by the French because he had defeated their raid from the sea on Acapulco; because, they said, he had violated an armistice at Puebla; and most of all because he had fought against them under Garibaldi in Rome in 1849 and was therefore classified in their minds as a godless Red. He was tried by court-martial and sentenced to death. General de Castagny, L'Hériller's superior officer, was apparently reluctant to have Ghilardi shot; he ordered L'Hériller not to carry out the sentence until Bazaine had confirmed it. Bazaine ordered Castagny to have Ghilardi shot at once.

A few days later Bazaine heard that Ghilardi was still alive and he wrote again to Castagny, ordering him to shoot Ghilardi. But Castagny did not transmit the order to L'Hériller, who now wrote directly to Bazaine asking what he was to do. On March 13 Bazaine wrote to L'Hériller that if his two letters to Castagny had gone astray, L'Hériller was to take this letter as authority to shoot Ghilardi immediately without waiting for orders form Castagny. Ghilardi was executed on March 16. He wrote a farewell letter to his wife in Lima, which Castagny sent to Bazaine, who arranged for it to be forwarded through the French consul in Peru.

The liberals suffered another loss less than three weeks later in the same area, in what was to become one of the most controversial incidents of the French occupation. According to Lieutenant Laurent, his company of the Chasseurs d'Afrique, under the command of Captain Crainviller, received a call for help from the Mal Paso ranch, about twenty miles south of Zacatecas, which was being attacked by a guerrilla band commanded by Chávez. The Chasseurs galloped to the ranch and engaged the guerrillas, who seized the women and children on the ranch and used them as cover from the French fire. The guerrillas succeeded in escaping. The Chasseurs found the corpses of seven women and three children on the battlefield, which made them "thirst for the blood of these wretches."

Two hours later an informer came to Crainviller and told him that Chávez's band was celebrating in the little town of Jerez, eight miles from Mal Paso. The Chasseurs arrived there at 4 A.M. and found 130 guerrillas asleep. They captured them all, including Chávez, before they could resist. Crainviller decided that Chávez and all his officers and NCOs above the rank of corporal should be shot and the others sent to forced labor on public works. The thirty-five men who were to be shot were taken back to Mal Paso in Laurent's charge so that they could be executed at the scene of their crime, in compliance with Forey's general order about the execution of bandits.

The condemned men made no attempt to escape but faced death with that philosophical resignation which guerrillas always showed at their execution and which always surprised the French. Both Chávez and his son were among the prisoners, walking together. The son had tears in his eyes, but the old man was unmoved. "We would be moved by the sight of this family scene," wrote Laurent in his diary, "by their heartrending last goodbye, by this old man with his resigned look who is trying to pass himself off as a martyr, if we were not at the same spot where this wretch cut the throats of women and children."

Crainviller and Laurent had anticipated the wishes of their commander-in-chief, who seems to have been misinformed about what had happened. On April 10 Bazaine wrote to Napoleon III that the first battalion of Chasseurs under Captain Crainviller had killed a hundred men and captured forty prisoners in an action at Jerez on March 25, and that the prisoners included Chávez, the former governor of Aguascalientes, "whom I will bring before a court-martial if he does not die of his wounds, because of his barbaric conduct toward the inhabitants who have submitted to the intervention."

The liberal writers strongly denied the allegations against Chávez. They claimed that Chávez and his men were a thoroughly disciplined unit who never looted or murdered, but were soldiers of the liberal army who had retreated to Zacatecas and could not possibly be regarded as guerrillas. The liberals said that the French invaders had shamefully murdered their prisoners of war, including the venerable Chávez, and had afterward invented this lie about the excesses at Mal Paso to justify their crime against the laws of war. There are certainly grave doubts about Laurent's version of events. He is confused about Chávez's name, insisting, incorrectly, that the old man whom he shot was called Chaviez, and must not be confused with another man named Chávez who supported the intervention. But there is no doubt that the man captured at Jerez and shot was named Chávez and that he was an eminent liberal leader. Even if we accept Laurent's version, it seems that the women and children did not have their throats cut by Chávez but were caught in the crossfire and unintentionally shot by the Chasseurs.

The French themselves were using the services of bandits a hundred miles away in the Tepic area. They had engaged as auxiliaries a band led by Lozada, a peasant from the district who had become a bandit after he had tortured to death one of Santa Anna's soldiers who had whipped his mother. The French admitted that Lozada had pillaged and committed worse atrocities on the local inhabitants; but they paid him $5,000 in return for the services of his 5,000 men during the last fortnight of March 1864. In his fifteen days of service he flushed out and killed many guerrillas. In due course he was rewarded by being given the rank of general in the Franco-Mexican army; he then decided to learn to read and write.

As a result of their winter campaign, the French had occupied many towns and were able to organize a referendum to decide whether the people of Mexico wished to have Maximilian as their emperor. Juárez called on the people to boycott the referendum; he announced that anyone who voted would be deemed to have collaborated with the invader and would be guilty under his decree of January 25. The majority of the inhabitants in the towns held by the French went to the polls and voted for Maximilian. The liberal propagandists claimed that the people voted under the glitter of French bayonets, and this view was widely accepted in the United States.

Henry M. Flint of Philadelphia, who lived in the North but sympathized with the South throughout the Civil War and soon afterward went to Mexico, saw things differently. He said that the glittering French bayonets had only kept open the way to the polls and had not influenced a single Mexican voter. He said the bayonets had protected the voters from the guerrillas, who would otherwise have murdered them for daring to try to vote. Flint thought that the French troops were much less guilty of intimidation than the Union troops in Maryland and Missouri, who had forced the Confederate sympathizers there to vote for Lincoln and the Republican candidates in the presidential election of 1864 and in other elections between 1863 and 1866.

The official results were certainly suspect. The regents announced that of the 8,620,892 population of Mexico, 6,445,564 had voted for Maximilian. This was absurd. No election could have been held north of Zacatecas or south of Tehuacán, where the French had not yet penetrated. And even in the central areas under their control, the French held the towns but not the villages, and the voting took place in only a few towns. The official figures were obtained by including in the vote for Maximilian the total population in all the states where elections had been held in the state capital. So there was undoubtedly fraud, and almost certainly some degree of force, in the election. But the official figures would impress Maximilian and assuage his conscience. They confirmed the glowing reports he had received from Gutiérrez and convinced him that he would be welcomed enthusiastically by the Mexican people.

⚜ 15 ⚜

THE FAMILY PACT

FRANZ JOSEPH AND RECHBERG had sadly accepted the fact that Maximilian would go to Mexico. At the end of January 1864 Maximilian visited Vienna, and Rechberg, in the course of a conversation with him, mentioned casually that before officially accepting the throne of Mexico, he would of course have to resign for himself and his heirs all his rights of succession to the throne of Austria and his financial rights as an Austrian archduke. This was the common practice when a prince of a reigning house accepted a foreign throne, but Maximilian was apparently unaware of it. He told Rechberg that he would not sign away his rights in Austria.

Rechberg reported Maximilian's remark to Franz Joseph, who said nothing about it, perhaps because he wished to put off having an unpleasant family quarrel with his brother. At the beginning of March Maximilian and Charlotte went to Paris, where they were given a great welcome. There were balls and banquets, and a reception that was attended by all the diplomatic representatives except the United States minister, William Dayton, who had received instructions from Washington not to go. As the reception was held on a Sunday, he was able to make up the excuse that diplomatic representatives of the United States never attended functions on a Sunday.

Maximilian established a warm relationship with Napoleon, and Charlotte became very friendly with Eugénie. In private discussions Napoleon and Maximilian agreed on the terms of a treaty between France and Mexico, by which Napoleon acceded to Maximilian's request that France keep 25,000 troops in Mexico for the next three years, and that 8,000 men of the French Foreign Legion remain there for eight years. Maximilian considered the agreement a diplomatic success, and he congratulated himself on it and on the friendly relations he had established with Napoleon; but he did not appreciate the financial obligations he was undertaking in agreeing to pay the cost of maintaining the French troops in Mexico.

Duke Ernest of Saxe-Coburg-Gotha (the brother of Queen Victoria's late husband, Prince Albert) attended one of the banquets in Maximilian's honor. Everyone seemed to be happy, especially Charlotte, but Duke Ernest thought that Napoleon looked pensive and anxious. After the dinner Napoleon took him aside and said, "A very bad business. If I were in his place, I would never have accepted."

From Paris, Maximilian and Charlotte went to London to visit Queen Victoria. "They are going to Mexico, which I cannot understand," wrote the queen in her diary.

The Mexican representatives were crossing the Atlantic, on their way to Miramar to proclaim Maximilian emperor of Mexico. On their way back to Miramar from London, Maximilian and Charlotte stopped in Vienna, where Maximilian was handed a document from Franz Joseph. The emperor demanded that Maximilian sign the family pact renouncing his rights to the Austrian throne; otherwise Franz Joseph, as head of the House of Habsburg, would not consent to Maximilian's becoming emperor of Mexico.

Maximilian was indignant when he read Franz Joseph's letter. He wrote back at once, telling his brother that he refused to sign away his rights in Austria; if Franz Joseph refused to permit him to become emperor of Mexico, Franz Joseph would bear the responsibility for preventing him from fulfilling his mission of ending decades of civil war in Mexico. Franz Joseph sent Maximilian a memorandum written by the eminent Austrian historian Alfred von Arneth, showing how, throughout history, princes who became kings of foreign countries always renounced their rights in their native lands and explaining the reasons for this very salutary rule. Maximilian still refused to sign.

Franz Joseph sent his cousin Archduke Leopold to Miramar to reason with Maximilian and to tell him that the emperor was quite determined not to allow him to go to Mexico unless he signed the family pact. Again Maximilian refused; he felt his brother was bullying him, and he would not give in.

On March 27, two days before the ceremony proclaiming Maximilian emperor of Mexico was to take place at Miramar, Maximilian decided to refuse the Mexican throne. He would leave Austria the next day for Rome to explain everything to the pope, and he would then retire to the island of Lacroma. He told Hidalgo, who had already arrived in Trieste for the ceremony, and Hidalgo immediately telegraphed the news to Napoleon III.

Napoleon could not believe it. After Maximilian had accepted the offer at the ceremony on October 3; after he had been received in

Paris as emperor-elect; after he had initialed his treaty, as emperor of Mexico, with Napoleon; after he had requested Napoleon to persuade the bankers to float a loan for Mexico on the London Stock Exchange and the Paris Bourse — how could he back out now? Eugénie was furious. She wrote a letter to Richard Metternich, the Austrian ambassador in Paris — which was handed to Metternich by Napoleon's aide at two o'clock in the morning — asking him to intervene with the Austrian government to prevent Maximilian from causing this "appalling scandal" for the House of Austria because of "a family matter of no importance compared with the confusion into which you throw the whole world." She ended her letter "Yours, in a most justifiable bad temper, Eugénie."

Napoleon hastily sent off a telegram to Maximilian. "Your Imperial Highness is bound in honor to me, to Mexico, and to the subscribers to the loan. Family quarrels cannot prevent Your Imperial Highness from fulfilling more exalted tasks elsewhere. Only think of your own reputation. A refusal now seems to me impossible." Metternich had never been keen on the Mexican project, but he was eager to avoid the scandal that would ensue if the quarrel between Franz Joseph and Maximilian became public. "The affair seems to me so undignified that it makes me groan," he wrote to Rechberg.

Napoleon followed up his telegram with a letter later the same day, in which he wrote a memorable sentence that would never be forgotten by Maximilian, by Charlotte, or by future generations. "Your Imperial Highness has entered into engagements which you are no longer free to break. What would you really think of me if, when Your Imperial Highness had already reached Mexico, I were suddenly to say that I can no longer fulfill the conditions to which I have set my signature?"

While Napoleon urged Franz Joseph to reach an agreement with Maximilian, Franz Joseph urged Napoleon to persuade Maximilian to sign the family pact. Napoleon appealed to King Leopold, who was staying with Queen Victoria at Windsor. But Leopold, who was really a little unbalanced where Charlotte and Maximilian were concerned, urged Maximilian to stand firm. He spoke about it to Queen Victoria, who wrote in her journal that Franz Joseph "has not behaved well."

But Napoleon had touched Maximilian on a point that always affected him deeply. Napoleon had written to him that "the honor of the House of Habsburg is in question." On the evening of March 28 Maximilian postponed the acceptance ceremony that was to have taken place the next day, but he abandoned his plan to go to Rome.

He offered Franz Joseph a compromise: he would sign the family pact if a secret clause was added by which Franz Joseph promised to restore to him his rights in Austria if he were driven out of Mexico.

Franz Joseph would not agree to the secret clause, but he promised that if Maximilian had to abdicate as emperor of Mexico, he would "take all measures to safeguard your position in my empire that I shall find compatible with its interests," and he would care for Charlotte and for any heirs that Maximilian and she might have if this were ever necessary. He also agreed to pay Maximilian an annuity of 100,000 gulden every year and to release him from the debt of 50,000 gulden he had incurred in building Miramar; to allow volunteers to be recruited in Austria for service in Maximilian's army in Mexico if Maximilian ever wanted them; and to provide an Austrian warship to take Maximilian to Mexico.

This was not good enough for Maximilian. He insisted on the secret clause. Charlotte went to Vienna and had a long talk with Franz Joseph, but he would make no more concessions. Rechberg wrote a little sharply to Maximilian that the emperor would not engage in any further haggling with his brother and that it was time His Imperial Highness complied with his august brother's wishes. Even King Leopold now urged Maximilian to give way, and Maximilian at last agreed to do so. On Friday April 8, with great resentment, he signed the family pact.

On April 9 Franz Joseph came to Miramar and spent several hours alone with Maximilian in the library while their brothers, Archduke Karl Ludwig and Archduke Ludwig Viktor, with Rechberg and other ministers and the chancellors of Hungary, Croatia, and Transylvania, waited in another room. When Franz Joseph and Maximilian at last emerged, they were both in an agitated state. Maximilian accompanied the emperor to his special train, which was waiting in the little nearby station of Grignano. They kissed each other goodbye with tears in their eyes. They were never to meet again.

And so the next day, Sunday, April 10, 1864, Maximilian was proclaimed emperor of Mexico by Gutiérrez de Estrada in the bedroom at Miramar; he signed his acceptance on the little marble-topped table that the pope had given him. It was undoubtedly the strain of the quarrels of the past three weeks and his mortification at having been forced to sign the family pact that caused him to collapse on his desk in the library a few hours after the ceremony, thus postponing for three days his departure for Rome and Mexico. He wept as he boarded the Austrian warship, the *Novara*, at Miramar; and after the festivities in Rome, as he crossed the Atlantic on the thirty-seven-day voyage from Civita Vecchia to Veracruz, he still felt the greatest resentment about the family pact.

In the ship he signed a protestation, drafted by Charlotte and witnessed by his'two closest advisers, the Belgian Felix Eloin and the Austrian Sebastian Schertzenlechner. In the protestation he declared that he did not recognize the legal validity of the family pact because he had not read it before he signed it and had been forced to sign by unfair pressure from eminent persons in several countries; in any case, a Habsburg prince could lawfully be deprived of his rights in Austria only by a resolution of the Austrian Parliament.

But at times during the voyage he managed to forget his grief and anger, and to think about the future that lay before him in Mexico. He began to write a long book on the rules of etiquette to be observed at his imperial court. His "Regulations for the Services of Honor and of Ceremonial at the Court" laid down every detail of the procedures to be observed at levées and receptions; the precise moment during the Maundy Thursday ceremonies at which the emperor should hand his hat to his aide and the empress give her shawl and fan to her lady-in-waiting; and who should hold the basin when they washed their hands.

On March 29, 1864, while Maximilian was considering whether to abandon the Mexican venture and retire to Lacroma, a banquet was held in New York, at Delmonico's Hotel at the corner of Fifth Avenue and Fourteenth Street — two hundred miles behind the front line along the Potomac, where 110,000 Union soldiers under their new commander-in-chief, General Ulysses S. Grant, were waiting to launch an offensive against the army of General Robert E. Lee that they knew would be long and bloody.

Four of the largest rooms in the hotel had been taken over for the evening — two for the reception, one for the dinner, and one for the orchestra. They were decorated with the Stars and Stripes and the Mexican tricolor, and a high pyramid of sugar was marked with the letters J U A R E Z. The guest of honor was Matías Romero, the minister of the Mexican Republic to the United States. A large band played throughout the evening, mostly Mexican music, "La Jaroba" and "La Sinolita" and other marches, but also "Yankee Doodle" and "Hail Columbia."

After all the other guests had taken their assigned places, marked by cards on which their names were surrounded by the national arms of Mexico engraved in gold, they rose to their feet as the chairman of the organizing committee, James W. Beekman, a descendant of the

Dutch family that had founded the city of New York two hundred years earlier, led Romero to the seat of honor on his right while the band played "La Tertulia." Other guests at the top table included the poet and journalist William Cullen Bryant, still active in support of liberal causes at the age of seventy; John Jacob Astor III; Hamilton Fish, a former governor of New York State and United States senator; the historian George Bancroft, who had been secretary of the navy and minister in London; the eighty-year-old Charles King, president of Columbia College; William E. Dodge, a leading figure in the Young Men's Christian Association; George Folsom, a former United States minister to Holland; Washington Hunt, a former governor of New York; the eminent lawyers David Dudley Field, Smith Clift, Henry E. Pierrepont of Brooklyn, and James T. Brady, the unsuccessful candidate for the governorship of New York at the last election; and Dr. Novarro, who had been the surgeon-general of the Mexican Eastern Army during the siege of Puebla.

The guests were served ten courses, listed in gold lettering on their menus of blue satin: oysters, chicken soup, hors d'oeuvres variés, game, salmon with sauce béarnaise, beef à l'Andalouse, salmi, pâté de foie gras, sorbet in Rhine wine, peacock truffles, artichokes and asparagus, Portuguese gâteau, Spanish biscuits, and fruit and dessert. Halfway through the meal, at 9 P.M., the chairman proposed a toast to the president of the United States, to which Field replied. Dinner was then resumed. After the dessert, King, amid great enthusiasm, proposed the health of Don Benito Juárez, the constitutional president of the Mexican Republic, to which Romero replied. In all there were sixteen speeches before the guests left, after midnight, to the sweet music of the Mexican song "Buenas Noches."

All the speakers harped on the same theme. The people of the United States applauded Mexico's fight for freedom against European monarchical despotism, and although this wicked rebellion in the United States made it impossible for the United States government to take appropriate action, the rebellion was about to be defeated in the forthcoming summer offensive, after which the American people would be free to deal with the invaders of Mexico. There were denunciations of the clerical party in Mexico, who were compared to the oppressors of past centuries from whom the founders of the United States had escaped by sailing to New England. Bryant declared that the United States had constituted itself "a sort of police of this New World" to warn off "the highwaymen and burglars of the Old World who stand at the head of its gates"; but there was only one reference to the Monroe Doctrine during the whole evening. Field, in replying to the toast to Lincoln, was careful not to embarrass the government; he assured the people of Mexico that the United States would "offer them all the encouragement which a neutral nation can offer."

One of the speakers at the dinner, Charles Astor Bristed, reminded the guests that the Saracens who had tried to conquer Spain had been driven out after eight hundred years, and said that he was sure the French would be driven out of Mexico "if it takes eight hundred years to do so." There was an interruption by another of the guests: "We do things faster nowadays. Say eight years." Even this shorter estimate was more than twice too long.

❈ 16 ❈

MAXIMILIAN ARRIVES

MAXIMILIAN HAD COME at last. He had appeared on the stage where his tragedy was to be played out, making his first entrance more than halfway through the play, when everything had already been determined and there was little he could do to change the disastrous course events were taking. After the initial French aggression and the execution of the guerrillas, Maximilian could never hope to win liberal sympathy in Mexico or the United States; he would not be able to retain the support of the Mexican Conservatives who had invited him to come if Napoleon III continued his policy of antagonizing the Church; and French troops would not stay in Mexico forever.

The *Novara* reached Veracruz on May 27, 1864, and Maximilian and Charlotte went ashore the next morning. There was an impressive official reception but no response at all from the people. The streets were empty, and the few individuals whom they encountered did not cheer and seemed not even to notice them. Charlotte was distressed and worried, but her gentlemen consoled her by pointing out that Veracruz was a liberal stronghold and that she and Maximilian would have a much warmer reception in other places. But things were worse in Orizaba, where little squares of paper were distributed bearing the words "Long live the Republic, long live Independence, death to the Emperor." It rained so hard at Córdoba, where they arrived in the middle of the night during a thunderstorm, that it was not until the next morning that a crowd of Indians were able to show their enthusiasm.

They certainly had a good reception in conservative Puebla, which delighted Charlotte, and there was almost as much enthusiasm in many other towns and villages through which they passed on their way to Mexico City. The Indians were especially ardent; according to the conservative spokesmen and Maximilian's supporters, they welcomed the tall, blond, blue-eyed Maximilian as their ancestors had welcomed Cortés 350 years before, believing that he was the fair-skinned God from the east, Quetzalcoatl, who, according to an old Indian myth, would one day come to save them. The Mexican liberals had not done much for the Indians economically, even if they had given them political freedom, and many Indians were won over to Maximilian's side.

On June 11 Maximilian and Charlotte reached the village of Guadalupe, a few miles from Mexico City. It was a glorious summer day with a cloudless blue sky. The aristocracy, the middle classes, and thousands of the common people had come out from the city to meet them, waving flags, throwing flowers, and cheering. After attending Mass in the Church of Our Lady of Guadalupe, they were entertained at a banquet and spent the night in Guadalupe before entering their capital the next day, June 12. There they were welcomed by even larger crowds. From early in the morning, 150 carriages filled with well-dressed ladies from the best Mexican families drove out toward Guadalupe, escorted by 500 gentlemen on horseback.

The emperor and empress drove into the city, with Bazaine and another general riding beside their carriage, preceded by a regiment of Mexican lancers led by Colonel Lopez, who afterward became, in the eyes of Maximilian's supporters, the traitor who delivered him to his enemies. Then came a troop of the French Chasseurs d'Afrique, singing their marching song "Escadron, marchons!," and another troop of French hussars. The imperial coach was followed by sixty carriages carrying high government officials and state, Church, and civic leaders. Maximilian and Charlotte went first to the cathedral to attend a *Te Deum*. After the service they walked from the cathedral to the government palace, cheered by a crowd of 100,000 people.

In the first few weeks after Maximilian arrived, there were even more festivities than there had been a year before when the French first came. There were balls, receptions, gala performances at the opera, and bullfights. Señor Barron gave a particularly lavish fancy-dress ball at his house in the Calle de San Francisco.

The French Colonel Blanchot attended a bullfight a few days after Maximilian's entry into the city. The crowds were shouting excitedly and encouraging both the bullfighters and the bull. When the bull fought back and struck at his tormentors, the people cried out, "Hurrah for the bull! Well done, bull!" A moment later they were shouting, "Kill the bull! Kill the bull!" When Maximilian and Charlotte arrived, the crowd received them warmly, crying, "Long live the emperor!" Blanchot wondered how long it would be before they would be shouting, "Kill the emperor!"

Maximilian and Charlotte took up residence in the government palace, but Maximilian did not like the climate of Mexico City, and soon moved to the palace of Chapultepec, which in 1864 was some four or five miles beyond the western limits of the city. The palace stood on a hill surrounded by a large park, where it had been built by the Spanish viceroy in 1785 on the ruins of the palace of the sixteenth-century Aztec emperor, Montezuma. The park still contained some magnificent trees, including several that were thousands of years old, though many of them had been cut down by Miramón during the War of the Reform in his preparations to defend Mexico City from attack by the liberals. Some inhabitants of the city thought that this action of Miramón's was a greater crime than his order to shoot the liberal prisoners at Tacubaya.

Maximilian had the palace rebuilt and enlarged, and Charlotte herself planned part of the garden. Maximilian drove every day from Chapultepec to the government palace in Mexico City along a road, built at his orders, that ran down from the castle through the park and the countryside to the Carlos IV Square in the city. It was known as the Emperor's Highway. In the afternoon Maximilian returned to Chapultepec and had dinner with Charlotte.

They had another residence at Cuernavaca, about thirty miles south of Mexico City. They had fewer opportunities to stay in their mansion of Jalapilla, three miles from Orizaba, as it was too far from the capital for Maximilian to visit frequently, though he preferred the warm climate of Orizaba to the cooler temperature in Mexico City. He hated the cold and loved the heat of the tropics.

Maximilian's daily routine was the same in all his residences. He rose at 4 A.M. and spent three hours dealing with correspondence in his candlelit bedroom (Veracruz was the only town in Mexico that had gaslight). He dictated letters to his secretary as he walked around the room in his blue flannel dressing gown, sipping a cup of chocolate and eating Vienna biscuits while two servants helped him dress and combed his hair and beard. At 7 A.M. he went for a ride on his horse Anteburro, in the Alameda when he was in Mexico City, in the park at Chapultepec, or in the country around Cuernavaca or Jalapilla, before having breakfast with Charlotte at 9 A.M. The rest of the day was spent in official duties, Cabinet meetings, state ceremonies, and audiences. Maximilian liked to go to bed soon after 8 P.M. when there were no evening banquets, receptions, or balls.

On formal occasions he wore either the military uniform of the commander-in-chief of the Mexican armed forces or court dress, with the Order of the Mexican Eagle or the Order of Guadalupe, which he instituted, or his Austrian Order of the Golden Fleece; but whenever possible he much preferred to wear informal clothes, a simple gray frock coat and a tall gray hat. In the cooler temperature of Mexico City and the cold lands, he nearly always wore a light gray overcoat, and even indoors and in his carriage he usually kept on his hat to protect him from the cold, for his long golden hair was thin on top. He was happier at Jalapilla, where he could wear white clothes and his Panama hat with its wide gold cord.

Wearing informal clothes was one of the few habits of which his subjects disapproved; they thought he did not dress and behave with the dignity they expected of an emperor. On the other hand, people condemned Charlotte for being haughty, and many stories were told about the empress's arrogant behavior and of the snubs she administered to people who ventured to be too familiar and dispense with the proper etiquette in approaching her. Her strong face, which showed her determination and character, sometimes made her look hard, but those who knew her better said this was a misleading impression. They denied the stories about her arrogance and said that in private she was charming and considerate to her friends and servants. In any case, she and Maximilian were bound to attract criticism from one quarter or another, and to become the object of malicious gossip, whatever they did.

Some of the difficulties were caused by differences in national customs. Charlotte was taken aback, and bridled a little, when the wife of General Salas was presented to her and, after curtsying, embraced the empress and offered her a cigarette. But Charlotte kept control of herself and politely told Señora Salas that her doctor did not allow her to smoke. This story went the rounds and was generally cited as an example of the empress's stuffiness, but Captain Laurent was first told it by Charlotte herself, who treated it as a great joke.

Maximilian could be very charming and had the knack of winning the affection of the people he met, even those who had originally been his political opponents. His principal private secretary, whose duty was to rise before 4 A.M. to be ready to work with the emperor on his correspondence, was the young José Luis Blasio. He first met Maximilian after his fifteen-year-old brother was captured with a band of guerrillas under the command of the Juárist leader Nicolás Romero and was in the notorious Martinica prison in Mexico City expecting to be shot. His mother took José to stand at her side as she waited with other petitioners for Maximilian to pass by and presented the emperor with a petition, signed by many people, imploring him to pardon her son because of his youth. The boy was released from prison a few days later.

Some time afterward, José Blasio was given a job in the office of

Maximilian's Belgian adviser, Eloin, and made such a good impression that Maximilian invited him to become his private secretary. After a little while Maximilian entrusted him with his secret ciphers. Maximilian said that he hoped Blasio would not betray his ciphers to anyone, because if he did, the secret police would find out about it, and Blasio would be sentenced to imprisonment for life. But it was not long before Maximilian realized that he could trust Blasio completely, for Blasio was absolutely devoted to him.

The emperor made a similar impression on Dr. Bandera, the head of the hospital at Pachuca, who was a good liberal and refused to attend the reception given for Maximilian when he visited the town. The next day Maximilian came to the hospital, praised Bandera's work, and offered to supply him with any funds he needed. Bandera was favorably impressed and accepted Maximilian's invitation to dinner that evening. Charlotte, too, knew how to win people over. When she met a lady in Puebla who haughtily refused her invitation to become her lady-in-waiting, Charlotte was so charming that the lady was sorry she had refused.

The efforts of Maximilian and Charlotte to ingratiate themselves with their subjects were helped by the fact that they were both excellent linguists. When some English visitors were presented to Maximilian and congratulated him on his fluency in English, he told them that he spoke ten languages. Apart from his native German, and French which he spoke as perfectly as every other European prince, he had learned to speak tolerably well every language of the subjects of the Austrian Empire, and could converse in Hungarian, Czech, Polish, and Croat. He also learned to speak English and Latin. As governor general of Lombardy and Venetia, he learned to speak fluent Italian, and as soon as there was talk of his becoming emperor of Mexico, he learned Spanish.

Charlotte's native language was French, but she learned at an early age to speak her father's native German, as well as English, which he had learned to speak fluently as a young man. After she married Maximilian and went with him to Milan and Venice, she learned Italian, signing herself "Carlotta" when she wrote letters in that language. She spoke fluent Spanish before going to Mexico, where she was, and still is today, "Carlota" to every Mexican. She signed herself "Carlota" when she wrote in Spanish, but remained "Charlotte" in her letters in French to her father, Eugénie, and her friends in Europe, and in her letters in German to Maximilian. She and Maximilian spoke Spanish as much as possible in Mexico, though in private they spoke to each other in German.

Soon after she arrived in Mexico City, Charlotte decided to improve the Alameda, and personally supervised the planting of flowers there. The Alameda had always been the rendezvous of the upper classes of Mexico City, with gentlemen riding on horseback and ladies in their carriages. Charlotte often visited the Alameda at the height of the morning get-together, and her bearing there, which some described as dignified and gracious, and others as haughty and arrogant, caused both favorable and hostile comment. She set the fashion in many things. Thanks to her example, Mexican women began to ride horses and to wear hats and crinolines, and some of them stopped smoking in polite society.

The emperor and empress held state balls quite regularly, though they did not enjoy them very much. Maximilian considered attendance at balls a painful duty, because it prevented him from going to bed at his usual time; but the guests enjoyed them greatly. They were attended by the elite of Mexico City society and by the officers of the French army, including General Bazaine, who prided himself on his dancing. The evening began with a formal presentation of the guests to the emperor and empress as they sat on a raised dais. Charlotte, who during the day usually wore dark dresses with high necklines, dressed in yellow silk for the balls, wearing many jewels and the ribbon of the Order of San Carlos across her breast. Her black hair, which reached to her waist when it was brushed out, was arranged in a simple coiffure. After the presentation, the dancing began. The empress usually opened the ball by dancing with Bazaine, while the emperor danced with Madame de Montholon, the wife of the French minister to Mexico.

Everyone in society wished to attend the balls, and there was great competition for tickets of admission. Sara Yorke loved the balls. The orchestra and the Austrian military band, conducted by the famous Viennese leader Saverthal, played quadrilles, waltzes, polkas, schottishes, and Mexican *habaneras* with style and verve. Supper was served at 11 P.M., and the food and wines were excellent. Maximilian and Charlotte usually retired early, but the ball continued until 3 A.M.

Maximilian much preferred informal luncheon and supper parties, which he gave for a few favored guests at the palace in Mexico City, and at Chapultepec, Cuernavaca, and Jalapilla. His Hungarian chef, Todos, who had accompanied him to Mexico, supervised the cooking, with the assistance of Mrs. Grill, the Viennese wife of his Italian valet; but there were strong differences of opinion as to whether the food was good or bad. There was equal disagreement about the quality of the sherry, Bordeaux, Burgundy, and Hungarian wines for lunch, and the Rhine wines and champagne for dinner. Maximilian was generous with the cigars, which were placed in open boxes on tables in nearly every room of all the palaces, and which he himself smoked almost continually.

The only drawback about these informal parties was the emperor's sense of humor, which was not to everyone's liking. Some of the guests did not appreciate his sarcastic jokes at their expense, or the little game he made them play in which those who lost at billiards had to crawl under the billiard table on their hands and knees, though when he himself lost, one of his gentlemen crawled under the table for him. Nor did all the guests enjoy his slightly dirty stories and his veiled references to their love affairs or to the scandalous rumors about their wives' infidelities. Sometimes he made jokes in German to his Austrian friends about the Mexican ministers and dignitaries present in the room. When Charlotte and his Austrian friend Baron von Malortie suggested to him that these jokes might cause offense, he laughed it off, saying that the Mexicans did not speak German and did not understand what he said. Malortie thought it quite possible that the Mexicans did understand these jokes in German. On some occasions, Maximilian behaved more like the naughty little boy who had embarrassed his elders at Schönbrunn by making rude remarks about distinguished foreign visitors than like the virtuous young prince who had drawn up the twenty-seven rules of good conduct that he still carried on his person.

Charlotte did not always enjoy Maximilian's jokes, especially when they touched on the marital infidelities of his generals and ministers, because she was deeply hurt by Maximilian's love affairs. He was no more faithful to her in Mexico than he had been in Vienna and Brazil. Rumors circulated about his mistresses, particularly about the beautiful eighteen-year-old daughter of one of the gardeners at Cuernavaca. Maximilian's impressive figure, his long golden hair and beard, his gentle, kind blue eyes, his soft voice, and his winning charm would have captivated many young women, even if they had not been stimulated and flattered at being wooed by an emperor. Charlotte's pride was hurt — Blasio called it "the pride of a beautiful woman" — and she was also sad that she was unable to have children, a problem she connected with Maximilian's infidelity. But his passing affairs, even the rather prolonged one with the gardener's daughter, could not compare with the very real and profound love that he felt for his wife. When the time came for them to be suddenly confronted with adversity and disaster, with madness and death, their love for each other was tested and proved.

A few months after Maximilian arrived in Mexico, he made a journey through the country, visiting the turbulent state of Michoacán and some of the areas from which the liberals had been expelled in the offensives of the past winter. He was warmly welcomed by at least part of the population, especially by the Indians; but on the journey he fell ill from malaria, being always prone to catch infectious diseases. During his absence Charlotte acted as regent, as she did later whenever he traveled through his empire. She showed great interest in state affairs and presided very effectively at the meetings of the emperor's council. The Cabinet ministers thought that she was a better chairman than Maximilian; she was quicker to see the point and make up her mind, and the meetings did not last as long as when Maximilian was in the chair.

Charlotte usually discussed with Maximilian his projects for improvements. He had great ideas but was able to put only some of them into practice, because he found it difficult to overcome the inertia, corruption, and obstruction of the government bureaucracy. He succeeded in pushing ahead with the program for extending telegraph lines and for building railways. Good progress was made in erecting the telegraph lines, but the extension of the railway beyond Camerone went more slowly. Work was often held up by the guerrillas, who blew up the track and attacked and killed the workmen. But it slowly moved forward, as did the extension of the only other railway that had so far been built in Mexico, the three miles of line from Mexico City to Guadalupe. After consulting Bazaine, Maximilian agreed to grant a contract to an English company to build a railway line from Tampico to Mexico City, for Bazaine believed that by the time the company was ready to start work, the district would have been cleared of guerrillas.

Maximilian issued a decree introducing the metric system into Mexico to replace the use of leagues and other old Spanish units of measurement, but the civil servants did not favor this and stopped the project. He was not much more successful in his schemes for improving the army and the national finances, though Napoleon III and Bazaine were very anxious that he should succeed in these. Napoleon's idea had always been that the French would show the Mexicans how to organize an efficient army so that Maximilian would be able to rely on his Mexican troops; then the French army of occupation could be withdrawn. But the French generals were not favorably impressed by the Mexican army. Some of the soldiers were very brave, at least in the face of enemy fire, though they tended to be more afraid of the bayonet; and a few of their generals, like Mejía and Miramón, were outstanding. But the ordinary level of efficiency, particularly on the administrative side, left much to be desired. Márquez believed that things would be greatly improved if he could get rid of the women

Maximilian, emperor of Mexico.
(Culver Pictures, Inc.)

Charlotte, empress of Mexico.
(The Granger Collection, New York)

Benito Juárez. *(Culver Pictures, Inc.)*

Right: Napoleon III and Eugénie.
(Brown Brothers)

The house in Oaxaca where Juárez lived from 1819 to 1828.
(Courtesy of Susan Adrian)

Fort Guadalupe at Puebla, scene of the fighting on May 5, 1862.
(Courtesy of Barbara Ridley)

General Leonardo Márquez.

Melchor Ocampo.
(Culver Pictures, Inc.)

Miguel Miramón. *(Index)*

General Porfirio Díaz. *(Index)*

Marshal Achille Bazaine.
(The Granger Collection, New York)

William H. Seward.
(The Bettmann Archive)

Lieutenant General Ulysses S. Grant, a
photograph taken by Matthew Brady
during the Civil War. *(The Bettmann
Archive)*

Major General Philip H. Sheridan. *(The Bettmann Archive)*

Prince Felix zu Salm-Salm

Princess Agnes Salm-Salm

Maximilian and Charlotte. *(Culver Pictures, Inc.)*

The Convent of La Cruz in Querétaro, Maximilian's headquarters during the siege. *(Courtesy of Susan Adrian)*

The following four photographs and drawings were sent to Queen Victoria by the British minister in Mexico on July 8, 1867.

Maximilian's prison in the convent at Querétaro. *(Reproduced by gracious permission of Her Majesty The Queen)*

The Convent of the Capuchins in Querétaro, where Maximilian was imprisoned. *(Reproduced by gracious permission of Her Majesty The Queen)*

Top Left:
The scene of
Maximilian's
execution.

Middle Left:
The soldiers
of the firing
squad who shot
Maximilian.

*(Both photos
reproduced
by gracious
permission of
Her Majesty
The Queen)*

Below:
An imagined
depiction by a
contemporary
artist of
Maximilian's
execution.
(UPI/Bettmann)

who accompanied their men in the army, but he admitted that he had found it impossible to achieve this.

One of the chief problems with the army was the lack of money to pay for it. No Mexican government had ever been able to afford to pay its soldiers a reasonable wage, and often the soldiers received no pay at all. There was therefore a great reluctance to enlist, and the ranks had to be filled by the *leva*, the compulsory recruiting carried out by press gangs. But no more money would be available for the army until the government finances were put in order, which Maximilian, like earlier Mexican governments, completely failed to do. Corruption in all branches of government service was endemic, and it was very difficult to stamp out.

Before the French and Maximilian arrived, Mexico was heavily in debt; had not this been the pretext for the intervention? But the debt more than doubled under Maximilian, rising from $81,632,760 in 1861 to $201,573,640 in 1866. The cost of the imperial household, and of all the balls and receptions, mounted up. When Juárez was president, he was accused by some of the radicals in his party of paying himself too large a salary and of spending too much money on banquets and on champagne at government receptions; but Juárez paid for it all out of his annual allowance of $30,000. Maximilian's household expenses were $1.5 million per annum, exactly fifty times as much as Juárez's.

Maximilian continued the policy, which Bazaine had begun, of encouraging cultural links between Mexico and France. He encouraged the work of the Scientific, Literary, and Artistic Commission, which Bazaine had appointed in March 1864, and naturally gave every assistance to French botanists who came to Veracruz to study the flora of the region, for he had always been interested in botany. Many books were imported from France, for the educated classes in Mexico had always learned to speak French; and a consignment of seventy-seven pianos was sent from Le Havre to Mexico in 1864.

For many years French repertory companies had come from Martinique to tour the little theaters in the provincial towns and to perform in the French theater in Mexico City. These companies came more often under the regency and the empire. There was always some French play being performed in Mexico City, and Bazaine often attended the performances. Other theaters put on plays in Spanish by contemporary Spanish and Mexican authors. On Charlotte's saint's day, November 4, 1865, the Teatro de Palacio staged a performance of José Zorrilla's play *Don Juan*, which Maximilian and Charlotte had read at Miramar when they were learning Spanish. Zorrilla added a few lines in praise of Maximilian for the occasion.

The Mexicans were disappointed that Maximilian and Charlotte rarely went to the theater or the opera, which the people enjoyed so much. The opera house, the former Teatro Nacional, now called the Gran Teatro Imperial, was nearly as large as Covent Garden in London, with excellent acoustics, and very comfortable, though it was sometimes a little cold in the evenings. All the audience sat in boxes, which extended around the whole auditorium, from stage level up to the roof. The boxes were open in front to within a few inches of the floor, so the ladies' toilettes could be seen by everyone. The sleeping children were also visible, for Mexicans usually took their family with them to the opera, and the eight-year-olds found it difficult to stay awake during the long operas, with several entr'actes, which lasted for four or five hours and finished about midnight. Normally all the seats in the Teatro Imperial were occupied except for the imperial box, which was nearly always empty, for Maximilian and Charlotte liked to go to bed early. The first time they went to the theater to see Halévy's *La Juive*, Maximilian fell asleep during the performance, and Charlotte nearly did.

The Mexicans never succeeded in persuading the greatest opera singers of Europe to perform in Mexico City. It was too far away, the journey took too long, and the singers had heard too much about the risks of yellow fever and of bandits on the road from Veracruz. Everybody knew the story of how a coach containing a troop of French actors was stopped in the forests near Orizaba by bandits, who forced the actresses to take off their clothes and dance naked in the moonlight before they were allowed to continue, unharmed, on their way. So the audiences in Mexico City had to be satisfied with less famous, but very competent, singers from Havana.

They were more enthusiastic about their own native prima donna, Angela Peralta, the first Mexican to become a professional singer. Many foreign visitors agreed with the proud Mexicans that if she had been born and lived in Europe, she would have won international fame. Whenever "La Peralta" sang at the Teatro Imperial in *La Traviata, Semiramis, Maria de Rohan,* or the new opera *Ildegonda* by the Mexican composer Melesio Morales, the house was sold out.

According to several observers in Mexico City, some men in the capital did not support Maximilian, but all the women loved him. This was an exaggeration, for there were some women who did not support him. One of these was La Peralta, who had always been an ardent liberal. When she appeared at the Teatro Imperial for a benefit performance, Maximilian and Charlotte paid one of their rare visits to the opera. La Peralta seized her opportunity. At the end of the performance, when she advanced to receive the applause of the audience, she draped herself in the national flag and sang a well-known liberal revolutionary song that had not been heard in public in Mexico City since the French arrived. The next time she sang at the Teatro Imperial the house was half empty, for the conservatives had decided to boycott her. Soon afterward she left the country for Cuba, and she was as great a success at the opera house in Havana as she had been in Mexico City.

✣ 17 ✣

The Capture of Oaxaca

MAXIMILIAN ATTACHED great importance to winning diplomatic recognition from foreign governments. His empire was of course immediately recognized by France, Austria, and Belgium, and soon other countries were sending diplomatic representatives to Mexico. The first to arrive was the newly appointed Swedish minister to the United States, Baron Wetterstedt, who visited Mexico on his way to Washington after Maximilian had sent a diplomat to pay a courtesy visit to the king of Sweden in Stockholm. After the usual uncomfortable and risky journey from Veracruz, Wetterstedt was able to console himself in the capital at the official receptions given by Maximilian and to enjoy the hospitality of Señor Barron at Tacubaya.

The king of Prussia reopened his legation in Mexico City and sent back Baron Wagner, who had formerly been minister to Juárez. King Victor Emmanuel of Italy, who wished to remain on good terms with Napoleon III, sent a minister to Maximilian, which did not please Garibaldi and the Italian liberals. Portugal, Spain, Russia, Holland, and Switzerland recognized Maximilian's empire, though they did not send ministers. The British government was more cautious, which distressed King Leopold. "My beloved Victoria," he wrote sadly to the queen on September 13, 1864, "England is now in Europe the only power that has *not* recognised Mexico." But British recognition was not long delayed. On October 31 the conservative politician and author Francisco de Paula Arrangoiz was received by Queen Victoria as Maximilian's minister to London, and by the spring of 1865 Peter Scarlett was at his post in the British legation in Mexico City.

The United States firmly refused to recognize Maximilian, and Maximilian refused to recognize the Confederacy, though Jefferson Davis's government was eager to enter into diplomatic relations with him. Maximilian had originally been in favor of recognizing the Confederacy; but when he was in Paris in March 1864 he had refused to meet Slidell because Napoleon III did not wish him to do so. Napoleon had no difficulty in making Maximilian play his part in the unofficial agreement between Napoleon and Seward that France would not recognize the Confederacy if the United States remained neutral with regard to Mexico.

But Seward was under heavy pressure from public opinion in the United States to do more to help Juárez. Romero was having considerable success in gaining sympathy for his cause. After the dinner in his honor in New York, he published the text of the speeches in both English and Spanish, distributing the Spanish text in Juárez's territory in Mexico and the English text in the United States. Romero persuaded Senator McDougall of California to move a resolution in the Senate requesting the United States government to demand an immediate withdrawal of all French troops from Mexico.

The chairman of the Senate Foreign Affairs Committee was Charles Sumner, who for many years had been one of the most eminent leaders of the struggle to abolish slavery. Sumner was a wise statesman. All his sympathies were with Juárez, but he realized that if Napoleon III came into the Civil War on the side of the Confederacy it would not help to defeat the Southern rebellion, to abolish slavery, or to preserve republican freedom in Mexico; and he did not wish to embarrass Seward and Lincoln. So he skillfully sidetracked McDougall's resolution.

Romero had more success in the House of Representatives. On April 4, 1864, Henry Winter Davis of Missouri moved a resolution in the House that it would be contrary to the accepted policy of the United States to acknowledge a monarchy on the American continent that had been erected on the ruins of a republican government. This resolution, which was distinctly milder than McDougall's in the Senate, was carried by a large majority. It caused great indignation in France and embarrassed Seward, who thought that it would upset his understanding with Napoleon III. When Dayton called on Edouard Drouyn de Lhuys, the French foreign minister began the conversation by asking him if he came to bring peace or war. Seward instructed Dayton to inform Drouyn de Lhuys that Congress did not decide United States foreign policy, which was entirely a matter for the president and the secretary of state, and that Lincoln and he would continue to pursue a policy of neutrality with regard to Mexico.

When Seward's note to the French government was published in *Le Moniteur*, liberals in Congress and throughout the United States were angry. The *Cheshire Republican*, the *Evening Post* (New York), and the *New York Herald* declared that Seward had brought the United

States to new depths of humiliation and had betrayed its interests and the cause of freedom in Mexico.

Lincoln was standing for reelection in November, and although the states of the Confederacy would of course be excluded from the voting, it was by no means certain that he would win the election. General George McClellan was standing against him as the Democratic candidate. At the beginning of the Civil War McClellan had been hailed as the military genius who would win the war for the Union, and though Lincoln had removed him after he had been unsuccessful in several campaigns, many of the soldiers who had served under him believed that he had been unjustly dismissed, and they were likely to vote for him. The radicals in the Republican Party were putting up General John Frémont as a candidate against Lincoln, and might well seriously split the Republican vote. The platforms of both McClellan and Frémont included a promise to help Mexico expel the French. Lincoln and Seward had to walk a tightrope to avoid provoking Napoleon III and losing vital votes.

In June 1864 the Republican Convention met in Baltimore, chose Lincoln as their candidate, adopted a platform that promised to defeat the rebellion and abolish slavery, and declared that "we approve the position taken by the Government that the people of the United States can never regard with indifference the attempt of any European Power to overthrow by force . . . the institutions of any Republican Government on the Western Continent." This placed Lincoln in a difficult situation, from which he emerged very skillfully. In the short reply to his party, in which he accepted the nomination, he referred to the clause in the platform that dealt with Mexico — the only one of the eleven paragraphs on which he commented. "While the resolution in regard to the supplanting of Republican government upon the Western continent is fully concurred in, there might be misunderstanding were I not to say that the position of the government, in relation to the action of France in Mexico, as assumed through the State Department and approved and endorsed by the Convention . . . will be faithfully maintained, so long as the state of facts should leave that position pertinent and applicable."

This carefully worded statement, while encouraging the liberals to believe that United States policy toward France might change one day, succeeded in reassuring Napoleon III. Seward's informal agreement with him was working very satisfactorily for the United States. At Seward's request, Napoleon agreed to seize some warships being built in France for the Confederacy, and to prevent them from putting to sea. By the summer of 1864, the newspapers in Richmond and Charleston were attacking Napoleon III and Maximilian, accusing them of having betrayed the interests of the Confederacy to the United States.

Politically, Maximilian was arousing opposition on all sides. He was in complete agreement with Napoleon III's policy of governing Mexico with a liberal dictatorship, though Napoleon sometimes felt that he was not a sufficiently vigorous dictator. But Napoleon approved of Maximilian's action in trying to win over the liberals and in standing up to the conservatives and the clergy by refusing to carry out their reactionary policies. Maximilian soon realized that there was no chance of winning over Juárez and the *puros* of the Liberal Party. It has often been said that when Maximilian was sailing to Mexico in the *Novara*, he wrote to Juárez, inviting him to come to Mexico City and join the imperial government, and that Juárez wrote in reply that he would never collaborate with Maximilian. But probably this is untrue, and Juárez's letter a forgery. No action that Maximilian could take would make the supporters of Juárez forget what he had done and who he was. The liberal minister of finance, José Maria Iglesias, who accompanied Juárez on his travels and edited his newspaper *El Periodico Oficial*, wrote in Monterrey three weeks after the emperor arrived in Mexico City that "Maximilian the early riser, Maximilian the pious, Maximilian the simple" was "Maximilian the usurper."

Maximilian hoped to persuade the moderate liberals to support his government, and he had some success. The moderate liberal lawyer José Fernando Ramírez, who had hitherto opposed the intervention, agreed to become Maximilian's foreign minister, to the dismay of the conservatives, who believed that he was a traitor and a Juárist spy. Despite this success with Ramírez, the main effect of Maximilian's policy was to antagonize the conservatives without conciliating the liberals.

The conservatives were disillusioned with Maximilian's attitude to the Church. He did not place a cross in his imperial crown and did not describe himself as emperor "by the grace of God" in official documents. Before he arrived, they had hoped he would reverse Bazaine's anticlerical policy, but they found that he was just as firm as Bazaine in insisting on religious toleration and in confirming the sales of Church lands by Juárez's government and the titles of the purchasers. Archbishop Labastida appealed to the pope. He was not disappointed in his hopes of support from Pius IX, who sent Monsignor Meglia to Mexico as papal nuncio.

Maximilian gave orders for the nuncio to be received with great honor at Veracruz and Puebla and at every stage on his journey, and welcomed him to the capital; but after the speeches, receptions, and banquets the two made no progress at all in their private talks about religious policy. After a few weeks of fruitless discussion, Maximilian issued a decree on December 27, 1864, while the nuncio was still in Mexico City, in which he declared that the Roman Catholic religion was to be the only official religion of the Mexican Empire, but that all other sects should have religious toleration, and that the confiscation and sale of Church lands by Juárez's government were recognized as valid. The nuncio issued a public protest and went back to Rome.

The pope backed the nuncio, but Napoleon III backed Maximilian and gave his official approval to a book by the Abbé Testory, the chaplain general of the French army in Mexico, in favor of religious toleration. Testory argued that if the pope could allow the Jews freedom of worship in Rome, the Mexican bishops should grant religious toleration to Protestants and other sects in Mexico. Even Eugénie, who was always accused by the liberals of being an Ultramontane, was in favor of religious toleration, and agreed with Charlotte that it was impossible for a modern ruler to return to the days of Philip II of Spain and refuse toleration. She did not object when Charlotte wrote to her that she thought the nuncio was a madman, and that she had made Bazaine laugh by asking him to throw Monsignor Meglia out the window.

The Mexican bishops would not accept religious toleration. "Mexico is exclusively a Catholic country," they wrote to Maximilian, "and the opposition of the people to religious toleration has always been manifested in the most unequivocal manner." Bishop Ormeachea told Maximilian that only 5 percent of the people of Mexico were in favor of toleration and that this 5 percent consisted chiefly of immigrants from Protestant countries. Father Miranda had argued that religious toleration might be a possible policy in Europe, but that in Mexico it would destroy the whole basis on which the Church rested. But Miranda had died of yellow fever in Puebla on his way home from Europe a fortnight before Maximilian landed at Veracruz. He had no illusions about Maximilian, and died fearing the worst for the Church in Mexico.

By the spring of 1865 the Mexican clergy were convinced that Maximilian was a Freemason. The rumor spread that he had joined a Freemason's lodge in Milan when he was governor-general of Lombardy and Venetia.

Maximilian decided to get rid of the two generals who were closest to the conservatives and the clergy and most hated by the moderate liberals. He sent Márquez on a mission to Jerusalem and Constantinople, and Miramón to Berlin to study the latest Prussian military tactics.

Maximilian continued his friendly correspondence with Napoleon III, and Charlotte and Eugénie exchanged very warm letters; but from the very beginning there was tension between Maximilian and Bazaine. Before Maximilian arrived in Mexico, Napoleon had told Bazaine that he would have to treat the emperor with deference and respect his authority. Bazaine had promised to do so, but he was used to giving orders to everybody in Mexico, including the regents and the archbishop, and it was not easy for him to have to submit to Maximilian. His behavior to Maximilian in public was impeccably correct, and Maximilian on his side gave many public demonstrations of respect and affection for Bazaine. But the friction between them began at once when Maximilian granted his new Order of Guadalupe to only some of the French officers on the list Bazaine had submitted to him.

On one point Maximilian and Bazaine were in complete agreement: Juárez and his supporters must be driven out of the areas they still controlled in the north and south. In September 1864, on Napoleon's orders, the French fleet captured Matamoros after General Santiago Vidaurri had entered into secret contacts with them. At the same time Bazaine's forces captured Monterrey and Saltillo. Juárez retreated another 450 miles to the northwest and established his new capital at Chihuahua.

Vidaurri had betrayed Juárez, but he had not gained any great reward from the French for doing so. On the contrary, he got involved in fresh difficulties, because a British agent managed to obtain documents proving that he had collaborated with the French. The agent sent the documents to Palmerston, who used them to obtain favorable concessions from Vidaurri for British merchants trading with Matamoros. Vidaurri complied with Palmerston's requests and asked him to do a favor for two of his friends in return. He also asked Palmerston to send him the incriminating documents. On April 20, 1864, Palmerston replied to Vidaurri in a courteous letter, expressing his "gratitude" and granting the favor. But he ended his letter, "You perfectly understand that I cannot remit to you the letters which compromise you with your Government: they are my guarantees for your fidelity." Vidaurri finally solved his problems by going to Texas, and on his return to Mexico openly joined Maximilian's side.

More of Juárez's leading supporters were deserting him. In June 1864 Zamacona, his former foreign minister, wrote from Saltillo to explain why he was giving up the struggle and going over to Maximilian. He had just seen a liberal officer, brandishing a whip, force a reluctant conscript whom he had press-ganged to take his place in the ranks of Juárez's army. On the other hand, Zamacona thought there was no use denying that thousands of Mexicans were willingly supporting Maximilian and the intervention. How otherwise could the French have kept open their lines of communication over such vast distances, extended the telegraph line from Querétaro to Veracruz, built the railway from Veracruz as far as Paso Ancho, kept the roads open, and run an efficient postal service? Zarco and Doblado also in effect left Juárez, though they disguised their withdrawal by saying that they were going on a propaganda tour of the United States.

After his success in the north, Bazaine planned an operation in the south, where so far the French had made very little progress. In Yucatán, the population was almost entirely Indian; they had stayed out of the struggle between the French and Juárez, and both sides, fully occupied elsewhere, had left Yucatán alone. Oaxaca was firmly in the grip of Porfirio Díaz, who, after escaping from the French, had raised an army of several thousand men and had established his headquarters in his native city. He was in control of most of the state of Oaxaca and made frequent raids into Guerrero.

The city of Oaxaca lies on a broad plateau surrounded by mountains. Until the invention of the airplane Oaxaca could not be reached except by crossing the high, forested mountain ranges, whether the traveler came from Orizaba, Puebla, Mexico City, or the Pacific coast. In 1864 there were no proper roads through the mountains, but only rough tracks that one could follow on foot, horseback, or mules; carriages and wagons could pass only with difficulty. The city itself was surrounded by walls. If Díaz withdrew his forces into the city, it would not be easy to take, even though many of the inhabitants were conservatives, whom the liberals kept down by force. The walls and defenses could be battered down by heavy guns, but how could heavy guns be brought through the mountains?

In July 1864 Bazaine decided to mount a major military operation to capture Oaxaca. He ordered the cavalry under General Brincourt to advance from Puebla against Díaz's army at Acatlán. Díaz retreated, and Brincourt advanced as far as Nochixtlán, less than fifty miles from Oaxaca City. Bazaine ordered him to halt there, for he would not be able to capture Oaxaca without artillery. Bazaine believed that Díaz had 7,000 men at Oaxaca; his intelligence was faulty, and in fact Diaz's forces were only 3,000 strong.

Bazaine decided to build a road from Puebla to Oaxaca City that could stand the weight of his cannons. His main force of 8,000 men began their march from Puebla and Tehuacán in October. After the engineers had built four or five miles of road, the army would advance that far and then wait until the engineers had built another five miles. The French hired the Indians of the district to help with the road building, and the Indians were eager to help, for they had been involved in some clashes with Díaz's troops, who had maltreated them.

By the beginning of January 1865 the whole French army, including the guns, were in place before Oaxaca City. Bazaine, who had just been made a marshal of France, arrived to take charge of operations. He began the siege on January 11. Díaz held out for a month by turning the city into a fortress, blowing up all the houses outside the city walls so that his view of the enemy should not be obscured, and making holes in the walls of other houses so that his men could pass from house to house during the street fighting for which he was preparing. But his difficulties increased every day. He was short of food and ammunition, a shortage made more acute when the supplies stored in the Santo Domingo monastery exploded, killing the commanding officer in charge. Many of his men deserted, though he shot four or five deserters every week. He sent his cavalry commander, General Trevino, to lead a sortie against the enemy; but Trevino deserted with all his men and joined the French. After three weeks Díaz's forces were reduced to 1,000 men.

On February 4 Bazaine bombarded the defenses for nearly twenty-four hours. On the eighth he decided to launch an infantry attack the next day. Díaz now had only 700 men left, and he realized that he could not hope to hold the city in street fighting against an enemy who outnumbered him by more than ten to one. At about midnight he rode to Bazaine's headquarters and surrendered his army and the city unconditionally. The French entered in triumph on February 9.

When Bazaine met Díaz, he told him that if he had surrendered earlier he would not have been considered a rebel against his emperor. Díaz said he was fighting for the lawful republican government of Mexico and had never accepted Maximilian as his emperor. Bazaine then reproached him for having broken his parole when he escaped after the fall of Puebla; Díaz replied that he had not given his parole when he was captured at Puebla. Bazaine apparently believed him, for he invited Díaz to have breakfast with him before sending him to Puebla under escort. Bazaine treated Díaz and all his men as prisoners of war, not as guerrillas or bandits, though Forey said, in a debate in the Corps Législatif in Paris, that Díaz ought to have been shot at Oaxaca as a traitor.

Díaz was imprisoned in Fort Guadalupe, which he had helped defend successfully against Lorencez's army on May 5, 1862. He was guarded there by Austrian volunteers, who had taken over the garrisoning of Puebla from the French. The Austrians were not very efficient, and Díaz escaped, eventually rejoining Juárez's forces.

Maximilian had been waiting impatiently for news of the capture of Oaxaca, and throughout the last three months Charlotte had been writing querulously to Eugénie, complaining of the dilatoriness and expense of the campaign and accusing Bazaine of incompetence. Maximilian and Charlotte completely ignored the difficulties of taking cannons across the mountains and the success of Bazaine's road-building operation. But many French officers also criticized Bazaine's tactics. They thought that Brincourt could easily have captured Oaxaca the previous August if Bazaine had not ordered him to stop at Nochixtlán, for Díaz had not yet fortified Oaxaca City, which at that time could have been taken by the cavalry alone. They said Bazaine had held back Brincourt so that he himself should have the glory of capturing Oaxaca. But if Bazaine overestimated the difficulties of capturing Oaxaca, there is no reason to think that he was guilty of anything worse than an error of judgment based on faulty intelligence. The year before, he had made no attempt to prevent Mejía from gaining the credit for the capture of San Luis Potosí and Guanajuato.

When the news of the capture of Oaxaca arrived at last, Maximilian was generous with his praise of Bazaine. He decorated him with the Grand Cross of the Order of the Mexican Eagle, and Charlotte asked her father to give him the Grand Cross of the Belgian Order of Leopold. Napoleon III was as delighted as Maximilian at the outcome of the campaign, and felt he could recall some of his troops to France. Nearly the whole of Mexico was now under Maximilian's rule; his sovereignty over Yucatán was clearly recognized when Charlotte went there in the autumn of 1865 and was welcomed enthusiastically by the Indian inhabitants.

But Maximilian was too angry to be able to enjoy his success. He had worked himself up into another rage against his brother. In November 1864 Franz Joseph addressed the Austrian Parliament, and in reviewing the events of the year he mentioned that Maximilian had become emperor of Mexico after signing a family pact renouncing his rights to the throne of Austria. This was the first time that the family pact had been made public, and Maximilian was furious that Franz Joseph had done this without consulting, or at least informing, him. He drafted a diplomatic note protesting the family pact, and referred to the protestation that he had made on the *Novara,* in which he claimed that his renunciation was void because it had been made under duress and had not been endorsed by the Austrian Reichsrat. He instructed his minister in Vienna to present the note to Rechberg, and he sent copies to the pope and to the governments of France, Britain, and Belgium. He published a statement in the semiofficial Mexican newspaper *L'Ere Nouvelle,* stating that his renunciation of his rights in Austria was invalid. *L'Ere Nouvelle* also published an anonymous letter in its correspondence columns that denounced the tyrannical rule of the Austrian government in Venetia.

This caused a diplomatic crisis. Rechberg unofficially told the Mexican minister in Vienna that if Maximilian's note was presented to him officially, Austria would break off diplomatic relations with Mexico. Napoleon III was annoyed when a copy of the note was officially presented to Drouyn de Lhuys, and told Metternich that he would not become involved in this absurd family feud. The Austrian minister in Mexico warned Maximilian that Franz Joseph was considering revoking his promise to Maximilian that he would care for him and Charlotte if they were expelled from Mexico, and that he might not permit recruitment in Austria for volunteers to serve in Mexico.

The Mexican minister in Vienna decided on his own initiative not to present Maximilian's note officially to Rechberg, and after some months the matter blew over. The incident did Maximilian no good in Mexico, for the people drew the conclusion that if he was so concerned with his rights in Austria, he must be expecting to be thrown out of Mexico or to return to Austria for some other reason.

Although he had no immediate plans to return to Austria, he still yearned for Miramar. Construction was continuing there in his absence. Maximilian had drawn up the plans for converting the bungalow into a two-story house before he left Miramar, and he wrote regularly to the man in charge of the work to ask how it was progressing, and to give new instructions.

He requested that the artist Karl Hase paint a mural around three sides of the new reception hall on the second floor. On the first wall there was to be a picture of the beginning, the ruins of the eleventh-century Happisburg Castle on the River Aar in Switzerland, where the Habsburg family originated and from which it acquired its name. The second wall would depict the midday glory, the Hofburg in Vienna. The mural on the third wall was to be the final destination, the palace of Chapultepec. Hase painted the mural just as Maximilian had ordered, but the emperor never saw it, for his final destination was to be not Chapultepec but Querétaro.

❊ 18 ❊

VICTORY OR DEFEAT?

MAXIMILIAN AND NAPOLEON III had won, or so it seemed. Mexico, like France, had a Second Empire to follow the First Empire that Iturbide had briefly established in 1822; the journalists and public speakers foretold that although the First Mexican Empire had ended with the emperor facing a firing squad, the Second Empire would survive, with the good will of France and Europe, to confound the United States and destroy the Monroe Doctrine. Bazaine welcomed the triumph of "all the friends of the intervention, all those who see with satisfaction that order has replaced anarchy. They have succeeded."

Maximilian's government had established its authority over all except four of Mexico's twenty-four states and territories, which were now called the provinces of the empire. Only Guerrero, Chihuahua, Sonora, and Baja California, which together had only 7 percent of the country's 8,000,000 inhabitants, had not been occupied by the Franco-Mexican army. In the south the liberal General Alvarez still held out at Acapulco and elsewhere in Guerrero along the Pacific coast. The French and imperial armies had not yet entered the three provinces of the northwest, although Juárez had hardly any regular forces there.

But two men did not believe that the French and Maximilian had won, or would ever win. One was Juárez and the other was Napoleon III. Juárez, in the face of one defeat after another, continued steadfastly to be sure of final victory; Napoleon, whose journalists proclaimed that the Mexican expedition was the greatest glory of his reign, had for eighteen months been telling his acquaintances in private that he had got into a mess in Mexico and wanted to get out of it as soon as possible.

The provinces of Chihuahua and Baja California were hardly worth invading, but Sonora was another matter. William M. Gwin, formerly a United States senator from Mississippi, had been trying for some time to interest Napoleon III in Sonora. After being arrested at the start of the Civil War on suspicion of being a Confederate sympathizer, Gwin was released and allowed to go to Europe. Arriving in Paris at the time when French troops were first sent to Mexico, he told Napoleon III and his ministers that Sonora was rich in silver and platinum mines, and he suggested that the French should reward themselves for their services in liberating Mexico from liberal tyranny by annexing Sonora and developing its riches with the aid of a company that Gwin and his friends would form for the purpose.

By 1864 Gwin had sadly reached the conclusion that the North would win the American Civil War, and this made him more determined to involve France in his schemes for Sonora. He hoped that the defeated Southern slaveholders might emigrate to Sonora with their slaves, who would provide the labor for developing the mines. He warned Napoleon that if France did not annex Sonora, the United States would do so when the war was over, for Maximilian's Mexican army would be unable to prevent them. But the United States would not dare to invade Sonora if it was a colony of France and the French army was there.

Napoleon was interested in Gwin's proposals, but there were difficulties. When Maximilian was proclaimed emperor of Mexico at Miramar, he took an oath that he would not cede any part of the national territory, and he was determined to keep his oath and not cede Sonora to France. Napoleon also thought that annexing Sonora might lead him into a war with the United States, which he was very eager to avoid. He had been told that there was a shortage of water in Sonora and that it would be difficult to keep an army there; and holding Sonora would in any case involve retaining many soldiers in Mexico, and he knew that public opinion in France wanted the troops brought home as soon as possible.

He decided that he would send an army into Sonora if only to capture the port of Guaymas on the Gulf of California. This would prevent Juárez, at Chihuahua, from using the port to receive smuggled arms from San Francisco or to communicate with his supporters at Acapulco; it would enable Napoleon to claim that another province had come under Maximilian's control. French experts could follow the army and study what would be involved in developing the province. An army duly invaded Sonora and captured Guaymas without encountering any serious resistance.

This certainly had the desired effect of interrupting Juárez's communications. Any illegal shipments of arms from San Francisco now had to be landed on deserted beaches, and postal communications became much more difficult. When Juárez in Chihuahua wrote to Romero in Washington, the letters had to be carried along the rough tracks through the sand of the northern desert to the little town of El Paso del Norte (today the city of Ciudad Juárez), across the Rio Grande to the village of Franklin (now the city of El Paso) in Texas and from there, passing to the west of Confederate territory, to Santa Fe and then by way of Kansas City to Washington. The letters usually arrived in six weeks, but sometimes took nearly three months. After the French captured Guaymas, Juárez had to use this route to communicate with Almonte in Guerrero and Porfirio Díaz in Oaxaca; from Washington the letters were taken by sea to Colón and, after crossing the isthmus to Panama, by sea to Acapulco. When Juárez heard that Díaz had escaped from Puebla and was leading the guerrillas in Oaxaca, he wrote to him from Chihuahua on November 12, 1865, reappointing him as commander-in-chief of the armies of the republic in the area; Díaz did not receive the letter till February 2, 1866.

The difficult communications at Chihuahua did not interfere with Juárez's supply of champagne or the excellent cigars that were sent to him and Lerdo from New York. On National Day, September 16, on the anniversary of the victory at Puebla on May 5, and on his birthday, March 21, Juárez attended banquets at which many bottles of champagne were opened and drunk before the guests settled down to listen to their leader's patriotic speeches. He was criticized at the time by the radicals in his party, and by the small groups of socialists in Mexico, for feasting in this way while his guerrillas were risking their lives and undergoing such hardships in Tamaulipas and Michoacán; in the twentieth century Marxist writers have repeated these criticisms. They have also labeled Juárez as a representative of the middle-class bourgeoisie in its struggle against the Catholic Church, the feudal landowners, and the dictatorship of Napoleon III. They point out that he failed to abolish the *leva* of the press gangs and the peonage that compelled the peasants to perform forced labor until they had paid off their debts to their landlords, which in practice meant permanent serfdom. During Juárez's lifetime, Marx and Engels were less critical of him.

The experts' report on Sonora convinced Napoleon that it would not be worth his while to annex it. On March 31, 1865, he wrote to Bazaine that he was sending Gwin from Paris to Mexico City to put his propositions about Sonora to Maximilian. Napoleon would leave it to Maximilian to take any steps about developing Sonora.

But Napoleon's propagandists could use the invasion of Sonora as new proof that the invincible French army was the best in the world. In April 1865 Favre and the opposition again raised the question of Mexico in the Corps Législatif. Rouher, as minister of state, defended the government's policy in Mexico so enthusiastically and eloquently that no one would have guessed that he had always opposed it in the secrecy of Cabinet meetings. He won great applause from the majority of the deputies when he described how our gallant soldiers, whom the opposition had denigrated, had advanced victoriously over immense distances in Mexico. "We have been to Acapulco, to Tepic, to San Blas, to Michoacán; perhaps we are already on the way to Guaymas" to plant there the victorious French flag, and the flag of the Mexican Empire which our soldiers carry. Rouher did not mention that they had since left Acapulco because of its unhealthful climate and that the liberals had recaptured the town and the port.

Favre asked why, if victory had been achieved in Mexico, the troops were not brought home. This was the question people were asking all over France. The reports of the *procureurs* from Caen, Lyons, Rouen, and Colmar all said the same: the war in Mexico was unpopular, and the people wanted their sons brought home soon. Rouher said that they would be brought home very soon, but the precise moment would be determined not by Juárez or by the disloyal opposition at home but by Emperor Napoleon III. Let our flag float in Mexico for a few months more in order to crush the last resistance and the final remnants of the revolutionary debris! Rouher obtained a majority for the government of 225 votes to 16.

The remnants of the revolutionary debris were far from destroyed. The situation seemed to have improved in the vicinity of Veracruz and Orizaba, where in July 1863 there were fewer incidents than at any time in the previous two years. The French had begun to congratulate themselves that Du Pin's force had killed all the guerrillas, when suddenly guerrilla activity in the neighboring province of Tamaulipas increased, and they realized that the "dissidents" and "bandits" of Veracruz had merely moved north. So in March 1864 Du Pin and the *contre-guérilla* were ordered to leave their base at Camerone and go to Victoria in Tamaulipas.

The French held the ports of Tuxpán and Tampico, and after capturing Matamoros they were in possession of all the ports in Tamaulipas; but the guerrillas swarmed all around, cutting off the garrison's food supplies, ambushing small groups of French soldiers who ventured out into the countryside, and sometimes raiding the ports and attacking the garrison, or sending agents to murder French soldiers in the streets. The French garrison in Tampico, having suffered many deaths from *vómito,* was temporarily withdrawn and evacuated by sea to Veracruz. The guerrillas then captured Tampico and held it for a few weeks until the French returned and took it. The guerrillas remained in Tampico long enough to arrest the local government officials who had held office under the French, try them by court-martial under the decree of January 25, and hang them in the town square.

The guerrillas in Tamaulipas produced a number of formidable leaders — José Maria Carbajal, Servando Canales, and Pedro Mendez. Carbajal, an Indian, was already an old man in 1864. He had not always been a high-principled liberal. According to some reports, in his younger days, before the American Civil War, he had been employed by the slaveholders of Texas to catch runaway slaves who escaped across the Rio Grande into Mexico. Carbajal and his men, in defiance of Mexican law, hunted down the slaves in Tamaulipas and restored them to their American masters for the whippings and other punishments that awaited them. But whatever Carbajal may have done in 1855, he was an invaluable asset to Juárez in 1864. Liberal intellectuals like Zarco and Iglesias could write stirring propaganda articles, and Romero was the man to handle the intricate diplomatic negotiations in Washington; but Carbajal was the guerrilla chief whom the liberals needed in Tamaulipas. Juárez allowed him a free hand, and Carbajal was loyal to Juárez.

In April 1864 Du Pin led the *contre-guérilla* from Tampico in a surprise attack on Carbajal, and a battle was fought at San Antonio, near the village of Soto la Marina. According to Kératry, the *contre-guérilla* had only 285 men against Carbajal's 1,200, but they defeated the guerrillas after a fierce fight in which the *contre-guérilla* lost eleven men killed and thirty-two wounded. Six of their ten officers were seriously wounded, including Du Pin's second-in-command, who was shot by Carbajal himself. Fifteen guerrillas were killed, including three United States citizens who had joined the liberal forces in Mexico and served as captains under Carbajal, and one French deserter who had been given the rank of major by Juárez.

Carbajal had two horses killed under him and received a painful wound, but he managed to escape and hid in a marsh all night with his wound unattended. Next day, after the *contre-guérilla* had left, he came out of the marsh and rode to Soto la Marina.

A few days later the *contre-guérilla* entered Soto la Marina, where they were welcomed by a prominent Mexican gentleman, Don Martin de Leon, the United States consul there. Leon invited Du Pin and his officers to an excellent dinner in his house. He told them he was Carbajal's cousin but had no sympathy with his political views. He said that he had met Carbajal in Soto la Marina the previous day, that Carbajal had told him how he had escaped after the battle at San Antonio by hiding in the marsh, and that Carbajal, having received medical attention for his wound, had then ridden off in the direction of Monterrey. This was a cool piece of double-bluff, for while Leon was telling this to Du Pin at dinner, Carbajal was hiding in a hut on his ranch a few miles away. The consul said goodbye to his guests and then went to the hut in the middle of the night, told Carbajal that the *contre-guérilla* had gone, and gave him a horse. Carbajal rode away to rejoin his men in the countryside.

The *contre-guérilla* were more successful a few months later, farther north at San Fernando. After the French had captured Matamoros and deprived the liberals of their last port on the Gulf of Mexico, the gunrunners from the United States had to land their cargoes on the deserted beaches near Soto la Marina and San Fernando. When the *contre-guérilla* entered San Fernando they encountered silent hostility from nearly everyone, but one of the inhabitants was prepared to talk when he was sure that none of his fellow townsmen were watching him. He told the *contre-guérilla* that Carbajal had been in San Fernando two days before and that he had seen Carbajal's men coming and going from a barn at the top of a cliff overlooking the sea not far from the town. The *contre-guérilla* went there and found 400 tons of gunpowder and 4,000 bullets and shells, all with markings that showed they had been made in the United States. The *contre-guérilla* could not move all these supplies, so they rolled them over the cliff and into the sea.

There was trouble all along the coast, from San Fernando in the north to Papantla in the mountains in the south, and inland around Victoria. The French had appointed a Council of Notables at Victoria to help the mayor govern the town. The guerrillas sent a warning from Soto la Marina that if any of the notables attended the inaugural meeting of the council he would be executed under the decree of January 25; but Du Pin forced the notables to go to the meeting protected by his men. Two French soldiers in Victoria were lured into a house by three local inhabitants, who killed them with revolvers and machetes. Du Pin had the murderers shot in the square after rounding up all their relations and forcing them to watch, and burned the house to the ground.

As Du Pin led his men back to Soto la Marina, he passed through the old Spanish town of Croy, which he knew was a center of guerrilla activity under a local chief, Ingenio Abalos. The guerrillas had left before the *contre-guérilla* arrived, but the mayor of Croy told Du Pin that a local beauty named Pepita was Abalos's mistress, and that he believed Abalos was planning to ambush the *contre-guérilla* as they left for Soto la Marina. Du Pin went to Pepita's house and asked her to reveal what she knew about the ambush. She refused to answer any of his questions.

Du Pin took out his watch and laid it on the table beside a strong piece of cord. He told Pepita that if she did not tell him all she knew within five minutes he would hang her from the beam in the room. She did not reply. As the minutes slowly passed, Du Pin saw her looking toward the door and thought that she might be planning to make a rush for it and escape; he drew his revolver and told his officers to do the same, and they all pointed their revolvers at Pepita. A look of fear came into her eyes for the first time, but she still said nothing. Then Du Pin announced that the five minutes were up, and he ordered his men to put the rope around her neck and hang her from the beam. When she felt the rope she broke down and confessed everything. An ambush had been planned, and she told them where it would be.

The *contre-guérilla* took her with them. They made her walk a yard or two ahead, with two of them immediately behind her, their revolvers pointed at her back. When they reached the place where Abalos's men were waiting, the guerrillas saw their leader's mistress and did not dare open fire. The *contre-guérilla* reached Soto la Marina safely and let Pepita go.

Pedro Mendez was as formidable an enemy as Carbajal. He was unique among the liberal guerrilla leaders in that he wore eyeglasses. He was tall for a Mexican and had the very small feet that his fellow countrymen admired. On the march and in battle he always wore a black vest, white breeches, boots with elaborately decorated spurs, a revolver strapped to his waist, a large sombrero, and green spectacles. According to the French, he was the most cruel of all the guerrilla leaders; no Mexican was willing to act as a guide or a carrier for the French in a district where Mendez was known to be operating. He drafted stirring propaganda leaflets denouncing the French and threatening collaborators, always ending with the liberal slogan "Liberty and Independence!" He distributed the leaflets in the path of the *contre-guérilla*.

At the end of November 1864 Mendez was operating near Victoria, and Du Pin set out to find and destroy him. The *contre-guérilla* discovered where he was, but they always arrived too late to catch him. Once they saw him sitting on his horse at the top of a hill, but he was out of range and had gone before the *contre-guérilla* got there.

As the *contre-guérilla* advanced, they found the corpses of collaborators and of a few French soldiers hanging from trees. At one point they came upon a newly dug grave in the middle of the road. On it was a cross to which a notice was attached: "Death to the French murderers!" One of the *contre-guérilla* indignantly tore down the cross and the notice. As he touched it, a bomb exploded, killing him, and as his startled comrades ran for cover, Mendez's men opened fire on them from their hiding place beside the road.

The inhabitants of Tampico were either sympathetic to the guerrillas or frightened of them, for they had not forgotten the collaborators who had been hanged in the town square. Du Pin thought that he should restore the morale of Maximilian's supporters, and terrify Juárez's, by showing that he could emulate the guerrillas. Risking the *vómito,* which had scared off other French regiments, he established the *contre-guérilla* headquarters in Tampico and made raids on the guerrillas in the neighboring villages. When he captured guerrillas, he did not hang them on the spot, but brought them back to Tampico with their hands bound and ropes around their necks. He took them to the town square in the early evening, when it was usually crowded with people, and hanged them from the trees in the square. He left their bodies hanging there all night, their faces to the sea, and took them down the next day.

After the execution, the people quickly left the square, and all the occupants of the houses in the square kept their windows closed, although it was a very hot summer night. The café in the square remained open. The owner said he hoped that the sight of the corpses of the bandits would not stop his customers from coming to his café as usual and spending an enjoyable evening eating and drinking on the sidewalk in front of the café. Afterward Kératry discovered that the owner of the café was an agent of the guerrillas who supplied them with information about the movements of the *contre-guérilla.*

Some of the respectable citizens of Tampico, especially the moderate liberals on whose support Maximilian was relying, were shocked at Du Pin's methods. They complained to the government in Mexico City, and Maximilian told Bazaine, who agreed that Du Pin's methods were irregular. Bazaine ordered Du Pin to comply with regulations and try suspected guerrillas before a court-martial, but this did not satisfy Maximilian (Charlotte much disliked Du Pin). Maximilian insisted that Du Pin be removed from his command and sent back to

France. Bazaine at first demurred, but when Maximilian insisted he reluctantly sent Du Pin home.

The officers and men of the *contre-guérilla* were angry. They were devoted to their leader, and his dismissal lowered their morale, for they thought it meant that Maximilian and Bazaine would henceforth be soft with the guerrillas, just when Du Pin's methods seemed to be achieving good results. Napoleon III sent them a good replacement, Colonel Galliffet to lead the *contre-guérilla*. Galliffet had become Napoleon's aide-de-camp, and he enjoyed court life, taking part in amateur theatricals at Compiègne, pursuing Eugénie's ladies, and marrying the most beautiful of them, Mademoiselle Lafitte. But he wanted to go back to Mexico; he told Napoleon that he had some scores to settle with the Mexicans who had wounded him at Puebla.

The *contre-guérilla* soon discovered that Galliffet was as tough as Du Pin, and the Mexicans, seeing the savagery of the blue-uniformed *contre-guérilla*, called them the "blue butchers." Many years later Galliffet was reproached for his ruthless suppression in 1871 of the Paris Communards, whom he had shot as happily as he had killed the Arab rebels in Algeria. He replied that he had far less compunction about shooting the Communards, because the Arabs at least believed in a God, even though it was not the true Christian God, whereas the Communards were godless atheists. He showed as much zeal in dealing with the godless liberal guerrillas in Mexico as he later showed in Paris.

In the autumn of 1865 Du Pin went to Biarritz and spoke to Napoleon III, who was so impressed by Du Pin's outspoken manner and by his achievements with the *contre-guérilla* that he sent him back to Mexico. But he did not reappoint him to his old command. Du Pin was given a desk job in Veracruz. He always denied the accusations of cruelty that had been made against him. He said he had been very merciful toward the guerrillas, for he always hanged them by the neck until they were dead, whereas the guerrillas, when they captured one of Du Pin's men, usually hanged him from a tree by his feet, facing the sun, and left him there until he died of thirst.

❊ 19 ❊

THE HUNT FOR ROMERO

MAXIMILIAN COULD NOT UNDERSTAND why the guerrillas had not been crushed. Charlotte wrote about her anxieties to Eugénie, who told her not to worry. Eugénie thought it would never be possible to stamp out the last traces of banditry in Mexico, and she believed that the dissidents did not pose a threat to the stability of the empire. But Maximilian was exasperated that they were so active, not only in distant Tamaulipas but in Michoacán, less than a hundred miles from the capital. Michoacán was an ideal theater for guerrilla operations. Dark forests covered the high mountainsides nearly all the way to the valleys; the mountaintops were often covered in thick mists; and during the summer rainy season, the torrential downpours every afternoon and the swollen rivers sometimes made the rough tracks in the valleys impassable to soldiers on the march. It was as easy for the liberal guerrillas in Michoacán to hold out against Maximilian's government as it had been for Márquez and his conservative guerrillas to avoid capture by Juárez's armies in 1861.

The leader of the Michoacán guerrillas was the almost legendary Nicolás Romero. The French, and Maximilian's followers, called all the guerrilla leaders "bandits," but they were not far wrong in Romero's case. Romero, unlike Chávez, Ghilardi, and Díaz, had never been a prominent politician or general in Juárez's regular army. He had emerged in 1863 as the leader of a band that attacked and robbed the French and Mexican collaborators within a hundred-mile radius of Mexico City, in Michoacán to the northwest, in Guerrero to the southwest, and near Texcoco and Tlaxcala to the northeast. He was able to justify his robberies as acts of patriotism and revolutionary zeal against the foreign invader, the reactionary oppressors, and the wealthy classes. He was regarded by many of the people as a heroic Robin Hood figure, a champion of the poor against the rich.

Romero was particularly popular among the lower classes in Mexico City, and also with middle-class liberals. The people organized secret collections of money for him. They stole arms from the government stores and sent them to him; in April 1864 30,000 rounds of small-arms ammunition were smuggled out of the city across Lake Texcoco and taken by a semicircular route south to Zumpango, where Romero collected them. Young men left their homes in Mexico City to join his band, and though their mothers were sad to see their sons incurring such danger, many women were fascinated by Romero, and hoped and prayed for his success.

Bazaine sent an army of French, Mexican, and Belgian units under the Mexican General Lamadrid to catch Romero. The Belgian and Austrian volunteers, on whom Maximilian and Napoleon III were relying to take over from the French army, were arriving. Four hundred Belgians reached Mexico City on December 14, 1864, and more arrived during the next six months. In all they numbered 1,543 officers and men under the command of Baron van der Smissen. The first of the 7,000 Austrians under Count Thun landed at Veracruz on January 22, 1865. They came from all parts of the Austro-Hungarian Empire, and included Italians, Poles, and Croats as well as Austrians.

Some of the Austrians formed their own *contre-guérilla* units independent of the French *contre-guérilla*. In April 1865 a company of the Austrian *contre-guérilla* under the command of Captain Czapek was attacked by a large force of guerrillas at Tetela, some seventy miles north of Puebla. "Our enemies fought us as if we were not men but wild beasts," wrote the captain. Seeing that they were surrounded and outnumbered, he surrendered after a long fight. The guerrillas took the prisoners into a nearby church and began killing them; but some of the guerrillas wished to spare their lives, and soon their commander arrived and stopped the killing. "The Austrians never shoot their prisoners," he said, "and nor will I, for I think that the Austrians will pay money to ransom the prisoners." Czapek was exchanged a few months later for some guerrillas that the Austrians had captured.

Another Austrian officer, Count Kurtzroch, was less fortunate. His company was attacked near Guadalajara by Antonio Perez's guerrilla band. The Austrians were driven into a church, where they defended themselves until the guerrillas set fire to the church, which forced them to surrender. Kurtzroch had been badly wounded in the legs and was unable to walk, so his comrades carried him out of the church on a stretcher. Perez was waiting outside the church. As the stretcher bearers carrying Kurtzroch passed him he drew his revolver, placed it on the forehead of the wounded man, and shot him dead.

The Belgian volunteers had come out of devotion to their Princess Charlotte after Maximilian had asked King Leopold to send them "for the special protection of the Empress, their fellow countrywoman." They called themselves the Chasseurs de l'Impératrice and went into action shouting, "Long live the Empress!"

The Belgian liberals objected to the volunteers' going to Mexico. A prominent liberal barrister and politician, L. van der Kerkhove, presented a petition to the Court of Appeal in Brussels in January 1865, in which he argued that the volunteers were violating the Belgian law against foreign enlistment and the constitutional principle of Belgian neutrality. A conservative barrister, J. B. Bonnevie, argued against Kerkhove, saying that it was perfectly lawful for Belgians to volunteer to serve in a foreign army provided that they had the consent of the king of the Belgians and that they were not fighting an established government. It was illegal for Belgians to volunteer to fight for Garibaldi against the king of Naples or the pope or to serve on either side in the American Civil War; but it was lawful for them to fight for Maximilian in Mexico, with King Leopold's consent, against a band of rebels who could not be considered to be a government, even if they were recognized by the United States, because they did not have a regular disciplined army.

In addition to his cold, legalistic logic, Bonnevie indulged in an emotional appeal, and asked Kerkhove and the judges not to insult brave men who were ready to risk their lives in defense of a Belgian princess. The court accepted Bonnevie's arguments, and king, legislature, and judiciary supported the enlistment of the volunteers. So the Neutrality Acts were enforced in the United States against Juárez and waived in Belgium in favor of Maximilian.

After going to Mexico City to salute the emperor and empress, who entertained their higher officers at dinners and receptions, the Belgian and Austrian legions set off to join Bazaine's army at the siege of Oaxaca; but before they got there they heard that Oaxaca had surrendered. They were then sent to Michoacán to help in the hunt for Romero.

When the Austrian and Belgian legions were operating on their own, they usually showed more restraint and humanity than their French and Mexican colleagues; when they served under Lamadrid, they were often shocked by their allies' ruthlessness. Lamadrid's men sometimes shot their prisoners and sometimes hanged them. They preferred to hang them because they thought that Mexicans considered shooting to be an honorable form of death, which was therefore no deterrent; but they believed that Mexicans feared the ignominy of hanging, though they continued to be amazed at their victims' stoical silence and resignation in the face of death. A man who was about to be hanged usually said nothing except to ask for one last cigarette. If he was pardoned and freed at the last moment, he was equally silent, walking away without a word.

Sometimes the prisoners were flogged in accordance with Napoleon III's directive. One man who was said to be a robber received sixty lashes with a cat-o'-nine-tails on his bare back and was then set free. He, too, walked off in silence. Some prisoners were not punished and were invited to join the Franco-Mexican army and fight against their former comrades. Many gladly agreed to do so.

Charles Mismer, an officer from Alsace serving in the French army, attended the court-martial of two Mexicans who were accused of entering the house of a married couple, dressed in soldiers' uniforms which they had stolen, and robbing them. The regulations were complied with; three officers sat as judges, there was an interpreter, and an officer who was a lawyer acted as advocate for the defense; but Mismer thought that the defense attorney handled the case rather badly, and that the interpreter sometimes translated statements incorrectly. He was not at all sure that the defendants really understood what was going on. When the president of the court told them they had been found guilty and were condemned to death, and would be executed within twenty-four hours, they replied, "*Este buen, Señor*" (Very good, sir).

The evening before the execution Mismer went to see the presiding officer and said he had doubts about the fairness of the trial. The officer laughed and told him not to worry. "Every Mexican," he said, "either is a guerrilla or has been one or will be one, so it can do no harm if we shoot those we catch."

But where was Romero? One day he was in Zumpango in Guerrero, but soon afterward he was attacking the town of Ixmiquilpan, north of Mexico City. Then he was in Michoacán, raiding Uruapan, Pátzcuaro, Zitácuaro, Maravatío, or Morelia. One day an informer came to Lamadrid and told him that a band of guerrillas was bivouacked around a cottage in a wood near Zitácuaro. Lamadrid sent a troop of cavalry to destroy them. Neither the informer nor Lamadrid realized that Romero himself was with the guerrillas in the wood, but the trumpeter of the cavalry troop was a Mexican who had once served as a guerrilla in one of Romero's bands and knew him by sight. The cavalry moved quickly and quietly and attacked the guerrillas before they could resist. Some of the guerrillas were killed, twenty were captured, and the rest, including Romero, escaped. But Romero could not find a horse and, knowing that the enemy were hard on his heels, he climbed a tree near the cottage and hid in the branches.

Lamadrid's men hanged the guerrillas they had captured, then settled down to enjoy a picnic lunch in the garden, very near the tree in which Romero was hiding. After a while the trumpeter spotted a cock who was strutting around the garden. He tried to catch the cock, which flew up into the tree where Romero was hiding. The trumpeter, determined to have that cock for his dinner, climbed the tree after it. He saw Romero and came down from the tree with a bigger prize than the cock.

They would probably have hanged their new prisoner at once if the trumpeter had not told the troop commander who he was. The commander was not going to hang Romero out of sight in a wood; he would take him back alive to Mexico City to show his superior officers, his comrades, his girlfriends, and the journalists what he had captured. They found Romero's mule, mounted him on it with his feet tied underneath, and sent him to Mexico City with an escort under the command of Captain Altwies of the Belgian Legion. When they arrived, Lamadrid took the mule as his prize and imprisoned Romero in the Martinica prison, where all the political prisoners were held.

The word spread at once throughout the city that Romero had been captured, and his court-martial was turned into a show trial. The president of the court was the French officer who had told Mismer that all Mexicans either were, had been, or would be guerrillas. Romero was assigned a competent French officer as his advocate; but Romero's friends discovered that a brilliant young Belgian advocate named Leroux, who had already made a reputation at the Brussels bar, was serving as a corporal in the Belgian Legion, and they offered him a fee of $1,000 if he would defend Romero.

Leroux accepted the brief and visited Romero in his cell. He was very impressed with Romero's courage, coolness, and intelligence. Romero told Leroux that he would plead that the court had no jurisdiction to try him because it had not been appointed by President Juárez, who was the only lawful authority in the Mexican Republic. Leroux knew that the president of the court would not allow the defense lawyers to make a political speech; if Romero insisted that he conduct the defense along these lines, he could not usefully accept the brief and the fee. If Romero wished to defy the court on political grounds, he could do it much better himself. So Romero defended himself at the trial, challenged the jurisdiction of the court, and denounced the intervention, the empire, and the Mexican traitors who served it. He was of course found guilty and condemned to death. Thousands of people in Mexico City signed a petition to Maximilian asking him to pardon Romero, but Maximilian refused.

Romero was executed with two of his officers by a firing squad in public in the Plazuela de Mizcalco in the capital on March 20, 1865. The authorities had heard rumors that the crowd would attempt to rescue him, so they placed the whole garrison of the city on the alert and packed the square with soldiers. The volley of the firing squad did not kill Romero outright, so a sergeant went over and finished him off with his revolver. The soldiers of the firing party put Romero's corpse into a coffin and took it away. As they moved off, the flimsy coffin broke. The liberals thought this was symbolic, as if Romero's corpse had moved and shattered the coffin as a last protest. The spectators dispersed in an angry silence.

Five liberal journalists published articles in obscure newspapers in Mexico City denouncing the execution of Romero and criticizing the conduct of his court-martial by the French officers. One of the journalists was a university student aged seventeen, who wrote that the French courts-martial were "sinister specters" in Mexico; the authorities discovered that another had written under a pseudonym and was in fact a government official.

Bazaine ordered the five journalists to be tried by a French court-martial on a charge of insulting the French army. He wrote to Marshal Randon, the minister of war in Paris, that when he first informed Maximilian about the prosecution the emperor was distressed, but he agreed that it was necessary after Bazaine had explained the reasons for it. The government employee was sentenced to a year's imprisonment and a fine of 2,000 francs; another of the journalists received a six-month sentence; two received three months; and the student received one month.

Favre and his colleagues raised the matter in a debate in the Corps Législatif in June. Rouher strongly defended both the execution of Romero and the imprisonment of the journalists. "The Honorable Monsieur Jules Favre has spoken about a trial which has taken place in Mexico and about the behavior of the French army, particularly about the behavior of a brave general, though I do not hesitate to proclaim him to be one of the noblest leaders of this army." The facts were that a man named Romero, whom the gutter press of Mexico City had presented as a martyr for his country and the cause of liberty, had been sentenced to death and executed for murder and robbery. A government deputy interrupted him: "So this is the man for whom the opposition are so solicitous!"

Rouher claimed that in a letter to Porfirio Díaz that had been intercepted, Juárez had written that bandits like Romero disgraced the cause for which the liberals were fighting. "In that case Juárez is a decent man!" cried an opposition deputy. Rouher ignored this interruption. Did Juárez really write this letter? If so, it is not surprising that it was not afterward published by his supporters. Whatever Juárez may have thought of Romero, he would not repudiate him now that thousands of people in Mexico regarded him as a hero and martyr.

Rouher went on to reveal something that caused great indignation on the government benches. He quoted from the reports in the American newspapers of the speeches made at one of the banquets in New York in support of the Mexican liberals. General Doblado had attended the banquet. Someone had proposed a toast: "To the death of Maximilian, tyrant of Mexico; to the death of the pope, tyrant of consciences; to the death of Napoleon III, tyrant of the whole world." This had been followed by a toast to the opposition deputies in the Corps Législatif in Paris "who oppose the emperor's tyranny."

But there was worse to come. Rouher told the deputies that the liberals in Mexico had distributed leaflets to the French army which, under the heading "Juárez and his friend Jules Favre to the French soldiers," called on them "to desert the flag of that tyrant who is called Napoleon III." Rouher ended his speech by calling on his audience to repudiate an opposition that could behave in such a way and to hasten, by their votes, the day when "French troops, not humiliated — how could they be? — but having triumphantly achieved their aim, will arrive amid the applause of the whole of France, to receive the crown of laurels which their courage has deserved." The applause as he sat down lasted for many minutes.

Rouher was right to feel worried about Doblado's visit to the United States in October 1864. As well as attending the banquet in New York, he had gone to Washington, where he had expressed a wish to meet General Grant, whom he much admired. As Doblado could not speak English, Matías Romero went with him as an interpreter. Grant was at the headquarters of the Army of the Potomac at City Point on the James River, only forty miles from the Confederate capital of Richmond. He had fought a war of attrition against Robert E. Lee during the terrible month of May 1864; outnumbering Lee by two to one, he had slowly advanced, despite heavy casualties, and Lee had finally withdrawn to Richmond and Petersburg. Grant was waiting quietly at City Point until his old comrade Sherman finished marching through Georgia and South Carolina and joined Grant in dealing the death blow to the encircled Confederate forces.

Seward gave Doblado and Romero a pass, and they sailed from Washington to City Point, where they met Grant on October 24. He provided them with accommodation in a tent very near his own, which Romero noticed was as simple as the tents of the private soldiers. Mrs. Grant was also in the camp and obviously gave her husband moral support in times of stress.

Grant told Romero and Doblado that he had fought in the war against Mexico and deeply regretted having been forced to play his part in that unjust and aggressive war. He told them how much he had liked Mexico and the Mexicans when he was stationed there after the war, and how strongly he sympathized with the struggle against the tyrannical oppression of Napoleon III and Maximilian. He said that if it had not been for the rebellion in the United States he would himself have raised a corps of volunteers to go to Mexico to fight for Juárez. He believed that as soon as the Confederates were defeated, the United States government should demand that Napoleon III withdraw his armies at once. Romero was greatly encouraged by Grant's attitude, for if the victorious commander-in-chief threw his influence on the side of intervention in Mexico, it would be difficult for Seward to continue after the war his policy of appeasing Napoleon III.

Grant raised the matter of Mexico several times in conversation with Lincoln and Seward, but they did not respond. Lincoln was not very interested in foreign affairs; he never left the United States, he spoke no foreign languages, and he seemed rather ill at ease when he attended receptions for eminent foreigners who were visiting Washington. He was thinking only about winning the Civil War and the problems of Reconstruction; he left foreign policy, including Mexico, to Seward, who seemed as indifferent as ever to the plight of the liberals in Mexico.

In December, Lincoln, having been reelected for a second term, said nothing about Mexico in his message to Congress. A few weeks later he entered into negotiations with Jefferson Davis's government about the possibility of ending the Civil War; but when the Confederates suggested agreeing to a negotiated peace and uniting to drive the French out of Mexico, he insisted on the unconditional surrender of the South and the abolition of slavery. As the world waited for Grant and Sherman to give the Confederacy the knockout blow, the French minister in Washington, Moustier, asked Seward from time to time whether United States policy in regard to Mexico was still the same. On March 17, 1865, Seward assured the French that there had been and would be no change in the United States policy of strict neutrality in Mexico. Baron Wydenbruck, the Austrian minister in Washington, had heard that when someone asked Lincoln about Mexico in a private conversation, he replied, "There will be no more wars while I am president."

Meanwhile the unofficial French representative in Richmond was trying to persuade the Confederate government to grant an export license to a French merchant to ship a large consignment of tobacco from his warehouse in the city to Europe, for Seward, eager as ever to please Napoleon III, had issued a permit for the tobacco to pass through the Union blockade. The French agent was still negotiating with the Confederates when Grant broke through the defenses of Petersburg. The Confederates then decided to set fire to their capital to prevent the munitions and stores in the town from falling into the hands of the Union army. The fire also destroyed the French merchant's warehouse and the tobacco he had hoped to export. The Confederate government did not trouble to apologize. They did not care in the least that French property was destroyed, for they felt that France had betrayed them in order to win United States neutrality in Mexico.

Maximilian and the French were in control of nearly the whole of Mexico. They had captured and executed Nicolás Romero in Michoacán and killed Pedro Mendez in Tamaulipas. But two months after Porfirio Díaz capitulated to Bazaine at Oaxaca, Lee capitulated to Grant at Appomattox. The news caused consternation in Mexico City and Paris.

❧ 20 ❧

WILL THE AMERICANS INVADE?

WHENEVER SARA YORKE went to a ball or a party in Mexico City, or met her friends in the foyer of a theater or the opera house, there was one overriding topic of conversation in May 1865. Has the American army crossed the Rio Grande? Are they marching on Mexico City? Will the French be able to stop them? When will they come? What will happen to us all if they come and bring Juárez with them?

The same questions were being asked in Paris. Lord Malmesbury, having left the Foreign Office and serving only as the opposition spokesman on foreign affairs in the House of Lords, had more time to travel. He went to Paris in May 1865 to see the preparations being made for the Great Exhibition, to be held in two years' time. Napoleon III was visiting Algeria, and Eugénie was acting as regent in his absence, which increased the general feeling of unease. On May 12 Malmesbury wrote in his diary: "News from Mexico is very alarming for the French, and produces great consternation in Paris, where the Emperor's return from Algiers is anxiously looked for." People believed that with the American Civil War over, many soldiers discharged from the United States army would "join Juarez, who will thus be more than a match for Maximilian with his French and Belgian allies."

The news of Lee's surrender on April 9 had reached Paris on April 24. Three days later it was known that Lincoln had been assassinated on April 14. A small group of Confederate sympathizers in Washington had planned to kill Lincoln and Grant when they attended a gala performance to celebrate the victory at Ford's Theater. At the last moment Grant had asked to be excused; he wanted to go home to Illinois for the first time since the end of the war. A few days earlier Seward had been thrown from his carriage when his horses bolted; he had suffered concussion and a broken arm and jaw and was confined to his bed.

At 10 P.M. John Wilkes Booth entered Lincoln's box at the theater and shot him. At exactly the same time a former Confederate soldier, Lewis Paine, went to Seward's house, bullied Seward's black servant into admitting him to Seward's bedroom, and stabbed the injured man in his bed before seriously wounding two of Seward's sons and three of his attendants and escaping from the house.

The assassination of the president caused great indignation throughout the world. Eugénie, in Napoleon's absence, sent a message of condolence to Mrs. Lincoln and the United States government. Maximilian seized the opportunity to write to the new president, Andrew Johnson, to express his sympathy and his desire to have friendly relations with the United States. Johnson did not reply, so Maximilian tried again, explaining that personal pride would not prevent him from acting in the interests of his empire and taking the initiative to improve relations between Mexico and the United States. Again Johnson did not reply, and he likewise ignored a third letter from Maximilian to "my great and good friend" the president of the United States.

Lincoln's death was an additional cause of worry to Napoleon III. Seward had assured him that Lincoln's policy of neutrality in Mexico would continue, but no one could be sure what his successor would do. Johnson was a stump orator from Tennessee whom Lincoln had chosen as his running mate in order to win the votes of the slaveholders of Tennessee who had remained loyal to the Union. During the presidential election campaign Johnson had indulged in some rabble-rousing phrases about Mexico. "You can get up no monarchy on this continent," he had told the cheering crowds. "An expedition into Mexico would be a sort of recreation to the brave soldiers of the Union, and the French concern will quickly be wiped out." Seward hoped that Johnson's speeches would not be reported in the French press or brought to the notice of the French minister in Washington.

People said that Johnson drank too much. John Slidell thought that after Lee's surrender the only hope for the South was that Andy Johnson, in one of his drunken outbursts, would insult Grant and that Grant and his supporters would then start another civil war in the North.

But the French soon discovered that there was nothing to fear from the new president of the United States. Johnson was undiplomatic, and something of a Yankee imperialist of the Manifest Destiny era, but he was certainly not a radical and had no more sympathy for

Mexico than he had for the blacks, the Abolitionists, or the radicals in Congress and in the Republican Party, who soon came into conflict with him.

Seward rapidly recovered from his wounds, and not long after his assailant, along with several of the other surviving conspirators, was sentenced to death by a military court, he was back at his desk in the State Department. On June 3, 1865, he sent another note to the French government in which he again assured them that there would be no change in United States policy with regard to Mexico.

Maximilian's supporters in Mexico City and in Paris felt a little happier. The panic of April and May subsided somewhat. They felt once again that Napoleon III had won and that Juárez had finally been defeated. This view was at last gaining ground in England. On July 17 Palmerston wrote to Maximilian "of the interest that all of us in this country take in the success of the great task which Your Majesty has undertaken, a success which would be beneficial for all Europe and would ensure the happiness of Mexico." He added that he believed the United States would be too busy recovering from its Civil War to disturb Maximilian before he had safely established his empire.

The Times of London, which had always supported the French intervention in Mexico, forgetting the battle of May 5 and the long defense of Puebla, had reverted to its original view of the weakness of the degenerate Mexican army. They thought that "the ease with which small bodies of the French defeat Mexican troops ten or even twenty times their number shows how complete is the demoralization among the followers of Juarez."

Juárez's guiding star, the Liberal Party's great Constitution of the republic of 1857, was becoming inconvenient. It laid down that the president of the republic should be elected by the people (by a complicated process of indirect election through an electoral college) every four years and should begin his term of office on December 1 following his election. The chief justice of the Supreme Court would be elected at the same time; if, at any time during his term of office, the president was unable to fulfill his duties, the chief justice was to act as president; and if, at the end of the president's term, it was impossible for any reason to hold a presidential election, the chief justice was to act as president until an election could be held.

According to these provisions of the Constitution, a presidential election should have been held at the end of 1860 and the new president should have begun his term of office on December 1, 1860; but on that date the War of the Reform was still in progress. Juárez, who had been elected chief justice in 1857, was acting as president, as he continued to do until the election was held in June 1861. At that time Juárez was elected president and General Ortega chief justice. Juárez took office on June 15, 1861.

On November 30, 1864, Ortega wrote to Foreign Minister Lerdo and asked when Juárez's term of office as president would end, on December 1, 1864, or December 1, 1865? Juárez and Lerdo immediately realized the significance of the question: Ortega was going to claim that when Juárez's term of office expired, it would be impossible to hold a presidential election with the foreign invader occupying most of the republic, and that Ortega, as chief justice, would become president until it was possible to hold the election.

Juárez knew he faced a dangerous challenge from Ortega, who not only had a case that was almost unanswerable in law, but was also the victorious general who had captured Mexico City and won the War of the Reform, who had scattered Márquez's guerrillas in Michoacán after two other commanders had been defeated and killed there, and who had heroically defended Puebla for two months against the greatest army in the world. But Juárez had no intention of making way for Ortega. Apart from the basic instinct of any strong leader to wish to hang on to power, he had good reason to think that he was the better leader of the national resistance to the invader and his puppet emperor. Ortega had shown at least a slight disposition to negotiate with Forey; and though some people might despise Juárez for being an Indian or a poor horseman, for having no military training, and for carrying prudence to a length that could sometimes be mistaken for cowardice, he was utterly resolved to carry on the struggle at all costs and never to submit to Napoleon or Maximilian. He had the knack of holding together his team of ambitious liberal politicians, argumentative journalists, jealous generals, and guerrilla leaders in the depths of the countryside.

Juárez and Lerdo dealt easily with the immediate problem. Lerdo coolly informed Ortega that the Constitution provided that the president's term of office should end on December 1 in the fourth year after his election, which would be December 1, 1865. But they knew that this only postponed the clash with Ortega, and Juárez wrote bitterly to his son-in-law Pedro Santacilia in the United States that Ortega was obviously intending to cause trouble and that he was determined to prevent him from doing so.

Ortega accepted Lerdo's interpretation of the Constitution and made no attempt to question Juárez's position as president for the time being. But he felt that he was doing nothing useful in Chihuahua, and on December 28, 1864, he asked Juárez's permission to go to the United States to raise a force of American volunteers to fight against the French. Juárez saw his opportunity to get rid of Ortega. He granted the request, and in January 1865 Ortega left for the United States, arriving in New York at the end of May.

Ortega found that he had to conduct his recruiting campaign in the United States without any help from Romero, who on Juárez's instructions refused to give him money or the authority to act on behalf of the Mexican republic. Juárez had told Romero that he did not trust Ortega to use the forces or money he might raise for the cause of Mexican independence. While Ortega was in New York, Colonel Allen of the United States Army brought a charge against him for raising money under false pretenses. Ortega believed that the charge had been instigated by Romero, acting on instructions from Juárez.

Ortega was acquitted of the charge and was about to return to Mexico at the head of a force of volunteers to fight against the French at Matamoros, when he heard of a decree Juárez had issued on October 28, 1865. Anyone who left Mexico with the permission of the government but remained abroad for more than four months without obtaining renewed permission was to forfeit any office he held and was to be arrested and prosecuted if he returned to Mexico. This law, of course, applied in Ortega's case.

On November 8, Juárez issued another decree prolonging his own term of office as president until such time as it would be possible to hold a presidential election throughout the republic. Ortega in the United States issued a proclamation denouncing Juárez's decree as illegal and unconstitutional and asserting that he, not Juárez, was now the lawful president of the republic.

Juárez and Lerdo justified the decree extending the president's term by an ingenious but farfetched argument: the provision of the Constitution that the chief justice should act as president applied only if the presidential election was rendered impossible by ordinary and temporary causes; it did not apply to a long-lasting and extraordinary event such as occupation by a foreign invader. The Constitution did not make any provision for such an eventuality, and the president was therefore free to take whatever measures he considered best to defend the Republic. Juárez had not put forward such an argument in 1858, when as chief justice he had used the provisions of the Constitution to take over the presidential powers when a presidential election was impossible because of civil war. Ortega rejected Juárez's argument because the Constitution stated that the chief justice should take over if the presidential election could not be held "for any reason."

Some of the Mexican liberals were unhappy about the extension of Juárez's term of office, but there was a strong feeling that they must stand by Juárez and not allow a split to develop in their ranks. Two prominent liberals who were in the United States supported Ortega; but all Juárez's commanders in the field, including Díaz, Escobedo, Carbajal, Regules, Mendez, and Corona, signed declarations approving the extension.

Maximilian's journalists and propagandists and the French made great play out of the situation. Even by the provisions of his own republican constitution, Juárez's tenure was now illegal; so how could the dissidents and bandits who fought for him claim to be the army of a lawful government and to be entitled to be treated as prisoners of war?

Maximilian and Charlotte were disappointed that despite the successes against the guerrillas they were still not crushed. "It must be said, openly, that our military situation is very bad," wrote Maximilian on June 29, 1865. Colonel Loizillon, who was still writing regularly to his parents, had hoped, after the capture of Oaxaca in February 1865, that he would soon be going home, but by April he was warning them that they must not expect him back just yet, for he was busy chasing the guerrillas in Michoacán, "and things are no better in the north."

La Barreyrie, the editor of the French newspaper at Orizaba, writing two years later saw 1865 as the turn of the tide. After the successes in the first half of the year, the French army seemed to be in complete control of Mexico, "but then the horizon darkened. The bands which no longer existed appeared again in the far distance. Soon they became more numerous, and in the end they ceased to be bands and became a veritable army corps."

Captain Timmerhans of the Belgian Legion could not understand it. "There is no region of Mexico," he wrote in the summer of 1865, "where the insurrection has not suffered a defeat which would have been decisive in Europe; but here . . . the setback is merely a blow inflicted by fate which good luck will put right next day."

These worries were forgotten temporarily that summer amid the festivities of Marshal Bazaine's wedding in Mexico City to a beautiful young Mexican girl, Señorita de la Peña, from one of the most aristocratic families in the country. She was seventeen and Bazaine was fifty-four, and he had met her for the first time at a ball in Mexico City only a few months before. His request to Napoleon III for permission to marry her had been granted with the warmest good wishes from Napoleon and Eugénie, who strongly approved of this new link at the highest social level between France and Mexico. Maximilian and Charlotte attended the wedding, and Maximilian gave Bazaine as a wedding present a country house and estate just outside the city, worth $100,000.

But the celebrations had hardly ended before news arrived from Tamaulipas that the whole province was in revolt on a scale that had not been seen anywhere since the beginning of the intervention. Carbajal's men were attacking all along the coast, at Nautla, Papantla, Tuxpan, Tampico, Soto la Marina, and San Fernando, right up to the suburbs of Matamoros, where General Mejía had taken command. The *contre-guérilla* was sent against them but did not have great success.

Alexander W. Terrell of Virginia had fought in the Confederate army in the American Civil War. When he heard that Lee had surrendered at Appomattox he made his way to Mexico and joined the *contre-guérilla*. He had witnessed some terrible things in Virginia during the Civil War, but he was appalled by the savagery of the fighting in Tamaulipas. He saw how Carbajal's guerrillas pounced unexpectedly on small units of French soldiers or seized their Mexican carriers, "whom they sometimes tortured and slew in a way not to be described. . . . The retaliation by the *contre-guérilla* was terrible, and often visited on non-combatants who were believed to be in sympathy with the guerrillas."

In Michoacán the guerrillas were led by two of Juárez's regular army generals, Arteaga and Salazar, who had fought at Puebla and had escaped to rejoin the liberal army in the north. On June 18, 1865, the guerrillas came down from the mountains and attacked the town of Uruapan, in a valley beside a quiet river and surrounded by avocado trees. They captured the town after a thirty-hour battle and arrested the mayor, Señor de Leon, and all the other local government officials who had been appointed by Maximilian's government. They pardoned the lower officials but put Leon, along with one of his chief officials and the commander of the local garrison, on trial before a court-martial. The defendants were condemned to death for violating the decree of January 25 and were executed by a firing squad.

Maximilian and the French could no longer deceive themselves that the great majority of the people of Mexico were on their side. Abbé Domenech, who was Maximilian's press secretary, had no illusions about this. "I have seen landowners, journalists, and scholars weep from despair at being obliged to rejoice at the success of our forces and at the death of their compatriots who had fallen under our bullets." In March 1865 someone put up a notice in the lobby of the luxurious Hotel Iturbide in Mexico City: "Wake up, Mexicans, and get rid at one stroke of this Austrian, this idiotic Maximilian!" It was quickly removed, but two days later another notice appeared in the same place: "Death to France! Eternal shame to that puppet who is named Napoleon III!"

Some French officers believed that many of Juárez's former officers and soldiers who had submitted to the regency or the empire under the amnesty and had been taken into the new imperial Mexican army were still liberals at heart and were betraying, or preparing to betray, Maximilian and the French. It was sometimes obvious that the guerrillas had obtained information known only to members of the Franco-Mexican army; and captured guerrillas were sometimes allowed to escape by the soldiers who were guarding them. The French wondered whether the surrender of so many liberal officers and soldiers was a trick, a calculated policy by Juárez to infiltrate the imperial army with traitors.

The new telegraph lines that the French had so proudly installed seemed to cause more harm than good. The telegraph should have made it possible to send orders quickly from army headquarters to the commanders in the field; but the chief engineer wrote to Napoleon III in August 1865 that messages from his office in Maximilian's palace in Mexico City took a long time to reach their destination because the Mexican telegraph clerks held up the messages for as long as possible in order to help the guerrillas. The clerks also disclosed the French messages to the guerrillas, who often knew about the enemy's plans before they reached the officer to whom they were addressed. Juárez's agents seemed to be everywhere.

Occasionally the people dared to make public demonstrations against the French. When the *contre-guérilla* entered Tlacotalpán, which had been so effectively cowed by Du Pin two years before, the people booed them and shouted: "Why have you come here?"

One incident in Mexico City particularly angered the French. In May 1865, when a fire broke out in a house, some French soldiers of the third Zouave Regiment entered the house to try to save some property and were trapped on the second floor. Their commanding officer insisted on going upstairs to rescue his men; as he reached the top of the stairs the floor collapsed beneath him, and he and two other soldiers fell into the fire below and died. He was acclaimed as a hero by the press, and thousands of French soldiers and Mexicans attended his funeral. As the funeral cortège passed by, a bystander insulted the hearse and cursed Frenchmen. He was arrested and tried by a court-martial, which sentenced him to five years' imprisonment with hard labor. Maximilian pardoned him and gave orders for his release after he had served six weeks of his sentence.

All the French officers and soldiers were incensed by Maximilian's action. In their eyes, it was the worst of many cases in which he had unwisely pardoned criminals who deserved to be severely punished. Both Bazaine and Napoleon III were annoyed that Maximilian commuted the death sentences of convicted guerrillas. In later years, some of Maximilian's admirers went so far as to say that he had never refused to pardon a guerrilla for whom a petition for mercy was presented. This was untrue; Maximilian had refused to pardon Nicolás Romero, even though many people had implored him to do so, and had refused to pardon several other guerrillas.

The case of the guerrilla leader Colonel Cano affected Maximilian's secretary Blasio. According to Blasio, when Cano was captured by the *contre-guérilla* they found papers on him that proved he was planning to assassinate Maximilian; however, assassination of important leaders does not seem to have been a method used by the Mexican liberals. Cano was sentenced to death by a court-martial. His beautiful young wife, who had a small child, came to the palace to beg Maximilian to spare her husband's life, but Maximilian said that it was for the court-martial, not him, to decide Cano's fate. She came again to the palace, but Maximilian refused to see her and told Blasio to send her away. Blasio, moved by her despair, advised her to wait at the roadside where Maximilian would pass on his way from Chapultepec to Mexico City and to present her petition to him there; but the footmen saw her waiting and told Maximilian, who ordered the coachman to take a different route. Cano was executed two days later.

But Maximilian did pardon more guerrillas than Bazaine would have wished. The French officers complained of the emperor's weakness and leniency. On one occasion, at a ball, Sara Yorke overheard Bazaine saying to a friend that he was tired of ordering his men to risk their lives hunting down and capturing guerrillas merely to give Maximilian an opportunity to show the world how merciful he was.

Napoleon III wanted to get out of Mexico. He was willing to admit to himself and to his friends in private that he had made three miscalculations about Mexico. He had not expected the resistance of the guerrillas to be so stubborn, for he had not realized that Mexicans did not mind being shot or even hanged; when he discovered this surprising fact, he hoped that the prospect of a flogging would deter them, but even the cat-o'-nine-tails had not proved effective. His second miscalculation had been about Maximilian, who he now realized was not a suitable choice. Napoleon approved of Maximilian's moderate liberal intentions and of his policy toward the Church; but he was not impressed by his lack of resolution, his utter failure to put Mexico's finances into any kind of order, his querulous complaints against Bazaine, and his habit of privately and publicly quarreling with Franz Joseph.

Napoleon's third and most serious miscalculation had been about the United States. He had believed that the South would win the American Civil War and that Maximilian would have as his northern neighbor not a powerful United States of America but a weakened Confederate States of America. He had hoped at the least that Maximilian would be firmly established in Mexico before the Civil War ended, and that once French troops had withdrawn from Mexico, the United States would accept and recognize Maximilian. He had also underestimated how successful Romero and the liberals would be in rousing public opinion in the United States to a sense of republican solidarity with Juárez.

It had never been part of his *grande pensée* that French troops remain in Mexico indefinitely. After he had conquered Mexico and destroyed Juárez's forces, he had hoped that Maximilian would be able to maintain himself in power with the imperial Mexican army trained by the French and with Austrian and Belgian volunteers. Then the French troops could come home. He knew from the secret reports of the *procureurs* that the people of France were expecting him to bring the boys home as soon as possible, and it was becoming very expensive to keep them in Mexico. It would also be useful to have them available if war broke out in Europe. Napoleon, like many other people in France, was beginning to fear Bismarck and the growing power of Prussia. The 40,000 troops in Mexico were not a large proportion of the total of 400,000 French troops in four continents; but if Prussian ambitions brought about a war in Europe, these 40,000 men would be much better employed along the Rhine than in Mexico.

By the Treaty of Miramar he had promised to keep 8,000 troops in Mexico for six years. But Maximilian had agreed in that treaty to pay all the costs of the French conquest of Mexico, amounting to 270 million francs at 3 percent interest per annum, plus 1,000 francs a year for each French soldier in Mexico, and 400,000 francs every time a French transport ship brought troops to Mexico. In addition he had agreed to pay all the debts owed by Mexico to French creditors, including the debt due on the Jecker bonds. When he was negotiating the treaty in March 1864 Maximilian had been too involved in his quarrel with his brother about his rights in Austria to realize that he was undertaking financial obligations he would be quite unable to fulfill.

Above all, Napoleon wished to avoid war with the United States. He did not think the United States would wish to go to war with France when it had only just ended its long and costly Civil War; but as long as French troops remained in Mexico there was a risk that

France and the United States might drift into a war neither of them wanted. But though from every point of view Napoleon wished to withdraw the troops, he did not want Maximilian to be overthrown and Juárez to win. If this occurred, it would be impossible even for Rouher and his zealous propagandists to hide from the French people the fact that he had suffered a humiliating defeat in Mexico.

He still believed that Maximilian would be able to maintain himself in Mexico if the French troops were withdrawn, provided that the United States recognized his government. American recognition would remove any prospect of Juárez's receiving military or financial aid from the United States, and the Mexican liberals would at last have to give up the struggle.

But Seward was not prepared to do this. He had clearly thought out the policy that the United States should adopt toward Mexico. He did not think it would benefit the United States to annex any more Mexican territory, for American investment in Mexico would in due course bring the country under the economic influence of its northern neighbor. He was as eager to avoid war with France as Napoleon was to avoid war with the United States. He wanted the French to withdraw their troops so that Maximilian and Juárez could fight it out themselves; he would do nothing to strengthen Maximilian's position against Juárez by granting him diplomatic recognition. He was sure that even if the United States refused to recognize Maximilian, Napoleon would withdraw the troops before long because he had so many reasons for doing so. The only thing that would stop the withdrawal was Napoleon's fear of losing face. The more pressure Seward put on France to withdraw, the more Napoleon and the French people would feel that it would be humiliating to submit to such pressure. So Seward would pursue a policy of masterly inactivity, neither intervening in Mexico nor recognizing Maximilian, waiting patiently till the French left, after which he could leave it to Juárez to defeat Maximilian.

This was not good enough for the liberals in the United States. They wished to drive the French out of Mexico as quickly and as harshly as possible and, by humiliating Napoleon III, help the cause of liberalism not only in Mexico but also in France and Europe. They did not believe that Napoleon would dare to go to war with the United States, as he would not be able to defeat the United States in a war on the American continent. Whatever Seward might say, there was no sign that Napoleon was thinking of withdrawing his troops from Mexico in the near future; the only thing that would make him do so was pressure from the United States.

⁂ 21 ⁂

ALICE ITURBIDE

MANY OF THE DEFEATED Confederate troops were crossing the Rio Grande into Mexico. Some of the younger men, who had served up to four years in the army, had never had a civilian job and did not wish to have one. They preferred to go to Mexico to take part in the fighting there. A group under General Shelby, marching south from Louisiana, did not really care which side they fought for in Mexico, though most of them sympathized with Maximilian rather than with Juárez and the liberals, and many had a romantic attachment to Charlotte. As they left Shreveport they heard that Lincoln had been assassinated; they cheered and fired cannon salvos in celebration until Shelby ordered them to stop. He wrote that he had stopped the salvos but "could not stop the exultation."

After crossing the Rio Grande they met some liberal guerrillas to whom they sold their cannons and most of their rifles. They were unhappy at being paid in "Juárez scrip," which they thought would probably be useless outside the immediate vicinity. As they marched south toward Monterrey they heard that the French commander there, General Jeanningros, had said that if he caught Shelby and his men he would shoot them for having sold arms to the guerrillas. Leaving his men, Shelby went to Monterrey and asked to see Jeanningros, to whom he explained that he had sold arms to the guerrillas because he had no other way of obtaining money with which to buy food for his men. Jeanningros was impressed and invited Shelby and his followers to enlist in the French army. Shelby said they would be very pleased to do so, and they served with the *contre-guérilla* in Tamaulipas.

William M. Anderson, a lawyer from Kentucky, also went to Mexico in 1865. His brother, Major Robert Anderson, had become a hero in the North as the commander of the garrison at Fort Sumter when it was fired upon by Confederate batteries to begin the Civil War; but William Anderson hated Lincoln and supported slavery, though he thought that the South was wrong to secede from the Union. After the war he wanted to explore the possibilities of large-scale emigration to Mexico from the former Confederate states.

Maximilian was lukewarm to plans for immigration from the Confederacy. He was being strongly urged to encourage it by Commander Matthew F. Maury, formerly of the Confederate navy, who had come to Mexico City; but Maximilian hesitated to accept Confederate refugees either as soldiers or as settlers to cultivate the land in Coahuila and Sonora. He thought they could be useful and knew Charlotte would be pleased to have them, for she had always sympathized with the Confederate states. But he still hoped to have friendly relations with the United States and did not wish to anger the government in Washington by encouraging their defeated enemies.

He agreed to allow a certain number of Southerners to settle in Sonora, and many of those who came brought their slaves. Maximilian could not permit slavery to be reintroduced into Mexico forty years after it had been abolished, particularly when he was planning to gain the support of the Indians in his empire by abolishing peonage. No Mexican government, whether conservative or liberal, had hitherto taken any step against peonage; but at the end of August 1865, when Maximilian was away from the capital, Charlotte presided at a Cabinet meeting and approved a decree abolishing peonage, which Maximilian endorsed in the decree of November 1. There were protests against the decree from all the landowners, including some who were supporters of Juárez, and they succeeded in preventing the decree from being put into immediate operation. Peonage continued in Mexico until the new revolutions of the twentieth century.

It was therefore particularly ironic that only a week after Charlotte issued this decree, Maximilian signed another one, on September 5, that established forced labor by former slaves on the lands colonized in Coahuila and Sonora by the immigrants from the Confederacy. The decree proclaimed that slavery did not exist in Mexico, but went on to state that black men and women could be hired as laborers on these lands for a period of five to ten years, during which time they would be obliged to perform the work assigned by their masters. They were not permitted to leave their employment; any of them who did so were to be sent to do forced labor on public works. Any worker who felt that he was being unjustly treated by his master could complain to the police, who would then investigate his complaint and ensure that he was not oppressed.

Juárez and Romero and their supporters in the United States immediately seized the opportunity to launch a propaganda campaign in which they accused Maximilian of reestablishing slavery in Mexico. In a note to the French government Seward stated that he was sure Napoleon III would not approve of Maximilian's action. Drouyn de Lhuys and Maximilian claimed it was unfair to say that the decree restored slavery; they tried to divert public attention by referring to Maximilian's decree abolishing peonage; but the forced labor in Sonora was a propaganda victory for Juárez.

Maximilian now seemed to have reached that stage in the career of a political leader when he commits one blunder after another. His idea of adopting Iturbide's grandson as his heir had very unfortunate consequences. Maximilian and Charlotte still had no children after eight years of married life, giving rise to many rumors. In their palaces, as was to be expected, they had their own separate state rooms and bedrooms; but Blasio noticed that when they traveled together, if they were lodged in a room with a double bed, Maximilian always slept on a camp bed in another room. The old stories of Maximilian's syphilis and of Charlotte's indignation about his love affairs were revived. Maximilian's valet, Grill, told Blasio in the strictest confidence about a secret door in Maximilian's bedroom at Cuernavaca. Some of the more beautiful ladies of the court were sometimes smuggled in through the secret door to spend the night with the emperor. Whatever the reason, there is no doubt that by 1865 Maximilian and Charlotte had accepted the fact that they would not have a child.

If the Second Mexican Empire was to endure, Maximilian had to have an heir, and he decided to adopt the grandson of Iturbide, the first Mexican emperor, Agustin I. When Iturbide was shot, his three sons and a daughter were taken to New York for safety. One of the sons married Alice Green, an American. In 1865 she was twenty-three or twenty-four, and according to John Bigelow, the United States minister in Paris, was possessed "of more than ordinary personal charms." She had a two-year-old boy, named Agustin after his grandfather the emperor. After her husband's death Alice married his brother Angel de Iturbide.

Maximilian believed that there was no better way of ensuring the succession than to arrange for it to pass to a Mexican child from such an illustrious family; but as in so many other areas, he only succeeded in annoying all the parties. The liberals, who had regarded Iturbide as a tyrant and had eventually shot him, considered Maximilian's adoption of his grandson as a deliberate affront; the conservative aristocracy were displeased that the child was from a family that had not lived in Mexico for forty years rather than from a resident aristocratic family that was known and respected.

Maximilian's plan was warmly welcomed by the child's aunt, Doña Josefa de Iturbide, who also lived in New York. In September 1865 Josefa, Angel, Alice, and other members of the family came to Mexico City, bringing Agustin with them. They all signed a contract with Maximilian by which they agreed to deliver Agustin to him for adoption in return for a large annual pension for each of them. In addition, Maximilian created Josefa a princess of Mexico. She alone of the members of the family would be permitted to live in Mexico; she was given a suite of rooms in Maximilian's palace and sometimes acted as his hostess when Charlotte was absent. The others agreed to leave the country and never return to Mexico. The child was handed over to Princess Josefa and his nurses in the palace. Maximilian, Charlotte, and Josefa all promised that they would write to Alice regularly to tell her how Agustin was progressing.

Nine days later, when Alice was on the point of leaving Mexico, as she had agreed to do, she decided that she could not bear the prospect of being separated from her little boy. On September 27, she wrote to Maximilian explaining that she had changed her mind and wished to cancel the agreement, and she asked him to hand back the child. She thanked Maximilian for all that he had done for him, "but I have so wept over this separation, I have undergone such bitterness during these nine days, that I have no words with which to explain to Your Majesty all the magnitude of my troubles. I thought that if I did not see my child I would lose my mind." Later that day a messenger from the palace called at her lodgings and said that she would receive a reply from the emperor in a few days' time.

Two days later, at 10 A.M., a carriage stopped before Alice's door and an officer of Maximilian's guard entered the house. He told her that the emperor would receive her at the palace and that the carriage was waiting to drive her there. She hastily put on her best *mantilla* and prepared to accompany him, but something about his manner aroused her suspicions. She said that she could drive to the palace in her landlady's carriage, but the officer replied that she would surely not be so discourteous as to decline the honor which the emperor had done her in sending his own carriage for her convenience. A little reluctantly Alice entered the carriage, and they drove off. Instead of going toward the imperial palace, she was surprised to find that they were driving out of the city. She said she supposed that the emperor must be at Chapultepec, and that they were going there, and the officer nodded. But soon she realized they were driving east, not west, and asked him where they were taking her. He did not reply.

Just past the outskirts of the city, the carriage stopped at a place where another carriage was waiting. The officer asked her to descend and enter the other carriage. Alice got out of the carriage and again demanded to know where they were taking her, but again she received no reply. She sat down on a stone beside the road and refused to enter the other carriage. The officer then ordered the footmen to lift her up and place her in the other carriage by force, and they drove off to the east. After a while the officer told her that she was being taken to Puebla, where her husband would be waiting for her, and that both she and he were being deported from Mexico.

When she arrived at Puebla she was handed a telegram from Maximilian telling her that Agustin had slept well and was happy. It was the only communication she received from Maximilian, Charlotte, or Josefa, though they had all promised to write to her regularly about the child. At Puebla she and her husband, Angel, were served with an order to leave the country on the next ship from Veracruz.

They left the next day for Veracruz, but stopped briefly at Orizaba, where Angel sent a letter to Maximilian:

> Sire, it is my duty to protest before Your Majesty against your forcible detention of my nephew the Prince Don Agustin against the wishes of His Highness's mother Doña Alicia G. de Iturbide. . . . I hope, Sire, that you will take measures for the restitution of the aforesaid Prince to the arms of his afflicted mother. I remain, Sire, with profound respect Your Majesty's very obedient servant, A. de Iturbide.

When the couple arrived in New York, Alice wrote to Bazaine to complain that Maximilian had abducted her child. She received a very kind and sympathetic reply from Bazaine, which is not surprising in view of the intense dislike Bazaine had by now come to feel for Maximilian. Alice then went to Washington, and had an interview with Seward.

Only a ruler as inept and unlucky as Maximilian could have handed such a propaganda gift to Juárez. Seward sent Alice to see Bigelow in Paris and instructed Bigelow to ask Drouyn de Lhuys to use his influence with Maximilian to help her recover her child. Seward, who was as anxious as ever to preserve good relations with Napoleon III, took care not to tell the press; but Alice herself was less discreet, and the story soon became public knowledge, though not all the details were known until Bigelow revealed them eighteen years later in an article in *Harper's Magazine*. On January 9, 1866, the *New-York Times* published the outline of the story under the headline "Maximilian Charged with Kidnapping an American Child"; other newspapers in the United States expressed their anger at the shameful treatment of a brokenhearted American mother by Napoleon III's Austrian puppet in Mexico.

When Bigelow raised the matter with Drouyn de Lhuys, the foreign minister at first took the attitude that the French government could not intervene in a personal dispute between Alice Iturbide and Maximilian; but after Bigelow had emphasized that he was merely asking Drouyn to act in an unofficial capacity on humanitarian grounds, Drouyn promised that he would write to the French minister in Mexico City and instruct him to urge Maximilian to return Agustin to his mother. But Maximilian would not be persuaded; he was probably influenced by Princess Josefa de Iturbide, who seems to have had a low opinion of Alice. He firmly refused to hand over the child. He would not be bullied by anyone, least of all by the French and by Bazaine. Were they not always denigrating him for being weak and irresolute? But on this occasion he had shown that he was capable of taking swift and ruthless action, even though it caused suffering to a mother, when it was a question of ensuring the succession to the throne on which the stability of the empire depended.

❆ 22 ❆

GRANT, SHERMAN

AND SHERIDAN

IN THE UNITED STATES, Lieutenant General Ulysses S. Grant was the hero of the hour. His photograph was everywhere displayed, and his name was used, sometimes as a pun, in slogans and advertisements. In Washington the banking house of Jay Cooke and Company hung a banner outside its office opposite the Treasury Department, bearing the words "Glory to God, who hath to U.S. Grant-d the Victory." The YMCA headquarters on Seventh Street was decorated with the slogan "God, Grant, Our Country, Peace." The hero himself was a modest, unassuming man who disliked the fuss and tried to avoid the publicity as far as possible; but he intended to use his position in the state and in the public eye to help Mexico.

Second only to Grant in the United States army and in public esteem was Major General William T. Sherman. The two men were close friends and had much in common. They had been at West Point together, for they were in the same age group, Grant being forty-three in 1865 and Sherman forty-five. They had both fought in the Mexican War, had afterward been stationed for a time in San Francisco and Oregon, and had then left the army under something of a cloud, Grant because he drank too much and Sherman because he was too outspoken to his superior officers. Both had rejoined the Union army at the outbreak of the Civil War. Both drank whisky and chain-smoked cigars.

Sherman's behavior to his superiors had again gotten him into trouble at the beginning of the war, and many members of the military hierarchy thought that this red-haired, neurotic, brilliant officer was a little mad. They had therefore promoted Grant over Sherman's head to be supreme commander in the West, with Sherman as his second-in-command. Sherman accepted the situation and at all times gave Grant his loyal support. Grant was grateful to Sherman for this, and the two men, after they had worked together during the bloodbath at Shiloh, the long siege of Vicksburg, and the lucky fluke that brought them victory at Chattanooga, became very close.

There was one difference between them, Grant was a liberal in politics, and Sherman was not. Sherman was opposed to the abolition of slavery, and, during the later stages of the Civil War, the enrollment of black soldiers in the Union army; after the war he was against giving blacks the right to vote. Grant was strongly in favor of abolishing slavery, of using blacks as troops, of giving them the vote, and of protecting their interests vigorously during Reconstruction.

It was therefore not surprising that Sherman and Grant disagreed about Mexico. When the French troops entered Mexico City in the summer of 1863 Sherman wrote to Henry Halleck, general-in-chief of the Union armies, urging him to use his influence to prevent the United States from taking any steps to stop the French. He thought that the United States, having the finest part of the North American continent, had no need to acquire Mexico, and that American interests would not be harmed if the French were there. "The Mexicans have failed in self-government, and it was a question as to what nation she should fall a prey. That is now solved, and I don't see that we are damaged."

After Sherman, the third most popular hero of the North in 1865 was Major General Philip H. Sheridan, who had been too young to fight in the Mexican War; he was only thirty-four in 1865. He had nearly been expelled from West Point for fighting with a fellow cadet, but by the time the Civil War broke out he had brought his fiery temper under control. During the fighting in Virginia he had emerged as a brilliant cavalry leader, defeating the South's crack cavalry commander, General Jubal A. Early. Sheridan was as keen a liberal in politics as Grant and supported the same causes; he too was eager to help the Mexican liberals get rid of Maximilian and the French.

Grant believed that Napoleon III would be persauded to withdraw his troops from Mexico only by a clear demonstration that the United States was prepared to help Juárez even if this meant war with France. He discussed the position with Seward and found that Seward was determined to continue the soft approach to France. When Grant spoke to Johnson, he realized that the president would follow the advice of his secretary of state with regard to France and Mexico. Grant then decided to act by himself and force their hand.

The victory parade in Washington was to be held on May 23. Johnson and Grant would stand on the rostrum to take the salute, while Sherman, Sheridan, and the other generals led the army past them. Six days before the Grand Review, Grant wrote to Sheridan that a force of Confederate rebels was still holding out in Texas and part of Louisiana. He ordered him to go at once to round up the rebels, first stationing a large force along the Rio Grande.

Sheridan was disappointed, for if he left immediately for Texas and Louisiana he would miss the Grand Review. He went at once to see Grant and asked if he could postpone his departure. Grant then confided that he had not revealed in his letter the real reason why he was sending Sheridan and his army to the Rio Grande, for he did not wish to put it into writing. He wanted to make the French believe that the United States was about to invade Mexico to help the Mexican liberals. Finding that Sheridan was as sympathetic to Juárez's cause as he was, Grant explained that he had not told the president the true reason for Sheridan's mission. He was sorry that Sheridan would have to miss the Grand Review, but it was essential that he set out at once for the Rio Grande before Seward discovered what was happening and persuaded Johnson to countermand the order. When Sheridan understood what Grant was up to, he was determined to go.

Sheridan established his headquarters at New Orleans, where he found that Grant had sent him 42,000 men. He stationed a force of cavalry under General Merritt at San Antonio and another under General Custer at Houston, but he concentrated the bulk of his troops under General Steele at Brownsville, where they faced Mejía's men at Matamoros across the Rio Grande. This had the effect that Grant and Sheridan intended: it caused renewed alarm in Mexico City and in Paris just when the panic was beginning to subside in view of Seward's assurances.

Captain Loizillon wrote to his parents in France that he was sorry to tell them he would not be coming home just yet, for there was going to be a war between France and the United States. Everybody in Mexico expected the Americans to cross the Rio Grande and invade. Loizillon could not understand why everyone was flapping about it, and he was disgusted that the greatest army in the world should be afraid of the Americans. Personally he hoped that the United States *would* invade; then the French could give the United States a good beating, which would make the Americans think twice about ever again invading Mexico and about allowing the filibusterers to slip over the border to help Juárez. The United States would be forced to recognize Maximilian and leave him in peace.

Captain Loizillon's superiors were not so happy at the prospect of war with the United States, and his emperor in Paris was more alarmed than anyone. Napoleon III worked out his plan of campaign if the United States invaded. The French would retreat 300 miles from the Rio Grande and establish a defensive line somewhere near San Luis Potosí. Napoleon hoped that the Americans, exhausted with long marches through country where dangerous diseases were rife, would be forced to capitulate, as the Russians had been at the end of their extended lines of communications in the Crimean War. But Napoleon was by no means sure that this plan would succeed, and he strongly hoped that war with the United States could be avoided. He ordered Bazaine to withdraw at once from the immediate vicinity of the Rio Grande to avoid any risk of an incident between French and American troops that might provoke a war.

Napoleon III was perplexed. The reports from Bazaine on the situation at Matamoros reached Paris at about the same time as Seward's note of June 3 assuring him that the United States had not changed its policy of strict neutrality in Mexico and friendship toward France. This confirmed his belief that he had got himself into a difficult position in Mexico and that the sooner he got out of the "Mexican wasps' nest" the better.

On June 16 Grant attended a Cabinet meeting at the White House and proposed that a note be sent to France demanding the immediate withdrawal of French troops from Mexico. Seward strongly opposed this proposal. He said that Napoleon III had already decided to withdraw from Mexico, that Maximilian would leave the country within six months, perhaps within sixty days, and that any ultimatum or threats would stiffen Napoleon's resistance and delay the departure of the French troops and Maximilian.

The matter was discussed several times during the next five weeks. The Cabinet was divided: Hugh McCulloch, the secretary of the treasury, and James Harlan, the secretary of the interior, agreed with Seward; but Edwin M. Stanton, the secretary for war, and William Dennison, the postmaster-general, supported Grant's position. Gideon Welles, the secretary for the navy, was not sure which side to support; he thought Seward had been "feeble and inefficient, but Stanton and Grant are, on the other hand, too belligerent."

Romero and his friends decided to increase the pressure on Seward and Johnson by organizing a series of public meetings in support of Mexico. A rally at the Cooper Institute in New York was addressed by Zarco and other Mexican and American liberal leaders. They linked the struggle against slavery in the United States with the struggle against absolutism in Mexico and Europe and demanded that "the torches of civil war in the United States be extinguished in the blood of the minions of Napoleon III."

While Bazaine was withdrawing his troops from the frontier to avoid a clash with Sheridan, Maximilian wished to know why Bazaine was allowing Juárez to remain at Chihuahua. Juárez had only a handful of soldiers with him, and a few troops of cavalry would be all that was needed to drive him farther north and out of Mexico altogether; if Juárez could be driven across the border, the guerrilla resistance in Mexico might collapse before the United States had time to help Juárez.

Bazaine agreed to Maximilian's proposal. By the beginning of August the danger of American intervention had receded. Sheridan's 40,000 men were still on the Rio Grande, but Seward kept reassuring the French that the United States would not go to war, and it seemed that he would, after all, prevent Grant from sending American troops to help Juárez. So Bazaine sent General Aymard to take Chihuahua. Before he arrived, Juárez on August 5 left for the north, accompanied as usual by his ministers and by Iglesias and the journalists. On the last day of every month Iglesias published an issue of *El Periódico Oficial,* in which he gave the text of the official decrees of Juárez's government, wrote stirring appeals to the people to continue the fight for freedom, mocked Maximilian, and gave news of the heroic struggles of their liberal comrades in Poland, Hungary, and Italy and in the American Civil War. From time to time the paper did not appear on the last day of the month. In the next issue Iglesias would explain that the previous month's issue had not been published because the government was being transferred to a new capital.

Juárez traveled for nine days in his little carriage along the 230 miles of rough track from Chihuahua to El Paso del Norte, past high mountains and cactus bushes to wide valleys between distant peaks and the sand of the northern desert. He and his staff and the journalists were escorted by 500 horsemen with five pieces of artillery. Although he had retreated a thousand miles from Mexico City and had reached the extreme limits of the republic, he managed to make his journey look like a triumphal visit to his people. When he entered El Paso, two horsemen rode ahead shouting, "Juárez is coming!" and all the inhabitants turned out to stare at him.

During his stay in El Paso he was often visited and interviewed by J. S. Bartlett, a young journalist of the *Boston Journal* who also held the position of United States collector of customs at the border. Bartlett kept a diary while he was stationed there, and fifty years later published an article in the *Bulletin of the Pan-American Union* in which he described his recollections of Juárez at El Paso. Bartlett loved the little Mexican town with its low adobe houses surrounded by vineyards and gardens, the Mexicans lying in the hot sun, the continual buzz of insects, and the herds of goats on the distant hills. Juárez occupied the best house in the town, on the eastern side of the square.

Whenever Bartlett visited, he was offered champagne after their talk; and he attended the balls, parties, and receptions that were frequently held in El Paso.

Across the border in Texas there was a United States garrison at Fort Bliss. The officers of the garrison often visited Juárez at El Paso and attended the balls and receptions; but when these officers invited Juárez to accept their hospitality at Fort Bliss, he refused, saying he would not leave Mexican soil until the country was rid of the foreign invader. So the American officers decided to hold a dinner for him in El Paso, and Juárez then accepted their invitation to attend. He realized that Maximilian and the French were hoping to drive him out of the country, and that a visit across the border would give them good propaganda. He was joined at El Paso by another 300 soldiers, and he acquired ten more cannons from the United States. These were placed in the square, and defenses were erected around the town in preparation for a French attack.

The attack never came, and Maximilian's supporters, both at the time and in later years, wondered why the French, having chased Juárez so far, did not drive him out of Mexico altogether. Juárez himself did not expect the French to come to El Paso. On August 17, 1865, three days after he arrived there, he wrote to his friend Jesús Teran, whom he had sent on a mission to Europe, "It is difficult for the enemy to come as far as here, and if he did, so much the worse for him, because he would not destroy the government, and our people would profit by his absence, as they did by his expedition to Chihuahua." This was indeed the tactic of the liberal guerrillas; when the French troops marched anywhere, the guerrillas attacked the place from which they had come.

According to Kératry, who always wrote with the object of vindicating the French army from aspersions made against it, there would have been no point in driving Juárez across the Rio Grande, for the French would have been unable to guard the whole line of the river and he could easily have returned to Mexico. It is more likely that when the French got to El Paso, Juárez would have moved away to some other place on Mexican territory that was not occupied by the French.

But another reason why the French did not go to El Paso was undoubtedly Bazaine's determination to avoid contact with Sheridan's army. It was simpler and safer for the French and Maximilian's supporters to say falsely that Juárez had left Mexico. The news was published in the press in Mexico City in September 1865 that Juárez had crossed the Rio Grande and taken refuge in the United States.

One writer reported that Juárez had been seen in Santa Fe, where he had established his headquarters.

Sheridan blamed Seward for the French attack that had driven Juárez to El Paso. He believed that Seward's soft policy toward France had encouraged Maximilian and Bazaine to launch the offensive against Chihuahua in August, whereas in May they had been drawing back from the border as they waited for the American invasion of Mexico. "As the summer wore away," wrote Sheridan, "Maximilian, under Mr. Seward's policy gained in strength. . . . The Republic under President Juárez almost succumbed." Sheridan thought it was time to frighten the French and Maximilian again. "I opened communication with President Juárez," he wrote, "taking care not to do this in the dark, and the news, spreading like wildfire" convinced everyone that he was only awaiting the arrival of reinforcements from San Antonio before crossing the Rio Grande.

✳ 23 ✳

THE BLACK DECREE

OCTOBER 3 WAS a fateful date for Maximilian. On October 3, 1863, he accepted at Miramar the offer of the crown of Mexico. On October 3, 1864, an earthquake struck his new Mexican empire and did extensive damage in some of the provincial towns. On October 3, 1865, he issued the decree that damned him forever in liberal eyes. For the third time in four weeks, Maximilian laid himself open to strong criticism. On September 5, he had issued the decree establishing forced labor in Sonora; on September 29 he had ordered the abduction of Alice Iturbide; and on October 3 came the Black Decree.

The day before the decree was published, he issued a proclamation explaining it. He stated that "the cause which has been maintained with so much courage and constancy by Don Benito Juárez" had been defeated by the national will. Even under his own Constitution, Juárez's presidential term had expired, and he had left Mexican territory. The imperial government had been lenient for a long time, and many persons had accepted the amnesty; but the resistance was now being maintained only by a soldiery that was in no way patriotic but was the debris which always remained after all civil wars. Henceforth the struggle would be between patriots and bandits. "The time for indulgence has passed, for it would only help the despotism of the bandits who burn villages, rob and murder peaceful citizens, poor old men and defenseless women. The government, strong and powerful, will henceforth impose inflexible punishment."

The decree itself provided that anyone who was found carrying arms or was convicted of being a member of an armed band, even if he claimed to have acted from patriotic or political motives, would be put to death within twenty-four hours without being permitted to send a petition for pardon to the emperor or to any other authority. When prisoners were captured in a military action, the commander of the unit that captured them could execute them on his own authority without a court-martial. The decree was to go into effect on November 15; anyone to whom it applied would be granted amnesty if he surrendered before that date, which was later extended to December 1.

The conservatives and the French army officers were angered by the phrase in the proclamation referring to Juárez's great "courage and constancy." The *contre-guérilla* had been shooting and hanging guerrillas for the last three years. Now Maximilian was stating that these bandits were men of courage and constancy and was implying that though it would be justifiable to execute them in the future, it had not been justifiable in the past. At the same time, the liberals were incensed by the provisions of the decree and Maximilian's justification of it by the lie that Juárez had left Mexico.

But the conservatives were pleased that Maximilian was at last taking firm action against the guerrillas, and though they did not like the proclamation they welcomed the Black Decree. *La Nación* declared that it had "put an end to the anxieties which for more than a year had alarmed the friends of peace and order. Today all lovers of public tranquillity, of morality, and of justice unhesitatingly applaud the energetic and stern attitude which animates His Majesty's Government." Only professional troublemakers who thrive in times of anarchy would condemn it.

There were strong protests throughout the United States against the Black Decree, and Seward protested in an official note to the French government. Drouyn de Lhuys deftly turned Seward's protest to his own advantage by suggesting that Seward make his protest to Maximilian, which would have implied that the United States recognized Maximilian as emperor of Mexico.

Maximilian's apologists have always felt that of all his actions the Black Decree was the hardest to justify. They claimed that Maximilian only issued the decree because he believed that Juárez had left Mexican soil and because he had been pressured into doing so by Bazaine. Blasio, who claimed that the Black Decree was less savage than Juárez's decree of January 25, placed the responsibility on Bazaine. But this was denied by Kératry, who always tried to exonerate Bazaine and the French army by blaming everything on Napoleon III and Maximilian, and by Paul Gaulot, Bazaine's literary executor. Kératry and Gaulot argued that Bazaine had no responsibility for the Black Decree, that it was Maximilian who thought of it and issued it.

From one point of view, too much importance has been attached to the Black Decree. According to the liberal propagandists, the French and Maximilian's army shot or hanged 40,000 people during the intervention, though others claim only 11,000 victims. Whichever figure is correct, the overwhelming majority were executed before the Black Decree came into force, because the Franco-Mexican army and the *contre-guérilla* did not succeed in catching many guerrillas after December 1, 1865. By this time the tide of war had changed in favor of the guerrillas, who were capturing, and often executing, the supporters of Maximilian.

It is quite impossible to exempt either Maximilian or Bazaine from responsibility for the Black Decree. Bazaine had for a long time been urging Maximilian to allow him to shoot or hang guerrillas without the emperor's intervention, but it was not Bazaine who was responsible for the decree. It was drafted by an employee in Maximilian's War Department and approved by Maximilian and the members of his Cabinet, seven of whom were present at the meeting on October 2. All of them were in favor of issuing the proclamation and the decree, and after Maximilian had signed it in their presence they all countersigned the decree, including the foreign minister, the moderate liberal Fernando Ramírez.

Bazaine did not know about the decree at this point, but that same day he visited Maximilian to discuss other business, and Maximilian showed him the draft of the decree and asked if he approved of it. Bazaine said that he warmly approved of it and suggested one small amendment, to which Maximilian agreed. Bazaine was particularly pleased that the decree permitted army commanders in the field to have the guerrillas executed immediately without giving them the time to appeal to Maximilian.

The other excuse put forward by Maximilian's supporters, that Maximilian believed Juárez had left the country, and that the liberal resistance was about to collapse, is equally specious. Even if Maximilian thought that Juárez had left Mexico, he certainly did not believe that the guerrilla resistance had ended. His statement in the proclamation that the remaining guerrillas were the last debris of the soldiery left over from the civil war was quite untrue. Every French commander knew that guerrilla activity had never been greater than in the summer and autumn of 1865; Maximilian had repeatedly written to Bazaine and Napoleon III expressing his alarm at their increasing strength and at Bazaine's failure to destroy them. Maximilian issued the Black Decree, not because he believed that the guerrillas were nearly beaten, but because he feared that they were getting stronger and hoped, by resorting to the most drastic methods, to destroy them before the United States had time to intervene on their side.

Four days after he issued the Black Decree the guerrillas, for the first time in some months, attacked a train on the railroad between Veracruz and Camerone. The train was guarded by a detachment of French and Egyptian troops, but the guerrillas killed them all. Many were killed with machetes, and it was perhaps because of the ferocious machete wounds that the French believed that the guerrillas had deliberately mutilated the soldiers' corpses. This aroused great indignation throughout the French army.

On October 11 Bazaine sent a circular to his officers in which he referred to Arteaga's shooting of government officials at Uruapan, to the murder of Captain Kurtzroch by Antonio Perez, and to the recent slaughter of soldiers in the train and the mutilation of their corpses. "I direct you to inform the troops under your command that I will not permit them to take prisoners. Every individual, whoever he is, who is taken arms in hand shall be put to death. There will be no exchange of prisoners in future. Our soldiers must realize that they must not lay down their arms to adversaries of this kind. What is now taking place is a war to the death, a struggle to the finish between barbarism and civilization. On both sides it is necessary to kill and be killed."

The next day Bazaine sent each of his higher commanders eight copies of the Black Decree to pass on to their inferior officers. "I need not tell you how important it is for us that this law is strictly enforced. His Majesty had several times previously decreed repressive measures, but nearly all of them remained a dead letter, because of the apathy of the authorities and because of the clemency in which the Emperor himself set the example. I have obtained His Majesty's promise that it will be different this time." He directed that whenever possible it should be left to Mexican officers to enforce the Black Decree, that French commanders should do so only when the security of their units would otherwise be threatened.

On October 13 Maximilian's Mexican soldiers, under the command of General Mendez, made a surprise attack on the forces of Generals Arteaga and Salazar at Santa Ana Anatlan in Michoacán, and the two generals and thirty-five of their officers and men were taken prisoner. Mendez pardoned most of them and gave them the opportunity of joining Maximilian's army. But Arteaga, Salazar, and three officers were tried by court-martial on a charge of murdering the three government officials at Uruapan in June. They were sentenced to death and, in accordance with Forey's decree of June 1863, the court ordered that they be executed at the scene of their crime. Mendez had not yet received a copy of the Black Decree or Bazaine's letter of October 11, but he decided to carry out the sentence of the court at once without giving Maximilian an opportunity to pardon the five men. He had his own private reasons for wishing to see the death sentence carried out, because one of the officials shot at Uruapan by Arteaga and Salazar was his relation.

The condemned men were taken from Santa Ana Anatlan to Uruapan. All of them except Arteaga were made to walk all the way on the journey, which took six days. Arteaga, although he was only forty and looked younger, was very fat and had been wounded in the fight at Santa Ana Anatlan. He was therefore allowed to ride, but not on his own sturdy horse, which had been appropriated by one of his captors. The horse he was given was weak and often stumbled on the almost impassable mountain paths and, as the saddle fitted badly, Arteaga suffered greatly from the jolting, which reopened his wounds.

They reached Uruapan on October 20, and the five men were shot the next morning. The execution squad was composed entirely of Mexicans in Maximilian's service. As Salazar faced them, he pointed to his heart and called out "Aim here, traitors!" They did, and he died instantly.

The liberals were indignant at the execution of Arteaga and Salazar, and made much of it in their propaganda, particularly in the United States. They published the letters both men had written to their mothers on the evening before their execution; these farewell messages aroused great sympathy for the victims and anger against Maximilian.

Arteaga and Salazar had been generals in Juárez's regular army and had fought at Puebla, and it was obviously quite improper to call them bandits. It was generally regarded as the first case under the Black Decree, although the decree did not come into force until December 1, six weeks after Arteaga and Salazar were shot. They were executed for murdering the government officials at Uruapan, something the liberals in the United States did not ordinarily mention. Some of the propaganda stated that Arteaga and Salazar had been responsible for the death of a relative of Mendez's and accused Mendez of having had them shot out of a desire for private revenge.

The Belgian Legion had been operating in Michoacán against the guerrilla band led by General Regules, a Spanish immigrant who had joined the liberals. When the Belgians entered Tacámbaro, they were told that Regules's wife was living in a house in the town. They went to the house and found Señora Regules nursing two guerrillas who had been wounded in a fight against the Belgians some days before. The doctor whom she had called informed the Belgian major that he believed that she had been sending information about troop movements to her husband. The major told Señora Regules that he was going to arrest her and her children and hold them as hostages for her husband's good behavior but that she and her children and her property would not be harmed. She said she was sure she could rely on the major to behave like an officer and a gentleman. The major offered her his arm and led her to the Belgian headquarters, while Dr. Lejeune, the medical officer of the Belgian unit, took the children by the hand. The sight of Señora Regules and her children being taken under escort to the Belgian headquarters caused great resentment among the inhabitants of Tacámbaro.

The arrest of his wife and children did not deter Regules from attacking the 251 Belgians with a force of 3,500 men, and after a fierce battle, in which both sides lost more than 100 killed, the Belgians surrendered. Dr. Lejeune was attending to some wounded soldiers when a guerrilla officer, Jesús Gomez, walked up and shot him dead. The guerrillas told the Belgians that Dr. Lejeune had been killed in revenge for the arrest of Señora Regules and her children, but others said Gomez had been drunk. When Regules heard what had happened, he placed Gomez under arrest and said he would be court-martialed for murdering Lejeune; but Gomez was apparently not seriously punished, for he was fighting in the guerrilla ranks a few months later.

The Belgian prisoners were not ill-treated and were told that they would be exchanged for guerrillas whom the French had captured. But the negotiations for the exchange dragged on throughout the summer and were still in progress in October, when Bazaine issued his order forbidding any further exchanges of prisoners and stipulating that all captured guerrillas were to be shot. A few days later the news arrived of the execution of Arteaga and Salazar.

A guerrilla officer told the Belgian prisoners that they would all be shot as a reprisal for the murder of Arteaga and Salazar; but he offered to spare the lives of any who would agree to sign a protest against the killing of Arteaga and Salazar. The Belgians all refused to sign and decided to try to escape at once. Their escape was foiled, but they found that one of the guerrillas was sympathetic. He promised to inform the liberal leader, General Riva Palacio, about their plight, for he knew that Riva Palacio was a humane man who did not like killing prisoners.

Riva Palacio ordered the local guerrillas to postpone the execution of the Belgians and he got in touch with Bazaine, who, despite his order of October 11, agreed to release some captured guerrillas in exchange for the Belgians, and the exchange took place two months later. Riva Palacio, unlike some of the other guerrilla leaders, had always treated his prisoners well. On November 16 the head of Maximilian's military cabinet wrote to Bazaine informing him that if Riva Palacio were captured, Maximilian wished him to be sent to Mexico

City and not put to death. "This is the only exception which, for special reasons, the Emperor intends to make to the decree of the Third of October."

In El Paso del Norte Juárez from time to time received letters from Jesús Teran, whom he had sent to Europe in October 1863. He did not give Teran precise instructions about what to do in Europe beyond telling him to contact European statesmen and to try to influence them in favor of the Mexican liberals and against Maximilian. Teran went to Cadiz, London, Florence, Rome, and Paris, and sent reports that eventually reached Juárez in El Paso. He remained in Europe until his death in Paris in April 1866, but he does not seem to have achieved any great success, and barely justified the living and traveling expenses he incurred, which Romero, in Washington, paid to him through a bank in London.

On September 17, 1865, Teran wrote from Berne to Baron de Pont, who had been a close confidant of Maximilian at Miramar and had acted as a go-between with Gutiérrez de Estrada in 1861 and 1862 when the question first arose of Maximilian's becoming emperor of Mexico. Teran stressed the claims of Juárez and the liberals to represent the people of Mexico. De Pont forwarded the letter to Maximilian, who on December 8 replied to de Pont. Maximilian obviously realized that de Pont would forward his letter to Teran, who in turn would send it to Juárez; since the story of Maximilian's letter to Juárez, and Juárez's reply, is an invention, this letter to de Pont is the nearest that Maximilian ever came to communicating with Juárez.

Maximilian wrote that he was convinced that "Teran is a real patriot, like his master" (Juárez); but he intended to pursue his task of regenerating Mexico without repeating the mistakes committed by Juárez when he was president, because Juárez "wished to destroy everything and reform everything." Teran had written that Maximilian was very unpopular in Mexico, and Maximilian admitted that this might be true, because he was introducing a new regime that could not at first be popular with everyone. "I will be happy if, on the twenty-fifth anniversary of my coming to the throne, I am loved and appreciated." He wrote that he very much wished to reach an understanding with Juárez, but that Juárez must first accept the decision of the majority of Mexicans who wished for tranquillity, peace, and prosperity. If, as Maximilian believed, Juárez desired the well-being of Mexico, he should come and play his part in the work Maximilian was pursuing; he would be received with open arms, like every good Mexican. But there could be no question of Maximilian's making any kind of armistice with the dissidents, "because there is no longer a loyal enemy, but only barbarous brigands."

From Berne, Teran went to Paris, where at the beginning of October 1865 he received an unexpected letter from a friend of Miramón's. To get Miramón out of Mexico, Maximilian had sent him to Berlin to study Prussian military tactics. The letter stated that Miramón, who was in Paris on his way to Berlin, would like to meet Teran and discuss certain matters with him. Teran agreed to the meeting. Miramón offered to return to Mexico and fight for Juárez if Juárez would appoint him commander-in-chief of the liberal armies of the central area, including Jalisco, Guanajuato, Querétaro, and Mexico City. Miramón said he believed that he would be able to persuade all of Maximilian's generals to follow his example and come over to Juárez's side, except Mejía, who would remain loyal to Maximilian. He said Márquez, who had been sent by Maximilian to Jerusalem and Constantinople, would shortly be coming to Paris, and Miramón was confident that he could persuade Márquez, too, to join Juárez.

Napoleon III's secret police discovered that Miramón had been in touch with some French liberals, including a man who was a friend of Jules Favre's, and the French War Office wrote to Bazaine in Mexico about it; but they added that there was no reason to believe that Miramón had met Favre or that he was disloyal to Maximilian and the intervention. Neither Maximilian nor the French seem to have suspected that Miramón, the handsome, dashing young general, the bitter enemy of the liberals, had made secret offers to join Juárez.

Teran wrote to Lerdo in El Paso del Norte informing him of Miramón's offer, and Lerdo referred the matter to Juárez. On January 22, 1866, Lerdo replied to Teran in a long letter that avoided giving Miramón a straight answer. While Juárez would always welcome any Mexican who joined the national constitutional cause, he foresaw that it would be difficult for Miramón to reach the territory occupied by the liberal forces and that his appointment to any command had better be postponed until his arrival. Juárez was obviously unwilling to commit himself. He could not trust either Miramón or Márquez, and in view of the help he was now getting from Sheridan's forces on the Rio Grande he might soon be in a position where he did not need the help of Miramón.

Charles de Cazotte, the French consul in San Francisco, was an energetic and enterprising man who was prepared to act on his own initiative. A great deal of useful information could be obtained in San Francisco by snooping around the warehouses on the waterfront or talking to sailors and travelers arriving from Acapulco, which Cazotte called "Juárez's last boulevard on the Pacific." Cazotte's agents discovered in May 1865 that a man named Henry Kastan, a German by origin, had come to San Francisco from Acapulco to buy twenty-two cases of arms to be sent to Acapulco for Juárez's guerrillas. The arms were to be sent in several small ships to lessen the chances of losing the whole consignment if they were captured by French warships on the journey.

The consul wrote at once to Admiral Macères, who was in command of the French fleet off the Pacific coast of Mexico, and warned him to be on the lookout for ships landing the arms at Acapulco or anywhere on the coast of Guerrero. Cazotte also learned that twice a week an Indian traveled from Mexico City to Guerrero and gave General Alvarez, the guerrilla leader, a report of the discussions in Maximilian's Cabinet. Several of Juárez's former generals who were living in Mexico City after submitting to Maximilian were also sending information to Alvarez.

In October 1865 Cazotte found out that Juárez's agents had bought a supply of arms, which were to be shipped from San Pedro and San Diego in southern California to Juárez. Cazotte went at once to see Major General MacDowell, the commanding officer of the military district of San Francisco, and asked him to stop the arms from being sent to Mexico. MacDowell wrote to General Mason, the commanding officer of the military district of southern California, and Mason issued orders to stop the shipment.

The ban on the export of arms from California to Mexico worried Romero. He told Seward that the United States embargo on arms had so drastically reduced Juárez's supply of rifles that it was surprising that the Mexican liberals had been able to continue their resistance to the French invaders. Now that the Civil War was over, he hoped that United States policy would change. He bought 21,000 rifles, two rifled batteries, and 3 million cartridges in New York for Juárez. The French minister in Washington, hearing of this, protested to Seward, who persuaded the president to ban the export of arms. The Philadelphia correspondent of *The Times* of London, who was a strong supporter of Maximilian, was delighted. "This virtually ends the Mexican contest," he wrote in a report published in *The Times* on November 27, 1865. "Juarez depends entirely upon aid from the United States, and the enforcement of the neutrality laws ends even his hopes of success."

Romero was shocked; was Juárez to be deprived of a chance to acquire arms even now, after the Civil War, when there was no excuse for appeasing Napoleon III? He went to see Grant and asked him to intervene with President Johnson. Would it help if Grant arranged for Romero to see the president without having to go through Seward?

Grant did not think Johnson would be of any help, especially if it meant overruling a decision by Seward. He thought of a better way of helping Juárez. He sent secret orders to Sheridan to supply Juárez with the arms he needed from United States stores along the Rio Grande. Soon the liberal guerrillas around Matamoros were well equipped. Sheridan afterward wrote that he had sent 30,000 muskets to Juárez from the United States arsenal at Baton Rouge alone.

General Mejía at Matamoros found that the guerrillas of Tamaulipas had come to Matamoros in strength and were actually besieging the city. From time to time they bombarded Matamoros with cannon. This was a new development, for Mejía had not expected the guerrillas to have cannon. He was sure that they had obtained them from Sheridan or from his subordinate commander, General Weitzel at Brownsville. During the last months of the Civil War, Weitzel had commanded a corps of black troops, which he had led into Richmond, to the great indignation of the white inhabitants, when the Confederate capital fell. Weitzel and his black soldiers were among the troops that Grant and Sheridan had sent to Brownsville in June 1865.

A French naval squadron under Admiral Cloué was sent to Matamoros to help Mejía. On November 2 the commander of Maximilian's warship *Paysano* saw a barge crossing from the Texas shore. He stopped it and discovered that it was laden with munitions being sent from the United States for the guerrillas in Tamaulipas. The *Paysano* captured the barge and brought it to the Mexican shore. Soon afterward a ship full of black soldiers of the United States Army came across the river to recapture the barge, but the *Paysano* opened fire on them and drove them away.

On November 7 Cloué sent the warship *Antonia* up the Rio Grande to help in operations against the guerrillas. He had given the commander strict orders to open fire only on guerrillas who were in Mexico, on the right bank of the Rio Grande, and on no account to fire into Texas, on the left bank, even if he saw Mexican guerrillas there. Suddenly the batteries on the Texas side began firing on the *Antonia,* whose commander, obeying orders, did not fire back. Mejía's men in Matamoros, hearing gunfire, realized what had happened and came out on to the jetty at Matamoros to cheer the *Antonia* when she arrived. Two of her crew had been wounded, and the side of the ship facing Texas was riddled with bullet holes.

Cloué and Mejía sent a protest to Weitzel, who disclaimed all knowledge of the incident. He said there were so many bends in the

Rio Grande that the position of the bullet holes in the *Antonia* did not necessarily mean that the shots had been fired from the Texas shore.

Mejía's men captured seventeen of the guerrillas who were besieging Matamoros. They were court-martialed and sentenced to death under the provisions of the Black Decree. On January 2, 1866, Weitzel wrote to Mejía asking him to pardon the guerrillas. Mejía replied the same day with a curt refusal. "I find myself bound to repulse haughtily your interference in the internal affairs of this country." He insisted that the sentence of the Mexican courts could not be interfered with, and he would not pardon these seventeen men, who had stolen thirteen carriages and thirty-six mules. "It would really be strange, General, if in the middle of the nineteenth century bandits and robbers obtained the help and protection of the civilized world." He added that if he received a similar request from Weitzel in the future, he would not reply to it.

Weitzel kept Mejía's letter. Eighteen months later he sent it to the newspapers, which published it when Mejía was on trial for his life at Querétaro.

At 4 A.M. on January 5, a force of black United States soldiers under General Crawford crossed the Rio Grande and attacked Mejía's garrison in the little town of Bagdad at the mouth of the river. Five of Mejía's men were killed and the others were captured and imprisoned in the town hall, while the black soldiers, according to the inhabitants of Bagdad, rampaged through the town, looting the houses of anyone who did not give them money, raping several women, and killing two of them. After a while Weitzel sent Colonel Hudson with 150 black soldiers to restore order and stop the misconduct of their army comrades in Bagdad; but they failed to do so, and some of the newly arrived soldiers joined in the looting. The United States troops left Bagdad two days later.

Seward was very angry about the raid. His friend and supporter Henry J. Raymond, the proprietor and editor of the *New-York Times,* denounced filibustering on the Rio Grande and "the thieves and cutthroats who took possession of Bagdad . . . under the shadow of the American flag." Seward persuaded President Johnson to order Sheridan to arrest Crawford and to dismiss Weitzel from his command at Brownsville. Sheridan was disgusted. "It required the patience of Job to abide the slow and poky methods of our State Department," he wrote.

But Napoleon III had had enough. At the beginning of November 1865 the United States minister in Brazil, James Watson Webb, who had been recalled to Washington, went to Paris on his way home to see his old friend Napoleon, whom he had met when the emperor was a refugee in New York in 1837. On November 10 Webb had breakfast with Napoleon, who told him that he wished to withdraw his troops from Mexico but did not know how to do so without losing face unless the United States would agree to recognize Maximilian's government. Webb said it would be quite impossible for President Johnson to do such a thing in view of public opinion in the United States. He thought that if Maximilian remained much longer in Mexico, thousands of Americans would go to Mexico to fight for Juárez. Webb suggested that Napoleon might consider withdrawing his troops from Mexico in stages over eighteen months, for this would make it clear to the world that he was withdrawing in his own good time and not under duress. "An inspiration!" said Napoleon.

Napoleon realized that the United States would not help him out of his Mexican embarrassment by recognizing Maximilian. But he had to bring the troops home to save the mounting costs of keeping them in Mexico, to appease the discontent in France about the Mexican expedition, and to avoid the growing risk of a clash on the Rio Grande with the United States. If the only way to achieve this was to sacrifice Maximilian, then Maximilian would have to be sacrificed. On November 29 he wrote to Bazaine, "We cannot remain indefinitely in Mexico, and instead of building theaters and palaces, it is essential to introduce order into the finances and on the highways. Let him know that it will be much easier to abandon a government that has done nothing to enable it to survive rather than to support it in despite of itself."

On January 15, 1866, Napoleon wrote to Maximilian that he had decided to withdraw his troops from Mexico, and on January 22 he announced it to the world in his message to the Corps Législatif. France, having performed her duty to civilization in Mexico, would begin withdrawing her troops, for Emperor Maximilian was now strong enough to stand alone. Nine thousand French troops would leave in October 1866, another 9,000 in March 1867, and the remaining 11,300 would be withdrawn in October 1867.

Maximilian was taken aback at Napoleon's decision and wrote to him in protest; but there could be no question of Napoleon's changing his mind. He was determined to cut his losses in Mexico, and no one supported him more strongly than Eugénie. Many years later, when she admitted to Paléologue that she had been largely responsible for the decision to intervene in Mexico, she said that she regretted nothing except that the project had failed. By the end of 1865 she knew that it had indeed failed, and she energetically supported the decision to withdraw. According to General du Barail, she was at first always eager to meet soldiers who had served in Mexico; after 1865 she showed no desire to meet them and tried as far as possible to avoid doing so.

In November 1865 Bazaine, pursuing his strategy of withdrawing from the frontier and concentrating his forces to meet a possible American invasion, ordered General Brincourt to evacuate Chihuahua. As soon as Juárez heard that Brincourt's forces had left, he moved south with his escort of 800 men and entered Chihuahua. Brincourt was unhappy about this, particularly because he feared that the liberals would kill all the government officials and civilians who had collaborated with the French during their occupation of the city. He appealed to Maximilian, who asked Bazaine to send a force to recapture Chihuahua. Bazaine agreed to do so.

As the French troops advanced on Chihuahua, Juárez retreated to El Paso. The New Year found him once again driven back to the last half mile of Mexican territory, but Napoleon's decision to withdraw from Mexico meant that Juárez had won. If the French troops withdrew and the United States did not directly intervene, the field would be clear for Juárez and Maximilian to fight it out without foreign intervention on either side; if it was only a question of fighting Maximilian, Juárez felt sure of the final result. He had retreated once again to El Paso, but he had every reason to celebrate by opening another bottle of champagne.

❈ 24 ❈

CHARLOTTE

GOES TO EUROPE

THE LIBERALS WERE WINNING everywhere. At the beginning of
1865 *The Times* had written that twenty Mexicans would surrender
to one French soldier, but by the beginning of 1866 Maximilian's
armies were surrendering to the guerrillas. The liberals had learned
how to fight and their morale was high; but the morale of Maximilian's army was shattered by the knowledge that the French were abandoning them. Bazaine and his officers saw no point in risking their
lives to hold positions if they were going to evacuate them within a
year. The French army therefore remained on the defensive, withdrawing to convenient assembly points and not fighting unless they were
attacked; the guerrillas usually took care not to attack the French, for
they knew that they would soon be leaving.

The liberals had less respect for the Austrian and Belgian legions,
which were intending to remain in Mexico indefinitely to fight for
Maximilian. The guerrillas attacked the Austrians and Belgians and
often defeated and captured them. They also attacked Maximilian's
Mexican soldiers, whom they regarded as traitors, and killed them, as
well as the civilians who had collaborated with the French and Maximilian's government in contravention of Juárez's decree of January 25.

Maximilian's cause had not been helped by the deaths of three
people in Europe in 1865. In March the duke of Morny died in Paris;
he had been one of the chief supporters of the Mexican venture when
it was first suggested in 1861. In October Lord Palmerston died in
England; he would have been more likely than his successor, Lord
Russell, to have supported France in a war against the United States
to prevent the enforcement of the Monroe Doctrine. In December
King Leopold died in his palace of Laeken in Belgium. If he had lived
for another seven weeks, he would have had plenty to say when

Napoleon III announced his intention of withdrawing his troops from Mexico.

Many American volunteers were going to Mexico, most of them soldiers who had been discharged from the Union army after the Civil War. Some of them, like the Californians in the Legion of Honor, went to fight for Juárez out of enthusiasm for the liberal cause, but Romero encouraged them by offering good wages, with large payments to the higher-ranking officers. By 1866 Seward could no longer enforce the Neutrality Acts and prevent recruiting, as public opinion in the United States would not have tolerated it.

Two leading American generals wished to go to Mexico to fight for Juárez. General John Schofield, at Grant's suggestion, would have gone if Seward had not sent him on a pointless mission to Paris simply to prevent him from going to Mexico. General Lew Wallace had distinguished himself in the Battle of Shiloh and had sat on the military court that sentenced Lincoln's assassins and on the war crimes tribunal that sentenced Henry Wirz to death for his brutalities as commander of the Confederate prison camp at Andersonville (Wallace later won greater posthumous fame as the author of *Ben Hur*). In the spring of 1865 Wallace crossed the Rio Grande and met Carbajal in Tamaulipas, and together they managed to cross the French lines and reach New York, where Carbajal took a break from his hazardous activities as a guerrilla leader to spend some months as a propagandist and recruiting officer for Juárez. Wallace was a firm believer in the Monroe Doctrine and in the liberal cause, but money played its part. When Carbajal invited Wallace to take command of a corps of American volunteers and offered him $25,000 if the liberals lost in Mexico and $100,000 if they won, Wallace rejected the offer; he agreed to take command only after Carbajal offered $100,000, win or lose.

A few of the discharged Union soldiers went to fight not for Juárez but for Maximilian, whose agents opened a recruiting office on Tenth Avenue in New York. One of them was Prince Felix zu Salm-Salm, the younger son of the ruler of a small German principality, who had fought for the Union during the Civil War. He had risen to the rank of major general and was appointed by Sherman to be military governor of Atlanta after the capture of the city.

Prince Salm-Salm had married Agnes Le Clercq in Washington during the war. Agnes was a beautiful young woman with a mysterious past. Some said her parents were French immigrants, and others said she was a Canadian by birth; most commentators agreed that before she met and married Prince Salm-Salm she had been a circus rider in New York.

Thanks partly to Agnes's charm and energy, Prince and Princess Salm-Salm had become well known in society in wartime Washington and knew most of the leading people in politics and the army. Before Agnes left for Mexico, she went to see President Johnson and told him that her husband was going to fight for Maximilian. Johnson said he feared that the United States would have to intervene in Mexico on Juárez's side but he personally sympathized with Maximilian; he wished Salm-Salm the best of luck in Mexico.

In the depressing days at Chihuahua in 1864, Juárez, like other members of his government, had sent his wife and children to the United States for safety. Doña Margarita Juárez lived very simply in New York, for like all the Mexican diplomats and refugees in the United States, she was short of money. In March 1866 she heard that Romero's mother, who had been her friend when they were both young women in Oaxaca, had fallen ill at the Mexican legation in Washington, and she went to Washington to help nurse her.

Doña Margarita found, to her great surprise, that the United States government was treating her visit as a major diplomatic event, a state visit by the wife of the president of the Mexican Republic, the loyal ally of the United States. A great reception was held in her honor at the White House, the first reception held there since the end of the period of official mourning after Lincoln's assassination. A few days later Seward gave what was called an unofficial dinner in her honor at his house, attended by many important personages. In a speech at the dinner, Seward said he was sure that the French troops would leave Mexico before the end of the year.

The last event of Doña Margarita's visit was a ball given by General and Mrs. Grant at their house. To everyone's surprise, President Johnson came, though it was unusual for him to accept invitations to balls. It was even more surprising to see that the French minister in Washington was there. Doña Margarita, tall, handsome, and dignified, was in her element, and the political and diplomatic significance of her reception in Washington was clear. But she wrote to Juárez that the press reports of her elegant dress and many diamonds were untrue. She had worn the simple dress that he had bought for her in Saltillo and no jewelry except her earrings.

The campaign in the United States against Maximilian and the French in Mexico continued. Napoleon's announcement that he would withdraw his troops by stages did not satisfy the radicals, for they did not trust him to keep his promise. Another great rally at the Cooper Institute in New York on January 6, 1866, was addressed by a number of well-known liberals, who demanded that the French leave Mexico at once. In the press a battle was waged between Raymond's *New-York Times* and William C. Bryant's New York *Evening Post,* which denounced Seward's policy of appeasing Napoleon III. The *New-York Times* claimed that Seward's brilliant diplomacy was working and was persuading the French to withdraw from Mexico, whereas the *Evening Post*'s belligerent attitude would draw the United States into war against the greatest army in the world. The *Evening Post* replied that it did not wish to go to war with France, but thought Napoleon would leave Mexico only if the United States pursued a firm policy and strengthened Sheridan's army on the Rio Grande.

A broadsheet was distributed in Washington in July 1866 with the heading "The Betrayal of the Cause of Freedom by William H. Seward." It asked why Seward allowed the soldiers of Napoleon III, "the direst foe of Democratic liberty in Europe, still to hold a great and friendly people in bondage in Mexico?" Seward should tell Napoleon to leave Mexico within ninety days, for 500,000 American soldiers would be ready to make him go; if Napoleon tried to start a war with the United States, he would provoke a revolution in France "which would inevitably hurl the blood-stained conspirator who now rules her from his ill-gotten throne. . . . Mr. Secretary, for the sake of the country, your own reputation, do not *talk* any more about the Monroe Doctrine, but in the name of justice, liberty, in the sacred name of God, *act* upon that doctrine and stop the flow of blood in Mexico."

Under pressure from American public opinion, Seward adopted a firmer attitude, especially when he became convinced that Napoleon III was determined to leave Mexico and would not go to war with the United States in order to stay. Napoleon hoped that Maximilian would find other troops than the French army to fight his battles in Mexico, and he encouraged Maximilian to enlist more foreign volunteers; but the United States used its influence to prevent these volunteers from going to fight for Maximilian.

The United States could now afford to adopt a much firmer attitude than it had done in 1863 about the recruitment of black troops in Egypt. In August 1865 the United States consul in Alexandria, Charles Hale, was informed that the khedive was planning to send another 900 Sudanese men to Mexico.

Hale protested strongly to the khedive's foreign minister against the plan to send 900 men to invade the territory of the Mexican Republic, the ally of the United States. He told the foreign minister that the United States, too, had black soldiers in its army, 100,000 of them, and that if Egypt sent black soldiers to invade Mexico, the United States might send their black soldiers to invade Egypt. The khedive's government became alarmed and asked France to withdraw its demand for the soldiers. When Bigelow raised the matter with Drouyn de Lhuys, Drouyn insisted that France had the right to enlist Egyptian soldiers, with the khedive's consent, without consulting the United States. But he agreed on this occasion to abandon the plan.

Maximilian looked chiefly to Austria to provide the volunteers needed for his army. In March 1866 his agents recruited 4,000 more volunteers in Austria, and it was announced that the first detachment, 1,000 men, would sail from Trieste on May 15. Seward instructed Motley to make a strong protest to Rechberg and to inform him that if the volunteers were allowed to sail, the United States would regard it as a hostile act and would break off diplomatic relations with Austria. When Seward read the draft of his note to Austria at a Cabinet meeting in Washington on April 17, his Cabinet colleagues were surprised at the firmness of his tone, which contrasted strongly with the soft language he had always used in his notes to France. McCulloch and James Speed, the attorney general, thought the wording of the note was too strong, and McCulloch as usual argued that the United States could not afford the cost of a new war; but Dennison, Harlan, and Stanton supported Seward's strong stand. Welles suggested that if they were going to adopt a tough policy, it would be better to do it with France than with Austria; they should seize the French head rather than the Austrian tail. Seward said that if Napoleon III did not carry out his promise to withdraw his troops by the stated date, he would get tough with France as well as with Austria.

Seward's draft of the note was approved and was sent to Motley in Vienna. When Motley read it to Rechberg, the Austrian government agreed to forbid the volunteers to sail to Veracruz, and to ban the recruitment in Austria of volunteers to serve in Mexico. Maximilian bitterly resented the Austrian decision and felt that Franz Joseph had once again betrayed him.

By the summer of 1866 Maximilian's situation looked very serious. In June Bazaine again ordered his troops to evacuate Chihuahua, and when Juárez heard this, he again left El Paso and moved south. When he arrived at Chihuahua on June 17, he was given a great reception. The following evening a great ball was held in Juárez's honor.

Maximilian was annoyed that his forces had again withdrawn from Chihuahua and that Juárez had been allowed to return there. He asked Bazaine to send an army to recapture Chihuahua and chase Juárez away. Bazaine refused. He had twice captured Chihuahua for Maximilian, and did not intend to lose the lives of any of his men in capturing it a third time; he would in any case be obliged to evacuate again when his troops were withdrawn from Mexico. By September he had decided to withdraw from the north and west of the country and to hold nothing beyond a line from Tampico to Guadalajara. He hoped at first to hold Tampico, but after it had been captured by the guerrillas, recaptured by the French, and again lost to the guerrillas, Bazaine made no further effort to retake it. He also evacuated Tuxpán. To the surprise of the traders and foreigners there, the liberals did not loot or misbehave in the captured town, and in a very short time Tuxpán's trade and prosperity were thriving as they had not done for many years.

Many of Maximilian's soldiers were deserting to the liberals, including some French soldiers and members of the Foreign Legion. The liberal generals distributed leaflets to the French, Belgian, and Austrian soldiers, offering them farm land in Mexico if they deserted and joined the liberals; alternatively, if they preferred, they would be given a passport to the Rio Grande.

> Soldiers, it is four years since they made you come here to fight against us, who only wish to live under republican institutions. They made you believe that the ridiculous throne of Maximilian could consolidate itself in our country. Soldiers, you have been tricked. Instead of a military walkover which you thought you would make in our country, you are finding that every one of our mountain passes produces liberal forces which are always ready to fight against you.

The liberals took many Belgian and Austrian, and a few French, prisoners. Apart from an occasional unauthorized act of brutality by some of their guards, the prisoners were well treated. The Franco-Mexican army no longer enforced the Black Decree or Bazaine's order of October 11, 1865. Captured guerrillas were now well treated in the hope that they would be exchanged for the French, Austrian, and Belgian prisoners in the liberals' hands. Bazaine negotiated several agreements for the exchange of prisoners with Díaz in the south, with Escobedo in Tamaulipas, and with Riva Palacio in the west.

Maximilian, seeing that Napoleon III and Eugénie were turning against him, wondered if his minister in Paris, Hidalgo, had been mishandling matters. He recalled Hidalgo and appointed Almonte to replace him. This suited Almonte, as it meant that he would be out of Mexico before Juárez occupied the whole country. Hidalgo was not happy about being recalled; he resigned from government service, quickly settled his business affairs in Mexico, and returned to Paris in time. As for the man who had first conceived the idea of sending Maximilian to Mexico, Gutiérrez de Estrada, he had remained in Europe during the years of the empire and certainly had no intention of returning to Mexico now.

Charlotte decided to go to Paris. She was shocked that the French troops were to be withdrawn, for she had written to Eugénie that although the Austrian and Belgian legions were rendering useful service, in times of crisis they were no substitute for the French soldiers in their "red trousers." She hoped that if she herself spoke to Napoleon, she would be able to persuade him to change his mind and not withdraw the *pantalons rouges.* On July 9 she left Mexico City on her tragic and extraordinary journey, which ended three months later with her lapse into incurable madness. She was accompanied by Foreign Minister Castillo, a number of officials, and her ladies, gentlemen, and servants. Altogether the traveling party numbered about fifty. Because of the danger from guerrillas and robbers, they were escorted by several hundred cavalrymen. Maximilian went with Charlotte as far as Ayutla, about twenty-five miles from Mexico City, where they said goodbye. They were never to see each other again.

1866

She stayed the first night at Puebla, where she behaved a little strangely; the members of her escort later, with hindsight, thought that she showed the first symptoms of insanity at Puebla. She had just retired to bed when suddenly, at midnight, she said that she wished to visit the house of Señor Esteva, who some months before, when he was the political prefect at Puebla, had entertained her there at a banquet. As she insisted, her ladies and gentlemen went with her to the house. Esteva had now been transferred to a post in Veracruz, but his servants opened the door and showed the empress around the empty house. She was very exuberant, and when they reached the dining room she told them that it was the room where she had been entertained at the banquet.

The journey to Veracruz took four days because the roads were in poor condition after the recent heavy rains. Charlotte became very worried that she would miss the boat at Veracruz, though her gentlemen assured her that the ship's captain had been ordered not to sail until she arrived.

She was received at Veracruz by Admiral Cloué, who escorted her to the launch that was to take her to the *Impératrice Eugénie,* which was waiting for her just outside the harbor. When she saw that the launch was flying the French flag, she became very indignant; she refused to enter the launch until they had found a Mexican flag to hoist over it. On the voyage across the Atlantic she was more silent than usual, and at times seemed very depressed.

She arrived at Saint-Nazaire on August 8 and went on by train to Paris. There was an unfortunate slipup upon her arrival in Paris, for Drouyn de Lhuys, Almonte, and the other ministers and dignitaries who had come to receive her went to the wrong train station. Her gentlemen had to hire a cab to take her to the Grand Hotel, where a suite of rooms had been reserved for her. The dignitaries who should have met her at the station arrived soon afterward and made their apologies.

She had hoped to meet Napoleon III at once, but was told that he was at Saint-Cloud and was too ill to see her. She probably thought that this was an excuse, but it was not; Napoleon had already begun to suffer from the stones that were to affect his health and perhaps his judgment, and from which he would die seven years later. Eugénie came to the Grand Hotel, and Charlotte discussed the situation in Mexico with her and with Drouyn de Lhuys, Marshal Randon, the minister of war, and the Austrian ambassador, Richard Metternich.

After some days Napoleon was well enough to see her at Saint-Cloud, but she was unable to persuade him to change his mind. Eloin told Maximilian that she had argued her case very skillfully, and that if anyone could have persuaded Napoleon to keep his troops in Mexico, it was Charlotte. But Napoleon remained adamant: the first batch of troops would return to France in October, the second batch in March 1867, and the remainder in October 1867.

Charlotte had another unpleasant experience in Paris. Alice Iturbide came to the Grand Hotel, and Charlotte reluctantly agreed to see her. When she was admitted, Charlotte was seated on a sofa. She did not offer Alice a seat, so Alice sat down, uninvited, on the sofa beside Charlotte. After Alice pleaded to have her child back, Charlotte told her to write to Maximilian about it. Alice said she had written many times but had received no reply. "Write again," said Charlotte, "and write politely."

Charlotte went on to Miramar, from where she wrote to Napoleon and Eugénie, thanking them for their hospitality in Paris; it was in every way a proper and conventional letter of thanks. She also wrote at length to Maximilian, telling him that her efforts had failed. In these letters she was bitterly critical of Napoleon. "To me he is the devil in person," she wrote, and added that when he said goodbye to her, he was "quite the amiable Mephistopheles" and kissed her hand. These phrases have been cited as a sign of her developing insanity; but if she had not gone mad soon afterward, no one would have thought that there was anything strange about these letters, which could have been written by any normal person who used strong expressions, half-seriously meant, about someone they did not like. No one has ever questioned John Motley's sanity, but in a letter written at about this time he described Napoleon III as the "prince of darkness, who for the time being has thought fit to assume the appearance of a sovereign of France and to inhabit the Tuileries."

Charlotte stayed for three weeks at Miramar, living not in the castle, where construction work was being carried on, but in the little cottage in the garden. She then went to Rome to see Pope Pius IX, and there she showed for the first time unmistakable symptoms of insanity. On September 30, at one of her private audiences with the pope, she asked if she could stay the night in the Vatican instead of returning to her hotel. Pius said that this would not be possible because no woman had ever stayed the night in the Vatican; she said that the Vatican was the only place where she would be safe from the agents of Napoleon III, who were trying to poison her. The pope had no doubt that her mind was unhinged. She pleaded so hard that he relented and allowed her to stay one night in the Vatican; the next morning he sent her back to her hotel under escort.

Later that day she was able to write her last letter to Maximilian: "Dearly beloved treasure, I bid you farewell. God is calling me to Him. I thank you for the happiness which you have always given me. May God bless you and help you to win eternal bliss. Your faithful Charlotte."

In the hotel she refused to touch any food or drink prepared by the hotel staff. She sent her maidservant out to buy some live chickens, which she kept tied up in her hotel room. The maidservant had to kill and cook the chickens herself to make sure that no one had poisoned them. Charlotte would eat nothing except the chickens and the eggs they hatched in her presence. She drove in her carriage with her lady-in-waiting to the Trevi Fountain and filled a crystal pitcher with water from the fountain and took it back to the hotel to drink.

Maximilian had sent Blasio to Europe to act as Charlotte's secretary, and he was with her in Miramar and Rome. She dictated letters to court officials in Mexico City, in which she accused the foreign minister, Castillo, and other officials who were with her in Rome of trying to murder her on the instructions of Napoleon III. Her gentlemen did not post these letters but wrote instead to her brother King Leopold II of the Belgians, who sent their brother the count of Flanders to Rome to take her back to Miramar, where she was treated by Maximilian's former physician, Dr. Jilek. He arranged for Professor Riedel, the leading mental specialist in Vienna, to go to Miramar to treat her. Leopold decided that her medical treatment and the isolation of Miramar were doing more harm than good, and he had her brought to Belgium, where she lived in the castle of Tervuren near Brussels. Her relatives sometimes reported that she seemed to be improving, but this was always followed a few months later by a relapse.

Charlotte's gentlemen had written to Maximilian that the empress was ill. They did not specify the nature of her illness but mentioned that she was in the care of Professor Riedel. When Maximilian was told that Riedel was the director of the lunatic asylum in Vienna, he understood at once what had happened to Charlotte.

Napoleon III now saw that there was a drawback to his plan of evacuating his troops from Mexico in stages. After the bulk of the troops had gone, would those still left be strong enough to resist an attack by the liberal forces? He therefore decided that instead of bringing the troops home in three stages, he would bring them all back in March 1867. This meant postponing the departure of the first French troops for five months, but they would all be out of Mexico seven months earlier than he had promised. He duly informed the United States government of his change of plan.

This was an embarrassment for Seward. He had been strongly criticized for having accepted Napoleon's assurances about withdrawing the troops, and if Napoleon now broke his promise to begin the withdrawal in October 1866, Seward would be denounced in the United States as Napoleon's dupe. He drafted a very strong protest to France, which he read out to his colleagues at the Cabinet meeting on November 22 and which he proposed sending as a telegram over the transatlantic cable that had been completed two months before.

The Cabinet members were very surprised. A year before, Seward had seemed so eager to appease Napoleon III and unwilling to run the slightest risk of war in order to get the French out of Mexico; now he was prepared to wave the big stick and risk war because the French departure from Mexico was delayed for five months. The continual pressure of public opinion had obviously had its effect on Seward, who now felt he had to be seen as taking a strong line; he may also have calculated that if Napoleon was not prepared to go to war to maintain Maximilian in Mexico, he would not do so now just because he received a sharp note from the United States. Only Seward and Alexander Randall, the postmaster general, were in favor of sending the note; President Johnson approved of it, but all the others thought it was too menacing.

In view of the opposition in the Cabinet, Seward agreed to come back the next day with a new draft that was not so threatening. At Seward's suggestion the president invited Grant to attend the Cabinet meeting, and Grant praised Seward's new firmness and thoroughly approved of the note. Stanton, who had thought the first draft a little too strong, also approved of the new wording, and it was agreed that Seward should send the note to the French government. It did not lead to war or delay the plans for the total withdrawal of French troops in March 1867.

Napoleon believed that Maximilian's best course was to abdicate and return to Europe, but this would mean that Mexico would fall into the hands of Juárez. Anarchy would prevail, and all the horrors that Napoleon had tried to prevent would come about. He would prefer to see the United States take over Mexico. He instructed his minister in Washington to suggest to Seward that when the French troops and Maximilian left, the United States should intervene to maintain law and order in Mexico. Bazaine agreed and sent a message through an intermediary to President Johnson: "The moral influence of the United States has destroyed the Empire, and thus the obligation rests upon the United States to keep Mexico from anarchy and protect the thousands of foreigners residing there." The idea was discussed in the press in the United States. American intervention in Mexico to restrain Juárez was favored by the opponents of liberalism who had been opposed to American intervention to help Juárez against the French.

Colonel Gagern, a German immigrant who was an officer in the liberal army, went to the United States at about this time. He met Grant, Sherman, and Sheridan and was impressed by their different personalities. He noticed that the three top American generals were all cigar smokers, but all smoked differently. Grant, who smoked fifty a day, hardly ever took his cigar out of his mouth, so that it was sometimes difficult to understand what he said. Sherman would nervously light a cigar, stub it out after a few puffs, and then light another one, so his room was littered with half-smoked cigars. Sheridan smoked slowly and lovingly like a connoisseur and stopped while he talked, so he was always relighting his cigar.

Gagern discussed the situation in Mexico with Sherman at army headquarters in St. Louis. Sherman interrupted him. "What would you say, Colonel," he asked, "if I were to come to your help with 50,000 of my blue boys?" Gagern said that he was not sure the Mexicans would like this. They would be delighted if Sherman's blue boys came and drove out the French; but if the blue boys came to Mexico, would the Mexicans be able to get them to leave after the French had gone? Sherman laughed. "Perhaps you are right," he said, "it would probably cause difficulties. It would in any case be better if you carry out your liberation by yourselves."

Seward was as opposed as Sherman to sending an army into Mexico. The only step he was prepared to take was to send Lewis Campbell, an official of the State Department, and a prominent army general to Mexico to discuss with Juárez the possibility of American troops helping to maintain order in Mexico. He asked Grant, in view of his interest in Mexico, if he would go, but Grant suspected that this was a trick to get him away from Washington and the center of power, and he refused. He suggested that Sherman should go in his place. Sherman was not at all keen to undertake the mission, but he agreed to go to please his friend Grant. In November 1866 Campbell and Sherman sailed from New York to Veracruz, where they stayed on their ship, for their instructions from Seward were that they should not intervene in Mexico until Maximilian had abdicated.

Rumors that Maximilian was about to abdicate had been circulating in Europe and the United States. But Maximilian could not make up his mind. He realized that Napoleon III hoped that he would abdicate; no one could reproach Napoleon for withdrawing his troops and leaving Maximilian in the lurch if Maximilian had already abdicated and left the country before the French troops did. But Maximilian was not going to abdicate to please Napoleon. He knew that Charlotte did not wish him to abdicate. Just before she left Mexico she told him that abdication, particularly by a young emperor aged thirty-four, would be an act of cowardice unworthy of a prince of the house of Habsburg.

In November he traveled to his favorite residence, Jalapilla, near Orizaba. The news spread at once that he was on his way to Veracruz to embark for Europe and that he would abdicate before he sailed. Reports in the press of his abdication reached Austria, and his mother, Archduchess Sophie, sent a telegram to Franz Joseph at Schönbrunn telling him that Maxi would be arriving in Europe very shortly. But Maximilian remained at Orizaba wondering whether or not to abdicate. While his French advisers and some of the Mexican moderate liberals in his government urged him to go, the conservative ministers urged him to remain at his post, for they realized that this was their last desperate chance of preventing a liberal victory and all that this would mean for them. Eloin wrote to him from Brussels urging him not to abdicate, and so did his mother, Sophie, and his brother Archduke Karl Ludwig from Vienna. Gutiérrez, from the safety of Paris, also urged him to do his duty and stay at his post.

Maximilian summoned his ministers to Orizaba, and on November 25 he held a Cabinet meeting at 10 A.M. He opened the meeting by saying that he wished to have their advice as to whether or not he should abdicate, then he left them to discuss it while he walked in the woods with his Jewish physician from Prague, Dr. Basch, collecting plant specimens. The ministers had a long discussion. According to Blasio, who was with Maximilian in Orizaba, when the question was finally put to the vote, there were ten votes against abdication and eight in favor of it; but Dr. Basch stated that the voting was ten to two against abdication, with only the two moderate liberals voting in favor. The confusion may be partly due to the complicated voting procedure by which some Cabinet ministers had two votes and others had only one.

When the ministers told Maximilian of their decision, he said he would continue as emperor until he could convene a special session of the Assembly of Notables, whose decision he would abide by. He also issued a decree repealing the Black Decree of October 3, 1865. His ministers pledged their loyalty. They did not like his proposal to refer the question of abdication to a Congress of Notables, but consoled themselves with the thought that it would be impossible, in existing circumstances, to convene a congress.

When Campbell and Sherman at Veracruz heard that Maximilian was not intending to abdicate, they obeyed their instructions and returned to New Orleans. Campbell waited there while he tried to find out where Juárez was, so that he could go to him, but Sherman went on to New York. He wrote to his brother that he thought Juárez was "away up in Chihuahua for no other possible purpose than to be where the devil himself cannot get at him. I have not the remotest idea of riding on mule back a thousand miles in Mexico to find its chief magistrate."

Maximilian returned to Mexico City and prepared to fight the liberals with the support of his loyal Mexicans. He was now relying on the support of the conservatives, including Miramón and Márquez, who had returned to Mexico. The liberals were overrunning all of Maximilian's empire. By the end of September they had captured Matamoros, Tampico, Tuxpán, Saltillo, Monterrey, Durango, Guaymas, Alvarado, and Tlacotalpán. In October Díaz captured the city of Oaxaca, and in November Mazatlán and Jalapa fell to the liberals. By the end of the year they were in Zacatecas, Guadalajara, Guanajuato, and San Luis Potosí. Maximilian and the French held only Veracruz, Orizaba, Puebla, Mexico City, and Querétaro.

But just when the liberals seemed to be winning everywhere, Juárez was confronted with a situation that threatened great harm to the liberal cause. In October 1866 Ortega announced that he was returning to Mexico at the head of a band of volunteers whom he would lead against the French and Maximilian's forces; he issued his proclamation as president of Mexico. According to law, Ortega was undoubtedly in the right, but political expediency demanded that he be prevented from splitting the liberal forces in Mexico.

As soon as Romero heard that Ortega was on his way to Mexico, he contacted Grant, who decided to stop Ortega. Grant sent instructions to Sheridan in New Orleans, who warned the commanding officer at Brazos de Santiago, near Brownsville, that Ortega and his companions would be arriving there by sea, and that they were to be arrested and held in custody until further notice. The orders were carried out, and despite his protests Ortega was imprisoned at Brazos. Meanwhile Matamoros had been occupied by General Canales, who supported Ortega; so Sheridan sent Colonel Sedgwick with some American troops to Matamoros, ostensibly to protect the safety of some American citizens there, but really to prevent Ortega from capturing the city and holding it against Juárez. Romero made a formal protest to the United States against the presence of Sedgwick's troops in Matamoros, and the troops were quickly withdrawn across the Rio Grande to Brownsville. But Ortega's supporters were sure that this was a put-up job and that Sedgwick had acted in collusion with Escobedo, who commanded the pro-Juárez forces at Matamoros. A local liberal commander at Saltillo declared in favor of Ortega, but he was arrested and shot by liberal troops loyal to Juárez.

After Ortega had been imprisoned for a month at Brazos, Sheridan, after consulting Escobedo, ordered his release. Presumably Escobedo and Juárez thought that with Ortega's supporters having been worsted at Matamoros and Saltillo, it was now safe to allow him to enter Mexico, where Juárez's supporters would be able to arrest him. Ortega went to Zacatecas and told the local liberal commander that he was the president of Mexico; but the commander, who supported Juárez, arrested Ortega and sent him to Saltillo as a prisoner. Ortega protested that he was legally president; but he had failed, and Juárez, who received declarations of support from nearly all his generals in the field, had won.

Juárez was moving south a little behind his armies. On December 10 he left Chihuahua and moved to Durango, and by January 22 he had reached Zacatecas. When Miramón heard that he was there, he thought of a daring plan. Zacatecas, far behind the front line, was guarded by only a small liberal garrison. He would lead a troop of cavalry deep into liberal territory, raid Zacatecas, and capture Juárez. Maximilian approved of the plan. He ordered Miramón, if he captured Juárez or Lerdo, to try them by court-martial and condemn them to death, but not to carry out the sentence without referring the case to him.

Miramón's plan nearly succeeded; but unfortunately for him, it was not true, as his supporters believed, that Juárez could not ride a horse. Juárez was warned just in time. He and his ministers quickly left Government House in Zacatecas, mounted horses, and rode off into the countryside. Miramón's men broke into Government House a quarter of an hour after Juárez had left, but they did not pursue him, for they had no idea in which direction he had gone. What would Miramón have done if he had captured Juárez? Would he have obeyed Maximilian's' orders? Or would he, as many people believed, have shot him on the spot and thought up some story afterward to explain his disobedience to Maximilian? Or would he have done what no one expected and renewed the offer he had made in Paris to come over to Juárez's side if Juárez appointed him to a high command in his armies?

Miramón's daring raid had caught the liberals off their guard, but Escobedo quickly assembled his forces and struck back at Miramón. A week later he defeated Miramón at San Jacinto, a little south of Zacatecas. The liberals captured more than a hundred prisoners in the battle, including some French and Austrian soldiers and Miramón's brother Joaquin. They herded all the prisoners together in an open space surrounded by liberal troops, and then took small groups of prisoners away and killed them by firing two shots into their heads. The remaining prisoners, hearing the shots, realized what was happening to their comrades; they shouted their defiance, and were prepared for death when it was their turn to be taken away. Some of them asked their guards why they were being killed and were told that it was in reprisal for all the captured guerrillas who had been shot by the French and the *contre-guérilla*. Lerdo afterward justified the killings by stating that all the prisoners executed at San Jacinto were criminals who had committed atrocities during their brief occupation of Zacatecas.

The French were about to leave. The foreign residents in Mexico City, and anyone who had played a prominent part in Maximilian's administration, were expecting the worst when Juárez reentered the city. They thought it was high time to go, and waited only to arrange transport to Veracruz. Sara Yorke and her family decided to leave because they had been so closely connected with the French. The social life in the city had sadly deteriorated after the empress went to Europe, and it had now almost ceased; but they tried to forget their worries and enjoy themselves with their friends during the last days. They knew they would never see their houses again and would certainly not receive any compensation for them. But at least their lives would be safe if the coach to Veracruz came in time and they avoided the guerrillas on the road.

The French marched out of Mexico City on February 5, 1867, three years and eight months after they had marched in. The people came out to watch them leave, standing in silence, with no one cheering or booing or making any kind of demonstration. Maximilian did not come out onto the palace balcony to see them go. Before Bazaine left, he had invited Maximilian to come with him and had reminded him that he could, if he wished, embark on a French ship that would carry·

him to Europe. Bazaine stopped for some days at Puebla. He sent a message to Maximilian that if he had changed his mind about leaving the country, he would wait for him at Puebla and escort him to Veracruz. But Maximilian had decided to remain in Mexico and to lead his army into battle against the liberals.

Before setting out on his campaign, he made arrangements to return Agustin Iturbide to his mother. He wrote to Alice that he could no longer care for her son and would therefore hand him over to her or to anyone whom she would nominate to receive him. He asked Archbishop Labastida to make the arrangements with Alice. Agustin was taken to Havana and from there to New York, where he was reunited with his mother after a separation of nearly two years.

❦ 25 ❦

QUERÉTARO

MAXIMILIAN LEFT Mexico City on February 13, not for Veracruz and Europe but for the north, with Márquez and a force of 2,000 cavalry. He was dressed in his favorite gray topcoat and white hat and rode his beloved horse Anteburro. He had decided to establish his headquarters for the coming campaign at Querétaro. Prince Salm-Salm went with Maximilian, but his beautiful and adventurous wife was not allowed to come. This annoyed her very much, for she had usually accompanied her husband on his campaigns during the American Civil War.

Maximilian was short of men, short of munitions, and short of money. Owing to his utter failure to organize an efficient military and financial administration, he was in a far weaker position than Juárez, who was now receiving all the arms that he needed from the United States. Maximilian was not discouraged, for Mejía had told him that wars could be won without money, merely by courage and resolution, and he was sure he could rely on the courage and resolution of generals like Mejía, Miramón, Márquez, and Mendez and their devoted followers. Some of his subjects were responding to his appeals for money; Señor Barron the banker gave him $100,000. But his army was far outnumbered by the liberals: he had 21,700 men to their 69,700.

On February 19 he reached the summit of Cuesta China, one and a half miles from Querétaro, and looked down on the city. He changed from his civilian dress into the uniform of a general of the Mexican army, with the Grand Cross of the Mexican Eagle on his breast, and dismounted from his gentle Anteburro to mount one of his other horses, the more spirited Orisgelo. As he entered Querétaro he was greeted by Miramón and Mejía, who had already arrived there with 3,000 men. The civilian population turned out to cheer him, with the beautiful ladies of the higher social classes being particularly enthusiastic. Maximilian's health gave out, as it often did at moments of crisis, and he was too tired to attend the banquet given in his honor that evening.

The next day Mendez arrived from Michoacán with another 4,000 men, bringing the total of Maximilian's forces in the city to 9,000. Maximilian knew that two liberal armies were advancing on Querétaro, one under Escobedo, who was coming from San Luis Potosí with 17,000 men, and the other under Corona, coming from Acámbaro with 18,000 men. The two liberal armies were 150 miles apart. Miramón proposed to Maximilian the idea of attacking the two armies in turn before they could unite. He thought that if he could first defeat Escobedo by a vigorous surprise attack, which would have a shattering moral effect on Corona's army, he could then march against Corona and defeat him. Márquez said that the plan was too risky, but Blasio believed that the real reason Márquez opposed it was that it had been proposed by Miramón, for there was no love lost between these two generals.

After the matter had been discussed at a council of war, Maximilian decided against Miramón's proposal and supported Márquez. Blasio was surprised at the extent of Márquez's influence over Maximilian; and it is strange that Maximilian, with his liberal ideas, should have issued a proclamation at this time in which he warmly praised "the brave General Márquez." Was Maximilian fascinated by the cruel and successful military chieftain of whose policies and actions he disapproved, just as he had been fascinated by the Albanian sailor who had told him of torturing Turkish soldiers, and by the brutal slaveholder in Brazil who had made his slaves endure the agonies of the *chicote* and the *palmatoria*?

The armies of Escobedo and Corona joined together at Querétaro and began the siege on March 6 with 35,000 soldiers and siege artillery which bombarded the city nearly every day. Maximilian's 9,000 men resisted valiantly and often made successful sorties to obtain provisions and to inflict a blow at the liberals' morale by defeating their troops in some local engagement. Maximilian's headquarters were in the Convent of La Cruz on a hill inside the city. The convent came under enemy fire, but Maximilian behaved with great coolness, and alarmed his officers by insisting on strolling slowly across the courtyard, where there was no cover from liberal shells and bullets. He also walked in the streets of the city, smoking his cigar, talking to the passersby and asking them for a light or offering them one from the tip of his own cigar. The women of Querétaro were as fascinated as the women of Mexico City had been by the tall figure, red-blond hair and beard, kind blue eyes, and gentle charm of the young emperor.

Maximilian and his officers realized that they could not hold out indefinitely at Querétaro; their only hope was that a relieving army could come to their aid and force Escobedo to abandon the siege. Maximilian decided to send Márquez to Mexico City to raise a new army that would march to the relief of Querétaro. In case he himself should lose his life at Querétaro, he appointed Márquez and two of the conservative ministers to be regents until a Congress could be convened to decide the future government of Mexico.

At dawn on March 22 Miramón led a sortie and attacked the liberals as a diversion while Márquez with a small escort slipped quietly out of Querétaro. The maneuver was successful. Márquez reached Mexico City, and by resorting to the *leva,* which Maximilian had banned, his press gangs forcibly enrolled young men in the army. He raised some of the money Maximilian needed by forced loans.

While the liberals were besieging Maximilian in Querétaro, the French troops in Mexico were assembling in Veracruz. Before evacuating a town, the French in most cases destroyed their armaments. They were bitterly reproached for this, both at the time and afterward, by Maximilian and his supporters. Why, if they felt obliged to abandon Maximilian, did they not at least leave their cannon, their rifles, and their ammunition behind for his army? Maximilian's supporters attributed this solely to Bazaine's malice and his hatred of Maximilian and of the Catholic party in Mexico.

Kératry, Gaulot, and Bazaine's supporters refuted this accusation. They said Maximilian's Mexican army was so inefficient that it would not have been able to arrange to collect the munitions if the French had left them behind. In every case when the French evacuated a town, the liberals occupied it almost immediately, long before Maximilian's army arrived; and if the French had not destroyed their ammunition when they withdrew, it would in every case have fallen into the hands of the liberal armies. But according to Porfirio Díaz, Bazaine offered to sell his stocks of ammunition to him, and destroyed the ammunition only because Díaz turned down his offer.

More and more French soldiers crowded into Veracruz, as the transport ships arrived in the harbor. This caused an acute shortage of accommodations, and rents and prices soared. In the overcrowded conditions, yellow fever and *vómito* claimed even more victims than usual, both among the French soldiers and the civilian population.

There were also civilian refugees in Veracruz. The foreign residents who had lived in Mexico, in some cases all their lives, as members of high society in the capital, or as mine owners in Guanajuato, San Luis

Potosí, or Zacatecas, or as prosperous landowners on their country *haciendas,* were leaving as quickly as possible before they were massacred by the victorious liberals. Sara Yorke and her party waited as patiently as possible for a ship that would take them to France. Sara met Colonel Du Pin in Veracruz. He was no longer hanging and terrifying guerrillas and their sympathizers, but was showing avuncular solicitude for Sara and the other young ladies, warning them not to leave their hotel because of the risk of sunstroke.

At the beginning of March the people of Veracruz heard that Díaz had captured Orizaba and Córdoba, thus severing all links between Mexico City and Veracruz. Only the French troops marching across country could now reach the port.

The evacuation was carried out efficiently. Bazaine himself sailed on the *Souverain.* Before leaving, he handed over the governorship of Veracruz to Maximilian's political prefect, Bureau, and the commander of Maximilian's forces, General Taboada. As Bureau and Taboada were in charge, and there was no danger that the liberals would get there first, Bazaine did not destroy the French munitions, but handed them over to Taboada for the use of Maximilian's forces.

When Bazaine landed at Toulon six weeks later, he found to his surprise that no official welcome had been arranged for him. This was on the orders of Napoleon III, who wanted the whole Mexican business forgotten.

The last French soldiers left on March 16, when the *Magellan* sailed from Veracruz at 4 P.M. with Admiral Cloué on board. There had been a storm during the previous night, and the sea was still rather rough. The sky was overcast. After passing the Isla de Sacrificios, with the building that had been the French military hospital, they could still see the white walls of Veracruz disappearing into the distance in the evening light. "We were leaving, at last!" wrote Naval Captain Rivière.

Puebla was held by Maximilian's army under the command of General Noriega, a zealous conservative and a friend of Márquez's. Díaz besieged Puebla, and on April 2 captured it by assault. After Díaz's men had captured the forts and breached the defenses, Noriega, thinking that further resistance was hopeless, surrendered unconditionally. Díaz let the other ranks go free and accepted into his army all who wished to join him; but he ordered that Noriega and all his 74 officers were to be shot as traitors under the decree of January 25. Díaz addressed the officers before their execution; he said that although they had not lived like men, they could at least die like men. He afterward said he hoped that his severity at Puebla would teach the enemy a lesson he would not have to repeat elsewhere.

On April 7 Díaz issued an order of the day to his troops, praising them for their capture of Puebla. With the rifles taken from the enemy, they had captured at the first attempt a city that "the best soldiers in the world" had been unable to take by assault. Kératry was stung by this comparison between the ease with which Díaz had captured Puebla in 1867 and the time that it had taken the French army to capture the city in 1863. He attributed Díaz's success to Noriega's treachery.

After capturing Puebla, Díaz advanced on Mexico City. Márquez was intending to lead the army he had raised to Querétaro to rescue Maximilian. But he knew that if he marched to Querétaro, Mexico City would fall at once to Díaz, which would be a terrible blow to the morale of Maximilian's supporters. He therefore decided to disobey Maximilian's orders and lead the new army against Díaz and to save Mexico City by defeating Díaz in battle.

The forces of Márquez and Díaz clashed at San Lorenzo on April 10. Díaz routed Márquez's men, who fled in all directions, though Márquez was able to retire in good order to Mexico City with 400 Austrians who had enlisted in Maximilian's Mexican army when the Austrian and Belgian legions left for Europe in January. Márquez now had no army to lead to Querétaro, so he decided to put Mexico City into a state of defense and hold it at all costs against an attack by Díaz. Within a few days Díaz had laid siege to Mexico City. He captured Chapultepec and established his headquarters in Maximilian's palace.

The defenders of Querétaro waited impatiently for the arrival of Márquez's relieving army and wondered why he had not come. Maximilian sent out scouts who were to slip through the liberal lines and bring back news of Márquez from Mexico City. Most of the scouts did not return. The few who did reported that they had found the bodies of the others hanging from trees along the road to Mexico City, sometimes mutilated and with notes saying that this fate would befall all traitors who carried messages for Maximilian.

Miramón sometimes returned from his daring sorties with a few liberal soldiers as his prisoners. He proposed that they be executed and their corpses displayed to their comrades in the besieging army in reprisal for the hanging of Maximilian's messengers by the liberals and for the shooting of his younger brother by the liberals near Zacatecas. Maximilian forbade any reprisals. He insisted that the liberal prisoners be kindly treated and that any who were wounded should receive as much medical attention in the hospitals as his own soldiers did. Maximilian's kindly nature would never have permitted acts of cruelty to be carried out before his eyes; but the liberals were not impressed to see the emperor who had issued the Black Decree showing mercy, at the eleventh hour, to the soldiers of an army that greatly outnumbered him and was obviously going to win very shortly.

By the middle of May the situation was becoming very serious for Maximilian. His supplies were getting low, and though he still retained the loyalty of many of the inhabitants of Querétaro, some of his soldiers were deserting to the liberals. His forces had been reduced by losses and desertions to 7,000 men, while the arrival of reinforcements had raised the liberal numbers to 41,000. Maximilian and his generals decided that their only hope was to try to cut through the enemy lines with their cavalry and to ride across country to Veracruz. Bureau was still holding out for Maximilian, and they thought it would be possible to find ships at Veracruz to take them to Europe. They decided to make the attempt on the night of May 14, but then postponed the breakout for twenty-four hours.

During the night of May 14 the liberal forces entered Querétaro, and Maximilian was awakened at 4 A.M. on May 15 to be told that the enemy were in his headquarters at the Convent of La Cruz. Maximilian's supporters afterward said they had been betrayed by Colonel Lopez, the commander of Maximilian's household cavalry. The emperor had been warned against Lopez, who on one occasion had murdered an Indian; but he had refused to believe the allegations and had completely trusted Lopez. He had been godfather to Lopez's son, and Lopez had been awarded the Legion of Honor by the French. Lopez denied that he had betrayed Maximilian; he said Maximilian had sent him to Escobedo's headquarters to discuss surrender terms and that the liberals had followed him when he returned to Querétaro and found a way through the defenses.

Maximilian, together with Blasio and a few of his officers, walked out into the courtyard of the convent and found it full of liberal soldiers in their tall shakos, who apparently did not recognize him. He mounted his horse Anteburro, and rode to the hill of the Cerro de las Campanas. He wished to die fighting, but his generals persuaded him to surrender, as resistance was hopeless. He and his officers rode down the hill until they met a liberal officer; he was a United States citizen who had come to Mexico to fight for Juárez. Maximilian told the officer who he was and that he wished to surrender to him. The officer accepted Maximilian's sword and led him to Escobedo, who ordered him to be imprisoned in his former headquarters in the convent. Maximilian asked to be taken back to the convent through the outskirts of the city and not through the main streets, and Escobedo granted his request.

The next day Escobedo visited Maximilian and asked if he wished to have any of his officers and servants with him in prison. Maximilian asked for Dr. Basch, Blasio, Prince Salm-Salm, and three others. His request was granted. He had fallen ill with dysentry, and Basch was worried. Basch asked to be allowed to consult with Dr. Rivadeneria, the chief surgeon of the liberal army. Rivadeneria examined Maximilian, and on his advice Maximilian was moved to healthier quarters in the Teresita Convent, and a few days later to the Convent of the Capuchins. When Baron Lago, the Austrian minister in Mexico, visited Maximilian on June 4, he found him confined in a cell that was about ten paces long and three paces wide. It contained a camp bed, a cupboard, two tables, an armchair, and four other chairs. A window looked out on the passage. At night a general and three colonels were on duty in the passage with revolvers in their hands. Miramón and Mejía, in nearby cells, were allowed to talk freely to Maximilian.

The liberal army behaved much better in Querétaro than the conservative citizens had expected. Shocking stories were being published in the press in the United States and Europe of atrocities committed by Escobedo's soldiers, who were said to be looting, raping, and murdering all foreigners. There were a few cases of looting, but these seem to have been isolated acts of misconduct. The liberal guards treated Maximilian with consideration and even with respect. At first they all referred to him as "the emperor," but afterward they were ordered to call him "Archduke Ferdinand Maximilian."

Mendez and several of Maximilian's other generals had gone into hiding in Querétaro. On May 16 Escobedo issued an order that anyone who had served as an officer in Maximilian's army would be shot when he was captured unless he surrendered to the liberal authorities within twenty-four hours. Most of Maximilian's officers thereupon surrendered and were imprisoned with the others. Mendez did not surrender. He knew that even if he gave himself up within the twenty-four hours, the liberals would show no mercy to the killer of Arteaga and Salazar.

A few days before the end of the siege of Querétaro, Mendez had quarreled with a hunchback tailor in the town. The tailor insulted Mendez, who then struck him across the face with a whip. After the liberals entered Querétaro the tailor saw Mendez in the street. He followed him to the house where he was hiding and informed the liberal authorities. They sent a company of soldiers to search the house, but Mendez hid in a recess under the floor. As the soldiers could not find him, they thought that the tailor had misinformed them. They were about to leave when one of the soldiers felt the ground give way under his feet, and he fell through the floor into the secret room where Mendez was hiding.

Mendez was executed on May 19. He was made to kneel on the ground while they shot him in the back, a method of execution that was sometimes used for army deserters. Both the Mexican conservatives and the French had occasionally executed liberal guerrillas in this way, but Mendez's supporters were indignant and pointed out that he had at least allowed Arteaga and Salazar to face their firing squads.

As the executioners were about to fire, Mendez half rose and turned to face them, kneeling on one knee. They opened fire, and several bullets struck him, but he was still alive. He raised his hand and pointed to a place behind his ear. The officer in charge of the firing squad obliged him; he walked over, placed his revolver on the point Mendez had indicated, and shot him dead.

The prisoners did not know what would happen to Maximilian. They heard rumors that he would be tried by a court-martial and executed; but Maximilian himself was confident that he would be set free if he agreed to return to Austria. From time to time Escobedo visited Maximilian. The prisoners thought he might be coming to inform Maximilian about his fate; but he merely asked him, formally and coldly, if he had any complaints or wished to make any request, and left after a few minutes when Maximilian said that he had no complaints or requests.

At the end of May Maximilian was informed that he was to be tried by a court-martial on a charge of treason against the Mexican Republic under the provisions of the decree of January 25, 1862. He had helped a foreign invading army to wage war against the republic; he had taken the title of emperor of Mexico, thereby seeking to overthrow the lawful government of the republic; after the French army withdrew from Mexico he had begun a civil war in February 1867 against the lawful government of the republic; and by appointing Márquez and his colleagues as regents in March 1867, he had again challenged the lawful authority of the republic.

Miramón and Mejía were informed that they were to be tried with Maximilian before the same court-martial on a charge of treason under the decree of January 25. Miramón was also charged with having waged war against the lawful government of the republic during the War of the Reform from 1858 to 1860, and with the murder of the prisoners and medical personnel he had ordered Márquez to kill at Tacubaya in 1859.

In accordance with the usual procedure under Mexican law, the accused men were examined before the trial by the fiscal, the prosecuting attorney. This was Lieutenant Colonel Manuel Aspiroz, a young man of twenty-eight who was an able lawyer. When Aspiroz questioned him in his prison, Maximilian claimed that the court had no jurisdiction to try him whether they regarded him as their emperor or as an Austrian archduke. He refused to answer any other questions. He afterward told his friends that when he heard the charges he found it hard to keep from laughing. But Aspiroz said that in the Republic of Mexico, archdukes, like everyone else, were subject to the law.

Mejía and Miramón denied that they had fought for the French until after the establishment of the regency in 1863, and claimed that during the War of the Reform, and under the regency and the empire, they had served the established government in Mexico City. Miramón denied that he had murdered the prisoners and the medical personnel at Tacubaya in 1859, saying that Márquez had killed them on his own initiative.

Maximilian was informed that he could choose lawyers to defend him at the trial. He chose Mariano Riva Palacio, Martinez de la Torre, Jesus Maria Vasquez, Eulalio Ortega, and Frederic Hall. Riva Palacio and de la Torre were leading advocates of Mexico City, and Riva Palacio was the father of Juárez's General Riva Palacio. Vasquez was a local attorney in Querétaro. Hall was a lawyer from the United States who had come to Mexico a few years before and had met Maximilian in Mexico City. He now came to Querétaro and offered to help in Maximilian's defense.

Princess Salm-Salm also arrived. She had been besieged in Mexico City, but managed to make her way to Díaz's headquarters to obtain his permission to visit her imprisoned husband in Querétaro. She did not tell Díaz that she wished to go there also to do what she could to save Maximilian. She was allowed to visit Maximilian and Salm-Salm whenever she wished. She was often brought to Maximilian by one of the officers guarding him, Colonel Villanueva, with whom she seemed to be on very friendly terms.

Agnes Salm-Salm offered Villanueva a bribe of $100,000 if he would allow Maximilian to escape. Villanueva said that escape would be impossible unless his colleague Colonel Palacios also connived at it. Agnes hoped she would be able to bribe Palacios too. As she did not have $100,000 available in cash in Querétaro, she would have to persuade Villanueva and Palacios to accept a promissory note. Villanueva agreed to accept the note if it were signed by Maximilian and countersigned by members of the diplomatic corps.

The Austrian and Prussian ministers, Baron Lago and Baron Magnus, were granted a safe-conduct by Díaz to pass through his lines to Querétaro. Maximilian asked them to countersign his signature on the promissory note. Lago rather reluctantly agreed, but Magnus said he could not associate himself with the offer of a bribe to an officer in the Mexican army without the authority of his government. His arguments impressed Lago, who changed his mind about countersigning the promissory note, and cut off his signature from the document.

Princess Salm-Salm set to work with Colonel Palacios, hoping she would have as much success with him as with Villanueva. She asked Palacios to escort her to her lodgings and invited him in. She made him promise on his word of honor that he would not reveal to anyone what she was about to say. After he had given his word, she offered him $100,000 if he joined Villanueva in allowing Maximilian to escape. He was taken aback, but as he appeared to hesitate, she pressed him, saying that she had no doubt that he was poor, like most Mexicans, and that $100,000 would enable him and his family to live, perhaps in the United States, in a luxury of which they could scarcely conceive. Palacios pretended to agree and discussed with her the details as to how the money was to be paid; but when he left her he went at once to Escobedo and revealed everything. It is clear from the accounts of the incident by Agnes Salm-Salm, Blasio, and Basch that it never occurred to any of them that a Mexican liberal officer might be incorruptible and unwilling to betray his general, his president, and his cause for a large sum of money.

The next day Escobedo issued an order expelling Princess Salm-Salm and all foreigners from Querétaro. He would not even allow the diplomats, Magnus and Lago, to remain in the city. Hall was also ordered to leave. He asked Escobedo to allow him to stay, as Maximilian had chosen him to be one of his lawyers at the trial; but Escobedo refused, and said that under Mexican law foreigners were not allowed to practice at the Mexican bar. Magnus, Lago, and Agnes Salm-Salm went to San Luis Potosí to intercede with Juárez for Maximilian's life. Magnus was angry with Agnes, for he thought that her well-meant but foolish action had made the situation much more difficult for Maximilian.

A story about Agnes Salm-Salm and Palacios circulated among the Austrian officers imprisoned at Querétaro. They said that when Palacios refused Agnes's offer of $100,000 to help Maximilian escape, she said to him: "What? Is a hundred thousand not enough? Well, Colonel, here I am," and began to undress. Palacios was so startled that he rushed to the door, but she had locked it, so he ran to the window and threatened to jump out unless she unlocked the door. The story, first published in 1924 by Count Corti, has been accepted and retold by all Maximilian's biographers ever since. Corti wrote that he obtained the story from Colonel Count zu Khevenhüller, who was an Austrian officer serving under Maximilian in Mexico, and that although Khevenhüller did not vouch for the truth of the story, Corti had no doubt that it was true, as it was virtually confirmed by Agnes's own account of her talk with Palacios; but she wrote nothing that could be implied as confirming Khevenhüller's story, which sounds like the gossip of an officers' mess.

Riva Palacio and de la Torre asked Díaz for permission to leave Mexico City to go to Querétaro to defend Maximilian at his trial. Díaz granted them a pass through his lines, and arranged with Márquez for a cease-fire for two hours to allow them to leave; but owing to a misunderstanding about the time of the cease-fire, their departure was delayed for several days, and they did not reach Querétaro until June 5. They were then informed that Maximilian's trial was to begin on June 7. They protested that this gave them less than two days in which to prepare the defense, and Escobedo agreed to postpone the start of the trial for twenty-four hours, but no more. The lawyers sent a telegram to Juárez and the ministers of justice and of war in San Luis Potosí asking for a longer adjournment. They were granted another five days but were told that the trial must begin on June 13.

Riva Palacio and de la Torre set off for San Luis Potosí, hoping to use their influence with Lerdo and Juárez, who were old friends. Both Lerdo and Juárez greeted them in a most friendly way; Juárez said how pleased he was to see them again after an interval of several years. They asked Juárez and Lerdo to postpone the trial for at least a month to give them more time to prepare the defense, and not to proceed against Maximilian under the decree of January 25, which they called a "cruel" decree and one that was inappropriate in his case. They also asked Juárez to pardon Maximilian and to commute the death sentence if he was convicted by the court.

Lerdo and Juárez said they had no feelings of hatred for Maximilian and no desire for revenge, but the process of law must take its course. Juárez eventually agreed to refer the decision to a meeting of his Cabinet; after the meeting he informed Riva Palacio and de la Torre that the Cabinet had decided that the trial must start on June 13 and that the charges under the decree of January 25 must be proceeded with. As to their request to pardon Maximilian and commute his death sentence, Juárez said that it would be improper for him to decide about a pardon until after the trial.

Riva Palacio and de la Torre returned to Querétaro as quickly as possible, and by traveling through the night were just able to arrive before the trial began. It opened at 8 A.M. on June 13 in the Iturbide Theater in Querétaro. The judges, advocates, and prisoners sat on the stage of the theater, and the auditorium was packed with members of the public, including reporters for a liberal newspaper, *La Sombra de Arteaga* (The Shade of Arteaga) — an ominous name from Maximilian's point of view.

Miramón and Mejía were present at the hearing, but Maximilian obtained a medical certificate which stated that he was too ill to attend. The court was composed of seven officers: a lieutenant colonel, who presided, and two majors and four captains. They were all young men.

The defense lawyers argued that the decree of January 25 conflicted with the Constitution of 1857, which provided that presidential decrees made under emergency powers must not impose the death penalty. Nor did it apply to Maximilian, who first came to Mexico after the republic had ceased *de facto* to exist. But Aspiroz had his answers ready. The restriction on the presidential powers imposed by the Constitution could be overridden in wartime; and Maximilian was subject to the decree of January 25, because it was a clearly recognized principle of international law that an alien who resides in a foreign country is subject to that country's laws. As an alien residing in Mexico, he was subject to the laws of the Mexican Republic, which had never ceased to exist.

The lawyers defending Miramón and Mejía argued that the two generals had merely carried out the orders of the established *de facto* government, which they had loyally served, believing in good faith that it was the lawful government of Mexico. Miramón's advocate pointed out that he had been abroad from 1861 to 1863 and so had played no part in the conquest of Mexico by the French; he revealed that Miramón had offered to fight for Juárez, and said, inaccurately, that Juárez had accepted the approach Miramón made through Teran. In their last pleas for their clients the defense attorneys appealed to the court to give a merciful verdict that would heal, not reopen, the wounds of civil war.

Vasquez made an impassioned plea for Maximilian. He said that history had condemned the trial and execution of Charles I in England and of Louis XVI in France. The French revolutionaries of 1830 and 1848 had acted more nobly in sparing the lives of Charles X and Louis Philippe, as had the government of the United States in not executing Jefferson Davis after the Civil War. He appealed to the judges, as officers of the valiant army that had fought so bravely for the noble cause of liberalism, not to sully that cause by a vindictive sentence in their hour of victory.

The seven officers did not take long to reach their verdict. There was a rumor in Querétaro that they were divided, and reached their decision by the presiding officer's casting vote; but this is very unlikely, and all seven publicly concurred in the verdict. On the evening of June 14, the second day of the trial, they announced that all three defendants had been found guilty and were sentenced to be executed by a firing squad. The execution would be carried out at 3 P.M. on Sunday, June 16.

❧ 26 ❧

THE NINETEENTH OF JUNE

THE DEFENSE LAWYERS had only forty-two hours in which to obtain a reprieve from Juárez. They left at once for San Luis Potosí, traveling through the night and arriving there on the morning of June 15. Baron Magnus had also gone to San Luis Potosí, as had Princess Salm-Salm. Riva Palacio and de la Torre went immediately to see Lerdo, and repeated to him all the arguments they had used in their final pleas to the court.

Lerdo was very courteous and listened patiently to all they had to say, but he was adamant in refusing to recommend a pardon. He said that if Maximilian were pardoned, it would be illogical and unjust to punish any of his subordinates for having carried out executions under the Black Decree; the people of Mexico, especially the army, would never tolerate it if all the crimes and cruelties that had been committed against the liberals in the past six years went unpunished. He also said that if Maximilian were allowed to return to Europe, whatever he might promise now, he would inevitably again become the center of new plots against Mexico by Mexican conservative exiles and European governments, all of whom would interpret the granting of a pardon to Maximilian as a sign of the weakness of the liberal government. Lerdo used the same arguments to Magnus, when Magnus made an appeal for clemency on behalf of the Prussian government.

Riva Palacio and de la Torre then went to see Juárez, who was as courteous and as firm as Lerdo and gave the same reasons for refusing the pardon. But when they pressed him and protested the short time between sentencing and the execution of the sentence, he agreed to postpone the execution for three days. The order for postponement was cabled to Querétaro.

Maximilian, Miramón, and Mejía spent their last days in religious devotions and reading. They were often visited by a local priest.

Miramón read his favorite book, Thomas à Kempis's *Imitation of Christ,* which he lent to Maximilian and Mejía. Maximilian read *The History of Italy* by the contemporary Italian historian Cesare Cantù. He wrote a farewell letter to his mother and to Princess Josefa Iturbide and several of his ministers. He did not write to Charlotte, for reports had reached Mexico that she was dead, and though some of the prisoners doubted it, Maximilian was convinced that it was true. He said that he wished to be buried beside her.

Miramón was the most resigned to his fate. "All my disquiet has ceased," he wrote in his diary. "God has decided that I must leave for the other world, and I will go there with the greatest tranquillity." His former mistress, Concha Lombardo, whom he had now married, came to see him in his prison at Querétaro, bringing their baby son, not yet a year old. She told Miramón that she was leaving for San Luis Potosí to intercede for his life with Juárez. Miramón would have preferred that she not make the attempt, which he knew would be unsuccessful, but he did not try to dissuade her from going.

Mejía seemed to the other prisoners to be less resigned than Miramón and Maximilian to the fate that awaited them. His friends were very indignant that he had been sentenced to death, and they accused Escobedo of great ingratitude for allowing it, because Mejía had once taken Escobedo prisoner and had allowed him to go free instead of shooting him. But this was somewhat misleading. Mejía had captured Escobedo and several other liberal generals in the autumn of 1863 when Bazaine had not yet decided to shoot regular army prisoners as guerrillas and was still treating them as prisoners of war; and although Mejía had not shot Escobedo in 1863, he had certainly shot the seventeen guerrillas at Matamoros in 1865 and had haughtily rejected Weitzel's plea on their behalf.

Maximilian had at last accepted that he would be shot. He told Miramón that when they faced the firing squad together, Miramón should stand on the right, as he had earned this place of honor because of his valor in the last campaign. It was agreed that Maximilian should stand in the center, with Miramón on his right and Mejía on his left. Maximilian, always fascinated by questions of protocol, was concerned with them on the eve of his death.

Maximilian's attitude to Miramón was typical of his trusting nature. He obviously had no idea that two years before, Miramón had offered to desert to Juárez, although Miramón's advocate mentioned this at the trial. On the other hand, Maximilian had changed his mind about Márquez, who he now believed had betrayed him by not coming from Mexico City with reinforcements to raise the siege of Querétaro. Three weeks before his death he told Basch that he would be prepared to forgive Lopez, who had betrayed him out of cowardice, but that he would like to hang Márquez, who had betrayed him in cold blood.

Márquez always served a double purpose for Maximilian and his followers as both a useful ally and a scapegoat. In 1859 and 1860 he was condemned by them all as the Tiger of Tacubaya, with whom they would have nothing to do. In 1862 and 1863 he and his 2,000 guerrillas were praised as valuable allies in the war against the liberals, which won the crown of Mexico for Maximilian. From 1864 to 1866 Maximilian kept him in Turkey and Palestine on an unimportant mission to please the moderate liberals. In February 1867 he was Maximilian's right-hand man, praised by the emperor in a proclamation as "the brave General Márquez," and on March 7 he was one of the three regents to whom Maximilian entrusted the empire. After May 31 he was the traitor responsible for Maximilian's capture and death.

On the evening of June 15 Maximilian, Miramón, and Mejía were given absolution, and they prepared for death the next afternoon. Then a telegram arrived from San Luis Potosí, and they were informed that the execution had been postponed to the morning of June 19. The victims and their friends thought that this was an act of cruel kindness on Juárez's part, that he was playing a game of cat and mouse with them.

In Europe and the United States there was much concern over Maximilian's fate. The foreign governments that wished to intercede for Maximilian's life had no diplomatic relations with Juárez's government; their representatives in Mexico City, who were accredited to Maximilian, were not in a strong position to intercede with Juárez, even if they had managed to reach Querétaro. So they addressed their pleas to the government of the United States. All the European powers believed that in view of the relationship between the United States and Juárez, Maximilian's life would be saved if Seward asked Juárez to pardon him. The Austrian and Prussian ministers in Washington requested Seward's intervention. Prussia had recently defeated Austria in the Seven Weeks War, and Bismarck was eager to reconcile Austria by doing all he could to please the Austrian government. He saw a good opportunity to do this by interceding for Maximilian.

Juárez received appeals for clemency from two of his ardent supporters in Europe. On June 5 Garibaldi wrote to him from Italy, and on June 20 Victor Hugo wrote from Guernsey in the Channel Islands. Both Garibaldi and Hugo had strongly supported the struggle of the Mexican liberals, but they were both opposed to capital punishment (though this did not prevent Garibaldi from sometimes ordering soldiers in his army to be shot on the spot for looting). Garibaldi urged the Mexican liberals, in the name of his martyred comrade, General Ghilardi, to show the world that they were morally superior to the reactionaries by sparing the life of Maximilian, the brother of Franz Joseph who had executed so many Italian patriots.

Hugo told Juárez that on December 2, 1859, he had written to the authorities in the United States to ask them to spare the life of the Abolitionist John Brown, who had been condemned to death for his raid on the arsenal at Harpers Ferry; he was now asking Juárez to spare the life of Maximilian. His plea for John Brown had failed, but Juárez, who was far nobler than the slaveholders in the United States, would not allow his plea for Maximilian to fail. "Maximilian will owe his life to Juárez."

In the United States, most of the press hoped that a pardon would be granted. The *New-York Times* was particularly strident in denouncing the atrocities allegedly being committed by the liberals in Mexico and in demanding that the United States prevent the murder of Maximilian. Some right-wing elements went so far as to demand that the United States send an army into Mexico to rescue Maximilian.

Seward assured the Austrian and Prussian ministers that the United States would ask Juárez to pardon Maximilian. But the United States had no minister in San Luis Potosí. Campbell, whom Seward had sent to Mexico with Sherman seven months before, remained in New Orleans, apparently because he did not know where Juárez was or how to make contact with him. As early as April 6, Seward sent a telegram to Campbell stating that "the capture of the Prince Maximilian in Querétaro by the Republican armies of Mexico seems probable," and that the liberals' severity toward their prisoners at San Jacinto raised fears that Maximilian and his foreign troops would suffer the same fate. This "would be injurious to the national cause of Mexico and to the Republican system throughout the world," so the United States government hoped that Maximilian and his men would be treated as prisoners of war. Seward instructed Campbell to go to Mexico, find Juárez, and tell him this.

But Campbell did not go to Mexico, and many statesmen and other observers in Europe saw his inaction as a sinister plot by Seward. They thought that Seward, not wishing to offend the European powers by refusing to intervene for Maximilian and not wishing to offend Juárez by doing so, was deliberately keeping Campbell in New Orleans so that he would reach Juárez too late to save Maximilian.

An American naval commander showed more initiative. When reports of the conditions in Veracruz reached Washington in February, the United States government sent the warship *Tacony,* under Commander F. A. Roe, to Veracruz to safeguard any American citizens who might be in difficulties there. The *Tacony* arrived off Veracruz a few days after the last French troops left. Only Querétaro, Veracruz, and Mexico City were still holding out for Maximilian, and Veracruz was besieged almost immediately by a liberal army under General Barranda. It was defended for Maximilian by General Taboada and Bureau. Knowing that Veracruz had always been a liberal city, and that many of the inhabitants must be in sympathy with the besieging army, Bureau enforced a rigid dictatorship, imprisoning anyone who showed any sign of opposition, and the prisons were full.

Roe got in touch with both the liberal and the imperial commanders at Veracruz and, not surprisingly, established better relations with Barranda than with Bureau. When he heard that Bureau was imposing a heavy emergency tax on all residents, including American citizens, he protested to Bureau, who in his turn protested Roe's contacts with Barranda and the liberals.

On May 16, Barranda informed Roe that the liberal army had captured Querétaro and that Maximilian was their prisoner. Roe believed that if the United States could spare the life of Jefferson Davis, Juárez could spare the life of Maximilian, but he was not optimistic that Juárez would do so. Roe knew what the liberal soldiers felt about Maximilian. He discovered that a white cord with a golden thread in it was hanging from the flagpole over Barranda's camp, and was told that a similar cord hung in most of the liberal army camps, to be used to hang Maximilian when they caught him.

Roe decided, without consulting his government in Washington, to take an initiative that he hoped would save Maximilian's life as well as end a great deal of suffering in Veracruz. A British ship, the *Jason,* and an Austrian frigate, the *Elisabeth,* were lying off Veracruz. Roe suggested to Captain Apsley of the *Jason* that they urge Bureau to offer to surrender Veracruz to the liberals in exchange for a pardon for Maximilian. Roe and Apsley agreed that the proposal would come best from the Austrian captain, and at Apsley's suggestion Captain Gröller went to Bureau. Gröller argued and pleaded with Bureau for half the night, but Bureau refused to agree, perhaps because he was afraid of General Taboada's reaction. Roe regretted that his attempt to save Maximilian had failed, because when he mentioned the matter to Barranda, the liberal general seemed quite sympathetic to the idea, though he was not at all sure that Juárez would agree to it.

In San Luis Potosí, Baron Magnus, Riva Palacio and de la Torre, Agnes Salm-Salm and Concha Miramón renewed their efforts to obtain a pardon for Maximilian and the generals. Juárez received Concha Miramón and told her that the grant of a pardon for her husband did not depend on him. "On whom does it depend, then?" she asked. "On the country, who wishes it," he replied. "I can do nothing." She left him in tears. A few days later she asked for another interview, but Juárez refused to see her again, telling Riva Palacio and de la Torre that it would only increase her pain, as he would again have to refuse her plea.

He agreed to receive Princess Salm-Salm in the little room opposite the bedroom which he shared with his wife in Government House. She went on her knees to him and implored him to pardon Maximilian. He gently raised her to her feet and told her he regretted that he would have to refuse her request. She burst into tears and sobbed hysterically. He was very distressed but would not change his mind. According to Agnes, he said to her: "If all the kings and queens of Europe were in your place, I could not spare that life. It is not I who take it but the people and the law, and if I should not do its will the people would take it and mine also."

At 1:30 P.M. on June 18, seventeen hours before the time fixed for the execution, Maximilian sent a telegram to Juárez asking him to pardon Miramón and Mejía, who had already endured the agonies of preparing for death before the postponed execution on June 16. He hoped that his own death would be enough to atone for any offenses the two generals might have committed. Juárez did not reply, but he had a final meeting that afternoon in San Luis Potosí with Riva Palacio and de la Torre. He told them he realized how painful it must be for them to have failed in their vigorous attempts to save their client's life. "Today you are unable to understand the necessity for this severity," he said, "or the motives of justice on which it is based. Only time will enable you to appreciate this measure. The law and the sentence are inexorable now because public safety requires it, and this will enable us later on to be sparing of the blood of those who have been led astray, which will be for me the greatest happiness of my life."

Apart from questions of law and justice, Juárez and his ministers had sound political reasons for refusing to pardon Maximilian. Romero stated them in a private letter to his friend Hiram Barney in the United States on May 31. If Maximilian were allowed to return to Europe, he would continue to call himself emperor of Mexico, he would set up a court and government in exile at Miramar, and every dissatisfied conservative Mexican politician would come to him and urge him to return to Mexico; he would one day make another attempt to become emperor, as Iturbide had. If they allowed Maximilian to return to Austria, "I am certain that no man in Europe would admit that we had acted from a magnanimous impulse, for feeble nations are never considered to be generous; on the contrary, they will say that we have acted through fear of public opinion in Europe, and because we dared not treat with severity a European Prince, *our sovereign*." But Romero did not rule out the possibility that if Maximilian were condemned to death, the sentence might be commuted to imprisonment for life.

The private and public comments of official Europe show that Romero was right. Queen Victoria's private secretary, General Grey, wrote to the foreign secretary, Lord Stanley, that "lawless as these Mexicans are," he hoped that "even they will pause before they outrage every European feeling by the murder of the Emperor." The "American correspondent" in Philadelphia of *The Times* of London, who regularly contributed antiliberal articles to the newspaper but was often misinformed about events in Mexico, wrote that "cruel as they are, the Mexicans can scarcely afford to kill Maximilian"; in an article published in *The Times* six days after Maximilian's execution, he wrote that Maximilian had been spared because " Juarez is afraid to shoot him."

Juárez knew, too, that pardoning Maximilian would have caused great indignation in the army. General Corona had written to him that there was a general feeling in the army that the safety of the republic depended on the government showing the necessary firmness. Juárez knew his soldiers carried cords which they said they would use to hang Maximilian. He had angered them by postponing Maximilian's execution for three days. When the news reached Querétaro that Maximilian was not to be shot on June 16, Colonel Palacios, who had been so badly misjudged by Princess Salm-Salm, went at once to Escobedo to protest. He offered to surrender his sword to Escobedo, saying that he could not use it for any useful purpose if pardons were to be granted to those who had attacked the sovereignty of the nation. "I hope," replied Escobedo, "that you will have confidence in the patriotism, the rectitude and the justice of the government."

The execution took place early in the morning of June 19 on the outskirts of Querétaro, on the Cerro de las Campanas, the hill where Maximilian had surrendered on May 15. Maximilian awoke before daybreak and prayed by candlelight at a little altar that had been erected in his prison cell. He put on a black frock coat and carried his white hat. Just before 6 A.M. he was taken to the Cerro de las Campanas, traveling in a carriage with a priest. His valet, Grill, and his Hungarian cook, Todos, neither of whom were under arrest, followed in a second carriage just behind him. They were his only close acquaintances who attended the execution, for Dr. Basch could not bear to go; but Magnus was present, and his report to Bismarck is the only one of the many conflicting accounts of the execution that was written by an eyewitness.

When they reached the Cerro de las Campanas they found more than 3,000 soldiers drawn up all around the square. Apart from the soldiers, there were less than fifty other onlookers. It was a beautiful morning, with a cloudless blue sky. As Maximilian alighted from the carriage he said to Grill that he had always hoped he would die on a beautiful sunny day. Maximilian, Miramón, and Mejía all walked firmly. Maximilian handed his handkerchief and his white hat to Todos and spoke to him in Hungarian, asking him to arrange for the handkerchief and hat to be taken to his mother.

As the three men faced the firing squad, they took up different positions from those that had previously been decided. The superstitious Mejía did not wish to stand on the left, because he remembered that the thief on Christ's left at the crucifixion had not repented. So Maximilian was on the left, Miramón in the center, and Mejía on Miramón's right. They stood with their backs to the remnants of a wall that had survived the bombardment during the siege, and looked out over Querétaro.

Maximilian made a short speech in Spanish. "Mexicans! Men of my class and race are created by God to be the happiness of nations or their martyrs." Then he said, "I forgive everybody. I pray that everyone may also forgive me, and I wish that my blood which is now to be shed may be for the good of the country. Long live Mexico, long live independence!"

A young officer was in command of the firing squad, and the six soldiers in the squad were even younger. The officer gave the order to fire. Six bullets hit Maximilian, and three of them inflicted fatal wounds. He died instantly, as did Miramón and Mejía. It was all over by 6:40 A.M.

The liberal newspaper, the *Boletin Republicano,* published the dry announcement: "At seven o'clock in the morning of the 19th instant, the Archduke Ferdinand Maximilian of Austria ceased to exist."

Later that same day, Bureau surrendered Veracruz to the liberal army.

Mexico City did not fall as easily as Veracruz. Díaz began the siege at the beginning of April; but Márquez was in charge of the defense of the capital, and he was determined to hold it to the last. He knew what he could expect if he fell into liberal hands. Generals Vidaurri and O'Horan were with him. He had an army of 4,000 men, many of whom had been press-ganged. Márquez issued a proclamation to the people. "I have undertaken the command of this beautiful city, and as you know me I think it unnecessary to say more. I am ready to sacrifice myself and would rather die than allow the slightest disorder."

By the end of May the siege had lasted for seven weeks, and food was running short. Márquez requisitioned all the food and distributed it to the people every day from a few centers. Women went out to get the food; men of military age stayed indoors in case they were seized by the press-gang for the *leva*.

Soon the food shortage was acute, and the people were rioting. Captain Kendall, an officer who had resigned from the British army to serve Maximilian, saw a starving woman try to force her way into a food warehouse that was being guarded by soldiers. One of the soldiers pushed the woman back and struck her in the face. The crowd leaped on the soldier and trampled him to death. Kendall saw a similar incident at another food depot, when a woman carrying a baby tried to seize some food. A soldier struck at her with his saber, cutting open her face and killing her baby. A moment later the soldier fell dead, stabbed by the knives of members of the crowd.

At the beginning of June the rumor spread that Díaz was allowing the civilian population to leave, and 3,000 people set out on the road to Chapultepec. But Díaz, like other military commanders at all periods of history, was not prepared to allow the defenders of a besieged city to rid themselves of useless mouths. He drove the people back into the city with gunfire. By this time fifty people were dying of starvation every day, and many more were dying from disease.

A father whose wife had died of starvation was living in his house with three small children. When their food ran out, he had no choice but to go and look for food, locking the door of his house to make sure that no one entered and harmed the children. As he walked through the streets searching for food, he was seized for the *leva* and marched off to an army barracks. He protested that he must be allowed to make some arrangements for the welfare of his children, but no one paid any attention. After three days, he was released. When he returned to the house he found that all three children had died of starvation.

Márquez's men were indignant with Díaz. Their sentries called out across the siege trenches to Díaz's men, taunting them with cowardice because they did not dare to launch an assault on the city and attempt to capture it by storm, but relied on bombardment and on starvation to force the defenders to surrender. The liberal soldiers hung up the corpse of a dead mule opposite Márquez's sentries, with a placard attached to it: "Meat for the traitors." Márquez's men replied by hanging up the corpse of an old woman who had died of starvation with a placard: "Meat for the cowards." Díaz had no intention of risking the lives of his men unnecessarily, and responded to the taunts by renewing the bombardment and continuing the siege.

At the beginning of June the news reached Mexico City that Querétaro had fallen and Maximilian was a prisoner. An envoy went to Díaz at Chapultepec and offered to surrender the city if Díaz guaranteed that the lives of Maximilian and his officers would be spared and that the foreign troops would be allowed to leave the country. Díaz promised that the foreign troops could go and guaranteed the lives of everyone except Maximilian, Márquez, and Vidaurri, whose fate, he said, did not rest with him. These terms were unacceptable to the defenders, and the siege went on.

On June 10 Márquez led a sortie of his cavalry in an attempt to obtain food supplies, but Díaz's men drove him back into the city. Some of Márquez's officers began to talk of surrender, but Márquez threatened to shoot anyone who engaged in defeatist talk. He imposed forced loans on the. wealthier inhabitants. He arrested those who refused to pay and imprisoned them on the top floors of buildings, where they would not only suffer from the summer heat but would be most likely to be hit by shells during bombardments by the liberal army. Then, on the afternoon of June 19, Díaz's men shouted out to Márquez's sentries that Maximilian had been executed that morning. The Austrians in the city immediately announced that they would not continue fighting now that the emperor was dead.

The civic authorities called a meeting of the military and civilian leaders. Several people demanded that negotiations be opened with Díaz to discuss surrender terms. To everyone's surprise, Márquez accepted the position and resigned his post as lieutenant of the empire, to which Maximilian had appointed him. He turned over command of the forces in the city to General Ramon Tabera, who immediately sent a message to Díaz that he wished to discuss surrender terms. Díaz insisted on unconditional surrender but promised to take the civilian population under his protection and to ensure that they were not harmed. He gave Tabera till 5 P.M. to accept his offer.

Tabera and his officers were still discussing whether to accept Díaz's terms when the time limit expired. Immediately the liberal guns began a tremendous bombardment, heavier than any to which the city had so far been subjected. After it had continued for several hours Tabera and his officers agreed to surrender unconditionally, and sent word to Díaz under a flag of truce. During the night of June 20 the surrender terms were signed by Tabera's envoy and Díaz in Maximilian's palace at Chapultepec.

Díaz rode into the city at 6 A.M. on June 21 at the head of 6,000 men. His troops kept good order and did not harm the civilians. He issued a proclamation calling on all officers and men in Márquez's army to surrender to the new authorities, stating that any who did not do so would be shot when they were captured. Most of Márquez's officers and soldiers surrendered and they were allowed to go free. But Márquez, Vidaurri, and O'Horan went into hiding in the city. Díaz ordered his troops to conduct a house-to-house search for them and offered a reward of $10,000 for the capture of Márquez.

Vidaurri hid in the house of his friend Mr. Wright, an American citizen. The story that Wright agreed to hide Vidaurri in return for money and then denounced him to the authorities when Vidaurri's funds ran out seems to be untrue. But when the liberal soldiers broke into Wright's house at midnight, they found Vidaurri in his bed. They beat the white-haired old man with their rifle butts. Wright's daughter cried out in horror and begged them to stop, but they paid no attention to her. Tying Vidaurri's hands behind his back with a lasso so tightly that blood ran from his wrists, they dragged him to the nearest army barracks and locked him up, wounded and bleeding, in the guardroom.

They came for him a few hours later, and at 4 A.M. took him to a piece of waste ground on the edge of Mexico City where all the filth of the city was collected. They blindfolded him and made him kneel on the ground. They were about to shoot him in the back of the head when one of the soldiers said that the piece of ground on which he was kneeling was too clean a place for him to die. So they took him to a spot where the ground was covered with horses' dung, made him kneel in the filth, and shot him there.

Márquez took a million dollars from the Treasury and hid, together with General O'Horan, in a mill on the outskirts of the city. After a while Márquez told O'Horan that he had an intuition that the liberal soldiers would shortly raid the mill and that they had better move. O'Horan thought they were safer where they were, so they agreed to separate, and said goodbye. Three hours after Márquez left the mill, troops arrived and arrested O'Horan.

Díaz would have wished to save O'Horan, but the government decided that he was to be court-martialed under the decree of January 25. O'Horan was sentenced to death and executed.

Márquez, always a survivor, preferred to kill rather than be killed. He made his way to the cemetery in Mexico City and hid for two days in a newly dug grave. Then he succeeded in making his way to Veracruz, from where he sailed to Cuba. He lived, unrecognized, for many years in Havana.

Juárez entered Mexico City on July 15, coming from San Luis Potosí by Querétaro, where he stopped to gaze at Maximilian's corpse. It was noticed that he did not offer Porfirio Díaz a place in his carriage when he entered Mexico City. Several observers thought that Juárez was received with less enthusiasm than when he arrived in January 1861 after his victory in the War of the Reform. Colonel Gagern, who agreed that Juárez's welcome was lukewarm, had great sympathy for Ortega and thought that the people did not cheer because they disapproved of Juárez's decree extending his own term as president and of his manipulation of the Constitution. Perhaps they were more affected by the sufferings they had recently endured under siege by Juárez's army.

27

"God Did Not Want It"

The news of Maximilian's death was published in the newspapers in New York on June 30 and reached Paris by July 1. Napoleon III was told about it just as he was leaving the Tuileries to make a speech at the prize-giving ceremony of his Great Exhibition. He made no reference to Maximilian's death in his speech and did not tell anyone; but by July 3 it had been reported in most newspapers in Europe. *Le Moniteur* reported on July 5 that Maximilian had been shot "by the wretches into whose hands he had fallen" and stated that his murder would arouse universal horror. The same day the president of the French Senate officially informed the senators that "a horrible crime has been committed against the laws of war, of nations and of humanity."

Favre and the opposition deputies thought it best to say nothing at this stage, but they raised the question of the government's Mexican policy in the Corps Législatif on July 10. After Thiers had denounced the Mexican expedition as a dreadful failure, Rouher replied. He said that the shocking news of Maximilian's murder proved how right the government had been to declare in 1862 and 1863 that one cannot negotiate with a Juárez. The Mexican expedition was a great idea, but it had not been properly understood and supported in France, and the emperor, being always responsive to the wishes of the French people, had felt obliged to bow to public opinion and recall the troops. The French army had in no way been discredited in Mexico, where it had marched victoriously over great distances and had won great victories. It was unfortunate that Napoleon III's grand project had failed, but "God did not want it; let us respect His decrees."

Several writers compared Maximilian to Louis XVI, which was a very sound comparison, for undoubtedly one of the chief motives of the Mexican liberals in putting Maximilian on trial and shooting him was the same that had animated the French revolutionaries in 1793 — to show that kings, like other men, would be tried and punished if they committed crimes against their people. The French journalist Adrien Marx thought that it could be said of Maximilian, as it had been of Louis XVI, that "it was to his concessions that he owed the loss of his scepter." Many others agreed with him that Maximilian had failed because he had not firmly repudiated the moderate liberals and put all his trust in the conservatives and the Ultramontanes of the Catholic Church until it was too late. Baron von Malortie thought he should have acted·like Philip II's duke of Alba, not like Schiller's Don Carlos.

Colonel Blanchot, who had returned to France after several years' service in Mexico, thought that Juárez, "this old Indian, revived by some primitive instinct of his redskin ancestors," was determined to have Maximilian's scalp. The bishop of Orléans, Dupanloup, denouncing a proposal to erect a statue of Voltaire, pointed out that Voltaire had been a liberal, like Garibaldi and Juárez.

Conservative journalists demanded that a joint European expeditionary force be sent to Mexico to punish Juárez, just as Britain was sending an army to Abyssinia to punish Emperor Theodore for outrages committed against British subjects. But Abyssinia did not have the United States as a friendly neighbor; and the French revolutionary, General Gustave Paul Cluseret, who had fought in most of the wars and revolutions in Europe and America during the last twenty years, could safely defy the governments of Europe: "Monarchy will never rise again in America. If Europe is not convinced of this, let her try again. We are ready."

For the French propagandists, the worst thing was that Europe had been defeated by the United States. "We went in the name of Europe to weaken America," wrote Charles d'Héricault, but "the Yankees have made Europe retreat." La Barreyrie, who had returned from Orizaba with the French troops, feared that the victory of the United States in Mexico was only the first step in the process, and that Europe was "on the eve of becoming the tributary, the vassal of America."

The Austrian, French, and Italian courts went into official mourning for Maximilian, but Franz Joseph did not make a very striking demonstration of his grief. Baron Goltz, the Prussian ambassador at Napoleon's court, thought that Maximilian's fate had caused more grief in Paris than in Vienna. The Viennese press duly paid tribute to Maximilian and lamented his death. The *Wiener Abendpost* saluted him as a martyr and as an artistic and sensitive man who had lived like a poet and died like a soldier. They believed he had in fact been the prisoner not of Juárez but of President Johnson and that the government of the United States was responsible for his fate.

The Prussian press, following Bismarck's policy of seeking a reconciliation with Austria, expressed grief and indignation. A writer in Berlin declared that the Prussian court and people were deeply distressed, and a Hamburg publication stated that every son of Germany would lament Maximilian.

Queen Victoria was very angry with Juárez, and regretted that her government did not protest more strongly. She was prepared to believe the worst about the Mexican liberals, and she naturally heard some grossly exaggerated stories from Eloin when he visited her at Osborne in the Isle of Wight at Christmas 1867. He told her that "the Mexicans were dreadful people devoid of all principle and truth, that the priests were very bad and immoral." The "horrid people" had trafficked in poor Max's body, "having sold bits of his skull, skin & hair!! Too disgusting & disgraceful!!"

In the United States, opinion was sharply divided. The *New-York Times* on July 4 published an editorial under the headline "The Mexican Savages and Their Crime," which denounced "the bloody tragedy enacted at Querétaro" by the hordes who called themselves liberals but who occupied a position beyond the pale of civilization. The newspaper returned to this theme day after day throughout July, attacking the Mexican liberals and singling out Escobedo as the special villain; the writers fabricated stories about his massacre of thousands of people in Querétaro and his call for the extermination of foreigners. In Buffalo a group of volunteers from a local regiment paraded through the streets wearing badges with the inscription "Poor Charlotte. We will avenge Maximilian. On to Mexico."

But in the House of Representatives, Mr. Shanks of Illinois moved a resolution congratulating Juárez on his victory over Maximilian and on all his recent actions, which were "eminently right and proper"; and the aged radical leader Thaddeus Stevens denounced "the clamor that has been raised against the Mexican government for the heroic execution of murderers and pirates." Senator Howard of Illinois, another prominent radical, said that Maximilian was "the most arrant felon of the age" and had received "just punishment." The *Evening Post* compared the outcry in the press over Maximilian's execution with their silence when liberal generals were being shot under Maximilian's Black Decree, and thought that "the execution of Maximilian was needed to warn royal adventurers . . . that their activities must not extend to America and that they have no business here."

These views were shared by a young French journalist, Georges Clemenceau, who was living in New York as the foreign correspondent of the Paris newspaper *Le Temps*. In a private letter, he wrote about Maximilian's execution in a way that he could not have done in *Le Temps*. As a republican and a democrat, he hated all these emperors, kings, archdukes, and princes. "Between us and these people there is a war to the death. They have tortured to death millions of us and I bet we have not killed two dozen of them."

Franz Joseph and his family hoped that Juárez would allow them to take Maximilian's corpse back to Austria to be buried with the other royal Habsburgs in the crypt of the Capuchin church in Vienna. Juárez's government agreed to this, but said that they could hand over the corpse only to a person who was properly authorized by Maximilian's family to receive it. Maximilian's supporters accused Juárez of using this excuse to cause endless delays; they told terrible stories of how, while Maximilian's corpse was being embalmed, it was insulted and manhandled by the liberals.

Franz Joseph ordered Admiral Tegetthoff, who had known and respected Maximilian when they served as officers in the Austrian navy, to go to Mexico to fetch Maximilian's corpse. Tegetthoff saw Lerdo and Juárez, who were courteous but raised many difficulties, and Tegetthoff had to stay in Mexico City for two months before finally leaving for Veracruz with Maximilian's body. He sailed with it on the *Novara*, the ship in which Maximilian and Charlotte had come to Mexico in 1864. He landed at Trieste and took the corpse to Vienna, where it was buried in the family vault of the Capuchin church on a snowy day in January 1868, in the presence of the Austrian royal family and the diplomatic representatives of most of the European courts; Charlotte was not in a fit state to attend the funeral.

The forecasts in the European press, and in many newspapers in the United States, that the liberals in Mexico would engage in a wholesale massacre of their opponents were proved wrong. After Díaz's executions at Puebla, only six people were put to death: Maximilian, Miramón, Mejía, and Mendez at Querétaro, and Vidaurri and O'Horan in Mexico City. All the prisoners captured at Querétaro and Mexico City were soon released. In September 1870 a general amnesty was issued under which all those who had supported the French and Maximilian were pardoned. One of the last prisoners to be freed was the unfortunate Ortega, who was detained under arrest for eighteen months at Monterrey; but in August 1868 he was set free after issuing a statement that although he considered that he had been right and had been unjustly treated, he would now accept that Juárez was the lawful president of the republic.

Mexico was for a time diplomatically isolated from Europe. During the wave of indignation following the news of Maximilian's death, the European governments declared that they would never enter into diplomatic relations with the bloodstained assassin Juárez; on his side, Juárez was determined not to make the first approach to any European government that had recognized Maximilian's empire. The first step was taken by Prussia, who in 1869 suggested to Juárez's government that trade relations be reestablished. Juárez agreed, and other European governments soon followed suit.

Juárez's relations with the United States were excellent. In 1868 Grant was elected president, and when he took office in March 1869 Seward was replaced as secretary of state. Later in the year Seward visited Mexico. He was warmly welcomed everywhere with banquets and speeches. There was a particularly lavish reception in Mexico City at the house of Señor Barron, who had succeeded as head of the bank when his father, Don Eustacio, died a few months after the liberal victory. He entertained Seward and Juárez on the same scale that his father had feted Forey and Maximilian.

Seward and Juárez praised each other in their speeches, and no one referred to their past disagreements, when Seward was placing an embargo on the supply of arms to Mexico. Juárez said that the people of Mexico were grateful for the help that the United States had given them during their struggle for freedom and independence. Seward said that Juárez was the greatest statesman he had encountered in the course of his career. This statement intrigued the journalists, for they knew that Seward had encountered many great statesmen in his career, including Abraham Lincoln. They asked him whether he really meant that Juárez was the greatest statesman he had known. Seward said yes and repeated his statement that Juárez was the greatest of them all.

Juárez showed his statesmanship in bearing no resentment of Seward's policy toward Mexico. Romero was particularly generous to Seward. He said in 1887 that while he and Grant had favored a quicker, direct approach to making the French leave Mexico, Seward had preferred the slower method in order to avoid the risk of war between France and the United States. Romero said he was now glad that Seward's way had been followed successfully.

Historians have been kind to Seward, usually claiming that his subtle and experienced diplomacy succeeded where the bullheaded approach of the generals would have failed; but Sheridan was justified in thinking that it was the presence of his army on the Rio Grande that made the French leave Mexico. The reaction of the French during the critical nine months between April 1865 and January 1866 shows that whenever Sheridan made a military demonstration in support of Juárez the French retreated, and whenever Seward sent them a reassuring note the French advanced. Other factors were certainly involved in the French decision to withdraw from Mexico. Napoleon's impatience with Maximilian, the high financial cost of the intervention, public opinion in France, and mistrust of Bismarck all played their part; but by far the most important reason was fear of war with the United States. The chief credit for getting the French to go must be given to Grant and to Sheridan, whom the conservative newspaper in Mexico City, *L'Estafette,* called the "sword of Damocles" which was always suspended over the head of Maximilian's empire.

In September 1870 Juárez heard that Napoleon III had been defeated and taken prisoner by the Germans at Sedan, and that his Second Empire had been overthrown by a revolution in Paris. The Third Republic was proclaimed, and a government was formed in which Jules Favre was minister of foreign affairs. Juárez sent a message of good will to republican France, and a French liberal sent Juárez some of Napoleon III's wines, which had been found in the Tuileries after the revolution of the Fourth of September. The surrender of Paris to the Germans was followed by the Commune, when the Communards, in reprisal for the summary execution of their soldiers by Galliffet, shot hostages chosen from among the wealthier classes in Paris. One of those shot was Jecker, who thus lost his life as well as his bonds at the hands of "Reds" and "anarchists."

During the Franco-Prussian War, Bazaine was in command of the army defending Metz. Believing that his situation was hopeless, he surrendered the city to the Germans. After the war the republican government had him court-martialed on a charge of abandoning his post to the enemy when he could have continued to resist. He was convicted and sentenced to death, but the sentence was commuted to twenty years' imprisonment. His Mexican wife organized his escape from the fortress of Île Sainte Marguerite, and he took refuge in Spain, where he died in 1888.

The only threat to Juárez now came from Porfirio Díaz, who stood against him in the presidential election of 1871. When Juárez was elected, Díaz declared that the result had been falsified by Juárez's government officials, and he led a revolution against him. The revolution failed, and Díaz was hiding in the mountains in Oaxaca when Juárez died of a heart attack in July 1872. Díaz continued his revolutionary uprising against Lerdo, who succeeded Juárez as president.

In 1876, Díaz marched on Mexico City, and Lerdo fled to New York. Díaz was elected president of the republic, and after holding office for four years, and ruling for another four years through a nominee, he was again elected president in 1884. He remained in office until 1911, having been re-elected for a seventh term at the age of eighty. Díaz modernized and developed Mexico with the help of foreign investors and established good relations with the European powers as well as with the United States. He was greatly admired by foreign governments and journalists. Here at last was the strong ruler Mexico had needed for so long, the ruler who would enforce law and order, develop railroads, and make Mexico a safe and profitable place for foreign capitalists. All agreed that Díaz had succeeded where Maximilian had failed. In 1867 Queen Victoria wrote that "it would be an eternal disgrace to us were we to entertain any diplomatic relations with such a bloodstained Government as that of the monster Juarez and his adherents." But thirty-nine years later her son King Edward VII made Porfirio Díaz a knight commander of the Order of the Bath.

One day in 1895 an old man of seventy-five arrived in Mexico City. He revealed that he was Leonardo Márquez, the Tiger of Tacubaya. He had become tired of living in poverty and anonymity in Havana; life there had no more enjoyment for him, and he thought he would have nothing to lose by returning to Mexico after twenty-eight years and placing himself at the mercy of his enemies. President Díaz was too busy dealing with the rising discontent among the people to take any action against his old enemy, and Márquez was not prosecuted or molested.

Márquez wrote a book in which he tried to justify himself against the accusations that had been made against him. He said Miramón had lied at his trial in Querétaro when he said that Márquez had killed the prisoners and medical staff at Tacubaya in 1859 in defiance of Miramón's orders. Márquez said he had merely carried out Miramón's orders. He also denied any responsibility for the murder of Ocampo in 1861, and said that his subordinate commander, Captain Cajiga, had kidnapped and killed Ocampo without consulting or informing him. He claimed that it would have been impossible for him to have led an army from Mexico City to relieve Maximilian at Querétaro. Márquez lived on unnoticed in the suburbs of Mexico City until his death in 1905. Escobedo had died three years before.

Díaz's failure to solve the problem of peonage led to the outbreak of a revolution in 1911. He fled to Paris, where he died in 1915. Two years later a Mexican named Sedano was executed in Paris by a firing squad on a charge of being a German spy during the First World War.

Sedano was the son of Maximilian and the gardener's daughter at Cuernavaca. The operation to catch and execute German spies in Paris was chiefly instigated by Clemenceau, who had rejoiced at the execution of Sedano's father at Querétaro fifty years before.

Eugénie escaped from Paris during the revolution of 1870 and fled to England. She survived Napoleon III by forty-seven years. When asked in her old age what she thought about the Mexican expedition, she admitted that she had been largely responsible for it, but she still thought she had been right; her only regret was that it had not succeeded. She was ninety-four when she died on a visit to Madrid in 1920.

Charlotte was still alive, living in Belgium, and still mad. No one has satisfactorily explained why an intelligent young woman of great determination and charm, and with a good deal of common sense, who had never shown any signs of insanity (and there was no record of insanity in her family) should suddenly have gone mad at the age of twenty-six. Several contemporary writers believed that she had been given a drug known only to the Indian tribes in Mexico, which caused people to go mad; they thought this drug had somehow been administered to her by an agent of Juárez at Puebla or somewhere else between Mexico City and Veracruz on her journey to Paris in July 1866. Queen Victoria blamed Napoleon III, who "has behaved very badly to poor Max, and I am afraid his behaviour to poor Charlotte has helped to bring on her madness."

Others have suggested that her grief at her childlessness and at Maximilian's love affairs and her anxiety about the threatening situation in Mexico affected her mind, though not every woman who experiences these sorrows, and not every empress who fears that she will lose her throne, has become insane. Her niece Princess Stephanie of Belgium (the widow of Franz Joseph's son Rudolf, who was found dead at Mayerling) often visited her in her old age. Stephanie believed that Charlotte's madness was greatly aggravated by her sense of guilt at having deserted Maximilian and left him to meet his fate in Mexico.

When Archbishop Dechamps broke the news to Charlotte that Maximilian had been shot, she reacted quite rationally, weeping at first and then accepting it sadly as the will of God.

In March 1879 a fire broke out in her residence at Tervuren during the night, and she had to be quickly evacuated. She seemed to enjoy the experience and said that the flames looked very pretty. After the fire she moved to the twelfth-century Bouchot Castle, where she lived for the rest of her life. She went for drives in her carriage in the park, but she never went outside the grounds. She often played the piano, which she still played well.

Her family visited her regularly and showed her great kindness. When Leopold II died in 1909, the new king, her nephew Albert, came to visit her regularly with his wife, Queen Elizabeth. She did not seem to realize that they were now the king and queen of the Belgians. Before Albert's accession to the throne he had been count of Flanders, and when they visited her, Charlotte would say, "The Flanders are here."

She understood her condition and sometimes referred to herself as "the mad woman." She usually spoke of herself in the third person and would say to a visitor: "Yes, Sir, one is old, one is stupid, one is mad. The mad woman is still alive" (*Oui, Monsieur, on est vieux, on est bête, on est fou. La folle est toujours vivante*). She never spoke about Mexico or Maximilian, but she would sometimes discuss other events of the past, like the German-Danish War of 1864, as if they were still taking place; at the annual party on her saint's day in November 1912, she asked why Maximilian was not there.

She died on January 19, 1927, at the age of eighty-six. The press of many countries reported her death and published obituaries informing younger readers who she was. The same newspapers contained reports of the protest issued by Pope Pius XI against a new decree by the Mexican government restricting the activities of the Catholic Church in Mexico, which had just emerged from another decade of revolutionary upheavals.

Charlotte was not quite the last survivor of those who played a part in the story of Maximilian and Juárez. One of the young soldiers in the firing squad that had executed Maximilian was still living in 1952, at the age of one hundred and eleven.

NOTES

1. DEPARTURE FROM MIRAMAR

PAGE

1–5 On the castle of Miramar, information from Dottoressa Rossella Fabiani and personal observation; for the events of Apr. 10–14, 1864, see Kollonitz, 1–5; Corti, 353–59; Foussemagne, 165; E. Domenech, *Histoire du Mexique,* 3:173–75. For the speeches of Gutiérrez and Maximilian, see Tavera, *Geschichte* 1:227–32; Hall, 85–92.

5 But the people there . . . back to Miramar. Gasparini, "Massimiliano nel Messico," 17.

2. GUTIÉRREZ LOOKS FOR AN EMPEROR

6 "All the most . . . worthy man." Kollonitz, 24–25.

8 In Mexico City . . . San Francisco. Bullock, 123–26.

8–9 In Mexico City . . . a few cents. Magruder, 43.

9 During the religious . . . his family. E. Domenech, *Le Mexique tel qu'il est,* 136–37.

9 Not surprisingly . . . inequality." J. Lynch, 23, 299, 302.

9 The Mexican conservatives . . . their history. Corti, 6.

10 The Inquisition . . . from error. Tambs, 179.

10 What most distressed . . . American hemisphere. Romero, *Mexico and the United States,* 287.

11 By 1794 . . . Frenchmen in Mexico. Rydjord, 61, 67, 93; Tambs, 179.

11 Hidalgo not only . . . and the state. Timmons, 184.

11–12 When Hidalgo's men . . . 14,000 of them. Domenech, *L'Empire au Mexique,* 22.

12 After he had . . . shot was fired. Roeder, 31.

PAGE

12 The Inquisition . . . survives today. Ibid., 36.

12 One of the charges . . . his possession. Ibid.

14 deplored the fact . . . forty years. Hanna and Hanna, 49.

14 "Every time . . . civil war. Lefèvre, 14.

14 Gutiérrez, after returning . . . and the guillotine. Hale, *Mexican Liberalism,* 27–29; Gutiérrez, *Carta,* 41, 54, 64, 67.

15 In 1842 . . . opposition of the United States. Corti, 29–33.

15 Gutiérrez appealed . . . from anarchy. Dawson, 84.

17 One book . . . the Pacific. Napoleon III, 2:461–543.

17 The prophets . . . 512 million. K. Hanna, 299.

17 In 1831 . . . Declaration of Independence. Bankhead to Palmerston, July 13, 1831 (Palmerston Papers, B.L., Add. MSS. 49964).

18 By 1852 . . . prescribe." Rippy, 26–28.

19–20 Lieutenant Ulysses . . . of Austria. Grant, 1:64, 162, 175, 179.

20 Had not the liberal . . . Santa Anna? Sanchez-Navarro, 28.

3. HIDALGO JOINS IN THE SEARCH

23–24 The benefactress . . . governor of Michoacán. Smart, 104–6; Roeder, 105–6; Valades, 21, 23.

24 The liberals told . . . against Dueñas. Valades, 402; Smart, 107; Roeder, 83.

24 Had not Christ . . . a holy group. E. Domenech, *Le Mexique tel qu'il est,* 128.

24–25 Dueñas himself . . . be our end." Roeder, 84.

25 He was born . . . for the Church. Juárez, 1:24–41; Smart, 29–34, 38–40.

25 for it could be . . . far below. Information from Señor Velasco of Oaxaca; personal observation.

25 but though he was . . . supported Santa Anna. Bulnes, *Juárez y les revoluciones,* 104, 126–36, 157, 160–61; Smart, 81.

26 Santa Anna, in . . . "can confirm this." Santa-Anna, 93.

26–27 Juárez went to . . . replied Juárez. Smart, 110–18.

27 The liberals also . . . for women. Callcott, 23–25, 33; Berry, 236.

28 "If a majority" . . . was an atheist. Roeder, 131–33, 135.

28 The ladies who . . . antiliberal zeal. Malortie, 299; Kollonitz, 223.

29 His forces . . . his supporters. Smart, 173, 178.

30 Eugénie seems . . . dangerous to go. Primoli, 760–61; Alba, 77–78; Beijens to Materne, Jan. 27, 1853 (RA: J.76/55); Filon, 23.

30–31 Not long after . . . to talk nonsense. Viel Castel, 2:243.

31 In September 1857 . . . the United States. Corti, 75; Barker, "Empress Eugénie," 12.

4. THE GENERAL AND THE INDIAN

32 "My sword is my influence." Gagern, 1:272.

33 As soon as . . . a month later. Smart, 180–81.

33 Some cynics said . . . army officers. E. Domenech, *L'Empire au Mexique*, 116; La Porte, 48; Kératry, *Maximilien*, 21; Prince Salm-Salm, 1:41; Blasio, 47; Loiseau, 256.

33–34 When he first . . . room in panic. Smart, 180; Roeder, 170.

34 But the conservatives . . . on the sofa. E. Domenech, *Le Mexique tel qui'il est*, 157; La Porte, 49.

34 Degollado called . . . "and peace." García and Pereyra, *Paredes y Arrillaga*, 263.

34 The conservative general . . . to go free. Ibid., 274–75.

34–35 As soon as . . . himself in action. Roeder, 199.

35–37 Miramón arrived . . . with the others. *Libro Rojo*, 200–14; Gagern, 1:276; García and Pereyra, *Paredes y Arrillaga*, 291.

37 A few days . . . "daughters of Mexico." Smart, 184–85.

5. THE GREAT POWERS BECOME INVOLVED

38–39 He thought that . . . the United States. Dawson, 6–8.

39 Their journal . . . Indian gods. *Saturday Review*, Apr. 7, May 26, 1860.

40 Gabriac came . . . Jecker bonds. Kératry, *Créance Jecker*, 10–12.

40 The *New-York Times* . . . "to the other." Roeder, 235.

40 President James Buchanan . . . Gadsden Purchase. Ibid., 194, 213–18; Smart, 192–203.

41 On December 14 . . . their country. Roeder, 214.

42 The news of . . . Napoleon III. Smart, 229; Reyes, 69–71.

42 On January 1, . . . "Northern Confederation." Connell, 296.

6. THE ARCHDUKE MAXIMILIAN

43 In July 1832 . . . in labor. Oddie, 209, 213.

43–44 Metternich became . . . allowed to meet. Ibid., 192–97.

44 "Not him!" . . . "mon petit choux." Hyde, 1; Wertheimer, 410.

44–45 Rumors about . . . believe this story. Oddie, 215.

45 On a very cold . . . at Schönbrunn. Wertheimer, 410.

45 When she was . . . Maximilian thrived. Oddie, 215.

46 "I could have . . . simply incredible." Redlich, 14.

47 "we call . . . above the law." Hyde, 14.

48 "1. Let the mind . . . or authority." Corti, 44–45.

49 His mother encouraged . . . nothing wrong. Bülow, 26, 28, 31–32, 39, 77–78.

49 As he was driving . . . "people of the south." Hyde, 22.

50 He was intensely . . . in Bohemia. Maximilian, 1:152, 237; 3:231.

50 In Albania . . . in Vienna. Ibid., 2:221–22, 224.

50 In Smyrna . . . "unbearably attractive." Hyde, 18.

50–51 At Gibraltar . . . "immorality of France." Maximilian, 1:234.

51 He loved . . . but not killed. Ibid., 1:186–201; 2:104–6.

51–52 He considered . . . "imperial etiquette." Hyde, 51–55.

52–53 Nine years . . . after a year. Woodham-Smith, 66–67.

53–55 When the little girl . . . *parvenus* in Paris. Hyde, 56, 59–64, 67–70.

55–56 "At Napoleon's . . . revolutionary polemicists." Corti, 81 (June 2, 1858).

56 who encouraged . . . "in its favor." Hyde, 73, 81.

56–57 When he stayed . . . and many slaves. Maximilian, 3:236–37, 324–26.

57 "the blacks . . . are born free." Hyde, 99.

57 But the marriage . . . "a people happy." Ibid., 106–7.

7. NAPOLEON III CHANGES HIS MIND

59 At that time . . . as a traitor. Duvernois, 100–102.

59 One prominent conservative . . . grant the amnesty. Scholes, 58–59; Roeder, 271.

59–60 Ocampo thought . . . "disobey and resist." Ibid., 125.

60–62 Ocampo went off . . . liberals had destroyed. Valades, 405–9; Roeder, 303–17; *La Bandera Roja*, June 11, 21, 1861; Smart, 246; García and Pereyra, *Paredes y Arrillaga*, 346–53, 360–63, 371–72, 381; Bibesco, 34.

62 From his headquarters . . . his achievements. García and Pereyra, *Correspondencia: 1860–1862*, 27–36, 73–75, 147.

63 In April 1861 . . . for our interests. Roeder, 284–285.

64 Rafael returned . . . years, not months. García and Pereyra, *Correspondencia: Sitio de Puebla*, 37–39.

64–65 In September 1861 . . . "he *will* accept." Corti, 99–101.

8. THE EXPEDITION TO VERACRUZ

66 When Hidalgo . . . suggested the idea. Barker, *Distaff Diplomacy*, 89–90.

PAGE

66 More than forty . . . "from myself." Paléologue, 99.

68–69 Rechberg wrote . . . "Mexico themselves." Dawson, 113.

69 As for the invitation . . . throne to Maximilian. Ibid., 134–35.

69 "Of course . . . the circumstances." Bock, 161.

69–70 "There is no" . . . been at war. Corti, 361–62 (German ed. 1:App. 3–4).

70 He wrote to Russell . . . any active support." Bock, 27.

70 "This project . . . expectations of support." Tavera, *Geschichte*, 77.

70 "Without at all . . . easy of attainment." Robertson, 173.

70–71 "We find ourselves . . . more imminent." Hanna and Hanna, 56.

71 On his way . . . Southern rebels. Miller, 230.

71 He proposed . . . for the payment. Hanna and Hanna, 54.

71–72 The Three Powers . . . occupation of Veracruz. Bock, 163.

72 Romero begged . . . told Romero. Hanna and Hanna, 39.

72 La Fuente waited . . . to invade Mexico. Bock, 129, 135, 141; Roeder, 343.

73 But Palmerston . . . yellow fever. Bock, 180.

73 He sent instructions . . . "if necessary." Ibid., 227.

73 But Russell instructed . . . "against Mexico City." Dawson, 133–34.

73 On November 1 . . . together to Veracruz. Bock, 219.

73 They arrived . . . San Juan de Ulúa. Hanna and Hanna, 40.

73–74 "Sailors and soldiers! . . . people follows it." Niox, 1:51.

74 Juárez entered . . . during the emergency. Lempriere, 90, 93–95.

74 "Mexicans! If they . . . from our fathers." *El Siglo XIX,* Dec. 18, 1861.

75 Charles Lempriere . . . miles from Veracruz. Lempriere, 2, 67, 85; Roeder, 380.

75 "Put yourself . . . I am seventy." Foussemagne, 106, 108.

76 In this last . . . Ferdinand Maximilian. Dawson, 215.

76 Maximilian wrote to say . . . "speedy remedies." Ibid., 151.

76 On October 24 . . . was to be welcomed. Leopold I to Queen Victoria, Oct. 24, 1861 (RA: Y.83/32).

77 Albert wrote . . . "fall into a trap." Prince Albert to Leopold I, Nov. 5, 1861 (RA: J.101/1).

77 Prince Leopold . . . "under your rule." Dawson, 212.

77 After keeping Gutiérrez . . . he would accept. Ibid., 147, 185, 188–89.

77–78 Labastida had already . . . "anarchy" in Mexico. Ibid., 186.

78 Maximilian went to see . . . with him to Mexico. Ibid., 190–91, 411–13.

78 Napoleon III agreed . . . services in Mexico. Corti, 149–50.

78–79 In January 1862 . . . anything at all. Dawson, 195–203.

79 He wrote to Rechberg . . . "from his tutelage." Ibid., 220–21.

79 By April 1862 . . . go to Mexico. Cowley to Russell, May 19, 1862 (RA: J.101/90).

9. SALIGNY WANTS WAR

80 The allies found . . . out of action. *The Times* (London), Feb. 18, 1862; Bock, 295–97.

80 The allied . . . of the high commissioners. Hanna and Hanna, 42.

81 At their first . . . to stop them. Wyke to Russell, Jan. 16, 1862 (RA: J.101/2).

81 The British claims . . . silver dollars. Kératry, *Créance Jecker,* 151.

81 The Mexican government . . . by that amount. Ibid., 19.

82 Wyke and Prim . . . Jecker bonds. Bock, 301.

82 And why was . . . interests in Mexico. Kératry, *Créance Jecker,* 18–19.

82 Even the French . . . Napoleon III himself. Bock, 303.

82–83 Prim afterward . . . negotiate with the government. Ibid., 301.

83 "I welcomed . . . except robbery." Juárez and Montluc, 60 (Sept. 29, 1861).

83 "My only merit . . . intervention necessary." Gaulot, 1:30.

83 Wyke, writing to Russell . . . to accept it. Bock, 301.

83 Russell agreed; . . . he replied. Ibid., 384, 675; Russell to Cowley, Mar. 10, 1862 (RA: J.101/55).

83 Napoleon III . . . troops in Veracruz. Bock, 346.

83–84 Juárez received . . . "a great nation." Wyke to Russell, Jan. 20, 1862 (RA: J.101/22).

84 He sent . . . Spanish commissioners." Niox, 85.

84 Juárez, though conciliatory . . . death penalty. Hall, 243–52.

84–85 During their seven . . . in four days. Niox, 97; *The Times* (London), June 27, 1859; Roeder, 417.

85 They halted . . . arrived in ambulances. Niox, 97.

85 On March 6 . . . Juárez's troops. Ibid., 103, 107.

85 The Spanish troops . . . port at Veracruz. Gaulot, 1:52.

86–87 In February 1862 . . . have been lost. Berry, 81; Colson to Lorencez, Apr. 15, 1862 (Niox, 138–39).

87 "Señor Merlin . . . Hotel Presidente. Berry, 82; information obtained at Oaxaca.

87 Miramón also arrived . . . go to Havana. Bock, 313.

88 Almonte also entered . . . reached the French camp. Lefèvre, i.214n; Bibesco, 76–77.

PAGE

88 Robles, who had . . . five hours earlier. Bock, 419.

88–89 Wyke regretted . . . party had done. Wyke to Russell, Mar. 29, 1862 (RA: J.101/97, no. 143).

89 Russell believed . . . "invaded their soil." Russell to Cowley, May 1862 (RA: J.101/86).

89 Saligny assured Jurien . . . Veracruz was liberal. Hanna and Hanna, 45; Niox, 106.

89 He showed Saligny . . . "we are lost." Roeder, 407.

89 Jurien was not . . . within a month. Bock, 420.

89–90 Prim tried . . . "and defend them." Gaulot, 1:48–51.

90 He sent an official . . . another commander. Niox, 144.

90–91 On March 20 . . . the battle zone. Bock, 428; Niox, 144.

91 To remove . . . claims against Mexico. Kératry, *Créance Jecker*, 19.

91 When Thouvenel . . . "for its instigators." Gaulot, 1:51–52.

91 On April 9 . . . the joint intervention. Wyke to Jurien de la Graviére, Mar. 27, 1862 (RA: J.101/97, encl. 4); compare Roeder, 420.

91 The high commissioners . . . start its operations. Allied Commissioners to Doblado, Apr. 9, 1862 (RA: J.101/102, encl. 5[1]).

91–92 Doblado, in reply, . . . force with force. Doblado to Allied Commissioners, April 1862; Doblado to Saligny and Jurien de la Gravière, Apr. 9, 1862 (RA: J.101/102, encl. 5[2] and 7[2]).

92 When Russell sent . . . "K. of Mexico." Wyke to Russell, Apr. 12, 1862 (RA: J.101/80); see also Wyke to Russell, Apr. 15, 1862 (printed dispatches, no. 2, in RA: J.101/102).

92 Wyke and Dunlop . . . the British government. Wyke to Russell, Apr. 29, 1862; Dunlop to the Admiralty, Apr. 28, 1862 (printed dispatches nos. 14 and 19[2], in RA: J.101/102).

92 It was almost . . . the Mexican Congress. Roeder, 423–24.

92 They did not object . . . "ratify these conventions." Russell to Wyke, June 26, 1862 (RA: J.101/111).

92–93 *The Times* . . . "lesson of self-government." *The Times* (London), Jan. 22, 1862; Roeder, 430.

93 When she heard . . . "in other countries." Bock, 431.

93–94 "Governments are no" . . . "be there already." Lefèvre, 1:67; Ollivier, *L'Expédition du Mexique,* 67.

94 In the autumn . . . "not well known." *French Opinion: Extracts,* Case, 311–12.

94 In March 1862 . . . "ruin the dynasty." Nassau Senior's journal (RA: K.57, Mar. 25, 1862).

94–95 General Lorencez had . . . "master of Mexico." Niox, 153, 155; Roeder, 441.

10. THE FIFTH OF MAY

96 "Mexicans! . . . if they dare!" Proclamation of Apr. 16, 1862 (Niox, 129–31).

96 General Almonte . . . Republic of Mexico. Almonte's proclamation, enclosed in Wyke to Russell, Apr. 21, 1862 (RA: J. 101/102, encl. no. 13).

97 There were 340 . . . Juárist barbarians. Niox, 138–41; Lefèvre, 1:238–40.

97 Prim, who was . . . be in Paris. Roeder, 429–30.

97–98 He stationed . . . thirty-six wounded. Ibid., 442; Niox, 157.

98 He had ordered . . . families in France. *The Times* (London), July 18, 1862.

98 Saligny, relying . . . people of Puebla. Roeder, 444.

98 His chief anxiety . . . conservative stronghold. Ibid., 448–49.

98 A few days . . . taken from the north. Ibid., 443–44.

99–100 On the morning . . . a great victory. Gaulot, 1:66–68; Roeder, 444–46.

100 "The national arms," . . . twelve prisoners. Gaulot, 1:71–72.

100 The French disputed . . . two to one. Ibid., 1:17 and note.

100 Zaragoza was disgusted . . . Fifth of May. Ibid., 449.

100–101 Lorencez assured . . . "before Puebla." Gaulot, 1:74–75.

101 That night . . . of their undertaking. Roeder, 450–51.

102 *Le Temps* wrote . . . in their honor. *The Times* (London), May 26, June 2, 1862; Lally, 450.

102 "Here we are . . . in Mexico City." Corti, 374 (German ed., 1:App. 12).

102 On the same day . . . "at the latest." Ibid., 373 (German ed., 1:App. 11–12).

102 The news about . . . for the information. Bock, 438.

103 The first reaction . . . "to Mexico City." *The Times* (London), June 19, 1862; Lally, 51.

103 Napoleon appointed . . . blaming Saligny. Gaulot, 1:88–89; Randon, 2:66–67.

103–4 On July 3 . . . "and its prestige." Niox, 212–16; Gaulot, 1:94–99; García, 983–84; see also Hanna and Hanna, 78–80.

104 "it would be . . . clerical reaction." Extract from *Le Trait-d'Union*, Apr. 14, 1862, enclosed in no. 8(1) in RA: J.101/102.

104 Zaragoza had . . . guerrilla warfare. Lefèvre, 255.

104–5 "There is no point . . . defend ourselves." Juárez and Montluc, 124.

105 In Tampico . . . in the street. La Bédollière, 1:51.

105 "The Mexicans . . . very expensive." Mérimée, 2(5):200.

11. SEWARD APPEASES NAPOLEON III

116–17 "The French government . . . troops to Mexico. Blumberg, "William Seward," 32–33.

117 The 500 blacks . . . the hot lands." Kératry, *Contre-guérilla*, 65n.

118 In the summer . . . United States army. Hanna and Hanna, 72, 75.

118 The French minister . . . Seward agreed. Ibid., 76.

119 The United States minister . . . him to Washington. Case and Spencer, 517–21.

119 He issued . . . through Matamoros. Hanna and Hanna, 160–63.

119–20 In March 1863 . . . fight the French. Rippy, 240–41; Hanna and Hanna, 160–63.

120 On January 19 . . . join the army. Hanna and Hanna, 76.

12. "PUEBLA IS IN OUR HANDS"

121 In February 1863 . . . 'live the Emperor!' " Niox, 247.

122 The French formed . . . the *contre-guérilla*. Kératry, *Contre-guérilla*, 11–13; Du Barail, 2:167.

122 The *contre-guérilla* . . . "not by persuasion." Rivière, 3–4.

122 Kératry wrote . . . lost much blood. Kératry, *Contre-guérilla*, 3.

123 Du Pin, instead . . . sent to Mexico. Stevenson, *Maximilian*, 261.

123 On February 14 . . . at Du Pin's order. Kératry, *Contre-guérilla*, 9–11, 51, 70–71.

123 Du Pin, wearing . . . leagues of him. Ibid., 11; Rivière, 16, 273–76.

123–24 Eleven days . . . never saw him again. Kératry, *Contre-guérilla*, 16–18, 21–22.

124–25 When Du Pin . . . left Tlaliscoya. Ibid., 25–40.

125 The inhabitants . . . the guerrillas. Ibid., 43.

125 The *contre-guérilla* . . . "order of things." Ibid., 52–54.

125–26 Du Pin was sure . . . in the area. Ibid., 58; Niox, 306.

126 There was one woman . . . lieutenant colonel. *The Times* (London), Aug. 13, 1863.

126 "The Emperor Napoleon . . . civilization." Gaulot, 1:106–7.

126–27 He decided . . . taken prisoner. Niox, 253, 260–61.

127 Forey had hoped . . . mine the houses. Ibid., 261–65.

127 By April 11 . . . siege to continue. Ibid., 266–67; Du Barail, 2:417.

127 During pauses . . . "you will conquer." Hugo, 2:253–55.

127 As the street . . . taken prisoner. Niox, 270–72.

128 One of the more . . . life was saved. Thomas, 42–43, 45, 61–65.

128 If the allies . . . La Soledad. Nassau Senior's journal (RA: K.45, Apr. 30, 1863).

PAGE

129 Forey sent the third . . . every year. O'Ballance, 79–81; Porch, 141–42.

129–30 Forey sent Bazaine . . . in all directions. Niox, 274–77.

130 The news of Comonfort's . . . rounds of ammunition. Ibid., 279–80; Du Barail, 2:445.

130 Ortega surrendered . . . prisoner by the French. Niox, 282.

130 They suggested to Forey . . . street fighting. Roeder, 505.

130–31 Forey offered . . . arrived in France. Niox, 281–83.

131 Napoleon III . . . 1,039 wounded. *The Times* (London), June 2, 5, 12, 1863; Gasparini, "Massimiliano nel Messico," 12; Niox, 283.

131 Napoleon wrote . . . "or for civilization." Niox, 283–84.

13. IN MEXICO CITY

132 On the night . . . the police force. Stevenson, 87–88.

132 When Juárez heard . . . defend the capital. Lefèvre, 1:286–87; *Cronista de Mexico,* June 3, 1863.

132–33 On the morning . . . through the night. Roeder, 511–12; *Independencia Mexicana,* June 15, 1863.

133 As soon as . . . law and order. Stevenson, *Maximilian,* 91; Dabbs, 52–53; Gaulot, 1:123.

133 When the people . . . "Death to Juarez!" Ollivier, *L'Expédition du Mexique,* 141.

133 The consuls . . . advance guard had entered. Dabbs, 53.

133 On the evening . . . enthusiastically at Puebla. Stevenson, *Maximilian,* 91–93.

133–34 Forey himself . . . classes were silent. Ibid., 96; Blasio, 41; Hanna and Hanna, 87.

134 Salas met Forey . . . than the French. Niox, 288; Stevenson, *Maximilian,* 97; *La Sociedad,* June 11, 1863; Gaulot, 1:124.

134 At the start . . . censor's office. García, 987, 994, 998; Lally, 61.

134–35 After Juárez left . . . of the Church. *Cronista de Mexico,* June 3, 1863; *La Sociedad,* June 10, 1863.

135 Sara Yorke . . . the lower classes. Stevenson, *Maximilian,* 94–96; Malortie, 175–77.

135 Forey did all . . . against the past." Hanna and Hanna, 104; *La Sociedad,* July 1, 1863.

135 Señor Don Eustacio . . . at Tacubaya. Kollonitz, 196–97; Bullock, 101, 128–29.

135–36 When they first . . . and his sword. Blasio, 42.

136 He restored . . . government in Mexico City. Stevenson, *Maximilian,* 102–3.

136 He nominated . . . president of the council. Gaulot, 1:134–36.

136–37 The reports . . . be coming home. Case, *French Opinion: Extracts,* 340–43, 346–47, 350.

137 Napoleon III had . . . to be true. *L'Empereur du Mexique,* 3.

137 The author of . . . "suffering humanity." *La Prise de Puebla,* 5, 9–10.

137 Prince Henry de . . . through Frenchmen. Valori, 36.

137 One writer believed . . . "was the second." *Où conduit l'expédition,* 10.

137 Another author . . . to arrest him. Arbelli, 13.

137 Napoleon's propagandists . . . the United States. Poussielgue, 12–13, 15.

137–38 On July 20 . . . through the town. La Bédollière, 2nd ed., 47; Le Saint, 107–8; *The Times* (London), July 22, 1863.

138 In Paris, which . . . throughout France. La Bédollière, 2nd ed., 50–51; *The Times* (London), Aug. 13, 1863.

138 "Napoleon the Third . . . Indian like Juárez." *Blackwood's Edinburgh Magazine* 96:72, 79.

138 *The Times* . . . "either hemisphere." *The Times* (London), June 13, 1863.

14. BAZAINE AGAINST THE CHURCH AND THE GUERRILLAS

139 In the first . . . Napoleon III. *Independencia Mexicana,* June 15, 1863.

139 Favre and Thiers . . . and Mexico City. Lally, 79–82.

139–40 "Negotiate with . . . San Luis Potosí?" Rouher, *Discours de Rouher du 17 janvier 1864,* 38.

140 In this grave . . . on September 8. Scholes, 92–99.

140 publication in Paris . . . of the Confederacy. Chevalier, *La France,* 10, 24, 27.

140 An English translation . . . Napoleon III himself. *New-York Times,* Sept. 25, 1863; Hanna and Hanna, 60.

140 The journalist . . . "strains he may." Kingsley, 3.

140–41 They chose 231 . . . 222 votes to 9. Gaulot, 1:138–39.

141 The people of . . . of the Assembly. Stevenson, *Maximilian,* 98; Kératry, *Maximilien,* 28n.

141 He wrote to . . . "noble efforts." Corti, 375 (German ed., 1:App. 13–14).

141 On August 8 . . . give this guarantee. Ibid., 377–78, 380–81 (German ed. 1:App. 15–18).

141 Napoleon confidently . . . "a few months." Corti, 380, 382 (German ed., 1:App. 17, 19).

PAGE

142 In a village . . . attack the train. Kératry, *Contre-guérilla*, 99–100.

142 but Napoleon III . . . as a punishment. García, 998; Buffin, 171; Kendall, 102–6; Lefèvre, 1:336.

143 He wrote regularly . . . soon afterward. Loizillon, 43–73.

143 He felt uncomfortable . . . Madame Hortense Cornu. Ibid., 97–113; Gaulot, 1:179–85.

143 Napoleon once wrote . . . sexual in it. Castelot, *Napoléon Trois*, 1:403.

143 But she was outraged . . . at the Tuileries. Nassau Senior's journal (RA: K54, Apr. 3, 1863).

143–44 A few weeks . . . in Mexico. García, 1028–29.

144 Saligny was furious . . . gift to him. Ibid., 1031–35; Gaulot, 1:192–93; Stevenson, *Maximilian*, 112–13.

144 Eugénie believed . . . a velvet glove. Corti, 844 (German ed., 2:App. 12).

144 Prevent the reaction . . . is in command. García, 1035.

144–45 Any act of hostility . . . within twenty-four hours. Lefèvre, 1:315.

145 In January 1864 . . . to be shot. García, 1091.

145 In March 1864 . . . "to that area." Ibid., 1112.

145 to prevent the Mexican . . . through the streets. Ibid., 1108–9, 1112–13, 1136, 1142–43.

145–46 When he heard . . . Juárez's territory. Ibid., 1060, 1121; Gaulot, 2:16.

146 He was quite . . . discipline the bishop. García, 1116–17.

146 There was trouble, . . . to admit them. Ibid., 1154.

146–47 One day . . . resistance collapsed. Ibid., 1085–86; Gaulot, 1:239–40; Dabbs, 81–83; Détroyat, 21–29.

147 Labastida wrote . . . "so many sacrifices?" Kératry, *Maximilien*, 80; E. Domenech, *Histoire du Mexique*, 3:158.

147 Gutiérrez, as spokesman . . . democratic republic." Gutiérrez, *Discorso en Miramar*, 2, 8.

147–48 He had submitted . . . received at Miramat. Corti, 260.

148 Maximilian said . . . constitutional sovereign. Tavera, *Geschichte*, 180–81.

148 After the ceremony . . . they approached it. Corti, 261, 263.

148 Napoleon III approved . . . even in Austria. Ibid., 389–90 (German ed., 1:App. 24–25).

148–49 Maximilian was now . . . Gulf of Mexico. Holdreth to Maximilian, July 1863 (Staatsarchiv, K 3/707).

149 In September 1863 . . . "not to do harm." "Conversations avec cher Papa," Sept. 12–19, 1863 (Staatsarchiv, K4/918, pp. 3, 6).

PAGE

149–50 "I have to state . . . the Arch-Duke." Russell to Bloomfield, Aug. 20, 1863 (RA: J.101/123).

150 On December 7 . . . Maximilian's expense. Corti, 295–96.

150 "without exception" . . . would soon come. Ibid., 283.

150 Wyke gave Napoleon . . . prestige in France. Ibid., 286–89; Dawson, 341–43.

150 His statement . . . "can I do?" Jerrold, 3:82.

151 Already in the autumn . . . in Austria. Maximilian's memorandum, Dec. 31, 1861 (Dawson, 411).

151 "a somewhat restless" . . . of his travels. Motley, 2:138.

151 In September 1863 . . . "Poor young man." Ibid., 2:143.

151 Motley reported . . . form of government. Rippy, 262.

151–52 Motley had to . . . discourage Maximilian. Sister M. Claire Lynch, 87.

152 Lieutenant Laurent, . . . devotion to duty. Laurent, 35–36.

152 Mejía was a small . . . near Querétaro. Malortie, 295; Rivière, 67.

152 Ten days later . . . "Indian people." García, 1075.

152 On January 5 . . . Guadalajara.

152–53 The French soldiers . . . their bayonets. Stevenson, *Maximilian*, 121.

153 In Paris . . . faithful wife. Mercer, 81.

153 Many liberals . . . about this policy. García, 1041.

153–54 Even Doblado . . . had already surrendered. Ibid., 1074–75, 1081, 1091, 1114.

154 General Ortega . . . intention of resigning. Smart, 298–99.

154 His illegitimate son . . . for San Luis Potosí. Ibid., 297–98.

154 Juárez's former leader . . . the French service. Duvernois, 204.

154–55 In March 1864 . . . consul in Peru. García, 1115; Laurent, 126; Lefèvre, 1:342.

155–56 According to Lieutenant . . . by the Chasseurs. Laurent, 135–36; García, 1140; Lefèvre, 1:280, 343–45.

156 The French themselves . . . to read and write. Loizillon, 188, 191–95; Bullock, 285–86.

156–57 Juárez called on . . . of January 25. Montlong, 8.

157 Henry M. Flint . . . between 1863 and 1865. Flint, 67–86.

157 The regents announced . . . state capital. Lefèvre, 1:257, 412–19.

15. THE FAMILY PACT

158 At the end of January . . . nothing about it. Corti, 320–21.

158–59 At the beginning . . . troops in Mexico. Ibid., 324–28; *The*

Times (London), Mar. 8, 10, 14, 17, 1864; Bigelow, *Retrospections*, 2:154.

159 Duke Ernest ... "never have accepted." Saxe-Coburg-Gotha, 4:168, 175–76.

159 "They are going ... cannot understand." Queen Victoria's journal, Mar. 14, 1864 (RA).

159 On their way ... not give in. Corti, 332–36.

159–60 On March 27 ... "set my signature?" Ibid., 338–40, 399–400 (German ed., 1:App. 32).

160 While Napoleon ... "not behaved well." Ibid., 348–50; Queen Victoria's journal, Mar. 30, 1864 (RA).

160 Napoleon had written ... "is in question." Corti, 341.

160–61 On the evening ... never to meet again. Ibid., 342–52.

162 In the ship ... Austrian Parliament. Ibid., 413–17.

162 He began to write ... washed their hands. Paso, 365–75.

162–64 Four of the largest ... "Say eight years." *Dinner to Romero,* 5–6, 8–48; *Gran Banquete,* 1–10, 31–32; see also Miller, 233.

16. MAXIMILIAN ARRIVES

165–66 The *Novara* ... Maximilian's side. Kollonitz, 85–88, 127, 135; Smissen, 23–25; García, 1159; Corti, 417–20; Stevenson, *Maximilian,* 125–28; Lefèvre, 1:385–89; *The Times* (London), July 14, 1864.

166 On June 11 ... 10,000 people. Blasio, 3–4; Kollonitz, 134–37; Stevenson, *Maximilian,* 127–28; *The Times* (London), July 30, 1864; *La Sociedad,* June 11, 1864; Flint, 93–101; Smissen, 27–28.

166 Then came a troop ... French hussars. Laurent, 21.

166 Señor Barron ... Calle de San Francisco. Magruder, 69–70.

166 The French Colonel ... "kill the Emperor!" Blanchot, 2:185–86.

167 palace of Chapultepec ... prisoners at Tacubaya. Blasio, 6, 30–32; Loiseau, 76–77; E. Domenech, *Histoire du Mexique,* 90; Anderson, 31.

167 They had another ... heat of the tropics. Blasio, 7.

167–68 Maximilian's daily routine ... wide gold cord. Ibid., 7, 9–10, 14.

168 Wearing informal clothes ... subjects disapproved. Mismer, 155–56.

168 On the other hand ... approaching her. Buffin, 107.

168 Charlotte was taken ... a great joke. Stevenson, *Maximilian,* 131; Laurent, 165; La Porte, 40.

168 His principal private ... a few days later. Blasio, 4–5, 13.

168–69　Some time afterward . . . imprisonment for life. Ibid., 5–6, 34–35.

　169　The emperor made . . . she had refused. Ibid., 18, 53–54.

　169　When some English . . . spoke ten languages. Kendall, 156–57; Blasio, 24.

169–70　Soon after she arrived . . . in polite society. Magruder, 58; Kendall, 150, 152; Loiseau, 81; Kollonitz, 170; Buffin, 107–8.

　170　The emperor . . . until 3 A.M. Blasio, 24, 36–38; Stevenson, *Maximilian,* 132–33, 223; Loiseau, 79–80; Blanchot, 2:188–90; Bullock, 102–3; Malortie, 194–97.

170–71　Maximilian much preferred . . . almost continually. Blasio, 23, 34; Kollonitz, 222; Malortie, 286–87; Castelot, *Maximilien et Charlotte,* 329.

　171　The only drawback . . . Maximilian's infidelity. Blasio, 17, 37–40; Malortie, 299; Blanchot, 3:235; Corti, *Vom Kind zum Kaiser,* 189.

　172　The Cabinet ministers . . . in the chair. Foussemagne, 225.

　172　He succeeded in pushing . . . cleared of guerrillas. Romero, *Mexico and the United States,* 115, 121; Stevenson, *Maximilian,* 133–38; Bullock, 19; García, 1095; Le Saint, 159–63; Kératry, *Contre-guérilla,* 295–99.

　172　Maximilian issued . . . stopped the project. E. Domenech, *Histoire du Mexique,* 3:239.

　172　Napoleon's idea . . . afraid of the bayonet. Kératry, *Maximilien,* 68–72.

172–73　Márquez believed that . . . to achieve this. Laurent, 36.

　173　Before the French . . . much as Juárez's. Kératry, *Créance Jecker,* 151–54; Lefèvre, 2:165–66.

　173　Maximilian continued . . . in 1864. Dabbs, 240, 244–47, 256n; García, 1120–21.

173–74　For many years . . . for the occasion. Gasparini, "Massimiliano nel Messico," 24–25; Dabbs, 255–56; Mismer, 187.

　174　The Mexicans were . . . Charlotte nearly did. Magruder, 63–65; Kollonitz, 149–50, 159, 202.

　174　Everybody knew . . . on their way. Kendall, 195–200; Valois, 72.

174–75　They were more enthusiastic . . . in Mexico City. Magruder, 64; *Cronista de Mexico,* Jan. 4, 8, 20, 1866.

17. THE CAPTURE OF OAXACA

　176　His empire was of course . . . not send ministers. Blumberg, "A Swedish Diplomat," 275–86.

　176　"My beloved Victoria" . . . in Mexico City. Leopold I to Queen

Victoria, Sept. 13, 1864; Scarlett to Russell, Mar. 1, 1865 (RA: Y.86/64; J.102/23); Lefèvre, 1:466.

176–77 Maximilian refused . . . regard to Mexico. Jordan and Pratt, 214.

177 After the dinner . . . in the United States. The Spanish edition (see *Gran Banquete*) had been published by June 16, 1864, when President Lincoln presented it to Congress; the English edition (*Dinner to Romero*) was published in New York in February 1866.

177–78 Romero persuaded . . . freedom in Mexico. White, 157–60; Rippy, 263–64; Bigelow, *Retrospections,* 2:179.

178 In June 1864 . . . "pertinent and applicable." Lincoln, 7:382, 411.

178–79 By the summer . . . to the United States. White, 163–65.

179 Though Napoleon sometimes . . . vigorous dictator. García, 1192.

179 It has often been said . . . letter a forgery. Smart, 431. The text of the forged letter is given in Roeder, 565–67.

179 The liberal minister . . . "Maximilian the usurper." Iglesias, 2:418 (June 30, 1864).

179 to the dismay . . . a Juárist spy. Blanchot, 2:194; Domenech, *Le Mexique tel qu'il est,* 214–16, 285–87.

179 He did not place . . . in official documents. Cleven, 325.

179–80 Maximilian gave orders . . . out the window. Détroyat, 31–111; Cleven, 327–55; Callcott, 62–68; Testory, 18; Corti, 150, 292, 849, 863, 877 (German ed., 2:App. 15, 26, 36).

180 The Mexican bishops . . . "most unequivocable manner." Cleven, 342.

180 Bishop Ormeacha . . . Protestant countries. Callcott, 61.

180 Father Miranda . . . the Church rested. Hanna and Hanna, 105.

180 By the spring . . . Lombardy and Venetia. Callcott, 61.

180 But the friction . . . submitted to him. García, 1166–67.

181 Vidaurri complied . . . "for your fidelity." Bigelow, 2:173.

181–82 In June 1864 . . . postal service? E. Domenech, *Histoire du Mexique,* 3:187–92.

182–83 Oaxaca was firmly . . . men as prisoners of war. Berry, 88–92; García, 1233; H. H. Bancroft, *Popular History,* 484–85.

183 Forey said . . . as a traitor. La Bédollière, 2:73–74; Kératry, *Maximilien,* 58.

183–84 Díaz was imprisoned . . . Juárez forces. García, 1294, 1308, 1317; Kératry, *Maximilien,* 58–59.

184 Maximilian had been waiting . . . capturing Oaxaca. Corti, 866, 869–71, 873, 888 (German ed., 2:App. 28–30, 32–34, 44); Loizillon, 296; E. Domenech, *Histoire du Mexique,* 3:283.

184 When the news . . . Order of Leopold. García, 1247; Corti, 883
(German ed., 2:App. 40); E. Domenech, *Histoire du Mexique,*
3:285; Gaulot, 2:77.

184–85 But Maximilian was . . . some other reason. Corti, 480–83.

185 Although he had no immediate . . . but Querétaro. Information
from Dottoressa Rosselli Fabiani; personal observation at Miramar.

18. VICTORY OR DEFEAT?

186 The journalists . . . Monroe Doctrine. Cuevas, 3, 6, 8, 16–17,
74–75.

186 Bazaine welcomed . . . They have succeeded." García, 1269.

186 Maximilian's government . . . states and territories. In 1861
Mexico consisted of twenty-four states in addition to the Federal
District of Mexico City. The states became provinces under
Maximilian. The population of Guerrero was 288,016; of Chi-
huahua, 156,070; of Sonora, 134,300; and of Baja California,
9,845 (Lefèvre, 5).

186 Napoleon, whose journalists . . . soon as possible. Jerrold,
4:343; Saxe-Coburg-Gotha, 4:176; Corti, 286–88.

187 The provinces . . . French army was there. Hanna and Hanna,
167–80; Rippy, 247–51.

187 When Maximilian . . . Sonora to France. Corti, 854, 861–62
(German ed., 2:App. 19, 25).

188 When Juárez in Chihuahua . . . until February 2, 1866. Knapp,
Life, 97; Berry, 238.

188 Juárez's supply . . . Lerdo from New York. Knapp, *Life,* 93.

188 On the National Day . . . critical of him. Juárez, 11:131–32;
Knapp, *Life,* 92–93; Bulness, *Verdadero Juárez,* 821–26.

188–89 The experts' report . . . developing Sonora. García, 1263.

189 Rouher, as minister . . . Cabinet meetings. Hanna and Hanna,
150.

189 He won great applause . . . 225 votes to 16. Rouher, *Discours
de Corta,* 42, 59, 61–62.

189 The reports . . . brought home soon. Case, *French Opinion:
Extracts,* 375, 377–78, 380.

189–90 The situation seemed . . . Pedro Mendez. Kératry, *Contre-
guérilla,* 92, 102, 104, 107–8, 110, 112.

190 According to some . . . that awaited them. Rippy, 173.

190–91 In April 1864 . . . men in the countryside. Kératry, *Contre-
guérilla,* 122–23.

191 The *contre-guérilla* were . . . into the sea. Ibid., 219, 222–23.

191 There was trouble . . . to the ground. Ibid., 203.

PAGE

191–92 As Du Pin led . . . let Pepita go. Ibid., 256–57.

192–93 Pedro Mendez . . . beside the road. Ibid., 241, 270–71, 274.

193 Du Pin thought . . . *contre-guérilla*. Ibid., 177–80.

193–94 Some of the respectable . . . achieving good results. Loiseau, 275; Rivière, 55.

194 Napoleon III sent . . . showed in Paris. Thomas, 72, 74–78, 133.

194 In the autumn . . . job in Veracruz. Gaulot, 2:221.

194 He said he . . . died of thirst. Kühn, 78n.

19. THE HUNT FOR ROMERO

195 Maximilian could not . . . stability of the empire. Corti, 865–66, 895 (German ed., 2:App. 27–28, 49).

195–96 He had emerged . . . for his success. García, 1142–43; Blasio, 4; *Libro Rojo*, 243–44.

196 The Belgian . . . January 22, 1865. Timmerhans, 15; Smissen, 41; Uliczny, 39, 48.

196 In April 1865 . . . Austrians had captured. Uliczny, 77–85.

196 Another Austrian . . . shot him dead. Stevenson, *Maximilian*, 152–53; Smissen, 114.

197 The Belgian volunteers . . . "live the Empress." Corti, 318; E. Domenech, *Le Mexique tel qu'il est*, 162; Timmerhans, 168.

197 The Belgian liberals . . . of the volunteers. Bonnevie, 11, 13, 30.

197 After going to Mexico . . . hunt for Romero. Smissen, 41, 64–65.

197–98 Lamadrid's men . . . off in silence. Bibesco, 9; Kératry, *Contre-guérilla*, 179.

198 Charles Mismer . . . "those we catch." Mismer, 172–75, 231.

198 But where was . . . or Morelia. García, *Archivo Bazaine*, 1092, 1142–43.

198–99 One day an informer . . . traitors who served it. Loiseau, 95–96; *Libro Rojo*, 245–46.

199 Thousands of people . . . Maximilian refused. Marx, 20, 22.

200 Romero was executed . . . an angry silence. *Libro Rojo*, 247–49.

200 Five liberal journalists . . . received one month. García, 1262, 1265, 1270; Rouher, *Discours de Rouher du 9 juin 1865*, 7–8.

200–201 Favre and his . . . for many minutes. Ibid., 6–11, 38–40.

201–2 As well as attending . . . appeasing Napoleon III. Romero, *Speech on 65th Anniversary*, 3–6.

202 Grant raised . . . did not respond. Grant, 2: 545–46.

202 In December . . . abolition of slavery. Hanna and Hanna, 211–13.

202 As the world ... "I am president." Bigelow, *Retrospections,*
2:411–12; Corti, 498.

202–3 Meanwhile the unofficial ... Mexico City and Paris. Case and
Spencer, 535–44.

20. WILL THE AMERICANS INVADE?

204 Whenever Sara Yorke ... Juárez with them? Stevenson, *Maximilian,* 169; Loizillon, 324; Corti, 903–5 (German ed., 2:App.
54–56); Callcott, 72.

204 On May 12 ... "Belgian allies." Malmesbury, 2:338.

205 Maximilian seized ... of the United States. Tyrner-Tyrnauer,
129–33.

205 "You can get up ... be wiped out." Stryker, 132.

205 People said ... in the North. Sears, 278.

206 On June 3 ... regard to Mexico. Bigelow, *Retrospections,* 3:57–
58.

206 On July 17 ... established his empire. Palmerston to Maximilian, July 17, 1865 (Palmerston Papers, Add. MSS. 48583).

206 They thought that ... "followers of Juárez." *The Times* (London), Sept. 29, 1864.

207–9 On November 30 ... approving the extension. Cadenhead,
331–38, 339n, 341n.

209 "It must be said ... is very bad." E. Domenech, *Histoire du
Mexique,* 3:297.

209 Colonel Loizillon ... "no better in the north." Loizillon, 314–
15, 317–18.

209 La Barreyrie ... "veritable army corps." La Barreyrie, 44–45.

209 Captain Timmerhans ... "right next day." Timmerhans, 188.

209 These worries ... worth $100,000. Stevenson, *Maximilian,*
123, 179; García, 1276–77, 1295–96; Gaulot, 2:140; Corti,
891–94 (German ed., 2:App. 46–48).

210 He had witnessed ... "with the guerrillas." Terrell, 68–69.

210 On June 18 ... a firing squad. Smissen, 114.

210 Abbé Domenech ... "under our bullets." E. Domenech, *Le
Mexique tel qu'il est,* 295.

210 In March 1865 ... "Napoleon III!" Lefèvre, 2:135.

211 Some French officials ... army with traitors. García, 1041;
Rivière, 55.

211 The new telegraph ... to be everywhere. García, 1301–2.

211 When the *contre-guérilla* ... "you come here?" Rivière, 169.

211 One incident ... of his sentence. Le Saint, 147–49; García,
1291; Gaulot, 2:155–56.

PAGE

212 In later years . . . several other guerrillas. García, 1168, 1195, 1204, 1218, 1220–21.

212 The case . . . two days later. Blasio, 58.

212 But Maximilian . . . merciful he was. Stevenson, *Maximilian*, 156.

213 The 40,000 troops . . . in four continents. *The Times* (London), Apr. 11, 1863.

213 By the Treaty . . . the Jecker bonds. "Treaty of Miramar," in Blasio, 193–96.

21. ALICE ITURBIDE

215 A group under General Shelby . . . in Tamaulipas. Edwards, 448–49, 451, 456, 459; Terrell, 65.

215–16 William M. Anderson . . . Confederate states. Anderson, 27:5, 32–33.

216 Maximilian was lukewarm . . . Coahuila and Sonora. Hanna and Hanna, 221, 223–26, 233.

216 but at the end of August . . . of November 1. Orozco, 21–22.

216 Maximilian signed another . . . was not oppressed. Ibid., 90–91.

217 Juárez and Romero . . . victory for Juárez. Hanna and Hanna, 232; Orozco, 13–14.

217 In their palaces . . . with the emperor. Blasio, 16–17, 21, 76–77.

217–19 Maximilian had to have . . . *Harper's Magazine*. Bigelow, "Heir-Presumptive," 735–42.

219 "Maximilian charged . . . American child." *New-York Times*, Jan. 9, 1866.

220 When Bigelow raised . . . over the child. Bigelow, "Heir-Presumptive," 743.

22. GRANT, SHERMAN, AND SHERIDAN

221 In Washington . . . "Our Country, Peace," Leech, 385.

221 They had therefore . . . his loyal support. Grant, 1:315.

222 There was one difference . . . during Reconstruction. *Sherman Letters,* 78–79, 83, 106, 115, 282; Stryker, 203.

222 When the French troops . . . "we are damaged." Sherman, 1:341.

222 He had nearly . . . a fellow cadet. Sheridan, 1:11–12.

222 He discussed . . . France and Mexico. Hanna and Hanna, 239–40.

222–23 Six days before . . . along the Rio Grande. Sheridan, 2:208–9.

223 Sheridan was disappointed . . . across the Rio Grande. Ibid., 2:209–11; Welles, 2:348.

223 Captain Loizillon . . . him in peace. Loizillon, 386.

223–24 Napoleon III worked . . . Crimean War. García, 1298.

224 "Mexican wasps' nest." Salomon, 175.

224 On June 16 . . . Grant's position. Welles, 2:317, 322, 332–33, 336.

224 Gideon Welles . . . "too belligerent." Ibid., 2:348.

224 A rally . . . "Napoleon III." *Proceedings of a Meeting*, 5–41 (quotation on p. 33).

225 Before he arrived . . . a new capital. Bartlett, 646; Iglesias, 3:3, 407, 475.

225–26 He and his staff . . . for a French attack. Bartlett, 641–58.

226 Juárez himself . . . "expedition to Chihuahua." E. Domenech, *Histoire du Mexique*, 3:338.

226 According to Kératry . . . returned to Mexico. Kératry, *Maximilien*, 82.

226 The news was . . . in the United States. Flint, 116.

227 One writer . . . his headquarters. Enduran, 133.

227 "As the summer" . . . crossing the Rio Grande. Sheridan, 2:215.

23 . THE BLACK DECREE

228 On October 3, 1864 . . . provincial towns. Kollonitz, 264; Le Saint, 133–34.

228–29 The day before . . . to December 1. Smissen, 103–12; Gaulot, 2:186–87.

229 *La Nación* declared . . . would condemn it. *La Nación*, Oct. 5, 1865.

229 Seward protested . . . emperor of Mexico. Hanna and Hanna, 263.

229 Maximilian's apologists . . . and issued it. Blasio, 61–62; Basch, 66; Hall, 153–54; Bulnes, *Verdadero Juárez*, 540; Kollonitz, 302; Kératry, *Maximilien*, 83–85; Gaulot, 2:187–89.

229–30 According to the liberal . . . 11,000 victims. Chynoweth, 52.

230 It is quite impossible . . . appeal to Maximilian. Gaulot, 2:188–89.

230 Maximilian had repeatedly . . . to destroy them. Corti, 913–14 (German ed., 2:App. 61–62).

231 On October 11 . . . "kill and be killed." Smissen, 114–16; Mismer, 198.

231 The next day . . . otherwise be threatened. García, 1318.

231–32 On October 13 . . . the next morning. *Libro Rojo*, 251–65; Smissen, 117; Loiseau, 201; La Bédollière, 3rd ed., 6.

232 The execution squad . . . he died instantly. Lefèvre, 2:268; *Libro*

PAGE

Rojo, 265–66; Mismer, 199. Mismer attributes the words "Aim here, traitors" to Arteaga.

232 Some of the propaganda . . . private revenge. E. Domenech, *Histoire du Mexique,* 3:334.

232–33 The Belgian legion . . . his prisoners well. Loiseau, 120–30, 221–25; Schrynmakers, 3rd ed., 368; Timmerhans, 97; García, 1287.

233–34 On November 16 . . . "third of October." Kératry, *Maximilien,* 320.

234 In El Paso . . . bank in London. *Mision Confidencial,* 6, 9, 12, 39–40, 85.

234–35 On September 17 . . . "only barbarous brigands." E. Domenech, *Histoire du Mexique,* 3:338–44.

235 To get Miramón . . . to join Juárez. *Mision Confidencial,* 45–47.

235 Napoleon III's . . . and the intervention. García, 1318.

235 On January 22 . . . until his arrival. *Mision de Teran,* 47–48.

235–36 Charles de Cazotte . . . stop the shipment. García, 1276, 1316–17, 1320–21.

236 The ban on . . . the French invaders. Romero, *Correspondencia,* 5:506–9; Miller, 235.

236 He bought 21,000 . . . export of arms. Cluseret, 16.

236 The Philadelphia correspondent . . . "hopes of success." *The Times* (London), Nov. 27, 1865.

237 Soon the liberal . . . Baton Rouge alone. Sheridan, 2:224, 226.

237 A French naval . . . drove them away. García, 1326–27.

237–38 On November 7 . . . the Texas shore. Ibid., 1328–31.

238 Mejía's men captured . . . life at Querétaro. E. Domenech, *Histoire du Mexique,* 3:374.

238 At 4 A.M. . . . two days later. Rivière, 133–34: 145–46; E. Domenech, *Histoire du Mexique,* 3:374–77.

238 Seward was very angry . . . "the American flag." *New-York Times,* Jan. 24, 1866.

238 Seward persuaded . . . command at Brownsville. *The Times* (London), Feb. 22, 1866.

238 "It required . . . our State Department." Sheridan, 2:217.

238–39 At the beginning . . . "An inspiration!" Hanna and Hanna, 272; see also Wellesley and Sencourt, 232.

239 "We cannot remain . . . despite of itself." Duniway, 321n.

239 On January 15 . . . in October 1867. Corti, 930–31 (German ed., 2:App. 75); Gaulot, 2:300.

239–40 Maximilian was taken aback . . . avoid doing so. Corti, 931–32 (German ed., 2:App. 75–76); Paléologue, 97, 103; Du Barail, 3:7–8; Barker, *Distaff Diplomacy,* 134.

240 In November 1865 . . . agreed to do so. Roeder, 627; Kératry, *Maximilien*, 131–32.

24. CHARLOTTE GOES TO EUROPE

241 *The Times* had written . . . one French soldier. *The Times* (London), Sept. 29, 1864.

242 Many American volunteers . . . higher-ranking officers. Hanna and Hanna, 298; Dabbs, 268.

242 General John Schofield . . . going to Mexico. Schofield, 378–93; Hanna and Hanna, 239–46.

242 In the spring . . . win or lose. McKee, 91–96, 101–14; Hanna and Hanna, 213–16.

243 Thanks partly . . . luck in Mexico. Princess Salm-Salm, 3–4, 175–76.

243 Doña Margarita Juárez . . . short of money. Miller, 236–37.

243 In March 1866 . . . except her earrings. Smart, 363–66; Roeder, 633–34; Deuson, 492.

243–44 Another great rally . . . Mexico at once. *New-York Times*, Jan. 8, 1866; *The Evening Post, New York*, Jan. 8, 1866.

244 In the press . . . on the Rio Grande. *New-York Times*, Nov. 17, 1865; Jan. 8, 11, 24; Feb. 6, 7; Mar. 12; Apr. 4, 17, 30, 1866; *The Evening Post, New York*, Feb. 7, 27; Mar. 8, 24, 1866.

244 A broadsheet . . . "blood in Mexico." *Betrayal of the Cause of Freedom*, unpaginated.

244–45 In August 1865 . . . abandon the plan. Blumberg, "William Seward," 34, 44–45.

245 In March 1866 . . . to serve in Mexico. X. Lynch, 87–89; Hanna and Hanna, 278–80; Welles, 2:485–86; Gaulot, 2:310.

245 When he arrived . . . in Juárez's honor. Juárez, 11:131–32.

245–46 He asked Bazaine . . . for many years. Ollivier, *l'Expédition du Mexique*, 271; Rivière, 207–8.

246 Many of Maximilian's . . . Foreign Legion. Stevenson, *Maximilian*, 200; Dabbs, 268.

246 The liberal generals . . . "to fight against you." La Garza's proclamation, Feb. 22, 1866 (Staatsarchiv, K 27, Kon. 2, f. 303–11).

247 Charlotte decided . . . "red trousers." Corti, 874 (German ed., 2:App. 34).

247 On July 9 . . . seemed very depressed. Blasio, 83–84.

247–48 She arrived . . . change his mind. Corti, 666–84.

248 Eloin told Maximilian . . . would be Charlotte. Foussemagne, 296–97.

248 Charlotte had another . . . "write politely." Bigelow, *Retrospections,* 3:508–10; Bigelow, "Heir-Presumptive," 744–45.

248 Charlotte went on . . . letter of thanks. Corti, 696.

248 She also wrote . . . kissed her hand. Ibid., 686.

248 No one has ever . . . "inhabit the Tuileries." Motley, 1:225, 231–32; White, 173.

249 Charlotte stayed . . . in the garden. Information from Dottoressa Rossella Fabiani; Blasio, 91–93.

249 She then went . . . hotel under escort. Blasio, 94–102.

249 Later that day . . . "Your faithful Charlotte." Corti, 711.

249 In the hotel . . . of Napoleon III. Blasio, 104–8.

249 Her gentlemen did not . . . to treat her. Corti, 715, 735.

249 Leopold decided . . . more harm than good. Foussemagne, 357–58.

249 Her relatives sometimes . . . by a relapse. Leopold II to Queen Victoria, Dec. 4, 1866 (RA: Q. 1/177); Foussemagne, 359–61.

249–50 They did not specify . . . happened to Charlotte. Corti, 735.

250 He therefore decided . . . change of plan. Bigelow, *Retrospections,* 3:581–2, 598–600, 617.

250 This was an embarrassment . . . the French government. Welles, 2:622–26; Bigelow, *Retrospections,* 3: 609–11.

251 He would prefer . . . order in Mexico. Bigelow, *Retrospections,* 3:618–20.

251 Bazaine agreed . . . "foreigners residing there." Schroeder, 20–21.

251 The idea was discussed . . . against the French. *New-York Times,* Oct. 8, 10, 11, 30, 1866; Apr. 11, 17, 20, 1867.

251 He met Grant . . . "liberation by yourselves." Gagern, 2:318–21.

251–52 The only step . . . Maximilian had abdicated. Hanna and Hanna, 285–89; Welles, 2:621–22; *New-York Times,* Oct. 30, 1866; Seward to Sherman, Oct. 25, 1866 (Sherman Papers, 19 [microfilm reel 11]); *Sherman Letters,* 280.

252 Rumors that Maximilian . . . the United States. *The Times* (London), Oct. 26, 1866; *New-York Times,* Nov. 6, 1866.

252 He knew that Charlotte . . . house of Habsburg. Corti, 638–41.

252 The news spread . . . Europe very shortly. Franz Joseph, 361; Leopold II to Queen Victoria, Dec. 4, 1866 (RA: Q.1/177); Wellesley and Sencourt, 316.

252 But Maximilian remained . . . at his post. Blasio, 114, 116, 118–19; Lefèvre, 2:345–46; Corti, 752, 770–72.

252–53 Maximilian summoned . . . convene a congress. Blasio, 115–18; Basch, 1:108–9, 124–25; Hanna and Hanna, 290; Corti, 751–53; Gaulot, 2:438.

PAGE

253 He wrote to . . . "its chief magistrate." *Sherman Letters,* 284.

253–54 In October 1866 . . . field, had won. Cadenhead, 341–43; Sheridan, 2:223–24.

254–55 When Miramón heard . . . he had gone. Blasio, 127; Prince Salm-Salm, 1:36; Schroeder, 57n; Gaulot, 2:503–4.

255 A week later . . . *the contre-guérilla.* Hans, 76–78.

255 Lerdo afterward . . . occupation of Zacatecas. Hall, 259–62.

255 The French were about . . . the last days. Stevenson, *Maximilian,* 202, 223, 229, 256–58.

255–56 The French marched . . . him to Veracruz. Blasio, 125–26; Kératry, *Maximilien,* 305.

256 He wrote to Alice . . . nearly two years. Bigelow, "Heir-Presumptive," 748.

25. QUERÉTARO

257 Maximilian left . . . American Civil War. Blasio, 129–30, 132, 135.

257 Maximilian was not . . . to their 69,700. Kendall, 243–45.

257–58 On February 19 . . . honor that evening. Blasio, 135.

258 The next day . . . these two generals. Ibid., 136–37, 140; Verdía, 63, 69–70; Basch, 2:28.

258 and it is strange . . . "brave General Marquez." Gaulot, 2:507.

258 by the Albanian sailor . . . and the *palmatória?* Maximilian, 2:221–22; 3:236–37.

258–59 The armies of Escobedo . . . of the young emperor. Blasio, 137–46; Prince Salm-Salm, 1:61.

259 In case he himself . . . government of Mexico. Lefèvre, 2:446.

259 Miramón led a sortie . . . out of Querétaro. Blasio, 147.

259 While the liberals . . . of the liberal armies. Duvernois, 315; Gaulot, 2:496; Kératry, *Maximilien,* 307–11; Blanchot, 3:425, 427.

259 But according to . . . down his offer. Blasio, 220; Romero, *Mexico and the United States,* 379.

259–60 More and more French . . . reach the port. Stevenson, *Maximilian,* 260–62, 265–66; Kendall, 208.

260 The evacuation . . . Mexican business forgotten. Kératry, *Maximilien,* 307, 311–12; Gaulot, 2:497.

260 The last French . . . Naval Captain Rivière. Rivière, 213.

260 Puebla was held . . . to repeat elsewhere. Kendall, 247; Smith, 247.

261 On April 7 . . . to Noriega's treachery. Kératry, *Maximilien,* 307.

261 After capturing Puebla . . . Europe in January. Hall, 177; Kendall, 297–312.

261 Maximilian sent out . . . messages for Maximilian. Blasio, 151.

261 Miramón sometimes . . . his own soldiers did. Ibid., 157; Kühn, 213; Hans, 75, 143, 226.

262 By the middle . . . for twenty-four hours. Blasio, 158–59.

262 During the night . . . granted his request. Ibid., 159–64.

263 The next day Escobedo . . . freely to Maximilian. Ibid., 165–68, 176; La Barreyrie, 73.

263 Shocking stories . . . murdering all foreigners. *New-York Times*, Apr. 15, 17, 25; May 29, 1867; *The Times* (London), May 11, 20, 1867.

263 There were a few . . . acts of misconduct. Blasio, 164–65.

263 At first they all . . . "Archduke Ferdinand Maximilian." Ibid., 169; Prince Salm-Salm, 1:216.

263–64 Mendez and several . . . shot him dead. Blasio, 170; La Barreyrie, 73–74; Hyde, 272–73.

264 The prisoners did . . . complaints or requests. Blasio, 171–72.

264–65 At the end of May . . . his own initiative. *Causa de Fernando Maximiliano*, 6, 10–66, 277, 446–61, 465–66; Lefèvre, 2:424–34; Hall, 223.

265 Princess Salm-Salm . . . the diplomatic corps. Princess Salm-Salm, "Diary," in Prince Salm-Salm, 9–67; Basch, 2:199–201; Blasio, 171.

265–66 The Austrian . . . from the document. Kühn, 229–49; Corti, 811–13.

266 Princess Salm-Salm . . . foreigners from Querétaro. Princess Salm-Salm, "Diary," in Prince Salm-Salm, 66–78; Basch, 2:200; Blasio, 174.

266 Hall was also ordered . . . the Mexican bar. Hall, 211–12.

266 Magnus was angry . . . difficult for Maximilian. Kühn, 243–44; see also Middleton to Stanley, June 23, 1867 (RA: J.102/82, 90).

266–67 A story about Agnes . . . an officers' mess. Corti, 812; Paso, 562–63.

267 Riva Palacio . . . before the trial began. Riva Palacio and La Torre, 16–67.

267–68 It opened at 8 . . . point of view. *Causa de Fernando Maximiliano*, 203; Basch, 2:239; D'Héricault, 291.

268–69 The defense lawyers argued . . . Sunday, June 16. *Causa de Fernando Maximiliano*, 173–481; Lefèvre, 2:424–50; Basch, 258; Corti, 816; Prince Salm-Salm, 1:291; Hyde, 284; Blasio, 175.

26. THE NINETEENTH OF JUNE

270 They left at once . . . cabled to Querétaro. Riva Palacio and La Torre, 69–71, 75–77, 80–91.

270–71　Maximilian, Miramón . . . buried beside her. Blasio, 175; D'Héricault, 353; Sanchez-Navarro, 277; Basch, 2:210.

271　Miramón was the most . . . dissuade her from going. Gasparini, "Massimiliano nel Messico," 190–91.

271　Mejía seemed . . . of shooting him. Corti, 820; Malortie, 215–17; Kühn, 276; *Causa de Fernando Maximiliano,* 218.

271　and although Mejía . . . on their behalf. E. Domenech, *Histoire du Mexique,* 3:374.

271　Maximilian had at last . . . eve of his death. Blasio, 178, 226.

271–72　Three weeks before . . . in cold blood. Basch, 2:183; Kühn, 240.

272　On the evening . . . cat and mouse with them. Riva Palacio and La Torre, 92–93; Blasio, 175–77.

272　All the European . . . Seward's intervention. La Barreyrie, 75; E. Domenech, *Histoire du Mexique,* 3:432.

273　Garibaldi urged . . . Italian patriots. Garibaldi, 2:392–93; Montlong, 120–21.

273　Hugo told Juárez . . . "life to Juárez." La Bédollière, 3:34.

273　The *New-York Times* . . . to rescue Maximilian. *New-York Times,* Apr. 11, 15, 17, 20, 25; May 28, 29, 1867.

273　As early as April 6 . . . tell him this. Tyrner-Tyrnauer, 139.

273　Many statesmen . . . plot by Seward. E. Domenech, *Histoire du Mexique,* 3:432; La Porte, 113.

273–74　An American naval . . . agree to it. Schroeder, 10, 13, 17, 26, 28, 37–39, 45–46, 56, 58–62, 64.

275　Juárez received . . . refused her plea. Gasparini, "Massimiliano nel Messico," 192; Riva Palacio and La Torre, 95–96.

275　He agreed to receive . . . "and mine also." Princess Salm-Salm, "Diary," in Prince Salm-Salm, 82.

275　At 1:30 P.M. . . . might have committed. Riva Palacio and La Torre, 94–95; Hall, 294.

275　Juárez did not . . . "happiness of my life." Riva Palacio and La Torre, 97.

275–76　Romero stated them . . . imprisonment for life. *Harper's Magazine* 66:747n (1883).

276　Queen Victoria's . . . "murder of the Emperor." Grey to Stanley, May 31, 1867 (RA: J.102/77).

276　The "American correspondent" . . . "afraid to shoot him." *The Times* (London), June 13, 25, 1867.

277　Juárez knew . . . "justice of the government." Verdía, 115–16; Schroeder, 45–46.

277　but Magnus was present . . . by 6:40 A.M. Kühn, 277–78; Blasio, 178–80; Basch, 2:219–20; Hall, 297; Corti, 820–23; Kendall, 333–45.

277 "At seven o'clock . . . ceased to exist." Translation of extract from *Boletin Republicano,* June 21, 1867 (RA: J.102/84).

277 Later that same . . . the liberal army. Schroeder, 103–4.

278 "I have undertaken . . . slightest disorder." Uliczny, 132.

278–80 By the end . . . harm the civilians. Kendall, 296–97, 319–31.

280 He issued . . . shot him there. Ibid., 351–53; D'Héricault, 383; Prince Salm-Salm, 2:141.

280 Márquez took . . . years in Havana. D'Héricault, 384–85; Kendall, 347; Blasio, 221.

281 Juárez entered Mexico . . . of the Constitution. Gagern, 1:361–69, 388; Roeder, 685.

27. GOD DID NOT WANT IT

282 The news of Maximilian's . . . "and of humanity." *New-York Times,* June 30, 1867; *The Times* (London), July 4, 1867; La Porte, 131–33.

282 Favre and the opposition . . . on July 10. La Bédollière, 3rd ed., 33–43.

282 After Thiers had denounced . . . "respect His decrees." *Discours de Rouher du 10 Juillet 1867,* 45, 65–66, 71–73.

282–83 Several writers compared . . . against their people. Treglown, 1; Schneider, 3; D'Héricault, 2–3.

283 The French journalist . . . "loss of his scepter." Marx, 18.

283 Baron von Malortie . . . Schiller's Don Carlos. Malortie, 310.

283 Colonel Blanchot . . . Maximilian's scalp. Blanchot, 3:509.

283 The bishop of Orléans . . . Garibaldi and Juárez. *The Times* (London), Sept. 12, 1867.

283 Conservative journalists . . . against British subjects. Treglown, 3–4; *Théodorus et Juárez,* 5–7.

283 "Monarchy will never . . . We are ready." Duvernois, 374. In Cluseret's French text the words "We are ready" were in English.

283 "We went in the name . . . made Europe retreat." D'Héricault, 399.

283 La Barreyrie . . . "vassal of America." La Barreyrie, 113.

283 Baron Goltz . . . lamented his death. Kühn, 298.

283–84 The *Wiener Abendpost* . . . for his fate. Hellwald, 601–2; Gasparini, "Massimiliano nel Messico," 207.

284 A writer in Berlin . . . lament Maximilian. Schneider, 32; Liegel, 178.

284 Queen Victoria . . . "disgusting & disgraceful." Queen Victoria's journal, Dec. 25, 1867 (RA).

284 In the United States . . . extermination of foreigners. *New-York Times,* July 2, 4, 6, 7, 8, 12, 14, 18, 23, 1867.

284 In Buffalo . . . "just punishment." *The Times* (London), July 22, 29, 1867.

284 The *Evening Post* . . . "no business here." *Evening Post, New York,* July 5, 1867.

285 In a private letter . . . "dozen of them." Monnerville, 54.

285 Juárez's government agreed . . . by the liberals. Kühn, 282–83, 330.

285 Franz Joseph ordered . . . the European courts. Tegetthoff, 342–57, 359–62, 367–70; Blasio, 185–87; Hyde, 301–3.

285–86 One of the last . . . president of the republic. Cadenhead, 343–46.

286 There was a particularly . . . the liberal victory. Seward, 414; Kollonitz, 196n.

286 Juárez said that . . . freedom and independence. Rippy, 279.

286 Seward said that . . . greatest of them all. Romero, *Mexico and the United States,* 361n.

286 He said in 1887 . . . followed successfully. Romero, *Speech on 65th Anniversary,* 7–8.

287 the conservative newspaper . . . Maximilian's empire. Callcott, 72.

287 Juárez sent a message . . . Fourth of September. Roeder, 714.

287 One of those . . . "Reds" and "anarchists." Bock, 476.

288 In 1867 . . . "and his adherents." Queen Victoria to Stanley, July 18, 1867 (RA: J.102/102).

288 One day in 1895 . . . Maximilian at Querétaro. Márquez, 17: 2–7, 33–72, 110–14.

288–89 Two years later . . . daughter at Cuernavaca. Hyde, 313–15.

289 When asked . . . Madrid in 1920. Paléologue, 97, 103.

289 Several contemporary writers . . . July 1866. Blasio, 84; Stevenson, *Maximilian,* 241–42; E. Domenech, *Histoire du Mexique,* 3:395; Détroyat, 151–53; Buffin, 208–9; Castro, 29.

289 Queen Victoria . . . "on her madness." Queen Victoria's journal, Dec. 22, 1866 (RA).

289 Stephanie believed . . . fate in Mexico. Princess Stephanie, 67.

289 When Archbishop Dechamps . . . will of God. Foussemagne, 361.

289 In March 1879 . . . looked very pretty. Ibid., 374.

289 She often played . . . still played well. Ibid., 380.

290 She did not seem . . . was not there. Ibid., 377, 380, 382.

290 She died . . . Catholic Church in Mexico. *The Times* (London), Jan. 20, 22, 1927.

290 One of the young . . . one hundred and eleven. Kühn, 330.

BIBLIOGRAPHY

MANUSCRIPT SOURCES

Foreign Office Archives, Mexico: Public Record Office, Kew.
Headquarters of the Army Papers, War Department Records: National Archives, Washington, D.C.
Maximilian of Mexico Archives: Hans-, Hof-, und Staatsarchiv, Vienna.
Palmerston Papers: British Library, London.
Royal Archives, Windsor Castle (cited as RA).
William H. Seward Archives: National Archives, Washington, D.C.
William T. Sherman Papers: Library of Congress, Washington, D.C.

NEWSPAPERS AND JOURNALS

La Bandera Roja (Morelia, 1859–1863).
Blackwood's Edinburgh Magazine (Edinburgh, 1864).
Boletin Republicano (Mexico City, 1867).
El Cronista de Mexico (Mexico City, 1862–1866).
The Evening Post, New York (New York, 1865–1867).
La Independencia Mexicana (San Luis Potosí, 1863).
La Liberté (Paris, 1867).
Le Moniteur Universel (Paris, 1864–1867).
La Nacion (Mexico City, 1865).
The New-York Times (New York, 1863–1867).
La Orquesta (Mexico City, 1862–1863).
El Pajaro Verde (Mexico City, 1863).
The Saturday Review (London, 1858–1867).
El Siglo XIX (Mexico City, 1861).
La Sociedad (Mexico City, 1863–1865).
The Times (London, 1858–1867).
Le Trait-d'Union (Mexico City, 1862).

PUBLISHED WORKS

Acton, J.E.E.D. "The Rise and Fall of the Mexican Empire." Lecture at Bridgnorth, Mar. 10, 1868. In *Historical Essays and Studies* (London, 1907).

Alba, Duke of. "La Emperatriz Eugenia." Lecture in Barcelona, 1947. In *Boletin de la Real Academia de Historia* 120:71–101 (Madrid, 1947).

Alvensleben, Max, Baron von. *With Maximilian in Mexico.* London, 1867.

Anderson, William Marshall. *An American in Maximilian's Mexico 1865–1866: The Diaries of William Marshall Anderson.* Ed. R. E. Ruiz. San Marino, Calif., 1959.

Arbelli, H. P. *Les Renards, les Dindons et le Mexique.* Bordeaux, 1863.

Arellano, M. R. de. *Ultimas Horas del Imperio.* Ed. A. Pola. Mexico City, 1903.

Arias, J. de Dios. *Reseña Historica de la formacion y operaciones del cuerpo de Ejército del Norte durante la Intervención Francesa.* Mexico City, 1867.

Arrangoiz, D. F. de Paula de. *Apuntes para la Historia del Segundo Imperio Mejicano.* Madrid, 1869.

Baedecker, K. *Southern Germany and the Austrian Empire: Handbook for Travellers.* Coblenz, 1868.

Baldensperger, F. "L'initiation américaine de Georges Clemenceau." *Revue de Littérature Comparée* 8:127–54 (1928).

Bancroft, F. *The Life of William H. Seward.* New York, 1900.

Bancroft, H. H. *A Popular History of the Mexican People.* San Francisco, 1887.

Barker, Nancy Nichols. *Distaff Diplomacy: The Empress Eugénie and the Foreign Policy of the Second Empire.* Austin, Tex., 1967.

———. "Empress Eugénie and the Origin of the Mexican Venture." *The Historian* 22 (1):9–23 (Nov. 1959).

Bartlett, I. S. "President Juárez at Old El Paso." *Bulletin of the Pan-American Union* 41:641–58 (Nov. 5, 1915).

Basch, S. *Erinnerungen aus Mexico: Geschichte der letzten zehn Monate des Kaiserreichs.* Leipzig, 1868.

Belleyme, A. de. *La France et le Mexique.* Paris, 1863.

Berry, C. R. *The Reform in Oaxaca 1856–76: A Microhistory of the Liberal Revolution.* Lincoln, Nebr., 1981.

The Betrayal of the Cause of Freedom by William H. Seward, Secretary of State. Washington, D.C., 1866.

Beust, F. F., Count von. *Memoirs of Friedrich Ferdinand Count von Beust.* London, 1887.

Biart, L. *Le Mexique d'hier et le Mexique de demain.* Paris, 1865.

Bibesco, Prince G. *Au Mexique 1862: Combats et Retraite des Six Mille.* Paris, 1887.

Bigelow, John. "The Heir-Presumptive to the Imperial Crown of Mexico: Don Agustin de Iturbide." *Harper's New Monthly Magazine* 66:735–49 (Apr. 1883).

———. *Retrospections of an Active Life.* New York, 1909.

Blanchot, C. *Mémoires: l'Intervention Française au Mexique.* Paris, 1911.

Blasio, J. L. *Maximilian Emperor of Mexico: Memoirs of His Private Secretary.* New Haven, 1934.

Blond, G. *La Légion Etrangère.* Paris, 1964.

Blumberg, A. "A Swedish Diplomat in Mexico, 1864." *Hispanic-American Historical Review* 45:275–86 (1965).

———. "William Seward and Egyptian Intervention in Mexico." *Smithsonian Journal of History* 1(4):31–48 (Winter 1966–67).

Blumenthal, H. *France and the United States: Their Diplomatic Relations 1789–1914.* Chapel Hill, N.C., 1970.

Bock, Carl H. *Prelude to Tragedy.* Philadelphia, 1966.

Bonnevie, J. B. *N'insultez pas les Gens de Coeur.* Brussels, 1865.

Buffin, Baron C. *La Tragédie Mexicaine.* Brussels, 1925.

Bullock, W. H. *Across Mexico in 1864–5.* London, 1866.

Bulnes, F. *Juárez y les revoluciones de Ayutla y de Reforma.* Mexico City, 1905.

———. *El Verdadero Juárez y la Verdad sobre la Intervención y el Imperio.* Mexico City, 1904.

Bülow, Paula von. *Aus verklungenen Zeiten.* Leipzig, 1924.

Burghclere, Lady. *A Great Lady's Friendship: Letters to Mary, Marchioness of Salisbury, Countess of Derby 1862–1890.* London, 1933.

Cadenhead, Ivie E., Jr. "Gonzalez Ortega and the Presidency of Mexico." *Hispanic-American Historical Review* 32:331–46 (1952).

Callahan, J. M. *American Foreign Policy in Mexican Relations.* New York, 1932.

Callcott, W. H. *Liberalism in Mexico 1857–1929.* Hamden, Conn., 1965.

Cambas, M. R. *Los Gobernantes de México: Benito Juárez.* Mexico City, 1972.

Case, Lynn M. *French Opinion on War and Diplomacy During the Second Empire.* Philadelphia, 1954.

———, ed. *French Opinion on the United States and Mexico 1860–1867: Extracts from the Reports of the Procureurs Généraux.* New York, 1936.

Case, Lynn M., and W. F. Spencer. *The United States and France: Civil War Diplomacy.* Philadelphia, 1970.

Castelot, A. *Maximilien et Charlotte du Mexique.* Paris, 1977.

————. *Napoléon Trois*. Paris, 1973–1974.

Castro, J. de. *El Emperador Maximiliano y su augusta esposa la Emperatriz Carlota*. Madrid, 1867.

Causa de Fernando Maximiliano de Hapsburgo que se ha titulado Emperador de México y sus llamados generales Miguel Miramón y Tomas Mejía. Ed. A. Pola. Mexico City, 1907.

Chevalier, M. *La France, le Mexique et les Etats Confédérés*. Paris, 1863.

————. *Le Mexique Ancien et Moderne*. Paris, 1863.

La Chute de l'Empire du Mexique, par Un Mexicain. Paris, 1867.

Chynoweth, W. H. *The Fall of Maximilian, Late Emperor of Mexico*. Ed. W. M. Laker. London, 1872.

Cleven, N. A. N. "The Ecclesiastical Policy of Maximilian of Mexico." *Hispanic-American Historical Review* 9:317–60 (Aug. 1929).

Cluseret, G. *Mexico and the Solidarity of Nations*. New York, 1866.

Connell, B. *Regina v. Palmerston*. London, 1962.

Corti, Egon Caesar, Count. *Maximilian und Charlotte von Mexico*. Zürich, 1924. English trans.: *Maximilian and Charlotte of Mexico*. Trans. Catherine Alison Phillips. New York, 1929. (The notes, unless otherwise stated, refer to the English translation. My quotations are from the German edition, which gives the documents in their original language.) Cited as Corti.

————. *Vom Kind zum Kaiser: Kindheit und erste Jugend Kaiser Franz Josephs I und seiner Geschwister*. Graz, 1950.

Coulter, E. M. *The Confederate States of America*. Baton Rouge, La., 1950.

Cuevas, J. de Jesus. *El Imperio: Opusculo sobre la situacion actual*. Mexico City, 1864.

Dabbs, J. A. *The French Army in Mexico 1861–1867: A Study in Military Government*. The Hague, 1963.

Dawson, D. *The Mexican Adventure*. London, 1935.

Détroyat, L. *La Cour de Rome et l'Empereur Maximilien*. Paris, 1867.

Deusen, Glyndon G. van. *William Henry Seward*. New York, 1967.

D'Héricault, C. *Maximilien et le Mexique*. Paris, 1869.

Dinner to Señor Matias Romero . . . on 29th of March 1864. New York, 1866.

Domenech, Emmanuel. *L'Empire au Mexique et la candidature d'un Prince Bonaparte au trone mexicain*. Paris, 1862.

————. *Histoire du Mexique: Juárez et Maximilien*. Paris, 1868.

————. *Le Mexique tel qu'il est*. Paris, 1867.

Domenech, Passena. *L'Empire Mexicain, la Paix et les Intérêts du Monde*. Mexico City, 1866.

Du Barail, General. *Mes Souvenirs*. Paris, 1894–1896.

Duniway, C. A. "Reasons for the Withdrawal of the French from Mexico." *Annual Report of the American Historical Association for the Year 1902* 1:315–28 (1903).

Duvernois, C. *L'Intervention Française au Mexique*. Paris, 1868. (Often attributed to Détroyat.)

Edwards, John N. *Shelby and His Men, or the War in the West*. Kansas City, 1897.

L'Empereur du Mexique. Paris, 1864.

L'Empire mexicain et son avenir considéré au point de vue des intérêts européens. Paris, 1865.

Enduran, L. *France et Mexique*. Limoges, 1866.

Engels, F., and K. Marx. *Der Briefwechsel zwischen Friedrich Engels und Karl Marx*. Ed. A. Bebel and E. Bernstein. Stuttgart, 1913.

Filon, A. *Recollections of the Empress Eugénie*. London, 1920.

Fleury, E. F. *Souvenirs du Général Cte Fleury*. Paris, 1897–1898.

Flint, Henry M. *Mexico under Maximilian*. Philadelphia, 1867.

Foussemagne, Countess H. de Reinach. *Charlotte de Belgique, Impératrice du Mexique*. Paris, 1925.

Franz Joseph. *Briefe Kaiser Franz Josephs I an seine Mutter 1838–1872*. Ed. F. Schnüder. Munich, 1930.

Frazer, Robert W. "Latin-American Projects to Aid Mexico during the French Intervention." *Hispanic-American Historical Review* 28: 377–88 (1948).

———. "Maximilian's Propaganda Activities in the United States, 1865–1866." *Hispanic-American Historical Review* 24:4–29 (1944).

Gagern, Carlos von. *Todte und Lebende: Erinnerungen von Carlos von Gagern*. Berlin, 1884.

García, G., ed. *La Intervención Francésa en México según el Archivo del Mariscal Bazaine*. Mexico City, 1975.

García, G., and C. Pereyra, eds. *Correspondencia secreta de los Principales Intervencionistas Mexicanos 1860–1862*. Mexico City, 1905.

———. *Correspondencia secreta de los Principales Intervencionistas Mexicanos: El Sitio de Puebla en 1863*. Mexico City, 1972.

———. *El Gral. Paredes y Arrillaga ... los Gobiernes de Alvarez y Comonfort*. Mexico City, 1974.

Garibaldi, G. *Edizione Nazionale degli scritti di Giuseppe Garibaldi*. Bologna, 1932–1937.

Gasparini, Lina. "Massimiliano d'Austria, ultimo governatore del Lombardo-Veneto." *Nuova Antalogia* 7th ser., 377:249–78, 353–87 (Rome, Jan.–Feb. 1935).

———. "Massimiliano nel Messico." *Nuova Antalogia,* 7th ser., 399:8–31, 169–213 (Rome, Sept. 1938).

Gaulot, P. *L'Expédition du Mexique*. Paris, 1906.

Gimenez, M. M. *Memorias del Coronel Manuel Maria Gimenez 1798–1878*. Mexico City, 1911.

Goldwert, M. "Matías Romero and Congressional Opposition to Seward's Policy Toward the French Intervention in Mexico." *The Americas* 22:22–40 (July 1965).

Gran Banquete dado al Ministro de la Republica Mejicana. New York (?), 1864 (?).

Grant, Ulysses S. *Personal Memoirs of U. S. Grant.* New York, 1885–1886.

Guedalla, Philip. *The Two Marshals: Bazaine, Pétain.* London, 1943.

Gutiérrez de Estrada, J. M. *Carta al Escmo. Sr. Presidente de la Republica.* Mexico City, 1840.

——. *Discorso pronunciado en el Palacio de Miramar el 3 de octubre de 1863.* Paris, 1863.

——. *Méjico y el Archiduque Fernando Maximiliano.* Paris, 1862.

Hale, C. A. "José Luis Mora and the Structure of Mexican Liberalism." *Hispanic-American Historical Review* 45:196–227 (May 1965).

——. *Mexican Liberalism in the Age of Mora 1821–1853.* New Haven, 1968.

Hall, Frederic. *Life of Maximilian I, Late Emperor of Mexico.* New York, 1868.

Hanna, A. J., and Kathryn A. Hanna. *Napoleon III and Mexico.* Chapel Hill, N.C., 1971.

Hanna, Kathryn A. "The Roles of the South in the French Intervention in Mexico." Address to the Southern Historical Association at Jacksonville, Fla., Nov. 13, 1953. In *The Pursuit of Southern History,* pp. 298–312. Baton Rouge, La., 1964.

Hans, Albert. *Querétaro: Souvenirs d'un officier de l'Empereur Maximilien.* Paris, 1869.

Hansard Parliamentary Debates. Official Report (House of Commons and House of Lords). London, 1858–1867.

Hellwald, F. von. *Maximilian I Kaiser von Mexico.* Vienna, 1869.

Hugo, Victor. *Oeuvres Complètes.* Paris, 1880–1890.

Hyde, H. Montgomery. *Mexican Empire.* London, 1946.

Iglesias, J. M. *Revistas Historicas sobre la Intervencion Francesa en Mexico.* Mexico City, 1868–1869.

Jauret, G. *Le Mexique devant les Chambres.* Paris, 1866.

Jecker, J. B. "La Créance Jecker." *Revue Contemporaine,* 2nd ser., 61:128–49 (Paris, Jan. 15, 1868).

Jerrold, B. *The Life of Napoleon III.* London, 1874–1882.

Johnson, A. *Dictionary of American Biography.* London, 1928–1936.

Jordan, D., and E. J. Pratt. *Europe and the American Civil War.* Boston, 1931.

Juárez, B. *Documentos, Discursos y Correspondencia.* Ed. J. M. Tarmayo. Mexico City, 1965–1971.

Juárez, B., and Montluc, J. P. A. *Correspondance de Juarez et de Montluc.* Ed. L. de Montluc. Paris, 1885.

Kendall, J. J. *Mexico under Maximilian.* London, 1871.

Kératry, Comte E. de. *La Contre-guérilla Française au Mexique.* Paris, 1868.

————. *La Créance Jecker, les Indemnités Françaises et les Emprunts Mexicains.* Paris, 1868.

————. *L'Empereur Maximilien, son élévation et sa chute.* Leipzig, 1867.

Kingsley, V. W. *French Intervention in America: Or, a Review of "La France, le Mexique et les Etats-Confédérés."* New York, 1863.

Knapp, F. A. *The Life of Sebastián Lerdo de Tejada 1823–1889.* Austin, Tex., 1951.

————. "Parliamentary Government and the Mexican Constitution of 1857." *Hispanic-American Historical Review* 33:65–87 (Feb. 1953).

Knowlton, R. J. "Some Practical Effects of Clerical Opposition to the Mexican Reform, 1856–1860." *Hispanic-American Historical Review* 45:246–56 (May 1965).

Kollonitz, Countess Paula. *The Court of Mexico.* Trans. J. E. Oliphant. London, 1868.

Kühn, J. *Das Ende des maximilianischen Kaiserreichs in Mexico: Berichte des königlich preussischen Ministerresidenten Anton von Magnus an Bismarck, 1866–1867.* Göttingen, 1965.

La Barreyrie, F. de. *Révélations sur l'Intervention Française au Mexique de 1866 à 1867.* Paris, 1868.

La Bédollière, E. de. *Histoire de la Guerre du Mexique: Puebla.* 1st ed. Paris, 1863.

————. *Histoire de la Guerre du Mexique 1861 à 1866.* 2nd ed. Paris, 1866.

————. *Histoire de la Guerre du Mexique, 1868: Mort et Funérailles de Maximilien.* 3rd ed. Paris, 1868.

Lally, F. E. *French Opposition to the Mexican Policy of the Second Empire.* Baltimore, 1931.

La Porte, M. A. de. *Maximilien Archiduc d'Autriche, Empereur du Mexique.* Lille, 1867.

Larousse, P. *Grand Dictionnaire Universel du XIX^c siècle.* Paris, 1866–1876.

Larrainzar, D. Manuel. *Algunas Ideas sobre la Historia y manera de Escribar la de Mexico.* Lecture to the Mexican Geographical and Statistical Society, Oct. 26, 1865.

Laurent, Paul. *La Guerre du Mexique de 1862 à 1866: Journal de marche du 3^0 Chasseurs d'Afrique.* Paris, 1867.

Leech, Margaret. *Reveille in Washington.* New York, 1941.

Lefèvre, E. *Documents Officiels recueillis dans la Secrétairie Privée de Maximilien: Histoire de l'intervention française au Mexique.* Brussels, 1869.

Lempriere, Charles. *Notes on Mexico in 1861 and 1862.* London, 1862.

Le Saint, L. *Guerre du Mexique 1861–1867.* Lille, 1867.

El Libro Rojo 1520–1867, by Vicente Riva Palacio, Manuel Payno, Juan

A. Mateos, and Rafaele Martinez de La Torre. Mexico City, 1905–1906.

Liegel, T. A. *Kaiser Maximilian I von Mexiko*. Hamburg, 1868.

Lincoln, A. *The Collected Works of Abraham Lincoln*. Ed. Roy P. Besler. New Brunswick, N.J., 1953.

Loiseau, M. *Notes Militaires sur le Mexique*. Brussels, 1872.

Loizillon, Lt. Col. *Lettres sur l'Expédition du Mexique: publiées par sa soeur 1862–1867*. Paris, 1890.

Loliée, F. *Frère d'Empereur: le Duc de Morny et la Société du Second Empire*. Paris, 1909.

Lynch, J. *The Spanish American Revolutions 1808–1826*. New York, 1986.

Lynch, Sister M. Claire. *The Diplomatic Mission of John Lothrop Motley to Austria 1861–1867*. Washington, D.C., 1944.

Magruder, H. R. *Sketches of the Last Year of the Mexican Empire*. Wiesbaden, 1868.

Malespine, A. *Solution de la Question Mexicaine*. Paris, 1864.

Malmesbury, Earl of. *Memoirs of an Ex-Minister*. London, 1884.

Malortie, Baron Carl von. *'Twixt Old Times and New*. London, 1890.

Márquez, Leonardo. *Manifiestos*. Mexico City, 1904.

Márquez de Leon, M. *Don Benito Juárez a la luz de la verdad*. Mexico City, 1885.

Martin, Theodore. *The Life of His Royal Highness the Prince Consort*. London, 1875–1880.

Marx, Adrien. *Révélations sur la vie intime de Maximilien*. Paris, 1867.

Masseras, E. *El Programa del Imperio*. Mexico City, 1864.

Maximilian. *Recollections of My Life by Maximilian I, Emperor of Mexico*. London, 1868.

McCornack, R. B. "Maximilian's Relations with Brazil." *Hispanic-American Historical Review* 32:175–211 (May 1952).

McFeely, William S. *Grant*. New York, 1981.

McKee, Irving. *"Ben Hur" Wallace: The Life of General Lew Wallace*. Berkeley, 1947.

Mecham, J. L. "The Papacy and Spanish-American Independence." *Hispanic-American Historical Review* 9:154–75 (May 1929).

Mercer, C. *The Foreign Legion*. London, 1966.

Mercier de Lacombe, H. *Le Mexique et les Etats-Unis*. Paris, 1863.

Mérimée, Prosper. *Correspondance Générale de Prosper Mérimée*. Ed. M. Parturier. Paris, 1941–1964.

Miller, R. R. "Matias Romero: Mexican Minister to the United States During the Juárez-Maximilian Era." *Hispanic-American Historical Review* 45:228–45 (May 1965).

La Mision Confidencial de Don Jesus Teran en Europa 1863–1866. Preface by G. Saldivar. Mexico City, 1943.

Mismer, C. *Souvenirs de la Martinique et du Mexique pendant l'intervention française*. Paris, 1890.

Monnerville, G. *Clemenceau*. Paris, 1968.

Montlong, W. von. *Authentische Enthüllungen über die letzten Ereignisse in Mexico*. Stuttgart, 1868.

Moreau, H. *La politique française en Amérique 1861–1864*. Paris, 1864.

Morel, Lt. Col. *La Légion Etrangère*. Paris, 1912.

Motley, J. L. *The Correspondence of John Lothrop Motley*. Ed. G. W. Curtis. London, 1889.

Napoleon III. *Oeuvres de Napoléon III*. Paris, 1869.

The New Catholic Encyclopaedia. San Francisco, 1967.

Nicolay, John G., and John Hay. *Abraham Lincoln: A History*. New York, 1890.

Niox, G. *Expédition du Mexique 1861–1867*. Paris, 1874.

O'Ballance, E. *The Story of the French Foreign Legion*. London, 1961.

Oddie, E. M. *Napoleon II, King of Rome*. London, 1932.

Ollivier, E. *L'Empire Libéral*. Paris, 1903.

———. *L'Expédition du Mexique*. Paris, 1922.

Orozco, L. C. *Maximiliano y la Restitucion de la Esclavitud en México 1865–1866*. Mexico City, 1961.

Où conduit l'Expédition du Mexique, par un Ex-Député. Paris, 1863.

Paléologue, M. *The Tragic Empress: Intimate Conversations with the Empress Eugénie 1901 to 1902*. Trans. H. Miles. London, 1928.

Parthe, E. *Die Intervention in Mexico und das neue Kaiserreich*. Leipzig, 1864.

Paso, Fernando del. *Noticias del Imperio*. Mexico City, 1987.

Perkins, D. *Hands Off: A History of the Monroe Doctrine*. Boston, 1941.

Porch, D. *The French Foreign Legion*. New York, 1991.

Poussielgue, M. *Ce qui va arriver au Mexique*. Paris, 1863.

Primoli, J. A. "L'enfance d'une souveraine." *Revue des Deux Mondes* 7(17):752–88 (Paris, Oct. 1923).

La Prise de Puebla. Paris, 1863.

Proceedings of a Meeting of Citizens of New-York to Express Sympathy and Respect for the Mexican Republican Exiles: Held at Cooper's Institute, July 19, 1865. New York, 1865.

Quinet, E. *L'Expédition du Mexique*. London, 1862.

Randon, César. *Mémoires du Maréchal Randon*. Paris, 1875–1877.

Redlich, J. *Emperor Francis Joseph of Austria: A Biography*. London, 1929.

Reyes, R. *Benito Juárez: ensayo sobre un caracter*. Madrid, 1935.

Rippy, J. F. *The United States and Mexico*. New York, 1926.

Riva Palacio, M., and R. M. de La Torre. *Histoire du Procès et de la Fin Tragique de l'Archiduc Maximilien d'Autriche*. Brussels, 1868.

Rivière, H. *La Marine Française au Mexique*. Paris, 1881.

Robertson, W. S. "The Tripartite Treaty of London." *Hispanic-American Historical Review* 20:167–89 (May 1940).

Roeder, R. *Juárez and His Mexico.* New York, 1947.

Romero, M. *Correspondencia de la Legacion Mexicana en Washington durante la Intervencion Extranjera 1860–1868.* Mexico City, 1870–1885.

———. *Mexico and the United States.* New York, 1878.

———. *Speech of Señor Don Matias Romero . . . on the 65th Anniversary of the Birth of General Ulysses S. Grant . . . at the Metropolitan Methodist Episcopal Church of the City of Washington on the 27th day of April 1887.* New York, 1887.

Rouher, E. *Discours de S. Exc. M. Rouher Ministre d'État dans la séance du Corps Législatif du 17 janvier 1864.* Paris, 1864.

———. *Discours de M. Corta . . . et de S. Exc. M. Rouher Ministre d'État* (Apr. 10 and 11, 1865). Paris, 1865.

———. *Discours de S. Exc. M. Rouher Ministre d'État dans la séance du Corps Législatif du 9 juin 1865.* Paris, 1865.

———. *Discours prononcé par S. Exc. M. Rouher Ministre d'État et des Finances dans la séance du Corps Législatif du 10 juillet 1867.* Paris, 1867.

Ruby, E., and J. Regnault. *Bazaine, coupable ou victime?* Paris, 1960.

Rydjord, J. "The French Revolution and Mexico." *Hispanic-American Historical Review* 9:60–98 (Feb. 1929).

Salm-Salm, Prince Felix. *My Diary in Mexico in 1867 including the Last Days of the Emperor Maximilian with Leaves from the Diary of the Princess Salm-Salm.* London, 1868.

Salm-Salm, Princess Felix. *Ten Years of My Life.* London, 1876.

Salomon, H. *L'Ambassade de Richard de Metternich à Paris.* Paris, 1931.

Sanchez-Navarro, C. *Miramón, el Caudillo Conservador.* Mexico City, 1945.

Santa-Anna, Antonio Lopez de. *Mi Historia Militar y Politica 1810–1874: Memorias Ineditas.* Mexico City, 1905.

Saxe-Coburg-Gotha, Duke of. *Memoirs of Ernest II, Duke of Saxe-Coburg-Gotha.* London, 1888–1890.

Scheffer, C. *La grande pensée de Napoléon III: les origines de l'expédition du Mexique 1858–1862.* Paris, 1939.

Schneider, F. *Maximilian's I Kaiserreich und Tod: von Miramar bis Querétaro.* Berlin, 1867.

Schofield, J. M. *Forty-Six Years in the Army.* New York, 1897.

Scholes, W. V. *Mexican Politics During the Juárez Regime 1855–1872.* Columbia, Miss., 1957.

Schönovsky, K. K. *Aus den Gefechten des Österreichischen Freicorps in Mejico.* Vienna, 1873.

Schroeder, S. *The Fall of Maximilian's Empire as Seen from a United States Gun-Boat.* New York, 1887.

Schrynmakers, A. de. *Le Mexique: Histoire de l'établissement et de la chute de l'Empire de Maximilien,* 1st ed. Brussels, 1882.

———. *Le Mexique,* 3rd ed., *Revue et augmentée.* Brussels, 1890.

Sears, L. M. "A Confederate Diplomat at the Court of Napoleon III." *American Historical Review* 26:255–81 (Jan. 1921).

Seward, F. W. *Reminiscences of a War-Time Statesman and Diplomat 1830–1915.* New York, 1916.

Sheridan, P. H. *Personal Memoirs of P. H. Sheridan, General U.S. Army.* New York, 1888.

Sherman, W. T. *Memoirs of General William T. Sherman.* New York, 1875.

The Sherman Letters: Correspondence between General and Senator Sherman from 1837 to 1891. Ed. Rachel Sherman Thorndike. London, 1894.

Smart, C. A. *Viva Juárez!* Philadelphia, 1963.

Smissen, Baron van der. *Souvenirs du Mexique 1864–1867.* Brussels, 1892.

Smith, G. *Maximilian and Carlota.* London, 1974.

Stephanie, Princess. *I Was to Be Empress.* London, 1937.

Stevenson, Sara Yorke. *Maximilian in Mexico: A Woman's Reminiscences of the French Intervention 1862–1867.* New York, 1899.

———. "Prince Louis Napoleon and the Nicaragua Canal." *Century Magazine* 64:391–96 (July 1902).

Stryker, L. P. *Andrew Johnson: A Study in Courage.* New York, 1929.

Tambs, L. A. "The Inquisition in Eighteenth-Century Mexico." *The Americas* 22:167–81 (Oct. 1965).

Tavera, E. Schmit Ritter von. *Die Mexikanische Kaisertragödie: die letzten sechs Monate meines Aufenthaltes in Mexiko im Jahre 1867.* Vienna, 1903.

———. *Geschichte des Regierung des Kaisers Maximilian I und die Französische Intervention in Mexico 1861–1867.* Vienna, 1903.

Tegetthoff, W. von. *Aus Wilhelm von Tegetthoffs Nachlass.* Ed. A. Beer. Vienna, 1882.

Terrell, A. W. *From Texas to Mexico and the Court of Maximilian in 1865.* Ed. Fannie E. Ratchford. Dallas, 1933.

Testory, Abbé. *El Imperio y el Clero Mexicano.* Toluca, 1865.

Théodorus et Juárez. Paris, 1868.

Thomas, L. *Le Général de Galliffet.* Paris, 1909.

Timmerhans, L. *Voyage et Opérations du Corps Belge au Mexique.* Liège, 1866.

Timmons, W. H. "José Maria Morelos: Agrarian Reformer?" *Hispanic-American Historical Review* 45:183–95 (May 1965).

Treglown, T. *Europe Insulted by the Murder of Maximilian.* Marazion, Cornwall, 1867.

Tyrner-Tyrnauer, A. R. *Lincoln and the Emperors.* London, 1962.

Uliczny, J. *Geschichte des österreichisch-belgischen Freikorps in Mexiko.* Vienna, 1868.

Valades, J. C. *Don Melchor Ocampo, Reformador de México.* Mexico City, 1954.

Valois, A. de. *Mexique, Havane et Guatemala: Notes de Voyage.* Paris, 1861.

Valori, Prince Henry de. *L'expédition du Mexique rehabilité au triple point de vue religieux, politique et commercial.* Paris, 1864.

Verdía, L. Pérez. *Impresiones de un libro "Maximiliano intime" por José L. Blasío.* Guadalajara, 1905.

Victoria. *The Letters of Queen Victoria, Second Series 1862–1878.* Ed. George Earle Buckle. London, 1926.

Viel Castel, H. de. *Mémoires du Comte Horace de Viel Castel sur le règne de Napoléon III.* Paris, 1883–1884.

Welles, Gideon. *The Diary of Gideon Welles.* Boston, 1911.

Wellesley, V., and R. Sencourt. *Conversations with Napoleon III.* London, 1934.

Wertheimer, E. de. *The Duke of Reichstadt.* London, 1905.

West, W. R. "Contemporary French Opinions on the American Civil War." *Johns Hopkins University Studies in Historical and Political Science,* ser. 42(1) (1924).

White, Elizabeth Brett. *American Opinion of France from Lafayette to Poincaré.* New York, 1927.

Wilson-Bareau, J., J. House, and D. Johnson. *Manet: The Execution of Maximilian.* London, 1992.

Woodham-Smith, Cecil. *Queen Victoria: Her Life and Times 1819–1861.* London, 1972.

❈ INDEX ❈